A BIRDWATCHING GUIDE TO

FRANCE

SOUTH OF THE LOIRE INCLUDING CORSICA

J. CROZIER

ARLEQUIN PRESS

ISBN 978-1-905268-02-3

First published 2000
Reprinted 2006

Arlequin Press, The Rea, Upton Magna, Shrewsbury SY4 4UR
www.wildlifebooks.com
© Jacquie Crozier
© All illustrations John Busby

All rights reserved. No part of this book may be reproduced, stored in a retrieval system or transmitted in any form or by any means, electronic, mechanical, photocopying or otherwise, without the permission of the publisher.

A catalogue record for this book is available.

CONTENTS

INTRODUCTION 5
    Area covered by this book 6
    Wildlife reserves and protected areas in France 8
    Bird organisations and twitch lines 10
    Travel information 11
    Southern France Site Calendar 17

BIRDING AREAS
Atlantic Coast 21
    Area 1   Lakes near Nantes 24
    Area 2   Bourgneuf Bay Maritime Reserves and Noirmoutier 27
    Area 3   Olonne Marsh 30
    Area 4   Aiguillon Bay 31
    Area 5   Île de Ré 35
    Area 6   Rochefort: Yves Marshes and Moëze Marshes 36
    Area 7   Île d'Oléron 40
    Area 8   Grave Headland (M) 41
    Area 9   Bassin d'Arcachon 41
    Area 10   Hossegor 47
    Area 11   Les Barthes and Orx Marshes 51
    Area 12   Hendaye 55
    Area 13   Camp de Poteau, Captieux (Landes) 56
    Area 14   Niort 57

The Pyrenees 59
    Area 1   Col de Méhatché 62
    Area 2   The western migration passes (M) 63
    Area 3   Gave de Pau – Artix Bird Reserve – a wetland site 65
    Area 4   Forest d'Issaux and Somport Pass 67
    Area 5   Ossau valley and Pourtalet Pass 67
    Area 6   Gavarnie 71
    Area 7   Néouvielle 73
    Area 8   The Lis and La Pique Valleys south of
                  Bagnères-de-Luchon 74
    Area 9   Port d'Aula 76
    Area 10   Ax-les-Thermes – the lower Ariège 78
    Area 11   Eyne – an eastern migration route (M) 81
    Area 12   Canigou and Prats-de-Mollo – La Preste Reserve 83

Mediterranean Coast 86
    Area 1   Perpignan and the Roussillon 88
    Area 2   Leucate (M) 94
    Area 3   Narbonne and Gruissan 97
    Area 4   Corbières 102
    Area 5   The Camargue 103

Area 6	The Crau and Vigueirat Marshes east of the Rhone	111
Area 7	Provence – Les Alpilles and Petit Luberon	118
Area 8	Provence – Mont Ventoux area	123
Area 9	Hyères, the Île d'Hyères and the Maures Hills	126
Area 10	The Eastern Mediterranean – Var River Mouth	138

Corsica ... 140

Area 1	The east coast: Lakes Biguglia, Urbino and Diane	144
Area 2	The southern mountains – Zonza and the Bavella Pass	147
Area 3	The south around Bonifacio	148
Area 4	The west coast – Ajaccio to Porto	149
Area 5	Porto to Galeria and Scandola Reserve	150
Area 6	The northwest – Calvi and the Regino valley	152
Area 7	Evisa, Aitone Forest and Col de Vergio	153
Area 8	Corte and the central valleys	154
Area 9	The north – Cap Corse (M)	156
Area 10	The offshore island reserves	157

The Alps ... 160

Area 1	The Maritime and Haute Provence Alps in the Mercantour National Park	163
Area 2	The High Alps (Haute Alps)	166
Area 3	Queyras Regional Park on the Italian frontier	170
Area 4	The Savoy Alps (Haute Savoie) Chamonix-Samoëns area	173
Area 5	The Jura Mountains	176

The Centre ... 180

Area 1	Angoulême	183
Area 2	Poitiers	187
Area 3	The Brenne	193
Area 4	Limoges	199
Area 5	The Northern Massif Central near Clermont-Ferrand	203
Area 6	The Southern Massif Central	207
Area 7	Lyons	212
Area 8	Montauban	219
Area 9	Toulouse	224
Area 10	Cévennes National Park	229

SOME SPECIAL SPECIES ... 239

BIBLIOGRAPHY AND RECOMMENDED BOOKS ... 258

CHECK LISTS

Birds	260
French bird-names	268
Mammals	276
Amphibians and Reptiles	278
Butterflies	279

INTRODUCTION

France is one of the largest countries in Europe, roughly four times the size of the British Isles. Its climate ranges from Mediterranean to Alpine, wet, windy Atlantic to cold Continental. Within all these very different climatic regions, there are also a great variety of habitats: wetlands, rivers, lakes, coastal lagoons, deciduous and coniferous forests, lowland and mountain heaths, urban areas and agricultural land.

Anyone planning a birdwatching trip to France may need to decide which species they especially want to see before choosing which area to visit, because France is so large and heterogeneous that bird species reflect this diversity. For example, the southern mountains hold quite different bird populations from the more northerly ones. Bird species in the Alps are surprisingly distinct from those in the Pyrenees. France has both long Atlantic and Mediterranean coastlines, and whilst many wetlands along both coasts are of international importance for the number and variety of migratory and wintering birds that use them, there is a noticeable difference in the bird species breeding in, say, the Camargue marshes compared to those on the rocky cliffs and islands around Brittany. The northeast has affinities with central and northern Europe, the southwest with Spain.

Great stretches of France are still largely rural but agriculture is big business nowadays and increasingly intensive. Modern agricultural practices discourage birdlife but away from the Paris and Aquitaine Basins, there are still very wild and unspoilt areas where traditional farming methods sustain wildlife, especially in the mountainous regions (the Pyrenees, Alps, Jura and the Massif Central). Tourism and a growing demand for "adventure" sports may be greater threats in these regions. Elsewhere France's huge army of "hunters" with their powerful parliamentary lobby and demands for an ever longer (July to March) shooting season is another threat to bird populations, with an additional danger posed by the hundred of tons of lead left by their shot each winter. However, after almost 20 years of lobbying by the LPO (*la Ligue pour la Protection des Oiseaux*), and other conservation bodies, France has recently awarded official protection to 71 bird species. Just how effective this protection will prove to be has yet to be tested.

On the positive side more and more small reserves are being created every year, often managed by LPO regional groups, and the LPO are encouraging farmers to manage their land for Little Bustards and Harriers. Each year some 400 volunteers search for Harrier nests and then guard over 1500 nest sites until the young fly. So in spite of the dramatic decline in a few species such as Little Bustard or Bonelli's Eagle, anyone birding France for the first time will still be amazed by the variety of species to be found in France as well as the sheer numbers of birds in many coastal and wetland reserves. 273 (51%) of the 535 European bird species breed in France and 350 species regularly winter there or pass through on migration*. France's situation in Europe makes it a very important migration route. For example, the total population of Spoonbills breeding in Holland crosses France on their way to Spain or

West Africa, as do more than 60,000 Cranes coming from Scandinavia, Germany and the Baltic. All northern Europe's White Storks migrate either down the Atlantic coast or the Rhône Valley. Besides common migrants, many rare or endangered species migrate though France: Black Stork, Corncrake, Little Bittern, Black Tern, Booted Eagle, and Red Kite among many others. Additionally, species that are either non-existent or rare in Britain such as Crested Lark, Serin, Black Redstart, Cirl and Corn Buntings, Montagu's Harrier, Honey Buzzard, Golden Oriole, Fan-tailed Warbler and Short-toed Treecreeper, to name but a few, are quite common and widespread. Six of France's woodpecker species (Black, Green, Grey-headed, Great, Middle and Lesser Spotted) are also widely distributed and can be found in both large and small woods throughout most of the country. Anyone interested in rarities will soon discover than France receives as many transatlantic vagrants along her Atlantic coast as does Britain while eastern overshoots and Siberian waifs turn up regularly throughout the country.

* *Figures taken from "Zones Importantes pour la Conservation des Oiseaux en France" published by the Ministry of the Environment and BirdLife International.*

Area covered by this book

The area covered by this book is roughly half of France south of a line running from the south bank of the Loire estuary on the Atlantic coast to Lake Geneva (Lac Léman) in the east. This division is partly climatic and geographic, as can be seen by the bird populations (for example, very few if any Fulmars, Black Storks, Grey-headed Woodpeckers, Rock Pipits, Collared Flycatchers, Icterine Warblers or Rooks breed south of this line [though the latter are rapidly expanding their range] while Short-toed Eagle, Eagle and Scops Owls, Rock Sparrow, Rock Thrush, Tawny and Water Pipits, Ortolan Bunting, Crag Martin, Fan-tailed, Orphean, Sardinian and Sub-alpine Warblers rarely occur north of it) and partly for convenience when grouping sites. It allows the entire Atlantic coast south of the Brittany peninsular to be included and covers the Alps and the Massif Central. It should be noted that there is also a clear east-west divide within this area with certain bird species: Nutcracker, Black Grouse, Rock Partridge, Fieldfare, Willow Tit, Pied Flycatcher, Lesser Whitethroat and Marsh Warbler, for example, only breeding in the east.

Division into areas and sites: France is divided into départements (departments or counties) and administrative regions. A region such as Aquitaine has five departments (Gironde, Dordogne, Lot et Garonne, Landes, and Pyrenees Atlantiques). Although some names, such as the Dordogne to refer to an area of France around the river of that name, are widely used by English speakers, often they are used quite loosely and not confined to the actual administrative department. Furthermore names can be confusing; the Loire department is on the opposite side of France to the Pays de Loire region. So as departments mean little to many British readers who could not find them easily on a map, this guide is divided into much more general areas (the Atlantic Coast and the Alps for example) or sites are grouped around main towns (the Toulouse area). If sites were listed under departments or even regions, then it would be easy to miss visiting a good site nearby because it occurs in another department. For example with sites in the Cévennes or the Massif Central, which cover several departments, or the Camargue, as the Petit Camargue is in a different region and even department to the rest of the marshland further east. However, a map showing the departments and regions is on page 16 as this can be a useful reference when travelling in France.

Site Maps: The large regions and main towns into which the book is divided are shown on the map of southern France on page 17. The section on each region opens with a sketch map showing numbered birding areas. Large areas are often divided into two or more sites and/or different itineraries described. The description of each area or site is accompanied by sketch maps where necessary, giving all the detail necessary to find the site. Because France is such an important country for migration, where a site is mainly of interest in spring and autumn when birds are on passage, then it is marked on the maps with **M** after its number. This does not mean that there is nothing of interest to see at other times of the year, but that its main importance is as a migration site.

Distances: Distances are given in kilometres, as these are the measurement shown on maps and road signs but for drivers with British cars a conversion table is given below. Occasionally the distances shown on the trip metres of different cars may show minor variations. Only very rarely is an exact distance crucial to find a site, usually a road junction or landmark is additionally given to help readers find the correct spot or turning.

Conversion Table Miles/Kilometres

Kilometres	=	Miles	Miles	=	Kilometres
0.1	=	0.06213	0.1	=	0.16093
0.2	=	0.12426	0.2	=	0.32186
0.3	=	0.18639	0.3	=	0.48279
0.4	=	0.24852	0.4	=	0.64372
0.5	=	0.31065	0.5	=	0.80465
0.6	=	0.37278	0.6	=	0.96558
0.7	=	0.43491	0.7	=	1.12651
0.8	=	0.49704	0.8	=	1.28744
0.9	=	0.55917	0.9	=	1.44837
1	=	0.62130	1	=	1.60930
2	=	1.24260	2	=	3.21860
3	=	1.86390	3	=	4.82790
4	=	2.48520	4	=	6.43720
5	=	3.10650	5	=	8.04650
6	=	3.72780	6	=	9.65580
7	=	4.34910	7	=	11.26510
8	=	4.97040	8	=	12.87440
9	=	5.59170	9	=	14.48370
10	=	6.21300	10	=	16.09300

Species
The more important species, or those of most interest to British birders, are listed in **bold type** under the description of each site. Obviously it is not possible to list all the species recorded for every site and so commoner birds, likely to be found in the habitat described, have been omitted. The text usually states whether the birds are to be seen in winter or summer but any reader unsure whether a species is resident or a passage or seasonal visitor should look it up in the check list at the end of the book or consult a field guide.

Special Species
The section on page 239 gives details of behaviour and habitat of those species likely to be of most interest to a non-French birder and suggests some sites where they are most likely to be seen. For example, if you particularly want to see White-backed Woodpecker, look up this species in the "Special Birds" section at the back of the book where you will read that they are easiest to locate between February and May but are very quiet at other times, that they favour a very restricted and local habitat of mature and decaying beech trees and that the Forest d'Issaux site in the Pyrenees is one of the most likely places to find them. Then turn to the Pyrenees section and read the detailed instructions as to location given under this site.

Tapes of bird-song
The use of pre-recorded tapes or CDs to attract birds is subject to much debate and arouses strong feelings on both sides. Whilst there is no doubt that many species (especially woodpeckers, owls and most warblers) react immediately to their calls being played and fly close to investigate, tapes should always be used with the greatest sensitivity and NEVER in the breeding season. It is besides counter-productive to play a recording more than once, or twice at the very most, as birds are never fooled for long. Once they have "sussed" you out, they will not continue to respond.

Tapes are most useful for familiarising yourself with calls before visiting an area where the species you wish to see are to be found. Calls and songs are by far the easiest way of locating birds. For example, you will be very lucky to find a Scops Owl or Corsican Nuthatch if you do not recognise their calls.

Sardinian Warbler

Wildlife Reserves and Protected Areas in France
There are some 140 Nature Reserves (*Réserves Naturelles*) in France, covering over 280,000 hectares. The aim is to have created 150 by 2000 as part of the Natura 2000

programme. Many of them are situated inside one of the six huge National Parks (*Parcs Nationaux*), which cover some 3830 square kilometres – but this is still only 0.7% of the country. On average five new Reserves are added to this network annually. Their specific purpose is to conserve the flora and fauna within the reserve. Some are state owned, some owned and run by local authorities, others managed by voluntary organisations, such as local naturalist groups or the LPO. Some belong to the *Espaces Naturels de France*, a non-profit making organisation. Many coastal reserves are owned by the *Conservatoire du Littoral* (Coastal Protection Society), a Government organisation dedicated to protecting the remaining natural areas of coastline and lakesides. It acquires such areas to ensure that they are preserved for future generations. 12% of the French coastline (750 km) is currently protected in this way but only small areas are reserves. Others called *Réserve Volontaire* are privately owned, sometimes by the Local Authority, and generally managed by the local branch of *Espaces Naturels de France* or the LPO. They are not always open to the public and indeed sometimes hardly accessible; certainly not all of them are of interest to bird watchers as they may be protecting invertebrates or a cave-system. When a reserve forms part of a site described in this book, it is either one that can be visited (though possibly only at certain limited times which are given) or parts of it can be viewed from public roads or footpaths.

As well as National Parks and Nature Reserves, there are also a large number (26) of regional natural parks or PNRs (*Parcs Naturels Régionaux*) such as the Haut-Languedoc and Haut-Jura; these cover some 7% of the country's surface. These are not intended primarily to protect wildlife but to maintain traditional human activities within a natural setting. Some sites will be found within these parks but often there is little or no protection (hunting is generally allowed) and/or too many tourists so they are not necessarily the best places for birds.

There are also areas designated as ZICOs (*Zones Importantes pour la Conservation des Oiseaux*) which are the equivalent of IBAs (Birdlife). As with other Important Bird Areas all over the world these are not automatically protected areas and although many of them are situated within Parks, both National and Regional, or form part of Nature Reserves, others have no protection whatsoever and are threatened by hunting, urbanisation, tourism or intensive agriculture. ZICOs range in size from a tiny airfield or lake of less than 600 hectares to a vast Ramsar wetland like the Camargue of nearly 80,000 hectares. Their inclusion as a ZICO depends on the rarity and/or number of bird species found there and French conservationists are working to have as many as possible designated a protected area. Currently, France is not doing very well at protecting bird habitat, and comes bottom in the European league table for the percentage of its territory (1.5%) designated as areas with special protection (ZPS) and most protected areas are along the sea coasts. Very few forested or agricultural areas are protected, putting at risk such birds as Woodpecker species, Black Stork, Hazelhen, Capercaillie,

Ortolan Bunting and Corncrake. Corsica is better protected, as all of its ZICO's except one have been made ZPS.

France is one of the most heavily wooded countries in the European Union, with some 28% of its land covered with forest. Over 100 ZICOs are forested or have forests within the zone. Some are private but the majority come under the aegis of the *Office National des Forêts*, which is State controlled and more or less the equivalent of the Forestry Commission. It manages over four million hectares of forests either for the State or for Local Authorities. This land also includes dunes, moorland, marshland and *maquis*. The *Code Forestier* ensures their protection in perpetuity. Unless there are signs to the contrary, or they are barred, it is possible to walk along most forestry tracks. Hunting is allowed in many of them, so be very careful from autumn to spring; cyclists and walkers are accidentally shot every year. (The storms in December 1999, when this book was almost completed, blew down an estimated 350 million trees and some of the forest sites described have been badly hit. How this may affect bird life in these woodlands is not yet known).

Contrary to what seems logical to many British birders, Hunting reserves (*Reserves de Chasse*) are areas where shooting is NOT allowed – at least for a certain number of years – to allow game populations to recover. After that period of time hunting starts again and another patch becomes a reserve. The *Office National de la Chasse* employs wardens and carries out studies on certain games birds, Capercaillie, Ptarmigan, Woodcock, partridges, as well as on deer and other game.

Bird organisations and twitch lines

France has a tiny percentage of the number of bird-watchers found in Great Britain (or indeed Holland or Scandinavia). The LPO (*la Ligue pour la Protection des Oiseaux*), the equivalent of the RSPB, is BirdLife's representative for France but has under 30,000 members. In spite of this, it runs a "twitch line" on 01 43 06 72 50 where you can listen to the latest rarity sightings – provided that you can understand rapid French and know the French names for birds (see checklist at the end of this book). Many keen birders seem to live around Paris or in the Camargue so a fair proportion of sightings come from these areas as well as reports from sea-watchers along the Atlantic and Channel coasts and Brittany (in autumn this is the French equivalent of the Scilly isles). However, there are active LPO regional groups that also record local sightings as well as organising guided walks around reserves in their area. Contact them if you are in their region. Alsace: 03 89 81 05 34; Champagne-Ardennes: 03 26 72 51 39; Franche-Comté: 03 84 76 04 50; Lorraine: 03 83 23 31 47; Loire-Atlantique/Vendée: 02 51 62 07 93; Ile-de-France: 01 49 84 07 90; Rhône-Alpes: 04 76 00 04 47

The LPO publishes two full-colour quarterly magazines, runs reserves, raises money to buy more land for reserves, cares for injured birds with centres for oiled birds in Brittany and for raptors in the Auvergne, has a continuing programme of protection for threatened species, (such as Montagu's Harriers, Storks, Little Bustard, Corncrakes) and fights the excesses and demands of the hunting-lobby (including taking to court hunters who have shot protected species). If you want to find out when any reserves they run are open, contact them at the address below or telephone 05 46 29 50 74. The British representatives of the LPO are currently Ken and Lys Hall, LPO (UK), The Anchorage, the Chalks, Chew Magna, Bristol, BS18 8SN. Tel: 01275 332980 Fax: 01275 332559.

The French equivalent of the British rarities committee is the Comité d'Homologation National (CHN), Corderie Royale, B.P. 263, 17305 Rochefort Cedex. Detailed reports of rarity sightings should be sent to them in the same way as ones are presented to the British committee. CHN will have the names and addresses of regional recorders who also like to be informed of rare birds in their areas.

Updating of sites

Though every effort has been make to ensure that site information is currently correct, by its very nature a book such as this constantly needs updating. New roads, building, tourist development or changes in farming practices may very rapidly alter sites and the bird populations they contain. The author and publisher would be very grateful if readers would let them know of any changes to, or problems with sites. In addition, readers may find that some of their favourite sites have been omitted. If they would care to send us details, the sites will be visited, included in future editions and their help acknowledged.

TRAVEL INFORMATION
Getting around

1. BY CAR: This book is intended for birdwatchers and people interested in wildlife generally, and it is assumed that they are either spending a holiday in one area or touring different parts of the country and either way would also like to visit some good birding spots. It would be difficult to reach many of the sites, which are usually way off the beaten track, without your own transport and most directions assume readers are travelling by car.

Roads, especially rural ones, are much less busy than in Britain and the motorways (except around Paris and other large cities) carry very little traffic compared to Britain and some northern European countries. However motorways are toll roads. Credit cards are accepted except on some very short, new stretches when you may have to pay a few Euros in cash. French motorways have many more petrol stations with pleasant restaurants, picnic and play areas than British ones. Additionally there are frequent *aires* along motorways with toilet and picnic facilities, often in very attractive surroundings. Some even have nature trails! Not all petrol stations will accept British credit cards, so beware of the 24 hour ones where you can only pay with a card outside normal opening hours. Such filling stations are often ones attached to supermarkets and are frequently the cheapest. Motorway petrol stations are the most expensive but will always accept any credit cards.

Bison Futé is an organisation that provides information on traffic flow and road conditions at busy times of the year. It also suggests *"itinéraires bis"*, alternative routes along less busy roads often through attractive countryside. These are indicated by green signposts and maps showing these routes are available at motorway toll booths during holiday periods. They are worth taking at any time of the year if you prefer driving along quiet roads. Their web site is http:/www.equipement.gouv.fr. Access "ROUTE" to check traffic conditions in advance.

2. PUBLIC TRANSPORT: There are good high speed rail links between large towns and the nearest stations to major birding areas have been given in the introduction to that region. However rural public transport is normally limited to the school bus run or a twice-daily bus service to the nearest town on market days, so buses may only run once a day – or week! Where it is possible to use public transport, this is stated.

3. CYCLING: When it is feasible to cycle, either by hiring bicycles or taking your own, this is mentioned in the text. Certain areas (the Camargue, the Brenne, the Dombe area north of Lyon and parts of the Atlantic coast, for example) are ideal for combining a birdwatching and cycling holiday.

Cycles can accompany you as luggage on TGV or InterCity trains in France only if they are folding models fitting into a 120 x 90 cm cover. Ordinary models must be checked into the rail depot and will travel independently of you, arriving anything between two to five days later (especially over a week-end). This service costs approximately 200 F. You can take cycles on some regional and local trains free of charge but each train carries only three cycles and the routes are limited. The Rail Express call centre (0990 848848) can tell you whether a specific line has trains with facilities for carrying bicycles. It is also necessary to obtain an up-to-date SNCF timetable and look for services with the bicycle symbol. The regional timetables are published twice yearly. They are available from European Rail Timetables (01909 485855).

4. WALKING: Long-distance walkers and climbers have their own guidebooks and maps, and many of the sites featured in this book are on or near the network of GR's (*Sentiers de Grande Randonnée* or long-distance footpaths) that criss-cross France. The Comité National des Sentiers de Grande Randonnée, 8 Avenue Marceau, 75008, Paris publishes guides to these footpaths. Where a birdwatcher can walk along these profitably for short or longer distances, this is also mentioned in the text, but this book is not intended primarily for the long-distance hiker. There are local footpaths near many of the sites featured and they are described if they lead to good birdwatching spots. However, anyone using them for long periods, especially in mountain areas, should purchase walking maps locally.

Accommodation

It is very rare not to be able to find a small, overnight hotel (cheap by British standards), however remote the area, near to where you wish to stop. The exception is high-season holiday periods (which include winter in the mountain regions) when hotels will be full, or totally out-of-season, when they may be closed. There are an increasing number of cheap chains (*Formule 1, Première Classe, Etap, Campanile*) to be found throughout France, mainly on the outskirts of the larger towns, often beside a motorway, and these are open all year round. Whilst these only charge between 140 F–250 F per night for a double-room, they are not usually to be found near any of the sites in this book, though they can be very useful when touring or on the way to a birding destination. *Mercure* and *Ibis* are slightly more expensive hotels, also to be found throughout the country, often near motorways.

In rural areas the *Logis de France* group of (usually) small, family-run hotels are excellent value and normally serve very good regional food. A book and map showing all their hotels can be obtained from 83, avenue d'Italie, 75013, Paris (Tel: 01 45 84 70 00 Fax: 01 45 83 59 66) or you can use their Internet site www.logis-de-france.fr. to find where hotels are situated and then make your bookings. Their Central Reservation telephone number is 01 45 84 83 84 or e-mail: info@logis-de-france.fr. *Logis* are frequently situated in small villages near Regional or National Parks, and one or several *Logis* will be found near almost all of the sites described in this book. They can be very useful for birdwatchers.

Gîtes ruraux are holiday homes to rent in country areas, useful for a family holiday or if staying in one place for a week or so. The Gîtes Panda are rural gites recommended by the WWF, often in or near reserves. There is a contact address for each department, which any French tourist office can supply but the easiest way to find out details of gites is through the Internet: Http://www.gites-de-france.fr. The head office is the Maison de Gîtes de France et du Tourisme Vert, 59, rue Saint-Lazare, 75439 Paris Cedex 09. Tel: 1 49 70 75 75 Fax: 01 42 81 28 53 and they publish an annual *Guide des Gîtes Ruraux* and another for Gîtes Panda. Phone for current prices.

Chambres d'hôtes are the French equivalent of Bed and Breakfast. These can now be found everywhere in France, especially in rural areas; they must meet certain standards and the ones listed in the official guide (current price 140 F, available from the address above) are very good and fulfil all the sanitary regulations. You will see the signs at farm entrances and on village houses. Some are also designated *table d'hôtes*, which means that you can have lunch or dinner there. These are generally farms as all products must be reared and processed by the farmer, except the wine, which is local – and may be a little difficult to drink! Local tourist offices will give you details of ones in the area but outside holiday periods there is usually no need to book in advance.

Camping There are an enormous number of campsites in France, especially in tourist areas where most of the sites in this book are to be found. Even quite small villages usually have a municipal campsite with electricity, water and toilets. Some of the large campsites near the coast are very sophisticated with every facility but are very full in summer. Only in early spring and autumn may it be more difficult to find a campsite open. Staying in a caravan/camping car outside campsites is forbidden in many areas. The French Camping-Caravanning Federation sells an annually updated guide to sites. Its address is 78 rue de Rivoli, 75004 Paris. Tel: 1 42 72 8

The French Tourist office in London will supply regional brochures, Gîtes and Chambers d'hôtes books and maps. The address is Maison de la France, 178 Picadilly, London W1V 0AL. Tel: 09068 244 123. Calls charged at 60p per minute. Fax: 0207 493 6594. Website: http://www.franceguide.com.

Health and emergencies

As France is part of the European Union, visitors from the UK should take form E111 from the Department of Health with them if they wish for reciprocal medical treatment. Otherwise make sure you are covered by a good travel and holiday policy. Emergency services for doctors, dentists and pharmacists can be contacted by dialling 15 (toll free). If involved in an accident, you dial 17 for police, 112 or 15 for medical help, 18 for the fire-service.

As the British do not have identity cards it is advisable to carry your passport with you in case the police stop you even though within the EU you theoretically need only produce valid identification. A passport is naturally essential for non-EU citizens. In case of emergencies there are British Consulates in Toulouse tel: 05 61 15 02 02, Biarritz tel: 05 59 24 21 40, Bordeaux tel: 05 57 22 21 10, Lyon tel: 04 72 77 81 70. The Consulate in Paris shares a telephone number with the Embassy: 1 44 51 31 00. The address is 16 rue d'Anjou, 75008 Paris.

Opening Hours

In small towns in the south most shops close from 12.00 to 14.00 and then stay open until (normally) 19.00. Large supermarkets on the outskirts of towns usually stay open during lunchtime but they may not open until 10.00. Most banks also close between mid-day and 14.00 but stay open until 18.00, except for Saturdays, which are mornings only Lunch and evening meals are served at standard European hours, 12.00–14.30 for lunch and 19.30–22.00 for dinner. Bars, which also serve tea, coffee and soft drinks, and can usually produce a croissant for breakfast, a sandwich or light snack, are open all day until late in the evening.

Maps

Blay-foldex series whole of France 1/1,000,000 is useful for planning tour; 15 regional maps 1/250,000 (2 cm=5 km) cover the country in sensible divisions and give enough detail to find your way to sites if used in conjunction with the sketch maps in this book. They are obtainable from almost any motorway shop and most petrol stations, though usually only the ones covering that area. The Michelin series gives more detail but using them means buying more maps, although the annually produced Michelin *Atlas Routier et Touristique* has the whole of France in one large book, on a scale of 1/200,000 (1 cm=2 km).

It costs about 120 F (£12) and is obtainable from any motorway shop, most bookshops and newsagents *Maison de la Presse*.

The National Geographical Institute (IGN) topographic maps 1/100,000 (1cm=1km) cover the country in 72 maps and are excellent if you need more details for any area. Walkers will need the larger scale IGN walking maps (cartes de randonnées) 1/50,000 or even 1/25,000. The ones covering the local area can be bought from any *Maison de la Presse*. Each scale has its own colour: for example 1/25,000 maps are from the "*série bleue*" and 1/100,000 from the *série verte*, so if you know the number you can ask for an "IGN série bleue numero..."

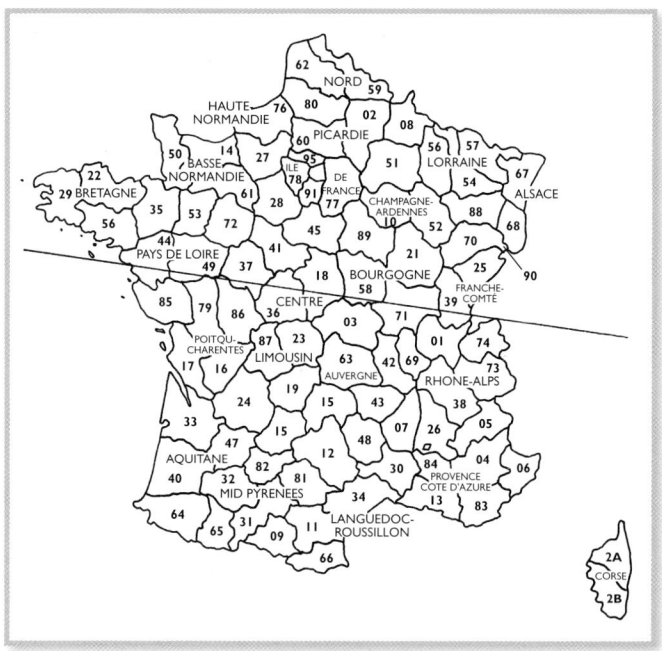

France showing Regions and Departments

01 Ain	23 Creuse	47 Lot-et-Garonne	71 Saône-et-Loire
02 Aisne	24 Dordogne	48 Lozère	72 Sarthe
03 Allier	25 Doubs	49 Maine-et-Loire	73 Savoie
04 Alpes de Haute-Provence	26 Drôme	50 Manche	74 Haute-Savoie
05 Hautes-Alps	27 Eure	51 Marne	75 Paris
06 Alpes-Maritimes	28 Eures-et-Loir	52 Haute-Marne	76 Seine-Maritime
07 Ardèche	29 Finistère	53 Mayenne	77 Seine-et-Marne
08 Ardennes	30 Gard	54 Meurthe-et-Moselle	78 Yvelines
09 Ariège	31 Haute-Garonne	55 Meuse	79 Deux-Sèvres
10 Aube	32 Gers	56 Morbihan	80 Somme
11 Aude	33 Gironde	57 Moselle	81 Tarn
12 Aveyron	34 Hérault	58 Nièvre	82 Tarn-et-Garonne
13 Bouches-du-Rhône	35 Ille-et-Vilaine	59 Nord	83 Var
14 Valvados	36 Indre	60 Oise	84 Vaucluse
15 Cantal	37 Indre-et-Loire	61 Orne	85 Vendée
16 Charente	38 Isère	62 Pas-de-Calais	86 Vienne
17 Charente-Maritime	39 Jura	63 Puy-de-Dôme	87 Haute-Vienne
18 Cher	40 Landes	64 Pyrénées-Atlantiques	88 Vosges
19 Corrèze	41 Loir-et-Cher	65 Hautes-Pyrénées	89 Yonne
2A Corse du Sud	42 Loire	66 Pyrénées Orientales	90 Territoire de Belfort
2B Haute-Corse	43 Haute-Loire	67 Bas-Rhin	91 Essonne
21 Côte d'Or	44 Loire-Atlantique	68 Haut-Rhin	92, 93 et 94: petite ceinture de Paris
22 Côtes d'Armor	45 Loiret	69 Rhône	95 Val d'Oise
	46 Lot	70 Haute-Saône	

Southern France – Main birding areas covered in the Guide

SOUTHERN FRANCE SITE CALENDAR

<u>January</u>   **Atlantic and Mediterranean** coastal sites for divers, sea duck and waterbirds. Check **Orx marshes** for wintering duck and cranes, possibly Spotted or Sea Eagles. Also **Camp du Poteau** and **Les Barthes d'Adour** (southern Atlantic Coast) for Cranes. Hard weather will bring many northern duck and geese to lakes and bays along the Atlantic coast both this month and next.

Les Baux (Camargue area) and **Montauban** for Wallcreeper and Eagle Owl.

Crossbills active in mountain conifer forests; Citril Finches flocking at lower altitudes.

<u>February</u>   Storks already nesting at **Teich** Reserve (Atlantic Coast). Buzzard and Goshawk displaying over forests. Alpine Accentor and Snow Finch still around ski stations in **Alps** and **Pyrenees**. Black and White-backed Woodpeckers noisy and active at **Forest d'Issaux** (Pyrenees); all wood-pecker species easy to spot in woodland sites while Buzzards and accipiters display overhead. Cranes return north at the end of the month; they cross the **Pyrenean passes** during good weather and may be seen at **Captieux**

Citral Finches

(Atlantic Coast) on their way north. Geese and plovers start leaving the **Atlantic coastal sites**.

March   **Atlantic and Mediterranean coastal sites** for dabbling ducks, waders and other migrants returning north. Spoonbill migration north peaks during the second week. Garganey may be spotted at the coast or on inland lakes. Great Spotted Cuckoo and early warblers at **Mediterranean sites**. Woodpeckers noisy and active in woodland sites, Crossbills also easy to see. Egyptian Vulture, Black Kite and Short-toed Eagle are early migrants. Flocks of up to 500 Black Kites can sometimes be seen crossing the **Pyrenees** from mid-month onwards.

April   Lower altitude sites: summer breeders arrive throughout month. Many species holding territory and early breeders already nesting.
    Last week: best time for **the Camargue** – waders, migrants and summer breeders. Bee-eaters back at colonies, Flamingos start nesting.
    Migration sites (**Leucate, Grave, Massif Central, Pyrenees, and Cap Corse**) for large flocks of Black Kites, hirundines and many passerines during the first half of the month. Montagu's Harriers return to breeding sites throughout the month.

May   First week: **the Brenne, the Camargue, inland Mediterranean sites, all coastal sites**. Migration of Honey Buzzards through passes and coastal migration sites continues all month. Rollers back at breeding sites around Mediterranean.
    Best period for summer and resident breeders at **Alpine and Pyrenean sites** below 1500 m, **Corsica**, the **Cévennes** and the **Massif Central**. Last two weeks: higher sites normally accessible for Rock Thrush, Citril Finch, Water Pipit and Alpine Accentor. Wallcreepers back at breeding sites.

June   Ideal period for all **mountain sites** over 1500 m, also **Corsica, Cévennes** and **Massif Central.**

July   Birds still active in highest areas: **the Pyrenees (Néouvielle, Gavarnie)** and **the Alps** for Ptarmigan, Snow Finch, and Alpine Accentor. Juvenile Crossbills and Citril Finch disperse. At the end of the month the first waders return from the Arctic to wetland sites.

August   The quietest months for birds, the busiest for tourists. Good for butterflies. Juvenile vultures flying: quite large flocks often seen feeding in non-breeding areas of **Pyrenees** and **Cévennes**. Nutcrackers easy to see in the **Alps**. During the last week, post-breeding migration gathers momentum; large numbers of Black Kites and Honey Buzzards cross the Pyrenees, especially at **Organbidexka and Eyne**. Some passerines such as Bee-eater can be seen along the **Mediterranean** and crossing the Pyrenees in flocks. Spoonbill migration south along the **Atlantic** coast peaks during the last ten days of the month. White Storks and a few Black pass through on migration this month. The numbers of waders along the western coasts increases.

September   Migration continues throughout month. Ospreys can be seen along the main river valleys, especially the **Allier** and **Loire** and at wetland sites. At **Organbidexka, Port d'Aula and Eyne** first two weeks best for variety of species crossing the Pyrenees: Short-toed and Booted Eagles, kites, storks, etc. Peak sea-watching period for shearwaters, Gannets, skuas, terns along the **Atlantic** coast. The end of the month (and the beginning of the next) is the best time to search for rarities on headlands along the Atlantic coast.

October   Migration continues at **Organbidexka** and the Basque passes. American vagrants still turning up along Atlantic coast; waders at **Atlantic** and **Mediterranean** sites. Northern populations of Little Bustards and Stone Curlews begin to flock and move south. Look for them on the plains south of **Niort** and north of **Angouleme** and the Reserve near l'Anglée in the **Poitevin Marshes** (Atlantic coast).

November   Migration of Cranes. Last week: large numbers of Cranes at **Captieux**, **Aquitaine (Atlantic Coast)**. Red Kite still passing through Pyrenean passes. The first wintering ducks and Brent Geese arrive at **Atlantic** coastal sites.

December   First week: Cranes still at above sites or moving through **Pyrenean p**asses. Geese, swans and geese at wintering sites. Intense cold will bring large numbers of Goldeneye, Smew, Eider and geese to the Atlantic coast and inland lakes. Divers offshore at **Atlantic and Mediterranean** sites.

Pyrenean sites including Gavarnie for displaying Lammergeiers and Golden Eagles; Snowfinches and Alpine Accentors around ski stations and lower passes in the **Pyrenees** and the **Alps**.

Spotted Eagle returns to the **Camargue** most winters.

Please note that the calendar suggests ideal times to visit various sites, though extreme weather conditions may affect timing. Except for specific periods mentioned, most species will be in these sites for some time before and after the suggested month. For example, Eagle Owls will be calling from late November, Wallcreepers will be at their winter sites by December, Lammergeiers may continue to display in January, woodpeckers are still active and calling in March and later, all coastal and lake sites are good throughout the winter months.

I would like to thank all those people, friends, wardens and other bird-watchers, who have helped with information on sites and birds, especially Brian Dore for all the driving and checking sites, Nigel Jones and Mike Witherick of Ornitholidays, Alex Clamens, Bertrand Delprat, Antoine Rouillon, Tony Williams and especially Marie-Jo Dubourg-Savage, who answered all my queries during the writing of this book, made many helpful suggestions and finally took the trouble to read the draft and correct any mistakes. I must take the blame for others that may have crept in later.

THE ATLANTIC COAST

Between the estuaries of the Loire and the Gironde, the Atlantic (or Bay of Biscay) coast forms a series of vast, shallow bays protected by several large islands with road links to the mainland. Although increasingly used for shellfish and oyster farming, the bays are still of international importance for the numbers of migrating and wintering waterbirds that feed on the mudflats. Because the bays are so shallow, tide levels are important for bird watching. The best conditions are a few hours before high tide, in the morning when the sun is in the east.

Tide-tables can be obtained from any tourist office and most hotels and campsites. At places such as Noirmoutier where the tide affects access, large boards display the times of high and low tides.

Behind the coast most of the marshes have been drained, so the countryside resembles the East Anglian fens or the Dutch polders. The sea is retained by dikes and the water meadows, criss-crossed by drainage channels and ditches and often flooded in winter, are the haunt of harriers, kestrels, lapwings and **Golden Plovers** in winter. Small areas of natural marsh remain, some now reserves (see sites 3-6).

WHEN TO VISIT: For most of the sites along this coast, mid-August to January and April to June are best. The beaches are very crowded in July and August but the inland marshes are reasonably quiet. As with most wetland sites, migration periods (March-May and August-October) will produce the greatest number of birds and species but all sites also hold good numbers of wintering **Brent Geese, Shelduck,** egrets, ducks and waders. Some interesting species also breed here, notably **Black-winged Stilt, Avocet, Kentish Plover, Bluethroat, Cetti's Warbler, Tawny Pipit** (very small numbers), **Crested and Short-toed lark.** Slightly further inland, both **Stone Curlew** and **Little Bustard** can be found but the latter is becoming very rare.

The most northerly headlands on the islands are excellent spots for sea-watching and they also attract migrating passerines in the spring. In August and the beginning of September, **Cory's, Great, Sooty, Manx** and large numbers of **Balearic Shearwaters** can be seen off this coast quite close inshore, together with **Storm** and **Leach's Petrel, Guillemot and Razorbill.** A few American gulls (**Sabine** and **Ring-billed**) are noted every year. In fact, there is always a good chance of rarities turning up along this coast, as well as in Brittany. The fact that few are reported probably reflects a lack of bird watchers rather than vagrant birds.

Accommodation: Although this is a very popular holiday area, most visitors stay in campsites or their holiday homes. There are surprisingly few hotels and rooms will need to be reserved during holiday periods while most hotels, outside the largest towns, are closed during the winter. One in Jard sur Mer and two in Noirmoutier stay open all through the year and further south there are year-round ones in Arcachon. There are ones belonging to the cheaper chains around la Rochelle, Rochefort, Bordeaux, Bayonne and Biarritz.

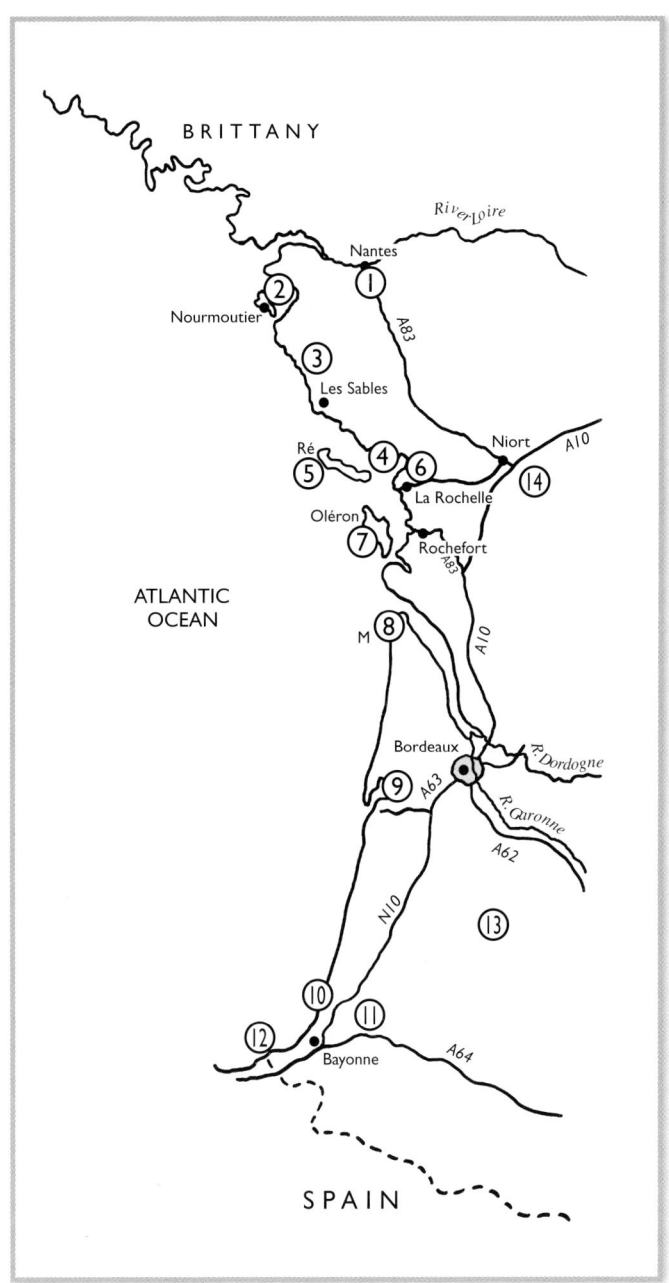

Atlantic Coast birding areas

Area 1	**Lakes near Nantes**	
	Site i	Cité des Oiseaux
	Site ii	Grand Lieu
Area 2	**Bourgneuf Bay Maritime Reserve and Noirmoutier**	
	Site i	Bourgneuf Bay
	Site ii	Ile de Noirmoutier
Area 3	**Olonne Marsh**	
Area 4	**Aiguillon Bay**	
	Sites i-iii the coast	
	Sites iv-v the Poitevin marshes	
Area 5	**Île de Ré**	
	Site i	Lileau-des-Niges National Nature Reserve
	Site ii	The Fier
Area 6	**Rochefort: Yves Marshes and Moëze Reserves**	
	Site i	Yves Marshes
	Site ii	Rochefort Sewage Works
	Site iii	Moëze Olèron Natural Reserve
Area 7	**Île d'Olèron**	
Area 8	**Grave headland** for spring migration	
Area 9	**Bassin d'Arcachon**	
	Site i	Teich Bird Reserve
	Site ii	Domaine de Certes salt-works and coastal trail
	Site iii	Près Salés d'Arès et de Lège-Cap-Ferret reserve
Area 10	**Hossegor lake** and nearby reserves	
Area 11	**Les Barthes d'Ardour and Orx Marshes**	
	Site i	Les Barthes
	Site ii	Orx Marshes
Area 12	**Hendaye**	
TWO INLAND SITES		
Area 13	**Camp du Poteau, Captieux (Landes)** for Cranes	
Area 14	**Niort** – plains to the south-east for "steppe" birds".	

Although very crowded in summer, anywhere in the areas would make a good combined family seaside/ birding holiday, with the advantage that August is a post-nuptial migration period.

Maps: Recta foldex nos. 3, 4 and 5 cover the whole coast from the north around Nantes to the Spanish frontier around Bayonne (this last also covers most of the Pyrenees to east of Toulouse and Ax). Also Institute National Geographique Topographic maps nos. 32 Nantes, 39 la Rochelle, 46 north of Bordeaux, 55 south of Bordeaux, 62 and 69 Spanish frontier area.

Area 1 **NANTES LAKES**

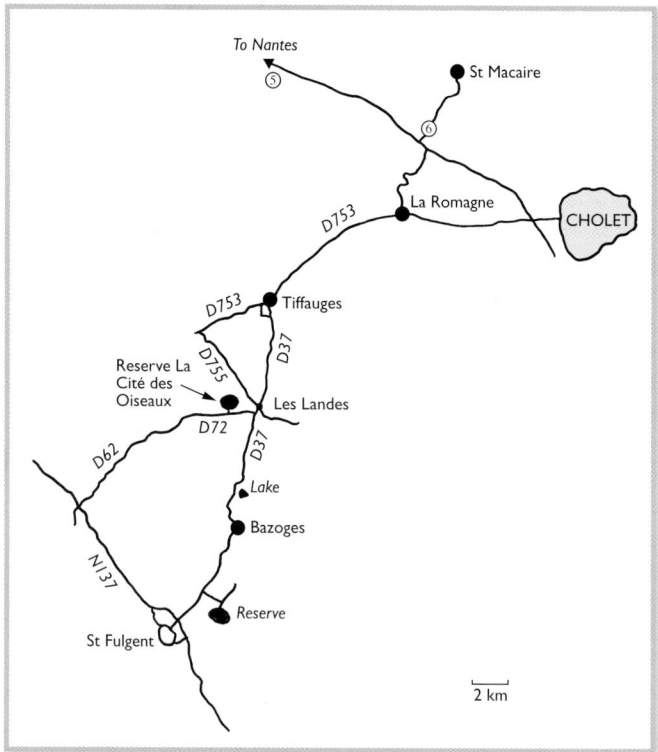

Atlantic Coast Area 1 Nantes Lake site i. Boucheries Lake

Site i. **BOUCHERIES LAKE**

The Réserve Ornithologique des Landes Genusson, also known as Boucheries Lake, is 45 km south-east of Nantes. It is now called and signed "LA CITÉ DES OISEAUX". Situated as it is just inland from Bourgneuf Bay and Grand Lieu, both very important sites for migratory and wintering birds, this small reserve can at times attract thousands of waders and duck. Autumn and the end of winter are the best times to visit this reserve when the numbers of breeding and wintering duck are swelled by many migrant species, including **Spoonbill**. A very cold spell in winter should also bring in some **Smew** or **Goosander**. **Hen Harrier** breeds nearby. (There are several other small lakes in this area, most of them either difficult to see from a public road or too much shot over).

ACCESS: To reach the reserve, leave Nantes on the N249 dual carriageway to Cholet. Get off at junction 6 (signed St-André, St-Macaire, etc and la

Romagne) and take the D91 south in the direction of this last village. In la Romagne, follow the "Toutes directions" signs and leave on the D753 signed Montaigu. Leave the D753 in Tiffauges village and take the D9 into the centre. At the end of the village, before a factory and silos, turn right onto the D37 towards les Landes. In Les Landes look for signs to BAZOGES and then take a right turn onto the D72 following the "La Cité des Oiseaux" signs. In 1.6 km turn right at the sign to the reserve. The "Cité" is also clearly signed from the N137 near St. Fulgent, which can be reached from the A83 motorway Nantes-Niort.

Since 1998 when the Vendée Council renamed and took over the management of this 54 hectare reserve, hides and marked walks have been constructed, as well as a visitors' information centre. This latter is open between 14-18h Monday-Friday, Sundays and holidays from 1st April to 31st May. Between 1st June and 15th September it is open from 10-12 and 14-19 every day. From 16th September to 15th October it is open between 14-18 Sundays and holidays. Groups can phone for a visit on 02 51 91 72 25 at any time. Reasonably up-to-date bird sightings are posted up. Even if you turn up outside these times, it is always possible to walk towards the lake and along the embankment on the left and scope the birds or walk through the woods towards the hide.

Another reserve managed by the Vendée Council is the 15 hectares of Les Renaudières Saint-Fulgent Espace Natural. There is a small lake, where **Purple Heron** may be seen in summer, and beech-oakwoods, good for woodland birds in spring. It lies some 2 km east of the D37 north of St. FULGEN and is clearly signed.

Site ii.
The largest lake near Nantes is **GRAND-LIEU**, some 10 km southwest of the city. It certainly looks a "big place" on the map and though most of it is now a reserve, access is still very difficult indeed (like many French reserves which are primarily for the wildlife, not for visitors) besides which a certain amount of shooting continues to be allowed. In summer the lake covers 800 hectares but in winter this may expand to over 3000 hectares. During wet winters, large stretches of land around the lake are flooded, ensuring that birds are very scattered over a huge area of water and lanes may be under water. Finally, a belt of vegetation around the lake hides much of it. However, local tourist pressure has resulted in the opening of visitors' centres. At Saint-Philbert-de-Grand Lieu on the D117 to the south there is a *masion du lac* and most recently and nearer to the reserve a *masion de la réserve naturelle* has just been opened at the village of L'ETIER, south-east of BOUAYE on the D85 to the north of the lake. The public is welcomed four afternoons a week and guided walks can be arranged. There is a permanent exhibition giving information about the fauna and flora of the lake and threats to their continued existence.

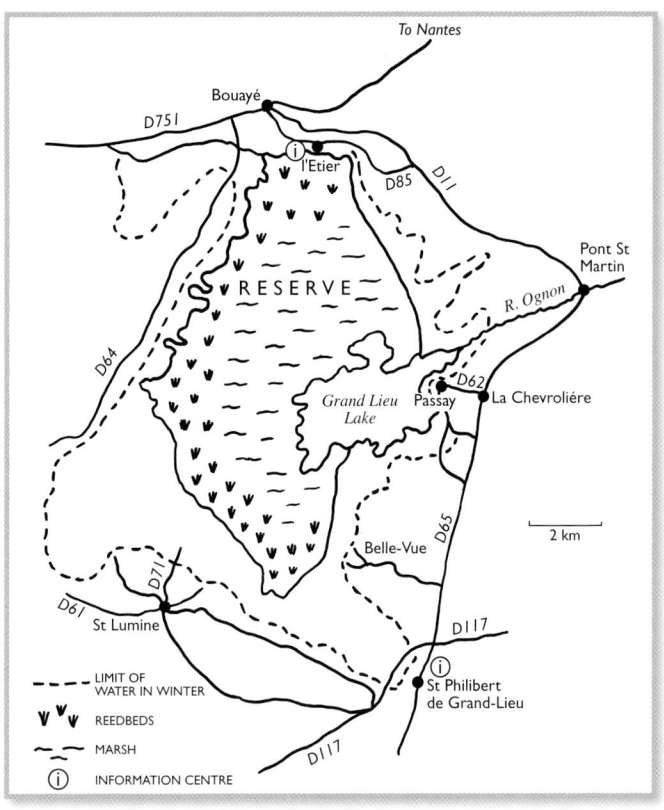

Atlantic Coast Area 1 Nantes Lakes site ii. Grand-Lieu

ACCESS: Lanes radiating from the villages of BELLE-VUE and PASSEY, both on minor roads north-west of the D65, seem to lead towards the lake, but then end at remote farm houses or circle back without getting anywhere near the water. There are also some tracks leading out of the village of St. LUMINE on the D64. It might be worth driving around some of these lanes and scoping the lake since thousands of duck winter here; terns and waders can be seen on migration and breeding birds include **Cormorant, Night-heron, Cattle and Little Egret, Grey and Purple Heron**, a few **Spoonbill** (one of only two sites in France, they have been breeding here since 1981), a few **Black Tern, Bluethroat, Bearded Tit** and **Sacred Ibis**. A single individual of this last species was first seen near the Spoonbill colony in 1990 and several couples have been breeding successfully since 1993. Breeding raptors include **Honey Buzzard, Black Kite** and up to 40 pairs of **Marsh Harrier**. In addition the largest heronry in France is found here but the hunting pressure on the unprotected marshland, the fact that hundreds of tons of grain are dumped into the lake to attract wildfowl and some 200,000 lead cartridges left behind each winter, is ruining the habitat.

Other fauna and flora: Otter and Genet are among the mammals found here and 37 species (some very abundant) of Dragonflies have been identified. There is a rich marsh flora.

Area 2 **BOURGNEUF BAY AND NOIRMOUTIER**

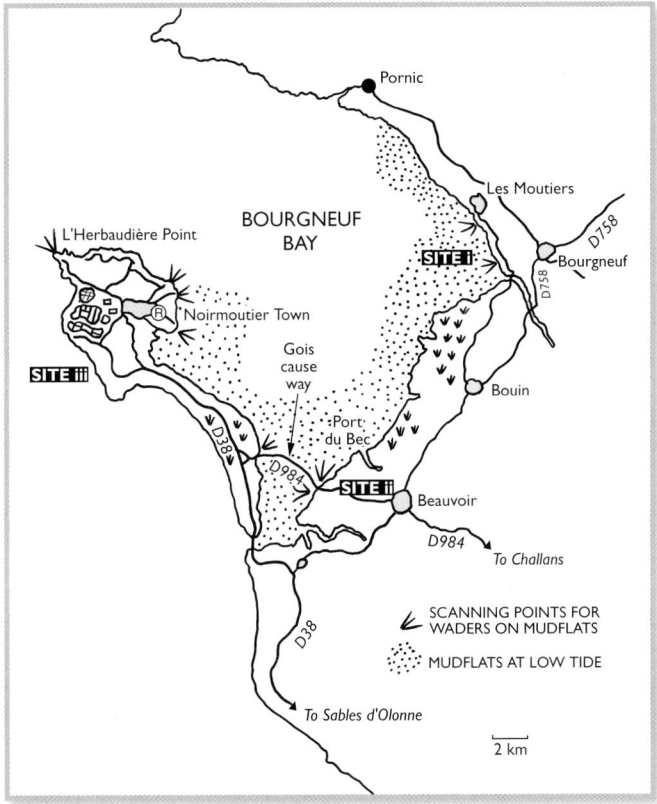

Atlantic Coast Area 2 sites i. and ii. Bourgneuf and Noirmoutier

Site i. **BOURGNEUF BAY**

Any road that leads to the edge of the bay and gives a view over the mudflats will allow you views of birds but the mud flats stretch to the horizon at low

27

Scop's Owl

tide and birds can be very scattered until an incoming tide drives them shoreward. The periods two or three hours before and after high-tide are best. Three good viewpoints are from a stretch of the D118 just south of LES MOUTIERS, where there is a coastal footpath, the little fishing PORT DU BEC (take the D51 from Beauvoir-sur-Mer) and the entrance to the GOIS causeway. The GOIS is a hard-surfaced road on a sandbar that links Noirmoutier island to the mainland. It is only safe to cross it at low tide. There is a large board on the right of the road giving tide times. Park here and walk left along the grassy top of the seawall or when the tide is receding venture a short distance out onto the Gois. Alternatively, especially at high tide, drive back 0.9 km. Turn left at the few houses known as Trente Salops. Turn left again directly after the last house towards the seawall. Park and walk along the wall. Even at low tide there will be scattered birds. In winter these include **Brent Goose, Shelduck, Curlew, Little Egret, Avocet, Oystercatcher, Grey Plover** and many smaller waders. In spring, look for **Bluethroat** among the Tamarisk bushes and along the ditches. **Marsh Harriers** fly over the polders, especially in winter, **Hen Harriers** are less common. **Montagu's Harriers** occurs in spring.

Site ii. ILE DE NOIRMOUTIER

Cross to the island, either by the Gois causeway <u>at low tide only</u> or the main D38 road. Stop where the causeway reaches the island. This is a good place for waders and grebes, as well as passage terns in spring. High tides drive them close inshore. With luck **Kentish Plover** may be seen in the polders just to the north. The sewage works just south of the Gois also attract terns and waders.

The northeast headland, L'HERBAUDIÈRE, is a good spot to seawatch, especially when large numbers of **Balearic Shearwaters** pass between July and September. Other shearwaters, skuas and many species of gulls are also likely to be seen in autumn. There are **Eider** and other sea duck and divers in winter. Look out for **Crested Lark** around this area. **Melodious Warbler** and **Bluethroat** may be found in the bushes around LUZÉRONDE, on the coast just south east of L'Herbaudière. The old saltmarshes and pans in the centre of the island between LUZÉRONDE and the town of NOIRMOUTIER have breeding **Black-winged Stilt, Avocet** and **Common Tern**, as well as **Bluethroat, Serin, Black Redstart, Cirl and Corn**

Bunting, Montagu's and **Marsh Harriers**. There is another sewage works off the D5 between these two towns, which may be worth checking for passage terns and grebes. It is possible to view from a car along some of the tracks that run from the D5 into the salt pans. **Hoopoe, Stonechat, Northern Wheatear** and **Blue-headed W**agtail are other species that may be found anywhere on the island **Short-toed Treecreeper** may be found in the woods south of L'EPINE as well as in the *Bois de la Blanche* in the north, where **Scops Owl** can also be heard in summer. The *Bois de la Blanche* is private, but it is possible to walk along the beach beside the wood. It may be worth searching for **Tawny Pipit** (rare) from the coast road west of L'EPINE.

A comparatively new reserve, and one of the best places on the island to birdwatch is MÜLLEMBOURG MARSH, which lies behind the Jetée Jacobsen, east of the town of Noirmoutier at the entrance channel to the port. The reserve is run by the LPO and the regional group organise guided visits but it is possible to scope the marsh (it is quite small) from the Jetty Jacobsen which runs from the outskirts of Noirmoutier separating the marsh from the sea. **Black-winged Stilt, Avocet, Shelduck** and **Kentish Plover** are amongst the breeding species; **Shelduck** and **Brent Geese** congregate here in winter and **Spotted Redshank** may be found among the many passage waders.

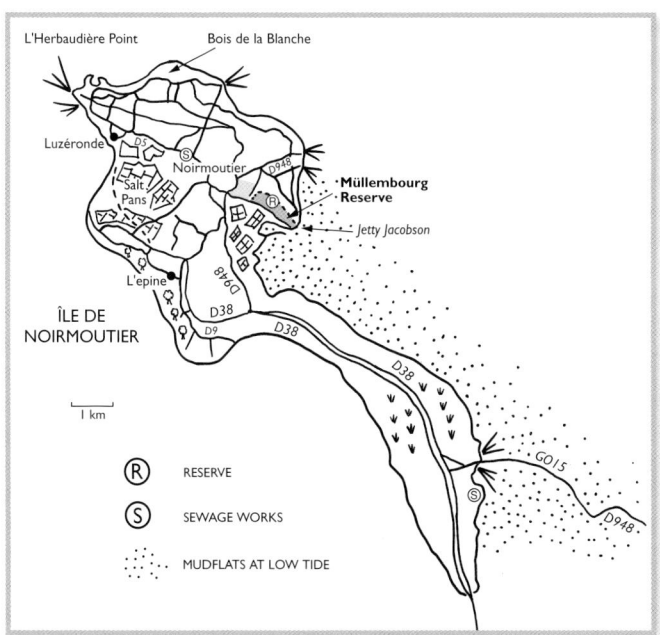

Atlantic Coast Area 2 site ii Île de Noirmoutier

Area 3 OLONNE MARSHES AND LES SABLES D'OLONNE

The **OLONNE** marshes, comprising pools, reedbeds and irrigation channels, lie due east of the D38 coast road north of LES SABLES D'OLONNE. They are separated from the sea by dunes and a belt of trees, the "forest of Olonne". Access is difficult as large parts of the marshes are private hunting areas and there are limited viewpoints from the roads.

A large colony of **Avocets** breeds in these marshes and can be seen all year round. Other breeding birds include **Black-winged Stilt, Redshank** and **Lapwing** while large numbers of **Shelduck, Pintail, Shoveler, Wigeon, and Gadwall. Cormorant** and **Coot** winter there and many waders stop off during migration. Naturally enough, most take shelter in the safety of the reserve and observatory run by the Association de Défence de l'Environment en Vendée.

ACCESS: Take the D32 from OLONNE-SUR-MER which is 5 km north of Les Sables. Turn left onto the D38 just after the railway line crosses the road. After 0.8 km turn left again and follow the tarmac to the tennis courts' carpark (0.5 km from the turn). Park and follow the signs to the observatory, a large hide overlooking stretches of water. Unfortunately it is only open daily between July 1st and August 31st (9.30–12.00 and 15.00–19.00) but phone 51.33.12.97 to visit at other times of the year. Part of the reserve can be scoped from the carpark outside the fence. The vineyards and bushes around are good for passerines.

Seawatching can be good from the lighthouse at the port of LES SABLES D'OLONNE. At the entrance to the town, follow signs to La Chaume, keeping the harbour on the left. Pass the old fort on the right and park here or near the old Priory of St. Nicolas at the tip of the peninsular. Walk along the jetty to the red (port) lighthouse which gives a wider view than from the green one.

This part of the coast is especially good for watching thousands of **Balearic Shearwaters** pass in August and September, while gulls, ducks and divers can be seen in winter, given the right weather conditions. **Lesser Black-backed, Herring** and **Yellow-legged Gulls** are all here in winter giving birders the opportunity to hone their identification skills on juveniles. Rarities turn up regularly, almost annually: **Little Gull, Caspian Tern, Sabine's Gull, Cory's and Great Shearwaters, Leach's Petrel** have all turned up between July and September. Severe storms in the Atlantic sometimes cause hundreds, even thousands of birds, notably Sabine's Gulls, to shelter in the harbour.

Pelagic trips are possible from SABLES D'OLONNE in old fishing boats. Trips last some 4 hours and go some 10 km out of port. These are not exclusively for birders but certainly give a better chance of seeing sea birds at close range than just seawatching from shore. Trips should be booked at the Tourist Office (tel. 51 32 03 28) several days (preferably a couple of weeks) in advance. Groups may be able to book a longer day trip.

Area 4 AIGUILLON BAY AND THE POITEVIN MARSHES

Although **AIGUILLON BAY** is smaller than Bourgneuf, the mudflats of this 6,500 hectare bay are one of the most important sites in France for wintering and migrating waders and wildfowl. Unfortunately it is quite difficult to reach the sea wall, especially on the north side of the bay, and a telescope is essential.

Site i.
One good viewpoint is from AIGUILLON POINT and the D46A (the Digue road) leading to it from L'AIGUILLON-SUR-MER. Stop at any lay-by along the D46A where there are steps up onto the sea-wall and scan over the river mouth.

At the point, walk across the dunes to the edge of the bay. An incoming tide brings in hundreds of waders: **Oystercatcher, Avocet, Grey Plover, Dunlin, Curlew, Knot, Black-tailed and Bar-tailed Godwit, Redshank, Spotted Redshank, Ringed Plover** in winter. All these plus **Spoonbill, Curlew Sandpiper, Ruff, Snipe, Wood and Green Sandpipers** in spring and autumn. Check the dunes for pipits and larks (**Tawny Pipit** on migration as well as a few elusive **Short-toed Larks**).

Site ii.
Another place to view the marshes and bay can be reached by taking the road (signed "St. Michel en l'Herm par La Dive") which joins the D46A to the D60 halfway between the Point and l'Aiguillon-sur-Mer. On reaching the D60 turn right. After 2.9 km the hard road finishes and a dirt track leads to the canal and dyke overlooking the salt marsh where there are **Greylag Geese** and waders at high tide. Walk along below the dyke towards the bay to scope the mudflats. There are always harriers over the fields in this area but numbers vary. In some winters **Hen Harriers** are numerous, in others very scarce. **Marsh Harriers** are more common. **Montagu's Harrier** and **Bluethroat** can be found in the breeding season.

Site iii.
The east side of Aiguillon Bay can be viewed from near CHARRON (take the D105 E2 signed "Port de Pavé" to the river mouth by turning right at the end of the village) or rather better at ESNANDES. Take the D105 coast road to Esnandes village and then the first right (D106E2) towards the estuary and Pointe St. Clement, past the Camping les Misottes and the well-signed Maison

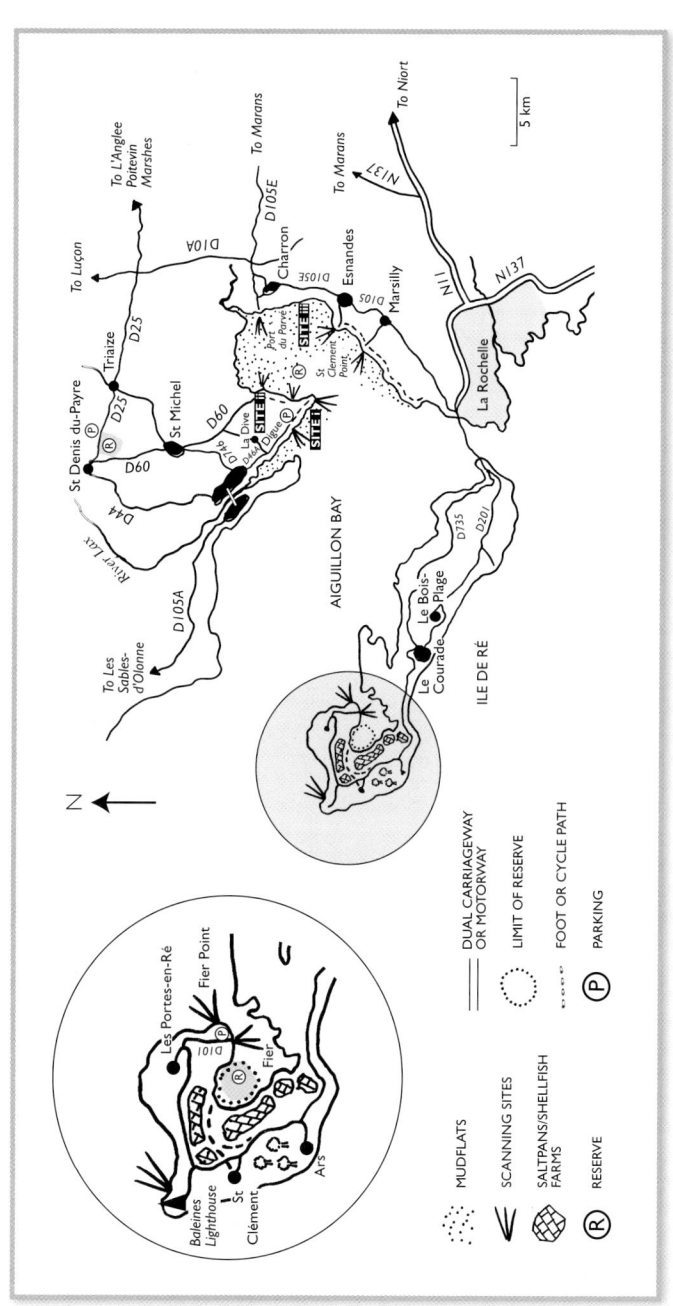

Atlantic Coast Areas 4 and 5 Aiguillon Bay and Île de Ré

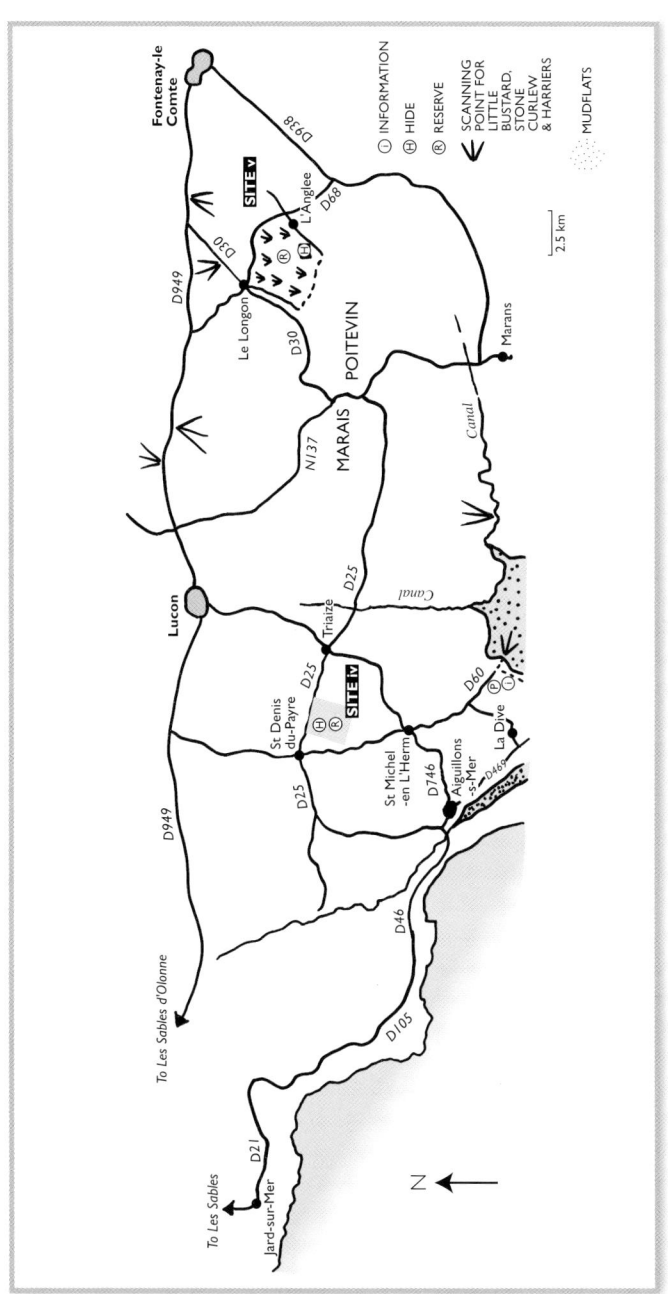

Atlantic Coast Area 4 sites iv. and v. Poitevin Marshes

de Mytiliculture (shellfish culture). On the coast are mudflats and a good area of salt marsh. Drive (or walk) up onto the little cliff on the left for a view over the bay. South of Esnandes there is only a narrow, rocky beach although a coastal footpath runs for miles along the south side of the bay with plenty of parking places.

Site iv.
The inland **POITEVIN MARSHES** can be best viewed from the Reserve Naturelle Michel Brosselin at ST. DENIS-DU-PAYRE. Take the D25 from St. Denis towards Triaize. The hide is 1.3 km from the end of St. Denis. It is only open to the public on the first Sunday of each month in the winter, every Sunday between 14.00-18.00 from March to June and daily between 10–12 and 15–19.00 from July 12 to August 31. Groups of 10 or more can arrange a visit anytime by calling or faxing 02.51.27.23.92. But it is possible to look into the reserve from the D25 road. **Black-winged Stilt, Black Tern** (irregularly), **Redshank, Bluethroat** and **Whinchat** breed on this 207 hectare reserve on communal grassland which floods in winter when it holds thousands of dabbling duck (mainly **Teal** and **Wigeon**) while hundreds of **Lapwing** and **Golden Plover** can be seen in the fields opposite. **Spoonbill, White** and **Black Stork** and many species of waders can be found here on passage.

Flora: In spring marsh plants including *Iris spuria,* Star Fruit *Damasonium alisma* and Adder's-tongue Spearwort *Ranunculus ophioglossifolius* as well as several orchid species, especially Loose-flowered *Orchis laxiflora* and Pyramidal *Anacamptis pyramidalis.*

Site v.
Further inland the local authority has erected a hide overlooking the east side of the communal marsh and flooded meadows that form the Reserve Naturelle Voluntaire du Marais Communal le Poiré-sur-Velluire beyond the village of L'ANGLÉE. A narrow canal and the Routes des Huttes and des Hollandaise lead from the hide and enclose the reserve, giving good views over it. To reach the hide take the D68 north from LE POIRÉ, after 1 km turn left at the first crossroads, and continue through the straggling L'ANGLÉE village (passing under a very low, narrow bridge). The hide comes into view just beyond the end of the village. **Lapwing** and **Golden Plover** are the most common birds on the reserve in

Short-toed Eagle

winter but waders use it during migration and small flocks of **Little Bustard** can be found here in autumn. Raptors include **Hen Harrier** in winter, **Montagu's, Short-toed Eagle** and **Black Kite** in summer.

Check the fields either side of the D949 between LUCON and FONTENAY-LE-COMTE (north of l'Anglée) as well as the D30 north of LA LANGON for **Little Bustard** and **Stone Curlew**.

A leisurely way to explore the inland Poitevin marshes is by boat or punt, with or without a guide. One or two hour trips leave from the villages of Coulon, La Garette, Arcais and St-Hilaire-la-Palud, all east of the previous sites and not far west of Niort. Check times and availability at any tourist office.

Area 5 ÎLE DE RÉ

ÎLE DE RÉ, joined to la Rochelle by the Sablanceaux toll bridge, effectively forms the southern side of Aiguillon Bay. It, like Noirmoutier further north and Ile d'Oléron directly south, contains a variety of habitats: saltpans, marshes, woods, cultivated fields, mudflats, dunes, rocky headlands and beaches that make them all good birding areas with a large number of species at any time of the year. An area of old saltpans in the north of Ile de Ré have been turned into a LPO reserve, providing some of the best and most accessible habitat along this stretch of coast, although there is no public access to the centre of the reserve and no hide as yet.

Site i.
To reach the LILEAU-DES-NIGES NATIONAL NATURE RESERVE, turn off the D101 onto a cycle track opposite a supermarket on the outskirts of Les Portes-en-Ré (signed "Déchetterie" – rubbish dump). (Unhelpfully, the sign to the reserve is only visible after the turn). Park by a large, dark wooden building. Follow the cycle track on the right, towards a large reserve notice board which lists recent sightings. Turn left here on to a narrower track, past a locked gate, then right and finally left again at the next gate to reach a large stretch of water, the almost enclosed bay called Fier d'Ars. At any time of the year, the obvious bird activity will lead you in the right direction. In the breeding season scan the old saltpans for **Black-winged Stilt, Avocet, Shelduck, Redshank, Little and Kentish Plovers, Common Tern, Blue-headed Wagtail** (very numerous in September and mid-March) and **Bluethroat** (some 12 pairs breed on the reserve), **Cirl Bunting** and **Hoopoe**. On migration and in winter waterbirds include **Spoonbill, Brent Geese, Shelduck**, dabbling duck, and (at high tide) many waders. **Divers, Great Crested and Black-necked Grebes, Red-breasted Merganser, Goldeneye**, sea ducks and gulls (Both **Herring** and **Yellow-legged, Lesser** and **Great Black-backed**) can be found on the Fier. The old wooden building can be seen from the reserve and it is possible to walk back towards it along the tops of the banks enclosing the pans, so making a circular walk or

you can return to the cycle track and continue south-west towards St. Clément-des-Baleines.

Contact the LPO (at the address and telephone number given in the Introduction) to find out dates of guided walks. In summer only there is an information centre, the *Maison des marais* at St. Clément-des-Baleines. Tel: 05 46 09 45 11.

Site ii.
The Fier can also be reached by continuing down the D101 south from LES PORTES-EN-RÉ to where the road ends in the large Patache carpark. Walk from here towards the sea. Alternatively, drive down the road that runs through the golf course west of the D101 (signed from the road). Park at the end and walk over the green to the bay.

Site iii.
Still in the north of the island, the Baleineaux or Baleines (whales) lighthouse on the north-west headland makes a good sea-watching spot, best in autumn and spring when Gannets, auks, petrels, shearwaters, skuas and many species of gulls and tern pass — often quite close to shore (**Little** and **Mediterranean Gulls, Caspian** and **Sooty Terns** and **Red Phalarope** have all been sighted). Divers, grebes and **Red-breasted Merganser** can be seen on the sea in winter and **Kittiwake** in the breeding season. A very few pairs nest near the lighthouse, the only breeding site in the region. The woods in the north and north-west attract migrant passerines as well as resident woodland birds. The D101 and the main road D735 both lead to the lighthouse, which is a popular tourist attraction.

Île de Ré is criss-crossed with cycle tracks and this is a good way of birding the island, especially the saltpans and Fier areas. There are two cycle hire shops in les Portes-en-Ré and others in Ars and St. Martin-en-Ré.

Area 6 OCHEFORT: MOËZE AND YVES MARSHES RESERVES

Île d' Oléron lies only some 20 km due south of Île de Ré but it is 90 km by road from la Rochelle to its northernmost point. However there are three good birding sites along the road between the islands which should not be missed if driving south.

Site i.
Roughly halfway (15 km–9.3 miles) between la Rochelle and Rochefort the N137 runs past the **YVES MARSHES** Nature Reserve managed by the Ministry of the Environment, local authorities and the LPO. Access is not very obvious but reasonable views can be obtained from roads running alongside the reserve and from the beach.

Turn off the N137 at LES 3 CANONS and drive towards les

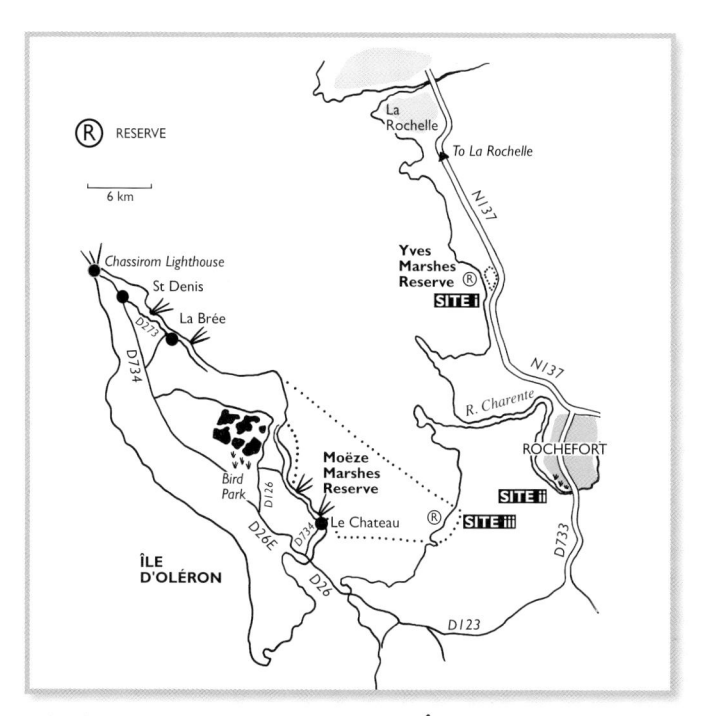

Atlantic Coast Areas 6 and 7 Rochefort and Île d'Oléron

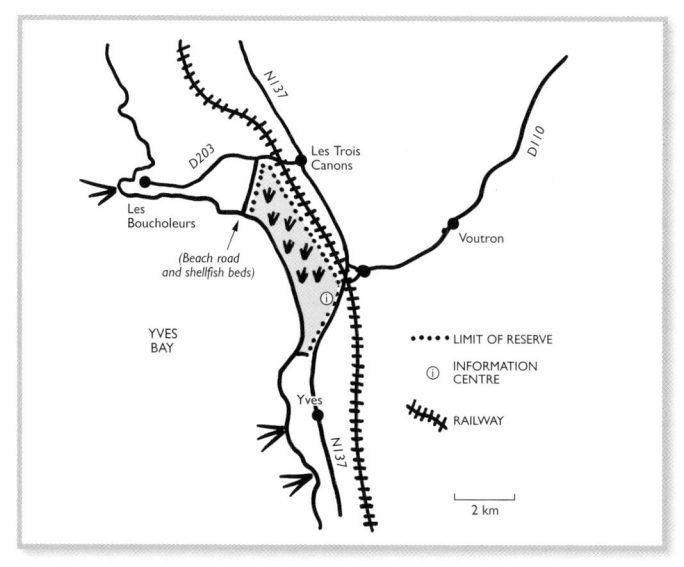

Atlantic Coast Area 6 site i. Yves Marshes

BOUCHOLEURS village (2.4 km) and park where there is a view over the seawall. Scan the beach or walk along it southwards for a couple of kilometres. It is possible to look over the dunes into the reserve as well as out to sea. Waders are driven shoreward by an incoming tide. They are plentiful during migration and in winter.

Alternatively drive 0.6 km from the 3 Canons junction towards les Boucholeurs. Just after the railway crossing turn left (signed *Mer et plage. Zone Conchylicole. Le Clapotis Bar*). The reedbeds on the left are part of the reserve and, tantalisingly, a hide can be seen. **Grebes** and **duck** can be seen on the open water; **Cetti's Warbler** is here year round and **Penduline and Bearded Tits** are found in the reeds in winter, *Acrocephalus* species in summer. There may even be a **Little Bittern**. **Marsh Harriers** hunt overhead. The same birds can be found in the degraded reedbeds on the right of the road where hunters place decoys from autumn to spring. This road also leads to the beach and this is perhaps a better place from which to start walking along the Reserve than Boucholeurs. Check the bushes where the road ends for migrant passerines.

Some 3 km south of the 3 Canons turning, the AIRE DE MAROUILLE is clearly marked beside the N137, just south of the D110 junction. There is a large parking area and it is possible to walk down to the beach or look over the marsh and pools. There is a *Maison de la Nature* here, with a permanent exhibition about the Reserve. You need to enquire here about access to the hides. It may not be open weekdays in winter.

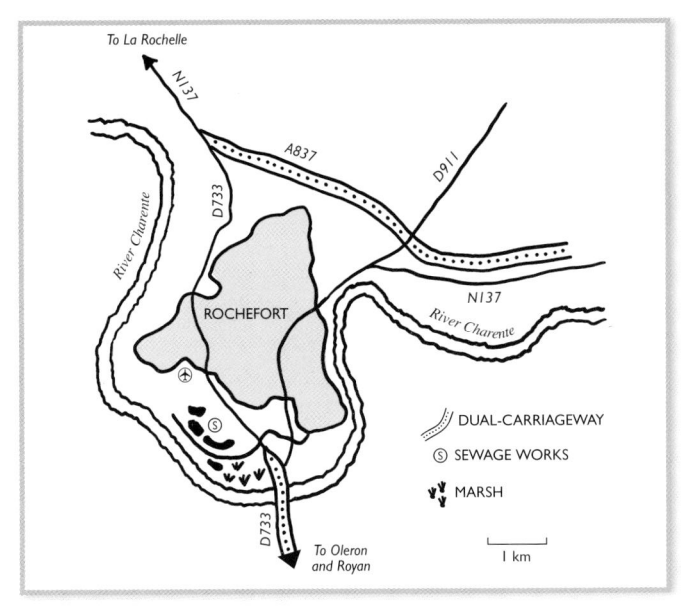

Atlantic Coast Area 6 site ii. Rochefort Sewage Works

Site ii.
The sewage works and settling pools on the southern outskirts of ROCHEFORT attract many waders, ducks and terns on passage, especially since the beds have been managed in collaboration with the LPO. In winter, hundreds of **Coot** and duck (up to 10 species) can be found on the ponds, 4 species of grebe and sometimes either **Grey** or **Red-necked Phalaropes** and small flocks of geese. The station is an important migration stop for **Black Terns** (and a few **White-winged Black**) in September with fewer **Whiskered Tern** in May. Sea terns may be seen in the summer. Some 20 species of waders have been noted during spring and autumn migration, including rarities. **Little Egret** roost nearby, **Night Herons** and **Spoonbills** are most likely to be seen at the end of summer, in May **Little Bittern** may be seen and in November, **Great White Egrets** are possible.

ACCESS: At Rochefort, coming from La Rochelle, take the D733 for Oléron-Royan. A road leading to the sewage works (*station de lagunage*) is signed just before the beginning of the dual-carriageway viaduct over the River Charente. There is car-parking space outside the works. An old road leading off to the right just before the work's entrance runs between the Charante river and several of the setting ponds, allowing views over them. It is only possible to get into the station on organised visits but footpaths and hides are in the process of being built to allow visitors views over the marshes from outside.

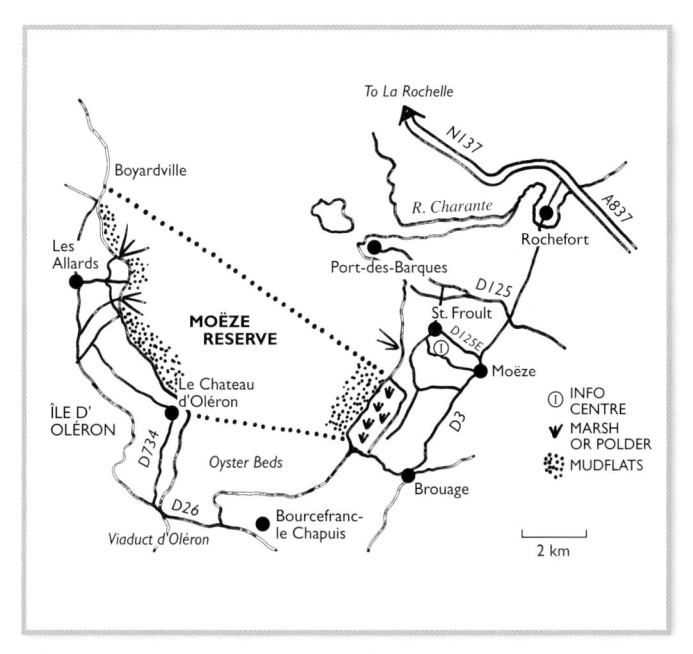

Atlantic Coast Area 6 site iii. Moëze Oléron Natural Reserve

Site iii.
The **MOËZE-OLÉRON** Natural Reserve comprises a huge area of sea, marsh and mud flats stretching between the mainland and the east coast of the Ile d'Oléron and a much smaller area of marsh on the mainland. Together with the other sites and reserves in this area, it forms part of a very important passage and wintering site for thousands of birds. Within a few years of the creation of the reserve, it had become the second most important French site for wintering waders, with more than 35,000 birds. The reserve is managed by the LPO, which organises guided walks in the spring and summer. The mudflats bordering Ile d'Oléron are best scanned from the island (see below) but it is possible to reach the mainland part of the reserve by taking the minor road south from St. Froult which runs along the eastern side of the reserve. There is a visitors centre between Moëze and St. Froult, just off this road.

Area 7 ÎLE D'OLÉRON

Take the N137 coast road south from la Rochelle for 30 km to Rochefort, then the signed toll road that loops through the Marenne marshes (stop at any lay-by and scan around – this is a good birding area) and across the bridge to the island. Oléron contains the same habitats and the same birds as Ré, but it is larger and more built-up. Development and oyster farms make access to the old salt pans and remaining marsh very difficult. The D734 runs the length of the island and the low cliffs beyond the lighthouse at CHASSIRON POINT, the extreme northern tip, are a good place to seawatch, especially in autumn when skuas, shearwaters and terns are passing close to land. There are nearly always **Mediterranean Gulls** here in winter as well as **Brent Geese**, waders and **Shelduck**. The woods shelter migrating passerines in spring and autumn and at high tide the beaches to the south-east of the lighthouse are good for waders. From the most northerly village, ST. DENIS, take the scenic (tourist) road that runs close to the shore with plenty of places to stop and scan the beach and out to sea, especially at low tide when birds are driven inshore. In the south, branch off the D26 as soon as you have crossed the viaduct and take the coast road to LE CHATEAU to scan the Moëze Reserve at low tide. From Le Chateau another minor road runs north towards Les Allards very close to the sea and it is worth taking this, stopping and scanning the bay frequently.

The **LES GRISSORIÈRES** bird garden/ nature reserve between Dolus d'Oléron and St. Pierre retains a small area of unspoilt marsh and there is a tower hide to view it from. It is clearly signed from the D734.

South of the Gironde estuary the shoreline changes; the coastline runs almost straight north to south with huge dunes lying just behind the beaches and further inland the extensive pine forests known as les Landes. The few coastal lagoons are not especially good for birds with the exception of the ones described below. It is only broken by one large bay, the Bassin d'Arcachon.

Area 8 GRAVE HEADLAND (M)

The N215 runs north from Bordeaux, parallel with the Gironde estuary for some 100 km, to the south side of its mouth. The southern tip, the Pointe de Grave, is a well-known pre-nuptial (March-May) migration site. However in recent years there have been quite nasty clashes between hunters and bird-watchers here. Nevertheless **White Stork, Honey Buzzard, Black Kite, Turtle Dove, Swift,** larks, pipits, finches and many other passerines can be observed from this headland when weather conditions are right.

Area 9 THE BASSIN D'ARCACHON AND TEICH BIRD RESERVE

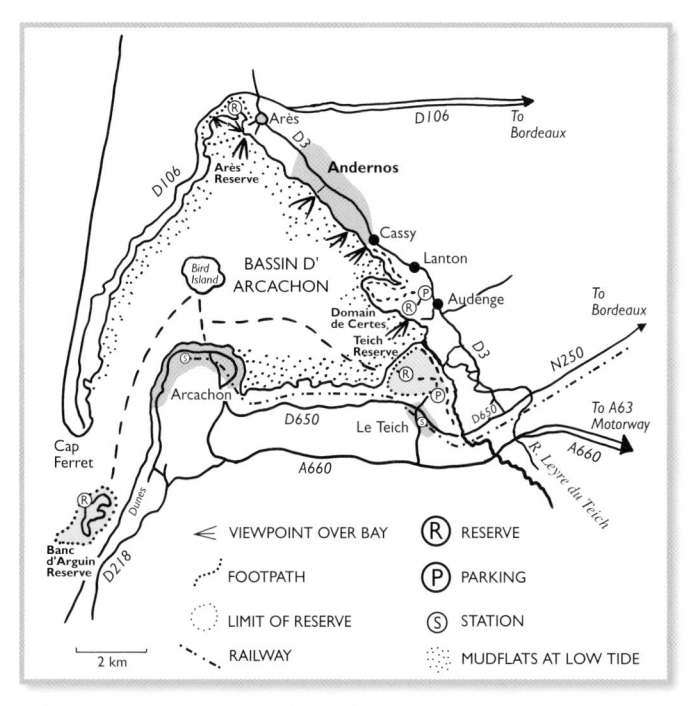

Atlantic Coast Area 9 Bassin d'Arcachon

Site i.

The Bassin d'Arcachon and the Banc d'Arguin (a sandbar reserve just off the coast south of the Bassin) are very important coastal sites. The **TEICH BIRD RESERVE** (*le parc ornithologique du Teich*) in the south-east corner of the Bassin it is one of the largest and best reserves open to the public in France.

In winter birds include large numbers of **Cormorant, Coot, Grey Heron** and duck (mainly **Shelduck** which also breed, **Wigeon, Teal, Pintail, Tufted** and **Shoveler); Garganey** occur in spring. **Great Crested, Black-necked** and (a few) **Red-necked Grebes** as well as the occasional **Great Northern** and **Black-necked Diver** may be seen on the bay in winter, with thousands of **Brent Geese. Mute Swans** are there year round. **White Stork** start nesting on their special platforms from the end of January. Waders (during migration and in winter) include thousands of **Curlew, Whimbrel, Bar and Black-tailed Godwits, Ruff, Knot and Dunlin, Oystercatcher, Ringed and Grey Plover. Spotted Redshank** is common during both migration periods, April-May and September-October, with fewer **Curlew, Wood and Green Sandpipers.** A few **Black Stork** occur on migration, as well as **Black-winged Stilt** and **Avocet** (some of the latter can be seen all winter). Up to a thousand **Spoonbills** (from the Dutch breeding population) may stop off here during migration (February-March and August-October) and a few overwinter; so occasionally do **Cranes** while **Great White Egrets** are regular winter visitors. **Night Heron** breed in the park. **Water Rail** can often be seen near the hides, especially in winter. Some 40 pairs of **Bluethroat** breed in the reserve and can be seen near many of the hides in spring and summer. In March, April and May, when their numbers are swelled by passage birds, the reserve's Guide says that they are "difficult to miss"! Other breeding species include **Night Heron** (in the flooded wood near the beginning of the trail) and **Little Egret,** while the woods hold breeding populations of **Black Kite, Short-toed Eagle, Wryneck, Golden Oriole, Short-toed Treecreeper** (often in the trees near the entrance), **Lesser Spotted Woodpecker** (more common than Greater Spotted) and **Nightingale.** Warblers breeding in the reserve include resident **Cetti's** and **Fan-tailed** (Zitting Cisticola) as well as **Savi's, Reed** and **Melodious** in summer. Great Reed only breed occasionally and are most likely to be heard on migration. **Bearded Tit** can be found in the reedbeds all year round but **Penduline** only occur in winter.

WHEN TO VISIT: There are birds to be seen all through the year at Teich but March, April and May and for waders September and October and to a lesser extent, August are probably the optimum times, as they are for most of the Atlantic coast sites.

ACCESS: Take the A63 motorway from Bordeaux to the Arcachon exit (22). Follow the dual carriageway A660 to the TEICH turning, which is 6 km after exit 2. (It is possible to leave the A660 at exit 2 and get onto the D650 but more complicated). The Teich Bird Reserve (*Parc Ornithologique du Teich*) is clearly signed from the Teich exit and all the way through the town to the carpark, a distance of 3.5 km from the A660 junction. Trains also run from Bordeaux to la Teich. The station is a short walk from the reserve.

A well-marked, dry path 5 km in length leads to the Bassin past reedbeds, woodland and large stretches of brackish water. The entrance ticket to the reserve includes a sketch map with information in English and French. There are 12 well-placed large hides overlooking the scrapes and marsh, facing different directions so that at any time of the day they give a view that is not directly into the sun. It takes at least 3 hours to walk the Bassin trail and is best in the morning with an incoming tide. (Tide times are given at the entrance). Some two and a half hours before high tide, waders start flying into the scrapes overlooked by hides 9 to 12 and remain until a couple of hours afterwards. Near the entrance there is also a shorter 2 km trail with three hides. The reserve is open every day until 22.00 in July and August, 19.00 in September and mid-April to the end of June and closes at 18.00 during the rest of the year. The current charge of 36 F for an adult is well worth the cost. There is a shop, toilets and a small restaurant near the entrance.

A stretch of the coastal footpath (*sentier du littoral*) runs along a raised path from just outside the park between the river Leyre du Teich and the Reserve boundary to the Bassin d'Arcachon and then along the sea wall. It gives good views over parts of the reserve as well as the reedbeds on the far side of the river, so that many of the same species can be seen as from inside the reserve and it can be used as a free alternative if, for example, you arrive near closing time. However, it is very popular at weekends so there may be some disturbance and it takes longer to reach the Bassin. There is good Bluethroat habitat along the path. The footpath and adjoining marsh are owned by the *Conservatoire du Littoral*.

Some three kilometres east of Teich on the D650, the *Conservatoire* has an Information Centre, the *Relais Nature du Delta de la Leyre*. Marked paths run along the river from here to the reserve, a distance of 4.5 km on foot, through some varied habitat: riverside, damp woodland, scrub and marsh and link up with the coastal footpath. Or you can make a 11 km round walk; worth considering if you want to stretch your legs.

It is also possible to hire canoes near the park entrance and paddle down the river into the Bassin and along to the Domaine de Certes (see below), which could be another way of birding the area.

Site ii.
Two further stretches of the coastal footpath are good for birding **ARCACHON**. The same species as listed above for Teich are likely to be seen. One signed trail runs from the village of AUDENGE, around the marshes, woods and old saltpans of the Domain de Certes, a large estate on the northern outskirts of the village now owned by the *Conservatoire du Littoral* and open to the public. The coastal path (*sentier du littoral*) is signed in the village, from a turning off the D3 (on the left if travelling north) just before the entrance to the Domain de Certes. The path leads athrough a variety of

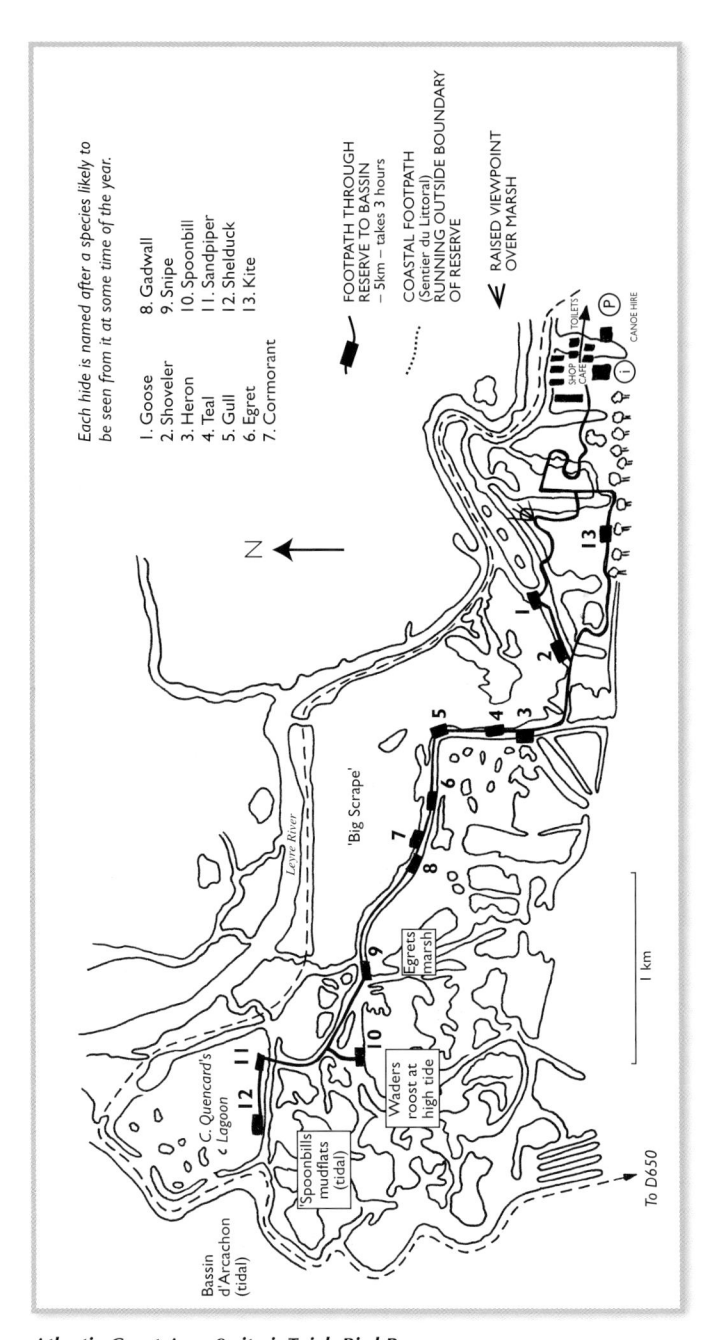

Atlantic Coast Area 9 site i. Teich Bird Reserve

habitats before eventually turning north along a sea-wall to LANTON, the next village north of Audence. The path continues north from Lanton. Again it is signed from the D3 which runs along the East Side of the Bassin. Any of the turnings signed "*sentier*" will lead to the Bassin from where you can scan the mudflats or walk some distance along the path. The two car parks north and south of the small marina at CASSY (follow the signs to the "port") on an inlet give good views over areas of salt marsh where birds roost at high tide.

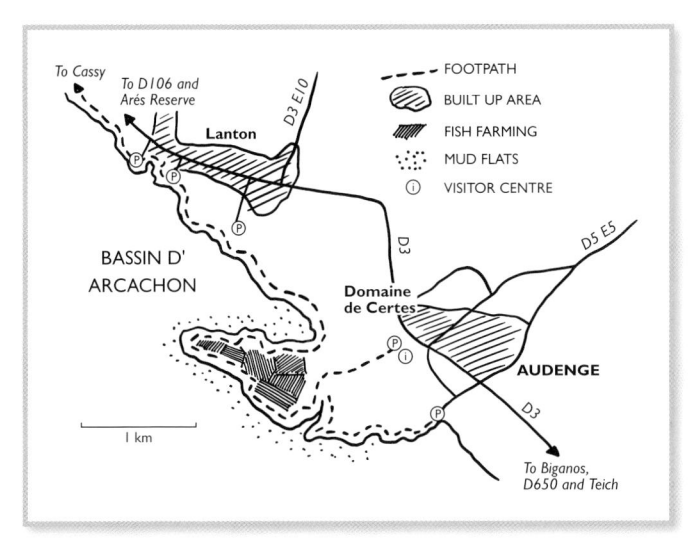

Atlantic Coast Area 9 site ii. Coastal footpath

Site iii.

At the northern end of the Bay of Arcachon is the 350 hectare **RESERVE OF PRÈS SALÉS D'ARÈS ET DE LÈGE-CAP-FERRET**. The Reserve contains dunes, some woodland, fishponds, mud flats and large areas of salt marsh. Most of the species listed above for Teich will also be found here. It is a good area for breeding **Bluethroat, Little Bittern, Wryneck** and reedbed warblers while many wildfowl feed there in winter and on migration. There is a large roost of **Little Egrets** in winter.

ACCESS: Continue north up the D3 to ARÈS. In the town centre, at the large roundabout with a church in the middle, take the *Rue du Port Ostréicole*, a small road immediately right of the one signed to the Poste and Plage. It is 0.8 km to the edge of the reserve and carpark beside the small shellfish port, from where part of the marsh can be scanned. A large map marks the start of the footpath around the Reserve.

The Reserve is wardened and between 15 June to 15 September there are two-hour plus guided walks leaving at 9.30 a.m. Monday, Wednesday and

Saturday. You can normally just turn up but for more information ring 0556 91 33 65. The emphasis may be more on plants than birdlife, as there are over 200 marshland plants in the reserve.

In July and August, boat trips from ARCACHON jetty circle round Bird Island in the Bassin or take you up the Leyre River. There are also day trips to the BANC D'ARGUIN reserve; where you can land, eat your picnic lunch and watch the breeding **Kentish Plovers** and terns as well as migratory waders who are starting to arrive in August. Bottle-nosed Dolphins *Tursiops truncatus* are often seen in the waters near the Banc d'Arguin.

Accommodation: There are hotels in all categories, several open in winter, and campsites near the resort of Arcachon some 20 km west. This is a good cycling area and there is a signed cycling route from Biganos to Lège, taking you off the D3. Bicycles can be hired in Audenge. Additionally, cycling is allowed along most stretches of the coastal footpaths.

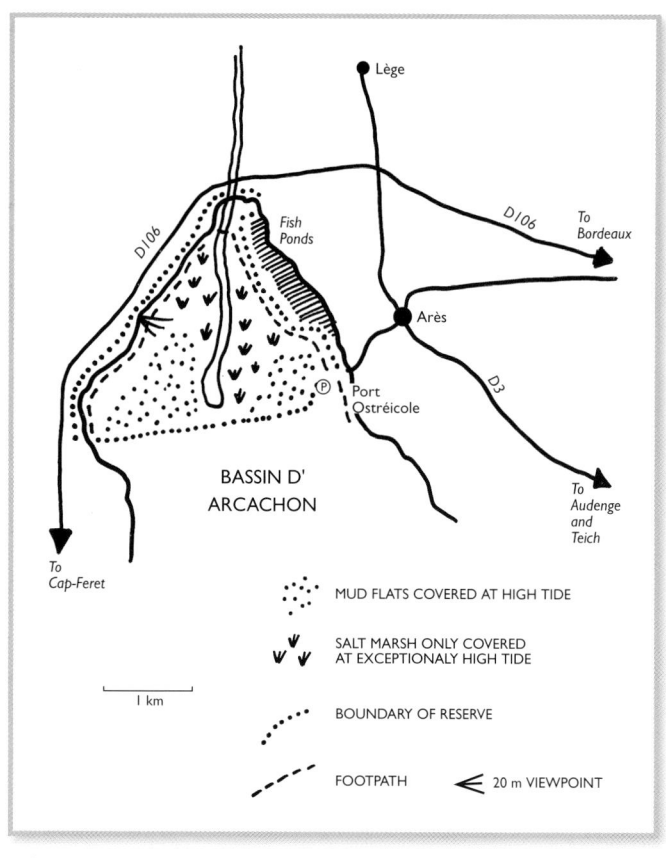

Atlantic Coast Area 9 site iii. Reserve de Près-salés d'Arés

Area 10 HOSSEGOR LAKE AND SEAWATCHING AT CAPBRETON AND BAYONNE

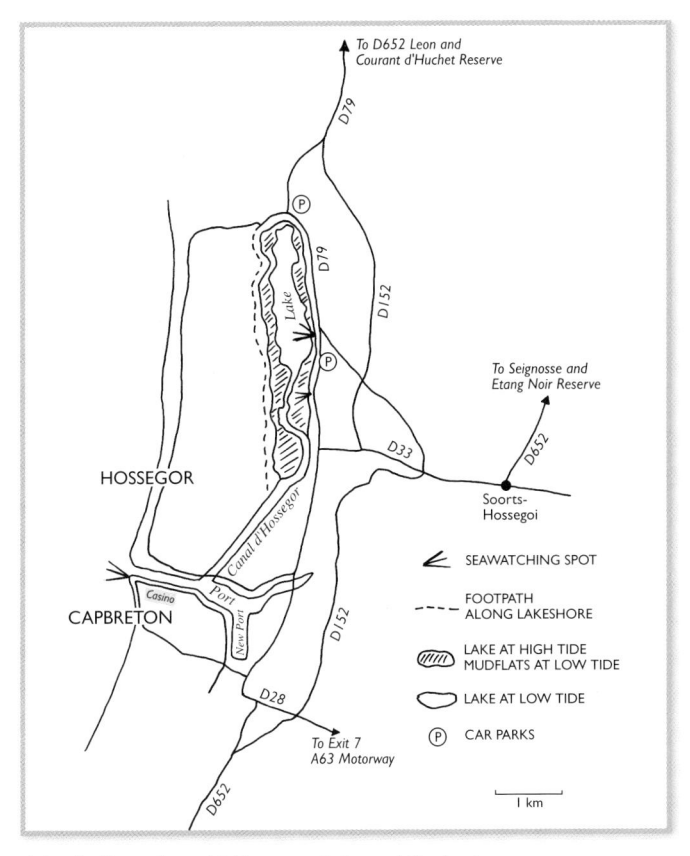

Atlantic Coast Area 10 Hossegor Lake and Capbreton

HOSSEGOR is a natural lake, some 20 km north of Bayonne. It is separated from the sea by dunes but linked by a canal at its south end so is tidal with large mudflats at low tide. It is a good site for **waders** and **gulls** during migration and in winter, when both **Great Northern** and **Black-throated Divers, Razorbill, Eider, Gannet, shearwaters** and **petrels** may be seen offshore in the right weather conditions. The coast here is a good spot for sea birds in winter. The best and most comfortable place to sea-watch is from the harbour-wall where the canal enters the sea at CAPBRETON, south of the lake.

Black-winged Stilts

WHEN TO VISIT: September to June. Avoid the summer holiday period. Mid-September to mid-October is best for waders and also, during stormy weather, sea birds.

ACCESS: Leave the N10 main coastal road, or the A-63 motorway (exit 7) at the junction signed HOSSEGOR-CAPBRETON. Follow the Hossegor-Capbreton signs and take the D28 towards Capbreton going straight over at roundabouts until some 2.5 km from the motorway junction there is a right fork onto the D152 signed to HOSSEGOR. In Hossegor look for signs to the "lac". A road runs close to the east side of the Lake, with several places to park and view the water and there is a footpath running around the lakeside to the west bank. The parking spaces on the south-east corner of the lake overlook mudflats and from here it is also possible to scope the far bank. The lake is much used in summer, so this is really only a migration and winter site, when many **waders (plovers, Curlew, Godwits, stint, Dunlin, sandpipers, Black-winged Stilt)** feed on the mudflats. This means that the lake is best visited just before and after low tide. Gulls also roost here at high tide. Whilst the majority are **Black-headed** and **Yellow-legged**, **Great Black-backed, Common, Mediterranean** and **Little Gulls** turn up and **Ring-billed Gull** is found regularly every winter. **Cormorants** and **divers** can be found on the lake in winter.

To reach the sea-watching site in CAPBRETON, which is good from September until February or March though best at high tide and during stormy weather, return to the junction of D28 and D152 and follow signs through the town towards "Centre ville". Follow the one-way system and head towards "le Port". Go past the pleasure port to the Old Port (*Port Vieux*) or follow signs to the Casino, which is near the river mouth. The road ends on the south side of the river. There is a short jetty but the best place to sea-watch is from the flat terrace roof over a small shopping arcade opposite the Casino. The terrace gives height for sea-watching or, if it is raining or blowing, the lower level provides shelter while still giving good views into the bay.

During bad weather **shearwaters, skuas** and **petrels** come right inshore to the area sheltered by the jetty. **Storm Petrel** breeds locally on rocky islands offshore from Biarritz and **Leach's Petrel** is regular in autumn. **Mediterranean Shearwaters**, **Skuas** and **Gannets** pass on passage in September, as do auks (mainly **Razorbills** but occasionally **Little Auks**). Storms in autumn bring in **Mediterranean** and **Little Gulls, Kittiwake** and in winter **Eider, Great Northern** and **Black-throated Divers**. **Sabine's Gull** is not uncommon.

North of Hossegor is an area of pinewoods, part of the famous Landes, where **Black Kite** and **European Nightjar** may be found in summer. Look for the latter at dusk in clearings or area where the trees are newly planted.

Some 15 km further south down the coast from Capbreton, the River Ardour (see next site) flows through Bayonne and enters the sea. An exceptionally long jetty (*digue*) has been built on its north bank and this also provides an excellent seawatching site as it is possible to walk along its top level some 15 feet above the sea for almost half a mile. Much the same species will be seen from here as at Capbreton but it is possibly a better site in calmer weather when birds are further out at sea. Warning – the jetty is closed during bad weather.

ACCESS: Leave the motorway A63 at exit 6.1 (the first exit north of Bayonne) and turn west onto the D85. 6.7 km from the motorway junction, turn right at traffic lights towards the industrial zone and port. Continue on this road for 2.5 km. It runs alongside a railway line on the left into the Port de Bayonne, through a factory area to Tarnos *Plage de la Digue* where there is a car park.

Other fauna and flora: There are two Nature Reserves fairly near Hossegor; both of which hold some bird species although they are mainly noted for their plants, amphibians and insects. The ETANG NOIR is about 5 km north of Hossegor Lake. Its name comes either from the black colour of its water or from the deep shade of the trees surrounding it. Whilst there are breeding **Night Heron, Water Rail, Coot, Great-crested Grebe** and some duck species, it is heavily hunted over in winter (when you will see more decoys that ducks on the lake), and is better known for its so-called "monster" frogs – *Rana kelpton grafi* that suffer from viral deformities caused by fish droppings – and outstanding aquatic and waterside vegetation (430 species of plants). It can be reached from the D89 between Le Penon and SEIGNOSSE and is well signed from the latter town. A wooden walkway allows access to the lakeside. There is an information centre and guided walks in summer.

Almost 25 km north of Hossegor, the RESERVE DU COURANT D'HUCHET is a protected stretch of river running from the Étang de Léon to the coast. It contains some fine riparian woodland, interesting plants (*Myriophyllum brasilense*, Swamp Cypress *Taxodium distichum, Hibiscus roseus*,

Royal and many other ferns) and a few good bird species: **Night Heron, Little Bittern, Kingfisher, Cetti's Warbler, Black Kite** breed; **Bittern, Marsh Harrier, Little Egret, Moustached** and **Black Terns** may be seen on migration or in winter. Dragonflies are numerous and include Banded Agrion.

ACCESS: The river can be reached by taking the coastal roads from the north of Hossegor lake, D79 and D652 to MOLETS-ET-MAA. Zero here. Turn left in the village towards the beach (*plage*) and almost immediately (0.3 km) turn right onto the D328 towards Maa and Pichelebe. At 4.6 km there is a small parking space on the left, just before a bridge, with a noticeboard showing a map of the reserve. A footpath leading left (west) along the south bank of the river starts from beside the map. It leads through woodland but in under a kilometre emerges into an area overlooking reed beds where **Little Bittern** may be seen. The path then continues in woodland for the remaining 7 km to the sea. Alternatively, from the car park, cross the bridge (Pont de Pichelebe) and take the footpath running right (east) along the north bank of the river towards another viewpoint some 2 km away and eventually the lake. There are also a couple of car parks beside the Léon Lake, of which only the west half is protected, and even this is much used by holidaymakers in summer. In July and August the reserve has an Information Centre near the southern carpark beside the lake (follow the signs from Léon village), opening hours 10-1, 3-6. There is some good woodland here too (**Short-toed Treecreeper** is common) and outside the holiday months there could be interesting birding from the lakeside footpath. During the summer the Centre will organise trips from the lake and down the Courant d'Huchet by boat, possibly the best way of seeing the river. Phone 05 58 49 21 89 outside the summer season or to arrange guided tours of the reserve.

Short-toed Tree Creeper

Accommodation: There are several hotels, including three *Logis*, alongside Hossegor Lake and many other hotels in Capbreton and all the surrounding villages as this is a popular holiday area. Hossegor is well supplied with cycle tracks that also run north through the pine forests and make this an excellent centre for a cycling holiday.

Area 11 LES BARTHES DE L'ADOUR AND MARAIS D'ORX

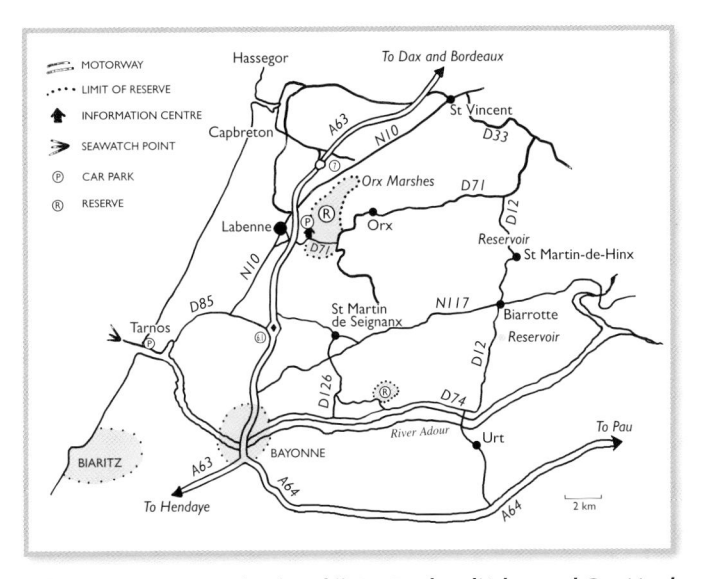

Atlantic Coast area 11 sites i. and ii. Les Barthes d'Adour and Orx Marshes

Site i.
Les Barthes is the name given to an area of marsh, flooded meadows, woodland, cultivated fields and reservoirs that lies to the north of the River Ardour where it widens and is dotted with islands some 10 km due east of Bayonne. A very small part of it is a reserve. The Marais d'Orx or Orx Marshes, to the north-west, can effectively be considered part of the same wetland complex and much of this latter area is a well-managed reserve. The variety of habitat makes for a large number of species and good birding throughout the year. **Night Heron, Little Egret**, **Spoonbill**, a few **White Stork, Honey Buzzard, Black Kite, Booted Eagle** and **Red-backed Shrike** are among the breeding birds. Most species of dabbling duck winter here, some in large numbers, but of more interest is the likelihood of seeing **Great White Egret**, up to a hundred or more wintering **Crane, Marsh and Hen Harrier** and, not least, the possibility of **White-tailed Sea Eagle** or **Spotted Eagle**. One or two individuals of the last two species regularly winter in the region but they move around this large area and may be found either near the river or round the larger stretches of water. On migration **Whiskered and Black Tern** may be seen over the marshland, as well as many **waders, Squacco Heron**, both **Black and White Storks** and **Red Kite. Black-shouldered Kite** has also been seen here; the first pair to breed

in France was discovered not far away. A **White Pelican**, presumably an escape, has been seen there recently. A **Spotted Eagle**, a regular winter visitor to Les Barthes reserve for some years, usually roosts in trees on the left of the further side of the reserve from the hide and can be seen between mid-December and the end of February. **White-tailed Sea Eagle** is much rarer but turns up regularly. **Great White Egret** is another rare wintering bird and in recent winters between 100 to 200 **Cranes** have roosted here, leaving to feed in nearby maize fields at dawn.

ACCESS: There is a small **RESERVE DES BARTHES** (Reserve Henri Sallenave) with a tower hide that gives excellent views over an area of marsh and seasonally flooded meadows south of St. MARTIN DE SEIGNANX. From the D74 which runs along the north bank of the river Ardour turn north onto the D126 signed to St. Martin. After 1.7 turn right (signed "Point de Vue – Reserve de Faune") and continue for 2.8 km (passing a small pool on the right) to where the road divides at a large farm. Take the right fork and in another 0.2 km there is an opening on the left and the tower hide is beyond a parking space on the left. The only indication that this leads to a reserve is a small green and white sign reading "*Grâce aux chasseurs cette espace naturelle est sauveguardé*". The name of the reserve is directly below the hide. Alternatively, from the D74 drive 3.2 km east from the St. Martin turning and just after an island in the river turn left (north) onto a minor road beside a Maison de Retraite, signed Rte. De Puntet (large sign) and Rte. De Lesgau (small sign). 1.1 km from the D74 is the turning to the reserve (just where the stream that has been running alongside the right side of the road stops). Unfortunately, unless some trees are lopped soon it will be impossible to see much of the reserve from the hide except in winter.

Another stretch of water, an artificial reservoir, lies just east of, and can be viewed from the D12, 1.5 km from the N117 at BIARROTTE. There is no access to the lakeside, which is hunted over, but reasonable views can be obtained from the roadside where there is a large lay-bye. **Little Egrets, Great-crested Grebe, Kingfisher, Purple** and **Grey Heron** can be seen in summer and duck in winter, as well as the possibly of any of the species mentioned above. In Biarrotte turn south off the N117 onto the D12 at Urt junction or continue along the D74 east along the River Ardour until it turns north at Urt and becomes the D12.

Site ii.
The **ORX MARSHES** Reserve is rapidly becoming one of the best birding sites in this part of France. The vast Orx marshes and lakes, probably formed when the River Adour flooded aeons ago, have been hunted over and fished since the early Middle Ages. There were various unsuccessful attempts to drain them dating back to the 17th century but it was only after the First World War that sufficiently powerful pumps were developed to dry them and allow maize to be grown. By the 1970's the cost of petrol and electricity made running the pumps uneconomic and gradually the marshes returned but were

again heavily hunted over. In 1989 some 800 hectares were acquired as a reserve, thanks to a legacy to the WWF, and are nowadays managed by local and regional authorities. As a comparatively new reserve, visitors' access is still limited though there are plans to build hides in the near future. The Visitors' Centre (*La Maison du Marais Tel: 05 59 45 42 46*), in a restored farm building beside the marsh, has excellent displays and leaflets showing the reserve's wildlife, a list of recent bird species and very helpful English-speaking staff. There is also a live video which shows the Spoonbill breeding area in a part of the reserve without close access. It is open from 8.30-12 and 14-17 during the week and on Sunday afternoons. A minor road, the D71, bisects the part of the reserve visible to visitors. The north part is open water with flooded meadows almost out of view in the extreme north. The south side is becoming overgrown by an invasive tropical plant *Ludwiga urugayensis,* which is proving difficult to eradicate. Its yellow flowers are attractive in summer and water birds seem to like it but it could become a menace.

ACCESS: Leave the A63 motorway at exit 7. At the Capbreton junction turn right (opposite direction to Capbreton – it is signed *Reserve naturelle* 10) In just under 2 km this road joins the N10. Turn right (south) onto the N10 and drive south for 5.5 km to LABENNE. In the village turn left at the traffic lights onto the D71 signed to the Reserve. (If you miss this turning there is another at the end of the village also signed to the reserve). The two turnings from Labenne meet just before the D71 crosses the motorway. From here it is almost 1 km to the Information Centre clearly signed on the right of the D71. There is a car park beside the centre. The D71 then swings right and crosses the marsh to its east side.

From the visitors centre it is possible to walk along the D71; there is a wide grass verge and plenty of lay-bys to view from. Footpaths also lead off north and south between the marsh and the canal bordering it. The path running around the southern half has plenty of openings giving views across the marsh. The north path is gated in under a kilometre but gives the closest views possible of the spoonbills and a small reedbed in the northern corner. It also allows one (just) to see a closed part of the reserve – the flooded meadows where geese feed in winter and which are grazed by Highland cattle. This side of the marsh is best birded in late afternoon and evening as you are looking east across the marsh. In the morning it is best to cross the marsh on the D71 and then walk along it northwards on the section that follows the east bank of the marsh or turn round and walk back westwards.

Besides the bird species mentioned above, both **Grey** and **Purple Heron, Little Egret** and **Night Heron** breed at Orx. Five pairs of **Spoonbill** bred in 1997 but since then water levels have been too low or storms have destroyed nests but a few birds can be see here all year round. 60-75 birds spend some time here during the autumn migration and up to 200 have been counted in September. **Black Kite** and **Hobby** breed nearby and can be seen over the water in summer, **European Nightjar** breed in clearings in the pine forests nearby. **Kingfisher** and **Cetti's Warbler** are found along the banks.

Ospreys are frequently seen on passage at the beginning of September as well as **Marsh Harrier**, which also overwinter. **Cranes** also spend time here. Migrating or wintering waders include **Curlew, Lapwing, Golden Plover, Sandpipers** and **Godwits**. Up to 240 bird species have been counted at Orx. Winter is definitely the best season at the Orx marshes when up to 10,000 ducks can arrive (though recently the numbers have been nearer 3-5000 due to the invasive yellow plant. They include dabbling ducks such as **Pintail, Wigeon, Shoveler, Garganey, Wigeon** and **Teal** and diving ducks such as **Tufted Duck, Pochard, Red-crested Pochard** and in hard winters both **Scaup** and **Goldeneye**. Some 1000 Greylag Geese winter here and up to 4000 may stop over here to feed up in early spring when they are returning from southern Spain, especially after a dry winter there. Among them may be **White-front, Bean, Barnacle** and **Pink-foot.**

Other fauna and flora: The mammal most likely to be seen at Orx is the naturalised Coypu but the marshes are also home to another introduced species, the Muskrat, as well as the very rare European Mink and possibly a few Otters trying to make a comeback. Genet, Polecat and Beech Marten are found nearby and hunt in the reserve but are strictly nocturnal. Roe Deer are also found in most of the pine forests of the Landes. Green Lizard, Stripeless Tree Frog and European Pond Terrapin are other inhabitants of the reserve, which is excellent for dragonflies (numerous species), and other insects.

<u>Accommodation:</u> There are four hotels, two of which are *Logis*, in Labenne. The coastal resorts of Capbreton and Hossegor with several hotels and campsites are not far away.

European Crane

Area 12 **HENDAYE**

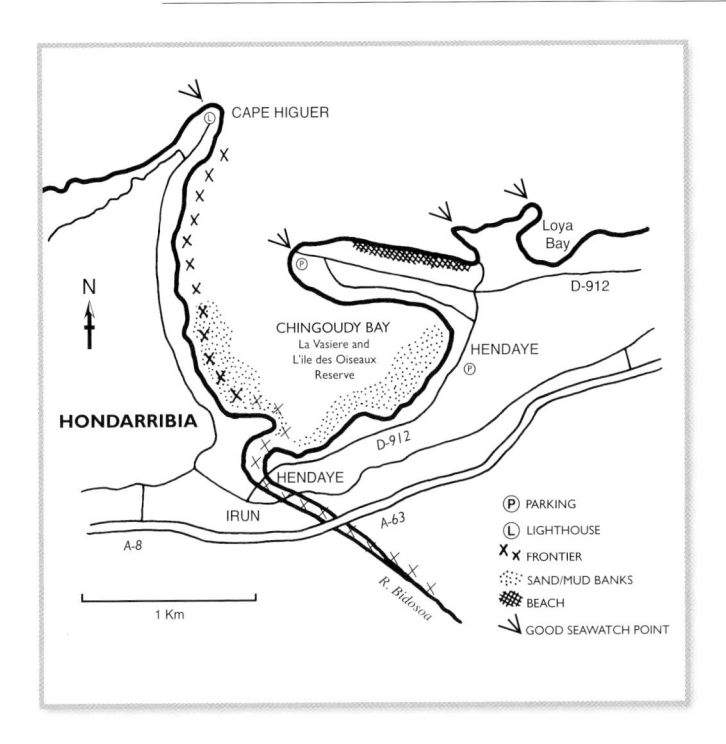

The seaside resort of Hendaye is situated on the north bank of the River Bidasoa, which forms the border between France and Spain. The gentle foothills of the Pyrenees rise up directly outside the town. Where the river enters the Atlantic, part of the CHINGOUDY ESTUARY has been turned into a bird reserve, LA VASIERE AND L'ÎLE DES OISEAUX. There is no access to "Bird Island" but good views of the mudflats can be had from the D912 which runs along the waterfront, with places to park. It is possible to walk all round the bay. There are always gulls present, mainly **Yellow-legged**, **Lesser Black-backed** and **Black-headed**, but also **Mediterranean** and a few rarities on passage. Plenty of **waders**, **Gannets** and **terns** pass through during migration, as do **Spoonbill, Avocet, Black-winged Stilt,** the occasional **Black Stork** and **Bluethroat**. The latter may be seen on the edges of reedbeds, in any patch of grass or even along roadside verges or from the end of August to October. When north or north-west gales drive seabirds inshore, **Great Northern Divers, Guillemot, Razorbill, sea-ducks, shearwaters** and **petrels** may be seen in the bay. A headland just north of the town beach, easily reached on foot, is a good spot for sea-watching.

A larger headland juts out to sea south of the river, in Spain, and this is an even better site to sea-watch. It is possible to drive over one of the bridges that separate Hendaye from its Spanish twin-town of Hondarribia where a road, not too easy to find, leads up along the bay to the headland, Cape Higuer, and the lighthouse (follow the signs for "*faro*"). This road gives good views down onto the bay. If it is raining, as it frequently is in the Basque country, there are two small bars beside the lighthouse from where one can look out to sea, protected from the worst of the weather.

<u>Accommodation:</u> There are plenty of hotels in both Hendaye and Hondarribia and a campsite right beside the lighthouse on Cape Higuer

Area 13 CHAMP DE TIR DU POTEAU, CAPTIEUX

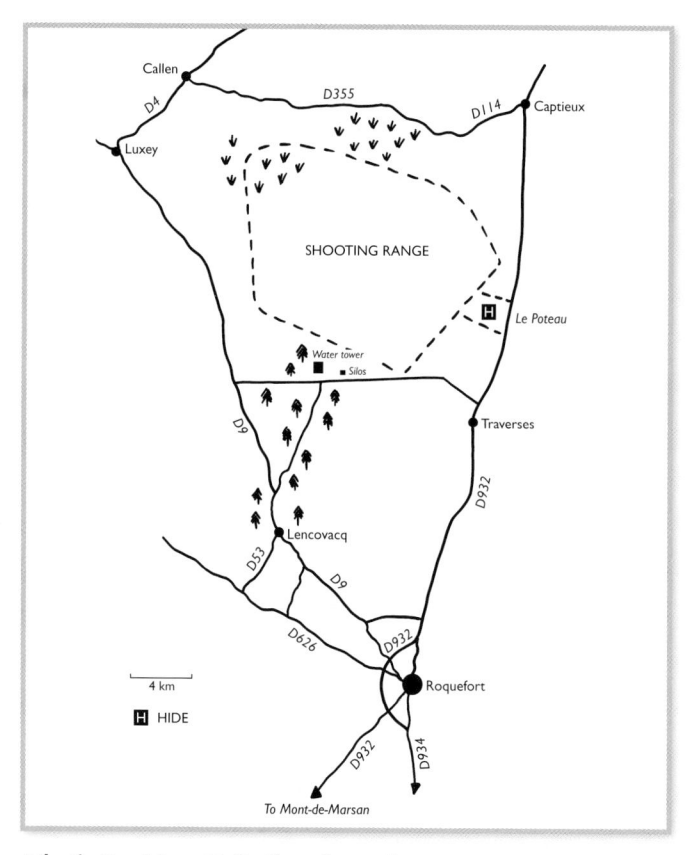

Atlantic Coast Area 13 Captieux Crane site

One of the most important stopovers for **Cranes** moving between Scandinavia and Spain is the military range near Captieux in les Landes. 30,000 Cranes may spend some time here on migration and up to 2,000 now winter here. Although much of this part of France is covered with pine forest, large fields have been cleared for growing maize and this is where the Cranes feed in the daytime. One area where you can be almost sure of seeing birds between October and March is just south of the range and north of the village of Lencouacq. Leave the village going northwards on the D9 towards Luxey and after 2 km take the first fork right (a minor road that runs through forest, only signed with the names of farms). After 6 km there is a crossroads by an old water tower. On the right is a large field with farm buildings "Co-op de Pau Sicapau". The **Cranes** may be feeding here. If they are not visible drive left down the track (firebreak no 53) to where you will see a large notice about the Cranes on the right-hand fence. There are usually Cranes in the fields both to the right and left. The right fork at the crossroads eventually leads to the hamlet of Traverses on the D932. Turn left (north) and some 3 km further north near le Poteau a hide has been erected for Crane watching. Cranes can fly long distances to feed, so if you fail to find them in the above areas look anywhere else around the shooting range shown on the sketch map. They often feed in maize fields.

In summer, **Short-toed Eagle, Hen and Montagu's Harriers** and **Tawny Pipit** breed in the open areas and **European Nightjar** in suitable parts of the forest (those recently planted or where the pines are widely spaced). Listen for them at dusk.

Accommodation: The nearest hotels (*Logis*) are at Roquefort 30 km or Mont-de Marsan 50 km to the south or Casteljaloux 30 km to the west.

Area 14 **NIORT**

The agricultural plains to the south-east of Niort are one of strongholds of the declining **Little Bustard** but there are probably only some fifty pairs breeding in a huge area, so finding them is rather a "needle in a haystack" task. Double that number of **Stone Curlew** also breed here as well as several pairs of **Montagu's Harriers**.

WHEN TO VISIT: All these species are migratory and the first two are present in this area between April and October. Montagu's Harriers leave during August. September/October is a good time to find Little Bustards and Stone Curlew as they gather in pre-migratory flocks of several hundred birds. In the spring, scattered birds are difficult to spot among the growing cereal crops but dusk is a good time to look for them as **Stone Cur**lew call just as it is getting dark and the Bustards often fly, or even display, in the early evening.

In winter, huge flocks of **Lapwing** and **Golden Plover** can be found in the fields, as well as flocks of passerines, especially **Skylark** and **Meadow Pipit**. **Hen** and **Marsh Harriers**, as well as a few **Merlin**, hunt over the winter fields together with numerous **Kestrels**.

ACCESS: An area that can be productive is around the village of PRAHECQ. The D740 runs south-east from NIORT through Prahecq and bisects the Bustard area. Minor D-roads radiate from Prahecq and other villages. Exploration of the many quiet minor roads leading to the villages of Triou, Tauché, Ste. Blandine, Brûlain, Juscorps and Fors, may give sightings if you park beside the road and scope the surrounding fields.

Further south, between NIORT and ANGOULÊME, is another cultivated area that is worth searching for the same species. The VILLEFAGNAN plains lie some 10 km west of Ruffec and 30 km north of Angoulême. Drive along the D19 between AIGRE and VILLEFAGNAN and again explore the minor roads radiating out from the village of SOUVIGNÉ, 5 km south of Villefagnan.

THE PYRENEES

WHEN TO VISIT: These sites are situated at altitudes ranging between 1000 to 2500 m. The majority are best visited between May and July. The trans-Pyrenean migration passes, areas 1, 2, 6, 8, 9 and 11 have the most concentrated passage during the post-nuptial migration and the optimum time to visit for the largest number of species is the last week in August and first two weeks in September, although migration starts at the end of July and at the western sites continues until November, when large numbers of **Crane** pass over the Pyrenees. This last species returns north at the end of February and the first few days of March but the pre-nuptial migration is more protracted and less concentrated than the autumn passage; **Storks** will start returning at the beginning of February while **Honey Buzzards** may still be crossing the Pyrenees at the beginning of June. Any of these sites can be good for pre-nuptial migration during March and early April. Anyone staying at the ski stations near areas 4, 5, 6, 7 and 8 during the winter will have a good chance of seeing **Snow Finch, Alpine Accentor** and **Alpine Chough** near the resorts and raptors displaying overhead. Woodpeckers and owls are always easier to hear and locate in woodland during February and March but the highest areas will be quite impassible in these months.

Alpine Chough

Area 1	Col de Méhatché
Area 2	The western migration passes (M)
	Site i Organbidexka
	Site ii Lindux and Lizarrieta
Area 3	Gave de Pau – Artix Bird Reserve – a wetland site
Area 4	Forest d'Issaux and Somport Pass
	Site i Forest d'Issaux
	Site ii Somport Pass
Area 5	Ossau valley and Pourtalet Pass
Area 6	Gavarnie
Area 7	Néouvielle
Area 8	The Lis and La Pique Valleys south of Bagnères-de-Luchon
Area 9	Port d'Aula (M)
Area 10	Ax-les-Thermes – the lower Ariège
	Site i The Beille Plateau
	Site ii Orlu Reserve
	Site iii The Gorges de la Frau
Area 11	Eyne – an eastern migration route (M)
Area 12	Canigou and Prats-de-Mollo
	Site i Canigou and the northern slopes
	Site ii La Preste Reserve – Prats-de-Mollo

Maps: The Pyrenees are covered in a series of eleven Institut Géographique National walking maps (*Cartes de randonnées pyrénéennes*) scale 1:50,000. Nos. 1 and 2 cover the western Basque country around Bayonne and the western migration passes, 4 the Gavarnie area, 5 the Néouvielle site, 6 the Port d'Aula, 10 Canigou and 11 the Roussillon coast around Perpignan. They show all footpaths and are essential if walking for any distance. The same Institute's Tourist or Topographic Maps numbers 69-72 cover the whole Pyrenees from west to east. No. 71 covers areas 9-11. One map, published by the National Geographic Institutes of both France and Spain covers the whole Pyrenees, both the French and Spanish sides, scale 1:400,000.

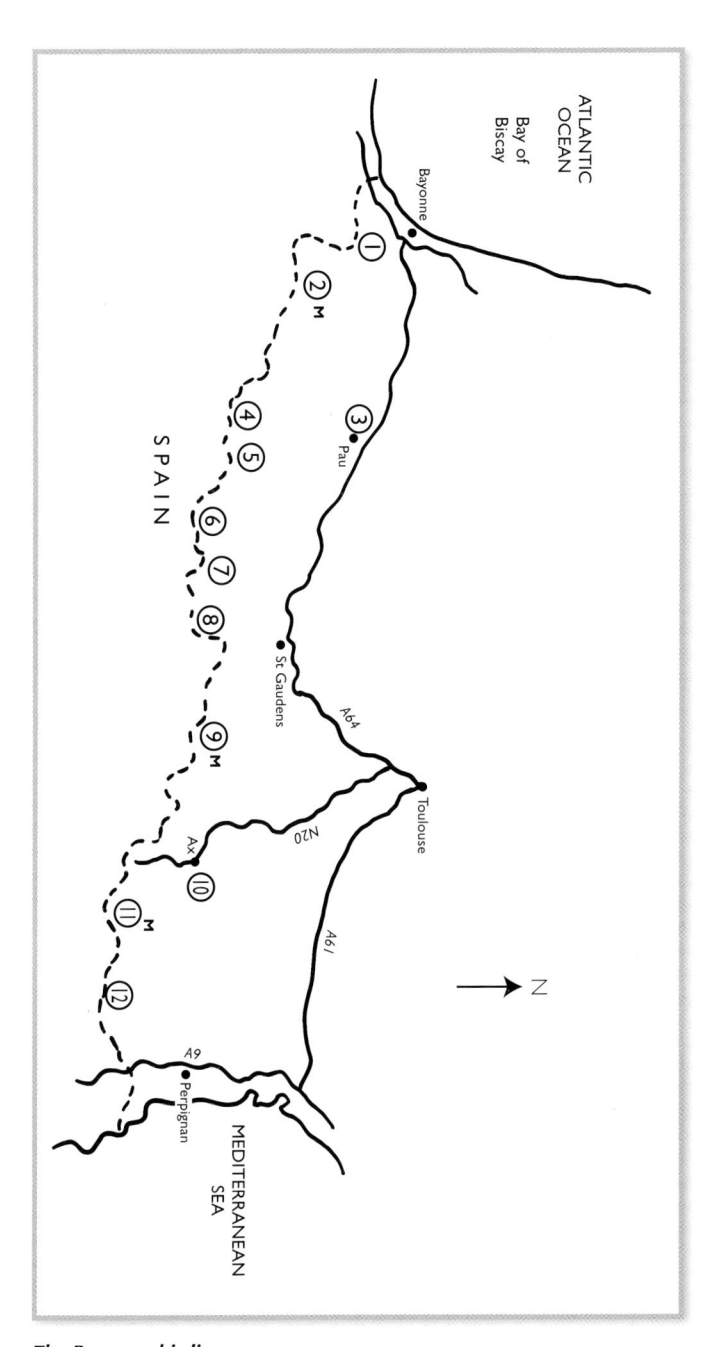

The Pyrenees birding areas

Area 1 **COL DE MÉHATCHÉ**

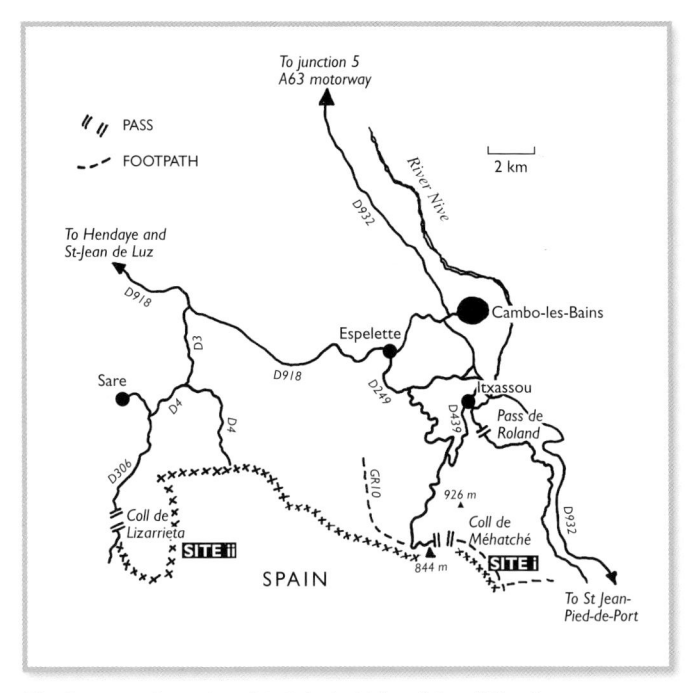

The Pyrenees Areas 1 and 2 Cols de Méhatché and Lizarietta

This pass is included as being the site of the nearest **Griffon Vulture** colony to the Basque coast and one where you can get very close to the birds. It is also situated in one of the most beautiful parts of the Basque country worth visiting for the scenery alone. Besides **Griffon Vulture, Lammergeier** have been seen here and both **Red** and **Yellow-billed Chough** may be observed flying over the hills, **Peregrine** and **Raven** also breed on the cliffs, **Dartford Warbler, Stonechat, Northern Wheatear** and **Whinchat** are among the passerines breeding on the moorland. Chiffchaffs found in nearby woodland are likely to be **Iberian Chiffchaff** and the pass is used by migrating **Honey Buzzards** and many hirundines and passerines at the end of August/beginning of September.

ACCESS: The pass is situated at the very end of an extremely narrow (often only one track with passing places), steep and winding dead-end road, which runs for almost 15 km from ITXASSOU, south of the D932 and CAMBO-les-BAINS. It can be quite confusing as there are many lanes leading only to farms turning off it. Leave the A63 motorway south of Bayonne at exit 5 and turn south onto the D932. It is 17.5 km from the junction to ITXASSOU. In this village take the second turning into the village centre, the D249 to ESPELETTE. Zero here. It is 14.5 km to the pass. Continue on the D249 but turn left off it in 2.6 km signed ARTZAMENDI/MONDARRAIN. Shortly after this bear left and in 0.3 km bear right. Ignore the dead-end road to the left both here and at the next fork where you also bear right. At 8.4 km from Itxassou take the right turn towards St. Pierre restaurant and Aizamendi. In just under 3 km turn right at fork and pass the St. Pierre restaurant. The final 3 kms. to the top of the pass are very steep and twisting. Keep left following the first "Venta Burkaitz" sign but after 2 km ignore the second "Venta" sign and take the left fork to the top of the Col de Méhatché, where you can park. Signs warn that valuables should not be left in your car and it is not permitted to drive off the tarmac roads. (The long hill or ridge, Artzamendi, to the left of the col has a radio/research station on top with a large white sphere on a building and a rectangular gridded "scaffolding" aerial. This can be seen from a long way back so if in doubt at a turning, make towards it). The long-distance footpath GR. 10 runs over the col almost to the top of a cliff where vultures nest. Follow its red and white markers towards the cliff; you will see birds flying as soon as you park. The GR. here is a reasonably level path over springy turf. Branch off it near the colony for a closer look. The GR. goes on to Bidarrai, some 2h30 walking. More productive is to make a circuit around the pass or down to the Col de Veaux, 4.5 km away in the direction you drove up.

The road back to Itxassou passes through some woodland with places where you can pull off the road and walk if you wish to do some woodland birding. Just south of Itxassou is a famous beauty spot, the Pas de Roland beside the River Nive on the D349. It is signed from Itxassou and it is also possible to reach the Col de Méhatché from here but the road is even narrower and it is advisable to take the route suggested.

Other fauna and flora: The moorland is grazed by small skewbald Pottock ponies, the local native breed. There is also an interesting heathland flora.

Accommodation: There are several hotels in Itxassou, including a *Logis* and many more in Cambo, a spa town.

Area 2 ORGANBIDEXKA, LINDUX AND LIZARRIETA

Autumn migration has been studied at these westerly passes since 1979 at Organbidexka and since 1987 at the other two. While there is still much to discover about trans-Pyrenean migration (when and why different routes are used by different species), and birds can be observed crossing almost every pass along the length of the Pyrenean chain at certain times, Organbidexka gives a visiting birder one of the best chances of watching mass movements of a large number of species.

All three passes are traditional sites for French hunters who shoot the huge flocks of pigeons that cross the Pyrenees in autumn; one possible reason for the decline of Turtle Doves. A conservation organisation, Organbidexka Col Libre (O.C.L) leases a former hunting site on the pass at Organbidexka and volunteers man the site from mid-July to mid-November. The area is classified as a reserve but this does not deter the hunters firing from their shooting butts nearby.

Honey Buzzard

Site i

Organbidexka (1355 m) is near the CHALETS D'IRATY, some 10 km west of LARRAU, along the minor road (a spur of the D18) leading to Iraty and Saint-Jean-Pied-de-Port. Larrau is about 4 km south-west of Oloron-Sainte-Marie. A small path leads to the observation site on the north side of the pass and when it is manned there are signs pointing to it but migrating birds can be seen from any vantage point on the grassy slopes above the road through the pass.

Some 10,000 **Black Kites** and 8,000 **Honey Buzzards** cross here, the majority during the last few days of August and the first week in September. The first two weeks in September are probably the best time to visit if you want to see a large number of species. In addition to the above two species, **Black Stork, Hobby,** all three **harriers, Osprey** and spectacular numbers of hirundines fly over. **Short-toed Eagle** numbers peak at the end of September, beginning of October. Most **Red Kites**, almost 3,000, cross in October and a similar number of **Cranes** in November.

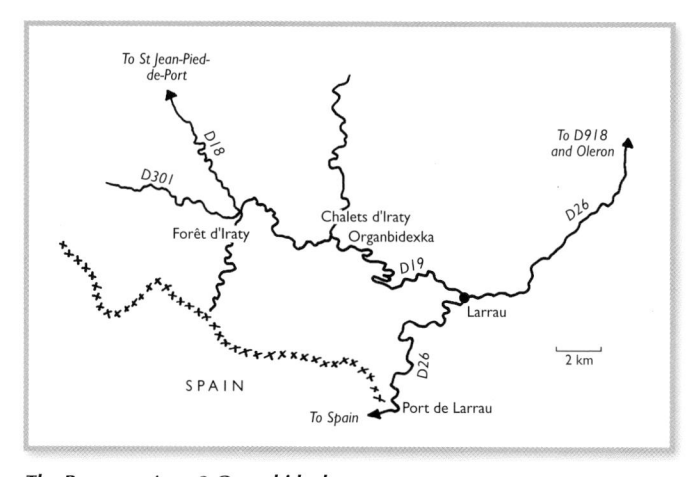

The Pyrenees Area 2 Organbidexka

Site ii.
Lindux and Lizarrieta, where O.C.L. also carry out counts, are slightly lower passes, further to the west. Lindux, near Roncevalles, is some 30 km south of Saint-Jean-Pied-de-Port and not very easy to reach but LIZARRIETA is on the D306 which leads from SARE (15 km from the coast at St. Jean-de-Luz, north of Hendaye) to the Spanish frontier (see map of Area 1). It is a low, accessible pass with some good birding habitat in the area if you can forget the line of gun butts. During the past few years, volunteers have camped at these passes in an attempt to deter the hunters; to try and count the number of pigeons, note their flight paths, check on the barrages of shots and the hunters' hides. More pigeons and **Cranes** fly over these westerly sites, otherwise they are used by the same species as cross at Organbidexka but in smaller numbers. Chiffchaff breeding in the woods here are likely to be **Iberian Chiffchaff**, although common Chiffchaff may pass though on passage.

Like migration watching anywhere, a good day depends on wind and weather conditions further north, not just at the pass. On some days birds may be passing over so high that they are mere specks, on other days you can watch for hours without seeing a single raptor, then suddenly flocks will start appearing on the horizon and thousands fly over right above your head.

O.C.L. can always use volunteers and welcomes visitors. Contact them at 11 Rue Bourgneuf F-64100 Bayonne. Tel: 05 59 25 62 03 or e-mail: ocl@wanadoo.fr.

Area 3 GAVE DE PAU – ARTIX BIRD RESERVE

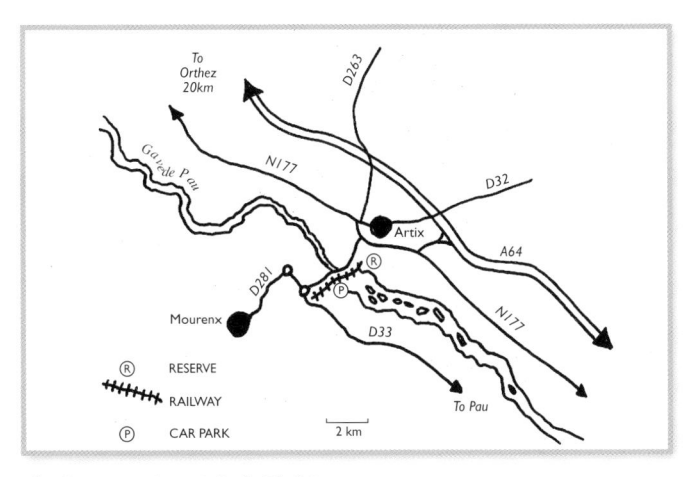

The Pyrenees Area 3 Artix Bird Reserve

The Artix Reserve is a wetland reserve formed by damming the Gave de Pau River. There are wooded islands, mud banks and open water. Most of it is inaccessible but there is a viewing spot on the south bank beside the bridge on the D281 between ARTIX and MOURENX.

In summer **Hobby, Purple Heron, Night Heron** (a few may overwinter), **Kingfisher, Squacco Heron, Little Egret, Common Sandpiper, Little Ringed Plover, Black Kite, Cetti's** and **Melodious Warbler** are among the species likely to be seen. **Marsh Harrier, Osprey, Crane, Pied Flycatcher, Penduline Tit, Black Tern** and various waders stop off here on passage while winter visitors include various species of duck, **Red Kite, Lapwing, Snipe, Reed Bunting, Redwing and Brambling**. There is a large heron roost on the islands and birds can be seen flying in and out at dusk.

It is possible to walk along the railway line over the bridge and then scramble down and follow the embankment. It is rather overgrown but will allow closer views of the far side.

ACCESS: Take the N117 from either PAU or ORTHEX and leave it where it by-passes ARTIX (roughly 20 km from either town). Turn south onto the D281 signed MOURENX. After a couple of kilometres this road crosses the river. Immediately you have crossed the bridge turn left over a railway line into the small parking space which leads to a small grassed area overlooking the reserve. There are seats, a telescope and information boards showing the birds and wildlife

Other fauna and flora: Coypu occur here and Wild Boar and Genet in the woods (unlikely to be see except at night). The European Pond Terrapin can be seen here between April and October, when it hibernates. Agile Frog *Rana dalmatica* and Iberian Green Frog *Rana perezi* both occur. This is a good site for dragonflies including *Libellula quadrimaculata,* Broad-bodied Chaser *L. depressa,* Golden-ringed Dragonfly *Cordulegaster boltonii* and Agrion species such as Blue-tailed Damselfly.

<u>Accommodation:</u> There are hotels in both Pau and Orthez.

Area 4 FOREST D'ISSAUX AND SOMPORT PASS

Site i
The forest lies to the west of the N-134 which runs from Oloron Ste. Marie to the Somport pass on the Spanish frontier through one of the loveliest Pyrenean valleys. Most woodland birds can be found in the forest but it is included here as one of the best sites for **White-backed Woodpecker**.

ACCESS: About 4 k. north of the village of BEDOUS, 26 km from the Somport, there is a turning west signed to LOURDIOS-ICHÈRE (this is much easier than trying to find your way through Bedous). Drive along this narrow road, passing through Lourdios village until there is a junction signed to Forest d'Issaux on the left. Drive south down this road, which passes through a rocky gorge that is a wintering site for **Wallcreeper**, until you come to another junction. Park here. The woodpeckers can be heard anywhere around here. Listen for their weak drumming, which has been likened to a creaking branch. They have been seen most frequently, however, from the small forestry track some 400 metres west of the junction. Take this track deeper into the wood. Stop at any areas with dead and fallen trees. The birds are easier to see in early spring when they are calling and before the trees are in full leaf. Early morning is the best time for these as for all woodpecker species. (See map page 68).

Site ii.
High altitude species can be found around the SOMPORT pass but the main road carries a lot of traffic. Walking above the ski station of ASTUN (just over the frontier) can be more rewarding. The road to Astun is clearly signed on the Spanish side of the frontier. **Snow Finch** and **Alpine Accentor** are often seen around the buildings in winter and early spring, **Water Pipit** and **Black Redstart** in summer. **Alpine Chough** are common and it is a good area for raptors, including vultures and **Golden Eagle**.

Accommodation: There are small hotels and camp sites in all the larger villages leading to the pass. The hotels in the ski resorts may be closed off-season. There are plenty of hotels in Jaca in Spain.

Area 5 VALLÉE D'OSSAU AND POURTALET PASS

Most of the Ossau valley is a protected area (it was created a "Réserve Naturelle" in 1974 mainly to protect two Griffon Vulture colonies) and forms part of the huge National Park of the Pyrenees, although Ossau lies west of the main part of the park and there is no east-west road link with the Gavarnie area (only footpaths for keen walkers). Pyrenean valleys run north-south and the roads follow them. Therefore a driver always has to go quite a long way north before meeting an east-west road. This is the case with Ossau.

ACCESS: The D934 follows the valley from its junction with the N134 at GAN some 10 km south of PAU and then climbs due south to its highest point at the Pourtalet pass on the Spanish frontier.

The turning to the first good birding site is 33 km from Pau at a pass where **Lammergeier** and other raptors are often seen. It can be reached by taking the minor D294 that runs from BIELLE to Bilhères and then continues west towards ESCOT and the N134. The roundabout is signed BIELLE and the Col de Marie Blanque/Bilhères en Ossau. Drive past Bielle and Bilhères villages and continue for a further 8-10 km up to any suitable parking places at the highest points of the col (1035 m) and scan. (If you continue on to Escot, another 10 km, this road joins the N134 running south up the Valleé d'Aspe where there are further good sites-see area 4 above)

Back on the D934 note the cliffs on the east of the road. They are the start of the vulture colony. Some 2.5 km further south turn left at the next roundabout following the sign to the "Falaise aux Vautours". The Observation and Information Centre is right beside a parking and picnic area with a map showing local walks. To the east you will see another tall limestone cliff. When the Reserve was created there were only 10 breeding pairs of **Griffon**

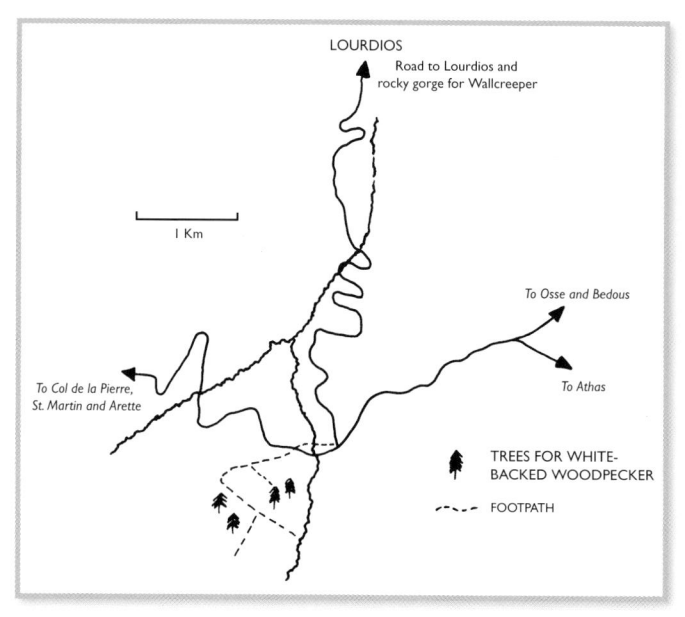

Area 4 The Forest d'Issau

Vultures; now there are well over 100 pairs and up to five pairs of **Egyptian Vultures**. **Peregrine Falcon** also breeds here. The first and last species can be seen flying above the cliffs at any time of the year; Egyptian Vulture arrives back in mid-March. Good views can be had by scanning with a telescope from the parking/picnic area beside the Information Centre. Access to the cliffs is prohibited during the breeding season January to August. If you want closer views, from inside the building it is possible to watch a live video, during the breeding period, of Griffon and Egyptian Vultures chicks in the nest while an ornithologist gives a running commentary. At any time of the year **Red Kite**

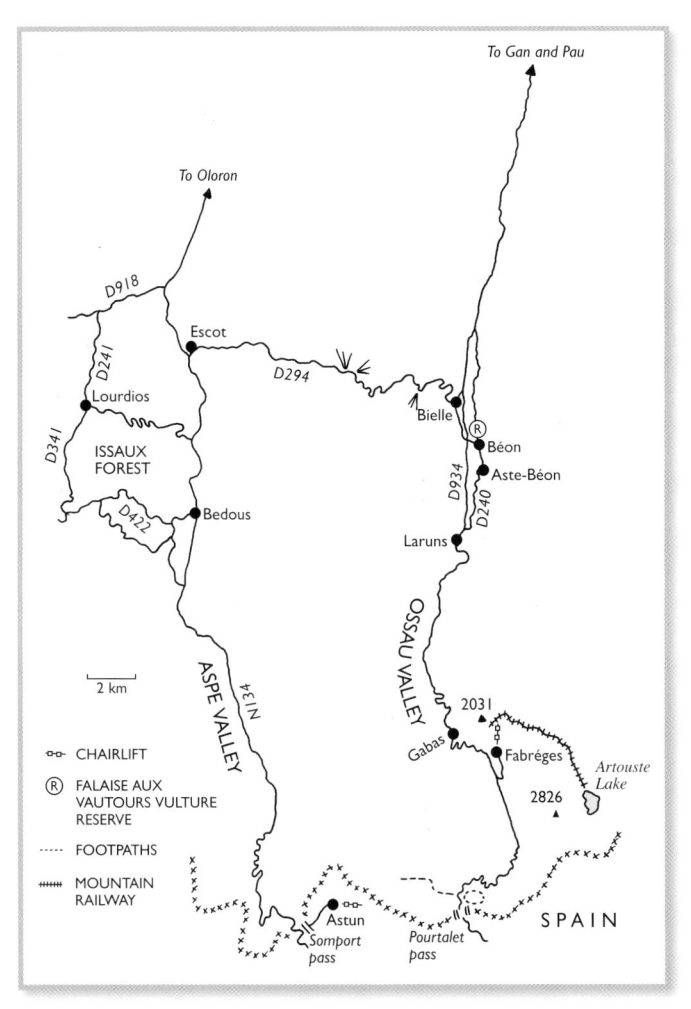

The Pyrenees Areas 4 and 5 Forest d'Issau and Vallée d'Ossau etc

Griffon Vulture

and **Raven** are often seen from here, and **Black Kite** and **Short-toed Eagle** from March to September; look for **Dipper** in the river here and further upstream. If you like, continue along the D240, which is a quiet road running parallel to the D934 so giving opportunities to stop and bird, until it loops back and rejoins the D934 in about 5 km.

The road starts climbing fairly steeply from now on and narrows as the cliffs close in each side of the road. It is difficult to park but where there is a lay-by scan the cliffs for **Wallcreeper** in the winter. There is a place to park just before the thermal spa of EAUX CHAUDES as well as more spaces in the village itself, and it can be quite productive to walk back below the cliffs. **Cranes** fly down this valley at the end of February or the beginning of March and can be seen from here or from the pass at the top.

Higher still the slopes each side of the road are covered with beech/fir woods. There are certainly both **Black** and **White-backed Woodpeckers** here but the hillsides are so steep that access is almost impossible. An easier site can be found in the next valley to the west – see area 4.

Four kilometres after Gabas (where there is a National Park Information Centre) and just after the dam, some cable cars can be seen on the left of the road beside a complex of buildings (hotels, restaurants, etc). This is FABRÈGES (1240 m) reached by a signed road which runs back from the south end of the lake. The cable car takes 12 minutes to reach Artouste station from where a small train runs every 30 minutes to Lake Artouste (2000 m). The track was built in 1924 to aid construction of Artouste dam. From here you can walk around the lake or use it as a starting point for longer walks. You are unlikely to see any birds that cannot be found at Pourtalet (see below) and it is very touristy in summer but it is an easy way to get among high mountain birds; you might find **Snow Finch** and **Alpine Accentor** among the scree slopes. And the views are wonderful. The cable car runs to the slopes of the Artouste ski station in winter and the train runs from the beginning of June to the end of September.

The D934 continues to the top of the pass and the border at POURTALET. Here, just across the frontier in Spain, are rows of cafés and "duty-free" shops. The French side is less commercial with just one restaurant and shop. Do not disregard this rather depressingly touristy end to a beautiful road. **Alpine Accentors** sometimes feed around the cafés in winter and can be seen around the rocky areas of the pass all year round. At any time of the year, park in the carpark on the French side and walk up towards the nearest cliffs or scope from the carpark. **Alpine and Red-billed Chough, Lammergeier, Griffon Vulture, Golden Eagle, Black and Red Kites, Rock Thrush, Water Pipit, Black Redstart** and **Northern Wheatear** are some of the species frequently observed from here. Check any sparrows as **Rock Sparrow** occurs here. **Wallcreeper** has been seen on the rocks, even those quite near the road, more frequently in spring and autumn. **Ortolan Bunting** and **Whinchat** are other species that can be found near the top of the pass. **Snow Finch** and **Alpine Accentor** are occasionally seen both before and after the breeding season, especially in March when the former can be observed flying between the patches of open grass that dot the snowfield. Afterwards walk down the pass a little way and turn off right at a small farm. Walk along a rough animal track towards the cliffs from here. There are no restrictions on entering Spain and just across the frontier, a broad track leads off right to some disused mines immediately before the first shop on the right "Venta Sancho". This is a good site for **Rock Thrush** and **Lammergeier** (if you failed on the French side), as well as Marmots and Chamois.

Other fauna and flora Marmots breed in holes among the rocks; listen out for their alarm calls – the shrill whistles fool many birders into speculation as to what species is calling! Isard (Chamois) can often be seen on the highest slopes above the pass, especially in spring and autumn. The alpine flowers at the pass are spectacular and can be seen without too much climbing. Mid-May to July is the best time for gentians, saxifrages, orchids and the Pyrenean Snakeshead Fritillary. Mountain butterflies are numerous; this is a good area for both Apollo and Clouded Apollo.

Area 6 GAVARNIE

The Cirque de Gavarnie is the best-known and most-visited site in the whole of the Pyrenees National Park. The scenery is certainly spectacular; waterfalls plummet thousands of metres from the top of a mountain amphitheatre which is streaked with snowfields, even at the height of summer. Birds and butterflies migrate through Gavarnie, as they do through most Pyrenean passes, but even outside the migration periods, Gavarnie is a good site.

The village of Gavarnie lies at the end of a no-through road, the D-923, from GÈDRE. Park in one of the many car parks in the village and take the well-marked track towards the Cirque. The path follows the river, where **Dipper** can be seen, through light woodland. There are **Citril Finch** here, as well as **Crested Tit** and **Crossbill** among the pines. **Alpine Swift** fly overhead. Keep checking the mountain ridges all round; **Griffon Vulture** are common in summer when there are flocks on the high pastures, **Golden Eagle** and **Lammergeier** can be seen year round. As you near the Cirque, search the cliffs and the small gorge for **Wallcreeper**, especially in spring and autumn. There is a hotel with a terrace at the end of the track; a good place to sit and watch for raptors. Footpaths lead on to the scree and snowfields below the rock walls; look for **Alpine Accentor** and **Snow Finch**. One footpath climbs westwards towards the Port de BOUCHARO, but this pass can also very easily be reached by car.

To drive to Boucharo pass, return to Gavarnie village and take the road signed to the ski-station. This leads upwards, through mountain moorland where **Black Redstart, Northern Wheatear** and **Water Pipit** are the characteristic species. **Rock Buntings** flit among the rocks and Marmots are very common. There are plenty of places to stop on the way up and a car park at the top of the pass. This is a good viewpoint, especially for migrating raptors in autumn. You can often look down on **Griffon Vultures** while **Alpine Chough** hang around the cars, hoping for scraps. Beyond the parking the road is blocked for vehicles but walkers can continue into Spain or to the footpath that runs up through the scree and snowfields. It may be worth walking a short way along this, before it climbs too steeply, searching among the rocks for **Alpine Accentor** and **Snow Finch**.

The third road leading from Gavarnie village is a very minor one along the Ossoue river. It eventually turns into an unsurfaced track leading up to a lake. Bird species are likely to be the ones mentioned above but the alpine meadows are a botanist's dream, making it is one of the best areas in the Pyrenees for butterfly species.

If you wish to continue eastwards from Gavarnie-Gèdre, towards Néouvielle, it will be necessary to drive over the Col du TOURMALET, where the birds and flowers are typical of bare mountain moorland, and then over the wooded Col d'ASPIN to ARREAU. **Snowfinch** can be found on the Col de Tourmalet in July-August. Check round the pylons on the slopes above the café, as well as the toll road to the observatory. The pinewoods on the latter pass are worth spending a little time in. **Crossbill** and **Crested Tit** are among the species that can be found there.

Area 7 NÉOUVIELLE

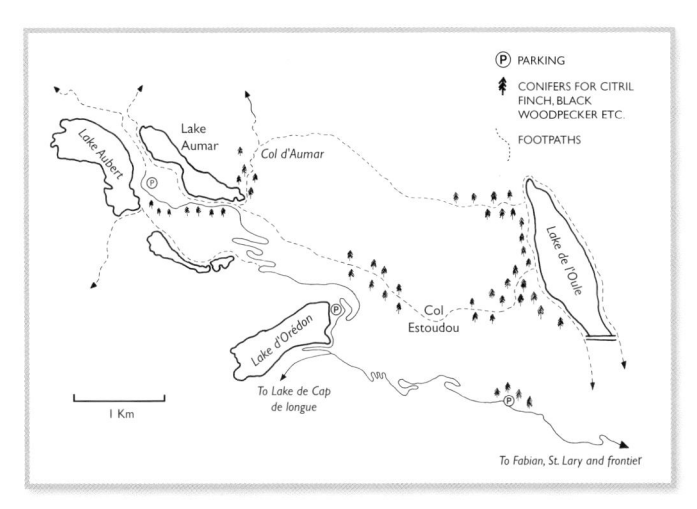

The Réserve Naturelle de Néouvielle

The Réserve Naturelle de Néouvielle (the name means "Old Snow") was created in 1935. It covers 2,313 hectares ranging in height from 1,800 to over 3,000 metres. It is easy to drive to above 2000 metres and the scenery is wild and majestic but although all the high Pyrenean species are to be found in the Reserve, actually seeing them is quite difficult, and involves a considerable amount of walking; even then, no sightings can be guaranteed.

A road up to the lake area of Néouvielle branches off the D-929 ARREAU-St. LARY road in the village of FABIAN, signposted to the Reserve. After 9.30 a.m. there is no entry to the final 6.4 km which is closed by a barrier, though you can leave at any time. It is worth going up to this top car park between Lakes Aubert and Aumar as **Citril Finch** are very common in the scattered pines here. If you arrive too late, there is a car park near the barrier served, in the summer season, by a shuttle-bus to the top car park.

From the top car park, footpaths lead in several directions. Several climb up to scree-covered slopes where **Alpine Accentor** and **Snow Finch** breed and can sometimes be found. One of the nearest sites is the COL d'AUMAR. Walk back along the road to the south-eastern tip of lake Aumar and climb up to the low pass on the left. Besides **Citril Finch**, there are **Siskin, Firecrest, Coal** and **Crested Tit** in the pines here and **Ring Ouzel** nearer the top of the pass. **Capercaillie** breed in the pinewoods but they are always difficult to see. They prefer the highest strands of pines. If there is still snow, you can sometimes see their traces. In summer, when the steep slopes are most accessible, there are many walkers and the birds are well away from the footpaths. **Black Woodpecker** is another forest species; look for them lower down in the taller forest, near the first two parking areas.

Other fauna and flora: Most mountain species – Isard, Marmot, Pine Martin, Red Squirrel and Pyrenean Desman among them – can be found within the Park. Look for the desman in fast-flowing, unpolluted mountain streams with rocky banks. The rare Seoanei's viper occurs in Néouvielle. The whole area is rich botanically; the Park publishes its own guides –"Fleurs du Parc National", showing 573 of the plants to be found here. There is a Botanical Garden on the Col du Tourmalet. Such an abundant flora hosts abundant invertebrates; butterflies include species such as the rare and local Gavarnie Blue and Glandon Blue. Many of the butterflies which occur on mountains can be found at Néouvielle (which has over 1,200 plant species), including the Apollo and many species of ringlet.

<u>Accommodation:</u> There are plenty of hotels and campsites in all the villages and small towns near the Park but in high season (July/August) it is almost impossible to find a room unless you have previously booked.

Area 8 THE LIS AND LA PIQUE VALLEYS SOUTH OF BAGNÈRES-DE-LOUCHON

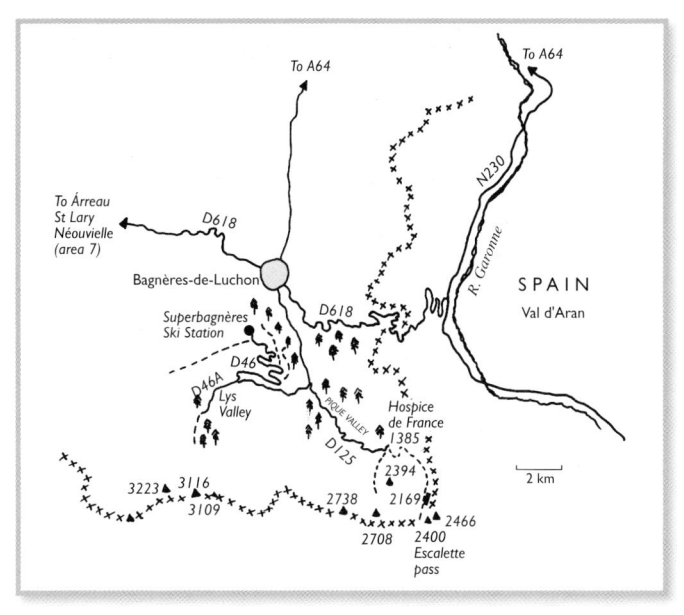

The Pyrenees Area 8 Lys and Pique Valleys

These two high mountain valleys run south of Bagnères-de-Louchon, east of the Vall d'Aran, where Spain extends into the north side of the Pyrenees. Their rivers run roughly parallel with the River Garonne and further north join it. It is an area of steep, narrow valleys clothed in predominantly beech and fir woods and is included here mainly because it is the most easterly site for **White-backed Woodpecker,** though the valleys are very dense and difficult to bird. **Capercaillie, Black, Green** and **Great Spotted Woodpeckers** also occur in these woods and all the tits, except Willow. **Siskin** also breed here, one of their few breeding sites the Pyrenees, as do **Crossbill**. **Citril Finch** can be found on the higher edge of the tree line. In the alpine meadows above the trees, especially around the ski station of Superbanères, **Northern Wheatear, Water Pipit** and **Black Redstart** are common. In the very highest areas **Alpine Accentor** and **Ptarmigan** can be found. There are fewer **Snowfinch** in this area than in the previous site but they occur; there are more when they disperse after the breeding season. **Raven** and **Red-billed Chough** can be seen over the ridges and with luck **Lammergeier**. **Short-toed Eagle** and **Honey Buzzard** are two more breeding species.

ACCESS: The D125 leads from the A 64 motorway west of St. Gaudens, signed to Bagnères. Follow it through town and continue south on it as it follows the La Pique river. Some 5 km from Bagnères, it forks. If you want to walk in the high mountains, take the left fork signed to Hospice de France. This very narrow road only allows cars to drive up for a couple of hours in early morning and down again mid day or after five. Several well marked footpaths run from the Hospice for anyone hoping to see high altitude species.

The right hand fork, the D46, ends at a series of waterfalls. Some paths lead into the woods but it is too touristy for many birds. The road to Superbagnères ski station leads off the D46 4 km after the fork. Follow this to the top where the species that like short grassland can be found. Look for **Citril Finch** where the trees start to thin out. One possible site for **White-backed Woodpecker** is off the *Route Forestière de Techous*, which leads off to the right just after the *La Carrière* sign as you drive up. Walk a little way up the forest road, listening and searching clearings with dead and fallen trees. The species has been heard calling near here.

Alpine Accentor

Area 9 PORT D'AULA

The **PORT D'AULA** (2260 m) is a pass on the Spanish frontier that is a notable autumn migration route. It lies within the Reserve de Mont-Vallier. From August to the end of October **Buzzards, Sparrowhawks, Red and Black Kites, Honey Buzzard,** all three **Harriers, Short-toed Eagles, Ospreys** and tens of thousands of hirundines fly over this pass. **Swifts** pour over at the end of July-beginning of August. **Black Kite** numbers peak during the middle of August, though they have been moving since the end of July. Most **Honey Buzzards** cross at the end of August and the beginning of September and account for 50% of the migratory raptors. **Griffon Vulture, Golden Eagle** and **Lammergeier** can be see throughout the year and, as at other high-altitude sites, resident mountain species include **Black Redstart, Alpine Accentor, Snow Finch** and **Ptarmigan. Rock Thrush, Water Pipit, Ring Ouzel** and **Northern Wheatear** are summer breeders. **Wallcreeper** certainly breeds on the highest cliffs but luck is needed to spot it. Check the cliffs to the right of the pass.

ACCESS: To reach the pass which is 18 km southwest of COUFLENS, take the D616 from St. GIRONS, then the D3 to SEIX and COUFLENS. This road follows the River Salat and the higher reaches of the valley are not only very attractive but the surrounding woods are also good for birding. Look for **Dipper** in the river. Just at the start of COUFLENS fork right, crossing the river, onto the very narrow D703 leading towards the COL DE PAUSE and the PORT D'AULA (signed). The road deteriorates some 5 km after Couflens and soon becomes a dirt track. It is inaccessible by car during the winter months (it is not snowploughed) and difficult, even dangerous, when the weather is bad (rain, low cloud, spring snow, summer thunderstorms). You will have to leave your car at the Col de Pause after 9 km and walk the remaining 9 km towards the Port d'Aula along the GR10 footpath (marked red and white) past the étang (mountain lake) d'Areau. The lake can be reached in about one hour but the pass will take at least three. Good birds can often be seen around the lake; passerines may rest here during migration and breeding species come to drink.

Red-backed Shrike is common along the road leading to Col de Pause. **Black Woodpecker** can be found in the woods near the Col de Pause. **Ptarmigan** are only likely to be found on the highest scree above the pass, together with **Snow Finch. Rock Thrush** can be found with **Black Redstart** on the rocks lower down, below the pass. **Alpine Accentor** is quite numerous beyond the lake. **Water Pipit** can be found around any streams or damp areas. **Northern Wheatear** prefers drier sites. The Pyrenean race of **Grey Partridge** may also be found on sunny, grassy slopes. **Raven, Red-billed** and **Yellow-billed Chough** and the raptors listed above can be observed throughout the area.

Other fauna and flora: Marmots and Isard (Chamois) are quite abundant. Look for Isard on the highest slopes and check Marmot holes among the rocks that dot the higher grassy slopes, though there are more on the Spanish side of the border. Other mammals include Wild Boar in the woods as well as Pine and Beech Martens. Red Squirrels (a very dark, almost black form) are common. Nine species of bat have been observed around the pass, including the large European Free-tailed Bat, which has a summer roost in the cliff on the right of the pass. A few Pyrenean Desman may still be found in the unpolluted mountain streams together with the Pyrenean Brook Salamander. A few years ago this area was where Brown Bears from Eastern Europe were released as part of a reintroduction scheme. One female was shot and the cubs have ranged widely, frequently crossing into Spain. So do not count of seeing any!

Over 130 species of butterflies have been recorded in this part of the Pyrenees; they include Swallowtail and Scarce Swallowtail, Apollo, Mountain Dappled White, Camberwell Beauty, Mountain Clouded Yellow, High Brown and Dark Green Fritillary, Great Banded and Rock Graylings, Spanish Brassy, Mountain, Piedmont, Lefèbvre's, False Dewy and Dewy Ringlets, Eros and Idas Blues, Tufted Marbled and Dusky Grizzled Skippers.

Accommodation: There are hotels in St. Girons and a couple of small ones in Seix, as well as Chambres d'hôtes. Summer campsites can be found along the Couflens valley and near Seix.

Black Woodpecker

Area 10 **AX-LES-THERMES –
THE LOWER ARIÈGE SITES**

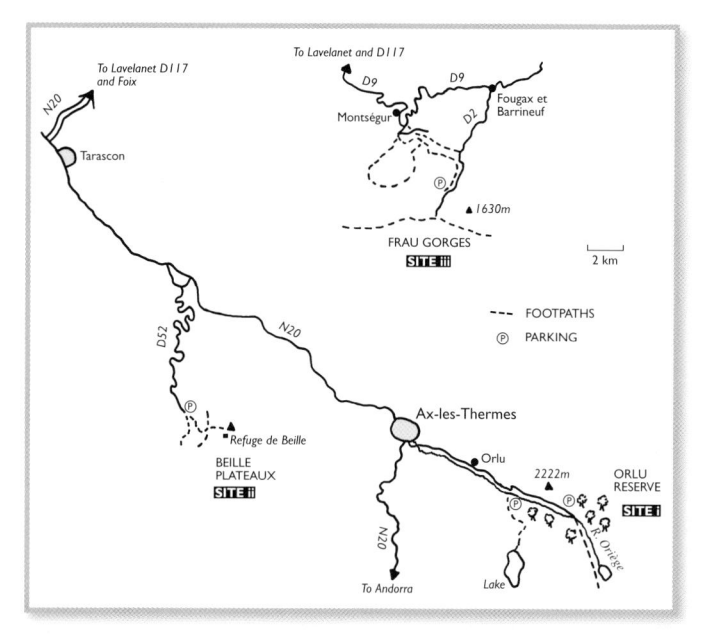

The Pyrenees Area 10 Ax-les-Thermes – the Lower Ariège

Ax-les-Thermes, a small spa town on the N20 leading to Andorra and Spain, is a convenient centre to explore three minor but interesting and different sites.

Site i.

The **BEILLE PLATEAU** (1780 m) lies some 12 km due west of Ax. This site is included because in winter the Beille forest contains a healthy population of **Capercaillie** and is one of the best places to see this species. Unfortunately, since the ski station was built, the population has suffered a sharp decline. The birds move down to the lower slopes during the breeding season but winter and lek in the scattered pines on the top of the plateau. Other forest species that are likely to be seen include **Crossbill** (a really good site), **Firecrest, Crested Tit, Siskin, Great Spotted** and **Black Woodpecker. Ring Ouzel** can be found near the edges of the woodland where the trees thin out or around clearings. Both **Red-billed and Alpine (Yellow-billed) Chough, Raven** and **Buzzard** can be often be seen flying above the open plateau, which is also a good migration and raptor observation spot. **Golden Eagle, Lammergeier, Griffon Vulture** (the last usually in summer) are all regularly seen, and occasionally **Egyptian Vulture,** while in autumn all the species listed for other Pyrenean migration sites may be observed. The best place to watch migration is from the open areas above the pines. **Skylark** and **Water Pipit** are common summer breeders on open ground, while **Dunnock** and **Linnet** nest in the low bushes.

ACCESS: The site is reached by leaving the N20 15 km north of Ax at a left turn signed to the plateau (or, if coming from Toulouse, take a right turn 8.5 km from Tarrascon). After 1.2 km turn left again in the village of les CABANNES towards Pech. A very minor road (well signed as Beille Plateau is a Nordic ski resort) twists up to the ski station for 17 km through mixed deciduous woods – oak, beech, chestnut and finally silver fir. Stop wherever there is a forestry track leading into them for some woodland birding. **Black Woodpecker** can be found where there are large, mature trees. The ski station is situated at the top of the plateau surrounded by mountain pinewoods, which gradually thin out. Park here (the road divides into numerous parking spaces) and go to the other side of the ski buildings. From the restaurant you will see where the pistes lead off into the pinewoods. **Crossbill** is very easy to see around the buildings. Follow the nature trail signed with black cut-out Capercaillies. It leads off the main piste and circles through the forest, past a wet, boggy area, through some clearings, listen for **Ring Ouzel**, and up onto the plateau to a spot where several trails or pistes meet. This is a good place to raptor-watch.

Winter (on Nordic skis or snowshoes), early spring or autumn are probably the best times to visit this site. **Capercaillie** is most likely to be observed at daybreak in spring, when they may be heard calling. Usually all you see is one flying away through the trees! Droppings under trees reveal roosting sites. To avoid disturbing the birds too much, please follow the RSPB guidelines set out under notes on this species at the end of the book.

Site ii.

ORLU, an ONC Reserve, lies just south east of Ax-les-Thermes. It comprises magnificent beech woods, pine forest and high mountain scenery. There is a high concentration of Chamois (Isard) and Marmots within the reserve and these attract raptors and vultures. The orphaned Brown Bear cubs (see Port d'Aula – Pyrenees area 9) were seen here during 1999.

ACCESS: To reach the reserve, take the N20 southwards and the first road leading off left after the end of the town (about half a kilometre from the centre), the D22, is clearly signed to Orlu National Reserve. Drive through Orlu village and just before the road ends at a large carpark (8.5 km from the centre of Ax), turn left and continue along this very minor road for about 5 km until it ends at a bridge over the Oriège river. A map here shows the various footpaths through the reserve. Check the high peak visible from the parking area; both **Golden Eagle** and **Lammergeier** are frequently seen around it. It is possible to make a day-long circular walk from here which will lead past several mountain lakes at altitudes above 2000 m and enable you to see all the high-mountain species described for other Pyrenean sites. But if you only want a short walk, then cross the bridge and continue along the main track. At first this runs uphill through beech woods, where the usual woodland species can be seen; they include **Marsh Tit**, quite rare in this region. When the path emerges onto open moorland, expect to see **Ring Ouzel, Water Pipit** and **Black Redstart**. There are always Marmots around the boulders on the rocky slopes from spring to autumn and Chamois (Isard) on the higher ridges. Continue walking for as long as you wish; the path continues to wind gently uphill. As you get higher, **Alpine Accentor** should be found on the scree slopes. Return the same way if you only want a short walk. Continue on the marked track if taking the circular walk. As this is a high-altitude site, it should only be visited late spring to early autumn.

Site iii.
The **GORGES DE LA FRAU** lie some 12 km due north of Ax (but considerably further by road).

ACCESS: Take the N20 northwards but turn off east onto the D117, 7 km before Foix (signed Lavelanet). 2 km before LAVELANET turn right onto the D9 in the direction of MONTSÉGUR. Montségur has a ruined Cathar castle perched high on a hilltop. However, to reach the gorge, drive through the village and continue on the D9 eastwards for 8 km to the village of FOUGAX ET BARRINEUF. Just at the entrance to the village the D2 road to the Gorge is signed right (south). It is a very narrow road running through woods alongside the river Hers for 6 km. Where it finishes a well-marked footpath takes over as the gorge narrows and starts to wind steeply uphill. From late autumn to early spring, look out for **Wallcreeper** on the cliff faces each side of the path; they are very close to the path on some sections. **Black Woodpecker** can be heard and seen in the gorge's woods; early spring is the easiest time to locate this species, as it is very vocal at this time. **Great** and **Lesser Spotted Woodpeckers** are also present, as are both **Short-toed** and **Common Treecreeper** and **Nuthatch**. Other woodland breeding birds include **Sparrowhawk** and **Goshawk, Buzzard** and **Honey Buzzard, Short-toed Eagle** (likely to be seen hunting over open ground). **Dipper, Grey and White Wagtails** can be seen along the river anywhere from Fougax. **Eagle Owl** breeds in the lower part of the gorge (listens for it at dusk early in the year) while **Tengmalm's Owl** is likely to be heard in May and June at the top end of the gorge. Both **Yellow-billed** and **Red-billed Chough** and **Raven** can be seen circling above the cliffs, and sometimes **Peregrine**, which also breeds near here. At 800 m the gorge is one of the lowest breeding sites for **Yellow-billed Chough** in the Pyrenees.

Other fauna and flora: Chamois and Marmots are very easy to observe, especially in Orlu Reserve. There are Red Squirrels in the woods and the very rare Pyrenean Desman has been found in the river of the Gorge de la Frau. The European Free-tailed Bat is found around the cliffs. All three sites are excellent for butterflies. This area is rich in orchids and both Black Vanilla and

Small White Orchids can be found on the higher slopes, while Pyramidal, Lizard, Fragrant, Lady, Burnt, Butterfly, Tongue and many Bee (*Ophrys*) species can be found in the meadows around Montségur.

Accommodation: There are hotels in every category in Ax-les-Thermes, and summer-only campsites nearby.

Area 11 EYNE – AN EASTERN MIGRATION ROUTE

The plateau near the village of Eyne is not only one of the more important migration routes across the Pyrenees but is also very easy to reach without hours of walking. In autumn up to 20,000 birds fly over the site, the majority **Honey Buzzard** and **Short-toed Eagle**. Other species include **Black Kite, Black and White Storks, Sparrowhawk, Hen, Montagu's** and **Marsh Harriers** as well as large numbers of **Bee-eaters** and quite a few **Dotterel**. The Bee-eaters often follow flocks of migrating dragonflies! Honey Buzzards cross early and most will have crossed by the end of August. Black Kites start in late July and peak 1st to 15th August. You are unlikely to see many of these two species after the end of August. Black Stork numbers peak during the last two weeks of September. Like all post-nuptial migration sites, weather conditions play a large part in determining whether the migration is high or low, spectacular or very disappointing.

Eyne used to be manned from August until early November by a team from O.C.L (see Organbidexka, Pyrenean site 1) counting the migrating birds. Recently they seem to have abandoned Eyne and concentrated their efforts on the west. However, Eyne is still a good site if you are in the area in early autumn. There are a variety of habitats on the plateau: hay meadows, pine woods, wooded streams, and several footpaths. It is a good area for **Red-backed Shrike.**

The best observation point is 2 km from the village where the plateau looks across the valley to Font-Romeu and the northern foothills. If coming from Perpignan take the N-116 through PRADES up to MONT-LOUIS and continue towards SAILLAGOUSE. Turn left after 2.5 km onto the D-33 signposted EYNE. In the village (do not at this point continue on the road to Llo) turn right onto the D-29 and after half a kilometre the path to the site is on the left just before a conifer plantation. If coming the opposite way from Saillagouse, the D-29 leading to Eyne is on the right after some 4 km and the site is then on the right before you reach the village.

Eyne Valley has fairly recently (1993) been classified as a Nature Reserve, extending from 1700 m just above the village up to the Finestrelles peak (2827 m), mainly because it is a famous botanical site with most of the eastern

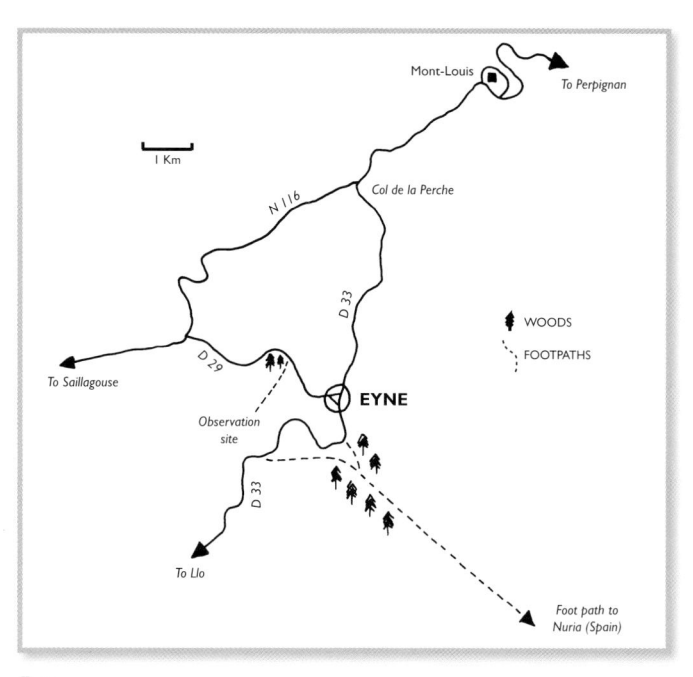

Eyne

Pyrenean specialities growing there. The Yellow Turk's-cap Lily *(Lilium pyrenaicum)* is especially fine in June.

To walk up the Reserve, return to the village and turn towards LLO where marked footpaths on the left lead up the Eyne Valley following the river towards the Nuria Pass, 8 km away. The path at first goes through pinewoods (where **Black Woodpecker, Goshawk, Crossbill and Crested Tit** can be found) that gradually thin out near the Refuge de Orry de Baix, about half way to the pass. **Citril Finch** is likely here. After this point all the high mountain bird species are likely to be seen: **Rock Thrush, Alpine Accentor, Alpine Chough** and **Golden Eagle**. When you reach the pass on the Spanish frontier with the Pic de Nuria (2794 m) on your right and the Pic d'Eyne (2786 m) on your left, **Ptarmigan** and even **Snow Finch** are possible. The return walk, with birding, is likely to take all day.

Other wildlife and flora: Isard (Chamois) may be seen from the pass, as well as Marmot and Moufflon. Wild Boar, Wild Cat and Genet occur in the woods but are unlikely to be seen in daytime. Mountain butterflies include the Apollo, Lefèbvre's, Dewy and Gavarnie Ringlets. Many species of Saxifrage will be found near the streams, *Viola diversifolia, Xatardia scabra* and *Senecio leucophyllus* in the higher screes.

<u>Accommodation:</u> There are a couple of small hotels in Eyne itself and others in Saillagouse and Mont-Louis as well as campsites nearby.

Area 12 CANIGOU AND PRATS-DE-MOLLO – LA PRESTE RESERVE

The **Massif de Canigou** comprises the highest mountains at the eastern end of the Pyrenean chain. Canigou itself at 2784 m is the highest peak but it is surrounded by three others over 2700 m in height and several slightly lower ones. Some 125 bird species breed there and these include Mediterranean species in the eastern foothills and alpine species on the high peaks. Its northern slopes are accessible from the N116 between Mont-Louis and Perpignan but although it is possible to walk over onto the southern slopes where the Nature Reserve is situated, this side is only accessible by car from the D115, which entails driving into Perpignan, then 20 km down the A9 motorway to Le Boulou before turning west onto the D115 – a distance of almost 100 km. In summer only it is possible to cross from the N116 to the D115 by the very twisty but scenic D618 or D13. Warning: these roads may be blocked by snow until quite late in the spring. All roads crossing the Canigou range are good birding areas and well worth exploring.

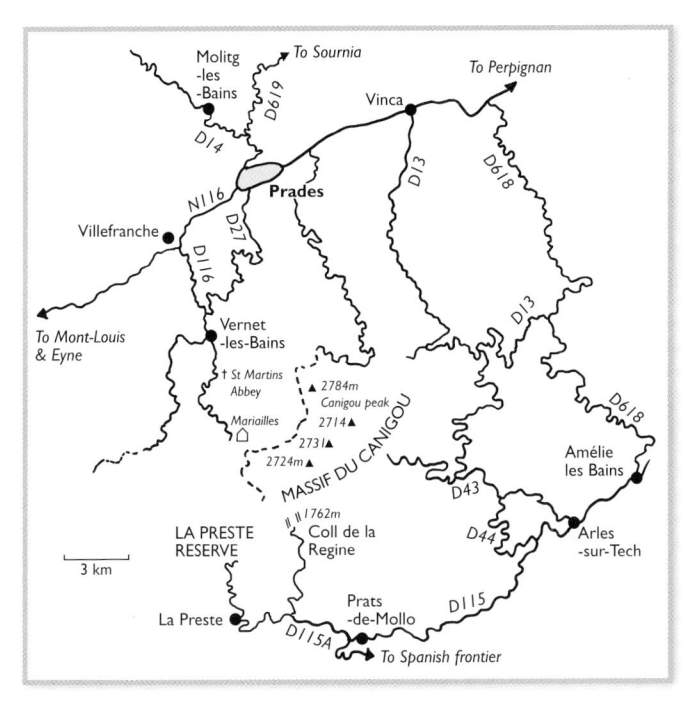

The Pyrenees Area 12 Canigou-La Preste Reserve

Site i. **CANIGOU and the northern slopes**.

ACCESS: The spa town of VERNET-LES-BAINS makes a convenient centre from which to explore the northern slopes and woods of Canigou. Leave the N116 at either VILLEFRANCHE-DE-CONFLENT or PRADES and then take the D116 from the former or the D27 from the latter, both signed to VERNET. Many species will be seen around Vernet: **Firecrest, Serin, Crested Tit, Bonelli's Warbler.** To reach the higher areas south of Vernet continue on the D116 towards the Abbey of St. MARTIN (clearly signed – a walk up to the abbey is good for all the woodland birds already listed) and then on to the COL DE JOU. It is possible to drive further on this very minor road when conditions are good, but better to park and walk along the GR10 footpath up towards the Marialles mountain hut. **Citril Finch** and **Black Woodpecker** are two species likely to be seen in the woods here. Both **Golden Eagle** and **Short-toed Eagle** are frequently sighted overhead.

The GR10 footpath continues around the slopes of Canigou to the peak but it is also possible to hire jeeps in Prades or Vernet that will drive up the rough track almost to the summit. **Short-toed Eagle, Buzzard** and **Golden Eagle** can also be seen from this route, as well as both **Red-billed** and **Yellow-billed Chough. Rock Bunting** and **Red-backed Shrike** are found among the shrubs once clear of the forest. The summit of Canigou is popular with tourists but **Water Pipit** and **Black Redstart** do not seem bothered by the disturbance. **Alpine Accentor** needs more searching to find among the scree slopes; it is very elusive during the breeding season.

The lower, sunnier slopes north of the N116 are good for more Mediterranean type species: **Sardinian, Dartford** and **Orphean Warblers, Woodchat Shrike** and **Cirl Bunting** can all be found in the *maquis* and trees along the N619 that leads from PRADES towards MOLITG and SOURNIA.

Site ii.

The **PRATS-DE-MOLLO – LA PRESTE** high mountain reserve is located in the extreme south-east of the Pyrenean chain, about 60 kms south-west of Perpignan. It is also the most southerly reserve in France, right on the Spanish frontier. Its northern limit extends to the high peaks in the Canigou Massif and adjoining its north-western slope is the Reserve of Py-Mantet, a mainly forest reserve on the northern slopes. The site is included because it is the best place to see mountain species if you are on the Mediterranean coast, as it is possible to drive up to over 2000 m, though the minor roads may be blocked by snow as late as mid-May.

ACCESS: Take the D-115 westwards from Le Boulou, which is 21 km south of Perpignan, to Prats-de-Mollo, a further 39 km. In Prats the very minor N-115A leads to La Preste. Turn sharp right just before the spa buildings. It is signed to the reserve but easy to miss as there are several other names. Follow this road, which becomes dirt higher up, as far as you can or wish and then walk. There is another track leading further west reached by continuing past the spa buildings and car park on left to where road forks. Take the narrow left-hand road (signed). Another road leading north branches off 2.5 km before La Preste at St. Sauveur; it leads up to the Col de la Regine (1762 m). Footpaths continue into the reserve from these roads and even without walking too far, many mountain species may be seen well.

The woodlands hold **Black Woodpecker, Crested Tit** and **Bonelli's Warbler** and even a few **Hawfinch,** often around the villages lower down; **Citril Finch** can be found where the trees start to thin out. **Rock Bunting, Rock Thrush** and **Alpine Accentor** can all be found around the highest slopes and **Ptarmigan** on the very highest screes. It is also an excellent site for both species of **Chough** and birds of prey: **Golden, Short-toed** and **Bonelli's Eagle** can all be seen here and occasionally **Lammergeier. Eagle Owl** also breed on some of the lower cliffs.

Other fauna and flora: There are Isard on the highest slopes; Wild Boar, Wild Cat and Pine Martin in the woods, all difficult to see as they are largely nocturnal. The rare blind scorpion *Belisarius xambeui* is found on some limestone outcrops in the reserve, which is excellent for mountain butterflies (species as listed for other Pyrenean sites); the rare and beautiful Spanish Moon Moth *(Graellsia isabellae)* is found in the pinewoods. The higher areas are excellent for alpine flowers.

<u>Accommodation:</u> On the south side there are hotels and campsites in both Prat de Mollo and la Preste, which are spa towns. On the northern side Vernet-les-Bains (also a spa) and Prades have hotels in all categories.

Lammergeier

THE MEDITERRANEAN COAST

Area 1	**Perpignan and the Roussillon**	
	Site i.	The Albères hills
	Site ii.	Canet, the mouth of the River Tech and Villeneuve lake
Area 2	**Leucate (M)**	
Area 3	**Narbonne and Gruissan**	
	Site i.	Gruissan lagoons
	Site ii.	The limestone hills of la Clape
	Site iii.	Pissevache lagoon
	Site iv.	Minerve
Area 4	**Corbières**	
	Site i.	Tautavel
	Site ii.	Lezignan-Corbières airfield
Area 5	**The Camargue**	
	Itinerary i.	The Petite Camargue
	Itinerary ii.	Saintes-Maries-de-la-Mer
	Itinerary iii.	Albaron/Domaine de Méjanes/La Capilière/ Tour de Valat etc
Area 6	**The Crau and Vigueirat marshes east of the Rhône**	
	Site i.	The Peau de Meau Reserve
	Site ii.	The Étang des Aulnes
	Site iii.	Entressen and nearby steppe areas.
	Site iv.	The northern Crau
	Site v.	The Vigueirat Marshes
Area 7	**Provence – Les Alpilles and Petit Luberon**	
	Site i.	Les Baux
	Site ii.	La Caume
	Site iii.	The Gorge de Regalon
	Site iv.	Font d'Orme
	Site v.	The Combe de Lourmarin
	Site vi.	The Durance Bird Observatory
Area 8	**Provence – Mont Ventoux area**	
	Site i.	Mont Ventoux
	Site ii.	The Dentelles de Montmirail
Area 9	**Hyères, the Iles d'Hyères and the Maures Hills**	
	Site i.	Pesquiers saltpans and lagoon
	Site ii.	Iles d'Hyères
	Site iii.	The Massif des Maures
Area 10	**The Eastern Mediterranean – Var River mouth**	

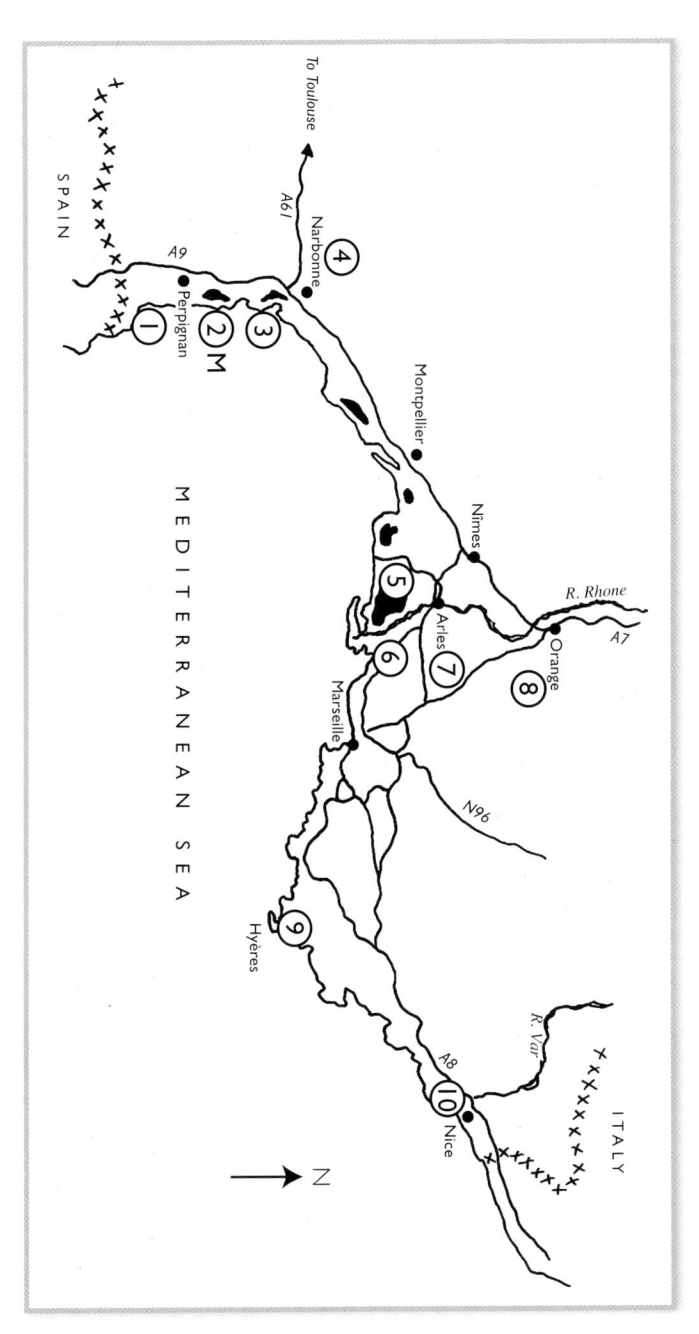

Mediterranean Coast birding areas

WHEN TO VISIT: Shallow, brackish lagoons, separated from the sea only by sand bars, stretch along the Mediterranean coast from Perpignan to Marseilles. All hold many of the same water birds, summer and winter but numbers and species depend on several factors: the degree of salinity or pollution, size of reedbeds, use for leisure pursuits, including hunting in winter and water sports in summer. Most will have Flamingos, Coots, Cormorants, Egrets and duck year round, with larger numbers in winter; Black-winged Stilts, Purple and Squacco Herons and *Acrocephalus* warblers in summer and many species of waders during migration. If time allows, most lagoons are worth checking out, especially in spring and autumn, though some are more accessible than others. If short on time, choose one of the sites described below. Inland from the sandy beaches and lagoons, stony *garrigue*-covered hills are the habitat of typically Mediterranean species such as *Sylvia* warblers, Black-eared Wheatear, Hoopoe and Bee-eater. Inland areas are best visited in spring. East of Marseilles, high cliffs drop sheer to the sea and here water birds are found only at estuaries.

As the above shows, there can be good birding along this coast in any month of the year but perhaps the best periods are April and the first two weeks of May, when both passage and summer breeding birds are present. The end of August and September can also produce large numbers of species. In winter there are overwintering waders and wildfowl as well as the chance of some rarities turning up.

Area 1 **PERPIGNAN AND THE ROUSSILLON**

Perpignan is the largest town situated in the north-west of this area, which runs from Canet-en-Roussillon, east of Perpignan, to the Spanish frontier in the south and is bounded on the west by the motorway A9 and on the east by the sea. The whole area covers some 100 square km and can be divided into two main sites, covering very different habitats: wooded hills and lakes and a river mouth.

Site i.
The **ALBÈRES** are the most easterly tip of the Pyrenean chain, becoming tamer and less dramatic just before they plunge into the Mediterranean as rocky headlands near Banyuls. They are still wild enough to be only partly accessible by road and to contain a good selection of wildlife in the evergreen oakwoods and *garrigue* covered hillsides. Both Cork Oak *Quercus suber* and Holm Oak *Quercus ilex* grow here, giving way to Sweet Chestnut *Castanea sativa* and Downy Oak *Quercus pubescens* higher up, with pines and Beech *Fagus sylvaticus* at the summits. Nearer the sea there are dry, rocky slopes.

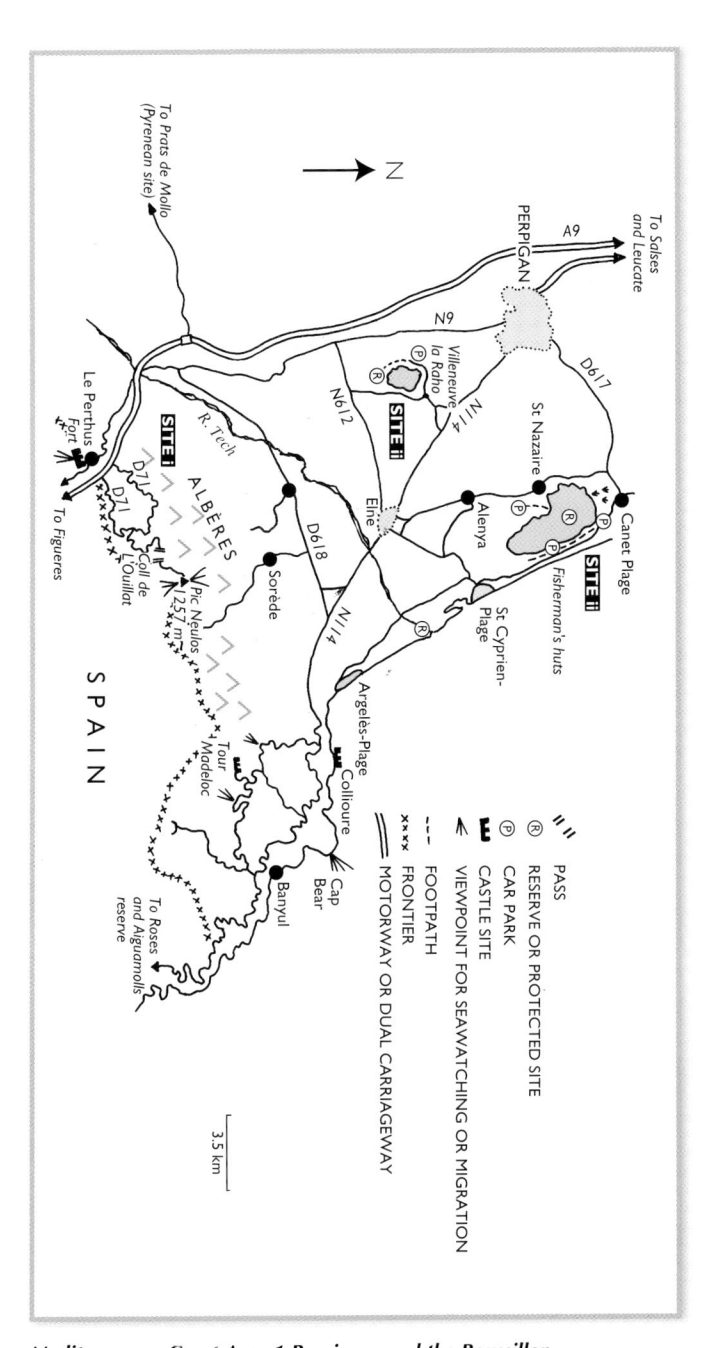

Mediterranean Coast Area 1 Perpignan and the Roussillon

This varied habitat accounts for the large number of bird species – a mixture of mountain and Mediterranean – to be found here: **Short-toed Eagle, Eagle Owl, Golden Oriole, Pallid** and **Alpine Swifts, Crag Martin, Short-toed and Thekla Lark, Rock and Blue Rock Thrush** (probably the best place in the south to see the two species close together), **Black-eared Wheatear, Serin, Woodchat Shrike, Short-toed Treecreeper** and **Crossbill**. The only **Black Wheatear** to be found in France used to breed near the Tour Madeloc, but their numbers have declined steeply and they may be gone by the time this guide is in print. The **Green Woodpeckers** here are of the Spanish race *sharpei*.

ACCESS: Road access to the Albères is at three points only. The western, most densely wooded side can be best explored from the frontier town of Le PERTHUS. Turn east off the N.9 on the northern outskirts of the town onto the minor D71, signed to the COL DE L'ULLAT (or Ouillat – names are in French and Catalan here). A circular route leads to the pass and down again but the GR10 footpath also follows this road, branching off after 4.8 km to climb more directly through the woods. It is possible to walk the whole way or park and walk for an hour or so. Birds likely to be seen are typical woodland species. Just below Pic Neulos (1257 m) on the Col de l'Ouillat, **Crossbills, Crested Tit, Bonelli's Warbler** and **Firecrest** can be found in the pines. In summer, check around the radio mast and rocky summit for **Rock Thrushes**. From November when the higher mountains are snows covered, small flocks of **Alpine Accentor** can be seen around the mast. The Col is also a good place from which to watch migration both in spring and late summer.

On the west side of the main road in Le Perthus, the Fort de Belleguarde dominates the town from the hill above. It is signed from the middle of the town. **Rock Bunting, Crag Martin** and **Serin** are three of the species to be found around the castle and it too is a good migration observation spot. **Honey Buzzards** pass low overhead in mid-May. **Crag Martins** breed under the motorway bridge at le Perthus!

The eastern, coastal slopes of the Albères can be reached from the coast road N114. At the COLLIOURE junction, exit 14, the minor D86 twists steeply up to the Tour Madeloc. This road is not for nervous drivers or those suffering from vertigo! It is advisable to walk as much as possible, certainly the last stretch up to the tower. On these windswept slopes, covered with heather *garrigue* and rocky outcrops, **Rock Bunting, Sardinian, Dartford** and **Sub-alpine** warblers are present (the latter in summer only) and **Rufous Bush Robin** has turned up occasionally during the spring migration. **Orphean Warbler** breeds in the Evergreen Oaks. The stony outcrops on the summits are where **Blue Rock Thrush and Rock Thrush** and, possibly, **Black Wheatear** can be found. (The nearest Spanish site for this species is around the lighthouse at Cap de Creus, near Roses, about two hours' drive down the coast road). **Black Redstart** and **Black-eared Wheatear** are relatively common. This is one of the few places in France where you may spot **Red-rumped Swallow** and **Thekla Lark**. The latter can be found from sea level up to 750 m on the hillsides above Banyuls. Unlike Crested Lark it often perches on boulders or bushes and can even be seen around the vineyards. **Ortolan Bunting** and **Tawny Pipit** are two other species that like these dry, sunny slopes; the latter species often to be found in recently burnt areas. Search among the Swifts for **Pallid Swift**; there are small colonies breeding along this rocky coast; the nearest in BANYULS. There may be the odd **Alpine Swift** among them.

Garganey

Site ii.
CANET, the larger lagoon, lies parallel with the coast, separated from the sea only by a narrow strip of sand and the coast road. From CANET PLAGE (due east of Perpignan), take the D617 south towards SAINT CYPRIEN PLAGE. A brackish lagoon, with variable salinity, some 5 km from north to south, most of Canet is surrounded by reed beds. It is best visited in April and May, though autumn can also bring large numbers of passage waders and duck (including **Red-breasted Merganser**) in winter. Winter is also the time to look for **Bearded** and **Penduline Tits** in the reeds as well as **Moustached Warbler** (the only warbler to overwinter, it is easier to locate at this season). In spring breeding **Great Reed and Savi's Warblers** arrive, together with **Purple Heron** and **Little Bittern. Greater Flamingo** can be seen most of the year, in numbers varying from several dozen to several hundred. In winter **Black-necked Grebe** outnumber **Great Crested**. Spring migrants include regular **Red-throated Pipit, Garganey, Black-winged Stilt** and good numbers of waders. It is the only site in France for **Purple Gallinule**, which have been breeding here in small numbers since 1996. They almost certainly came from Canet's "twin" reserve of Aiguamolls d'Emporda in Spain, an hour's drive south towards Roses, where they were reintroduced and have been breeding successfully for over 10 years. (If you really want this species and fail to find them at Canet, then they can always be seen on Cortalet scrape by the Information Centre at Aiguamolls).

Audouin's Gull

It is possible to park at various places along this road and walk towards the lagoon or across the beach to sea-watch (best in autumn or winter when **Balearic Shearwater, Razorbill and Gannet** can often be seen and gulls may include **Mediterranean** or a lingering **Audouin's**). About halfway along there is parking besides some "traditional" fishermen's reed huts. From here a 4 km "Discovery Trail" leads north along the shore, starting by two hides. Both give good scope views across the lagoon. The one by the river mouth is also good for herons and breeding **Little Tern** and **Kentish Plover**. Several pairs of **Little Bittern** nest and are usually seen flying over the reeds. The trail leads through Mediterranean seashore vegetation, helpfully labelled. **Fantail** and **Cetti's** warblers are common in the scrub, as are large flocks of finches in winter. Where there are openings in the reeds, check carefully along the water's edge for **Purple Gallinule** and **Water Rail**. On the outskirts of Canet, look among the starlings for **Spotless Starling**; one of the few places in France where it is now breeding.

On the west side of the lake there is another protected site, the **DELTA DU RÉART**. To reach it, continue driving south towards St. CYPRIEN. On the outskirts, turn right signed ALENYA. Pass a golf course on your right. In Alenya village, go straight across the first roundabout and at the second turn right in the direction of CANET/St. NAVAIRE. At the crossroads by the traffic lights, turn right again. At the Elf petrol station on the outskirts of St. Navaire village, turn right and follow the tarred track that curves right for half a kilometre. Park by a barred gateway with a "Delta du Réart" sign. A longish walk along the footpath beside the canalised River Réart leads through open grassland with scattered trees, reed beds and saltmarsh. **Marsh Harrier** is more numerous in winter. Look for **Roller** and **Lesser Grey Shrike** in spring. This area is best during migration periods. **Red-throated Pipit** is regular on passage in April.

Between St. Cyprien-Plage and Argelès-plage to the south, the coast road D81 crosses the River Tech as it flows into the sea. The Conservatoire du Littoral protects most of the land around the river mouth from the road down to the beaches; the reserve is known as **MAS LARRIEU**. The reedbeds, marsh and riverine woodland shelter many bird species, especially on migration, when **Lesser Grey Shrike, Great Spotted Cuckoo, Collared Pratincole** and **Red-rumped Swallow** all turn up quite regularly. Many of the species mentioned above can also be found in the reserve. **Penduline Tit** breed in the poplars and **Melodious Warber** in the thickets.

ACCESS: South of the river tracks lead to two parking places with information boards, There is a visitors centre near the entrance. Access is limited but there are reasonable views from the roads.

If there are few ducks on Canet, try further inland at **VILLENEUVE**. This is a smaller, artificial lake much used for sailing and water-skiing. Surprisingly, in view of its popularity, it is very difficult to find.

ACCESS: Easiest access is from the N114. Halfway between PERPIGNAN and ELNE the village of VILLENEUVE (VILLANOVA) DE LA RAHO and "le lac" are clearly signed. If coming from Elne (4 km to the south), turn right off the dual carriageway to go left over the road-bridge. The D39 leads to the village 2 km to the west. Do not turn into the centre of the village but continue past it towards the lake (signed). Go past the large car-park on the lake edge (it is for the recreational part of the lake). 1km further on turn left, following the lake south. Continue on this narrow road, past the Rives du Lac campsite for a further kilometre to a parking/picnic spot by the lakeside in a small grove of pine trees. (Recognise it by a sign forbidding wind surfing ("planche à voile").

Only the south-west, wooded corner of the lake is a reserve. It can be viewed by walking along the lakeside track to where it crosses the lake on an embankment. Villeneuve is best visited in winter, when the south end holds large number of duck, mainly **Common Pochard** with a few **Red-crested Pochard** among them, **Great** and **Black-necked Grebes** and the occasional **Black-throated Diver**. In spring and autumn there are usually plenty of waders and migrating raptors include **Honey Buzzard**.

Other fauna and flora: This is a wonderful area for botanists, with sub-alpine, woodland and Mediterranean plants in a relatively small area. Orchids are well represented; especially spectacular are the Tongue Orchids (*Serapias lingua*) in April. Butterflies go with flowers, and this area's varied habitats means a long list. A few Hermann's Tortoise can still be found in the hills. There is a marine reserve along the coast between Banyuls and Cerbère with a visitors centre opposite Banyuls port.

Accommodation: This is a popular tourist area and there are large campsites all along the coast as well as plenty of hotels (all categories) in Perpignan and the seaside towns. Collioure makes an attractive base and is quiet out of season.

Area 2 **CAPE LEUCATE AND THE CHÂTEAU DE SALSES – a migration site**

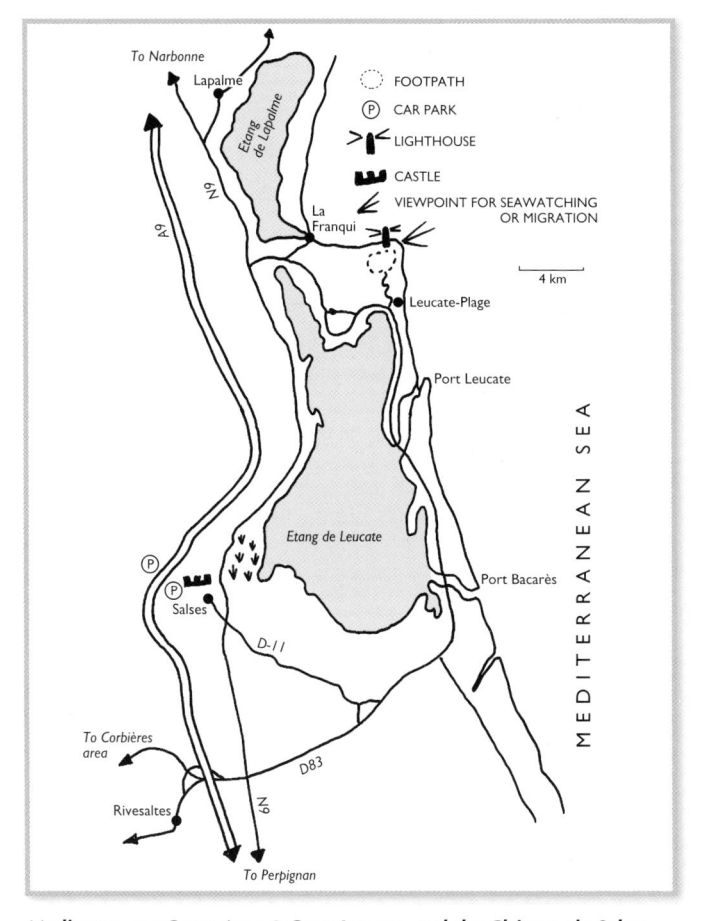

Mediterranean Coast Area 2 Cape Leucate and the Château de Salses

The site by the lighthouse on the cliffs at **LEUCATE** has long been recognised as a very important spring migration spot, but numbers (and observation) depend entirely on the *tramontane*, a cold, very strong north-westerly wind that blows frequently in spring. No raptors will cross the coast here while it is blowing, though any that have arrived just before it starts up may be kept grounded. Once it changes direction or calms down, then raptors may start passing in large numbers. March to the end of May is the migration period and the beginning to middle of April the best time for raptors, especially **Honey Buzzard**. Up to 20,000 raptors, mainly **Honey Buzzard** but also **Black Kite, Marsh Harrier** and **Sparrowhawk**, as well as hundreds of thousands of passerines can cross the coast here at this period and this has caused conflict between conservationists and hunters. As at any migration point, numbers of birds depend on wind and weather conditions; you may stand all day and see nothing, the birds may be so high they are only specks or, on a perfect day, thousands of birds may pass low overhead in flock after flock for hours on end. **Honey Buzzard** and **Black Kite** are the most numerous migrant raptors but **Short-toed Eagle** and **Marsh Harrier** also cross here, as do a few **Ospreys**. Some rarities have been observed here, such **as Lesser Kestrel, Eleanor's Falcon, Pallid Harrier** and **Black-shouldered Kite** while several **Red-footed Falcons** are seen most years. The last named and **Red-throated Pipit** do not usually turn up until the end of April or May. Passerines include thousands of **Chaffinches, Serins, Swallows, Swifts** and **Bee-eaters**. **Red-rumped Swallow** is regularly noted here. The trees and bushes around the lighthouses can be full of warblers after an overnight fall. Even on a bad day, the limestone plateau around the lighthouse can be good for some unusual species: **Spectacled Warbler** can be found in the thin scrub behind the lighthouse, **Blue Rock Thrush** is also often near this area**, Short-toed and Thekla Lark, Black-eared Wheatear, Hoopoe** and **Orphean Warbler** all breed here and **Great Spotted Cuckoo** is usually quite easy to find in spring. The best place to watch migration is a little south of the lighthouse. The clifftop is an excellent sea-watch site and **Black-necked Divers** and **Shearwaters** can often be seen in the bay beyond la FRANQUI beach in winter and early spring.

ACCESS: To reach the lighthouse, leave the N9 or the motorway at the second exit north of Perpignan. Follow the signs for LEUCATE village. Drive through the village and drop down to the coast. At 8.2 km from the motorway exit turn left – signed "Phare" and "Centre de Vacances". A climb of 1.3 km up onto the plateau brings you to the lighthouse.

North and south respectively of the cape lie the lagoons of LAPALME and LEUCATE. Whilst not as good for birds as Canet, they are worth checking while in the area. **Avocet** and **Black-winged Stilt** breed in the saltmarshes and **Moustached Warbler** in the reeds. LAPALME lagoon to the north is the easiest to bird and less disturbed. Return from Leucate village to the N9 junction. Turn north towards Narbonne and after almost 4 km take the first turning right towards Lapalme village. This minor road runs along the salt marshes on the north-west shore of the lagoon. There is a parking spot opposite the minigolf course just before the village. If you continue north it is possible to drive up towards the entrance to the salt works (Salines du Midi) and scan the salt pans. **Audouin's Gull** has been seen here, **Kentish Plover** breed. Numerous **Yellow Wagtails** can be seen in spring and sometimes a few **Red-throated Pipits** are among them. Check the stony cliffs on the side opposite the lagoon for **Thekla Lark** (only a very few) and **Blue Rock**

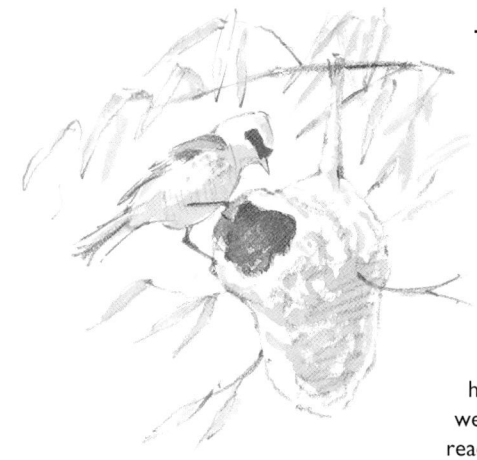

Penduline Tit

Thrush. A road signed to la FRANQUI leads off from the Leucate road and gives access to the southern end of the lagoon. The turning is just where the railway crosses the road. Turn towards the signed Camping Municipal and walk along the lakeside road. This end is best during migration periods.

The 16th century fortified castle of SALSES, an impressive historic monument, is at the south west of Leucate lagoon. It can be reached from the village of Salses on the N9 or from the A9 motorway as a footpath leads from the Salses picnic area ("aire") north of Perpignan. Hole nesters such as **Jackdaw**, **Hoopoe**, **Kestrel** and **Rock Sparrow** breed here (the latter near the main entrance) and the surrounding scrub is good for *Sylvia* warblers. **Great Spotted Cuckoo** can often be found here. The salt marshes with **Black-winged Stilts** and other water birds can be reached from here. A large reed bed called *Grandes Sagnes* can be found north-east of Salses village. It is a good site for **Bearded Tit, Reed Warbler, and Moustached Warbler. Penduline Tit** winters here. The LEUCATE lagoon is not particularly noteworthy for birds but can often hold quite large numbers of **Black-necked Grebe** while the settling pans around PORT-BARCARÈS (which can be seen from the road) have turned up rarities in the past.

Continuing north on the N9 from SALSES, the road runs near the lakeshore for 11 kilometres, where at LES-CABANES-DE-FITOU the D50, a very minor road, runs off west (left) to the villages of FITOU, TREILLES and FEUILLA, a distance of about another 11 km. It is worth driving along here slowly, stopping frequently. **Spotless Starling** have started nesting here in small numbers, **Thekla Lark** can sometimes be spotted on the right between Treilles and Feuilla and **Blue Rock Thrush** is common on the rocky escarpments. Other species that can be found near the rocky cliffs are **Eagle Owl, Alpine Swift, Crag Martin** and **Rock Bunting**. (From TREILLES the D27 leads back to LEUCATE, so enabling a circular tour to be made).

Other fauna and flora: The limestone plateau around the lighthouse has an interesting Mediterranean flora.

<u>Accommodation:</u> There are plenty of campsites, notably at La Franqui, and hotels near Salses as well as several of the cheaper chain hotels near the motorway junction.

Area 3 NARBONNE AND GRUISSAN

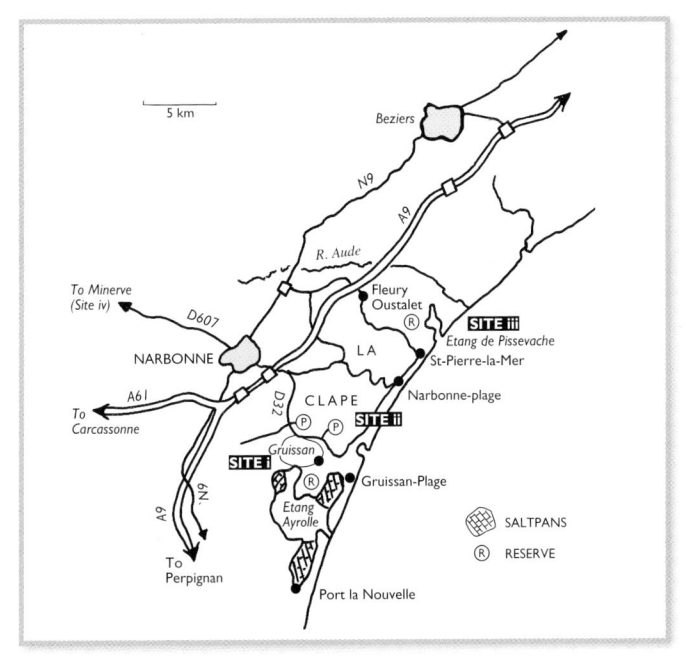

Mediterranean Coast Area 3 Narbonne and Gruissan

East of Narbonne along the coast (from south to north) are three good sites plus another inland:

Site i.
Gruissan lying between two lagoons, the smaller one of the same name and the Etang de l'Ayrolle.

Site ii.
The limestone hills of la Clape

Site iii.
The small lagoon of Pissevache and surrounding *garrigue*

Site iv.
An inland site some 30 km away, good for Mediterranean warblers, shrikes and buntings.

While Leucate is noted for its pre-nuptial migration and is best in spring, in GRUISSAN the post-nuptial migration is more remarkable, starting with Swifts at the end of July and continuing until October. This is not to dismiss the spring; April or early May produce the greatest number of species. During the post-nuptial migration periods, when the prevailing wind is north-west, Bee-eaters, Storks (about 500 White but increasing numbers of Black Storks), some 10,000 raptors and hundreds of thousands of passerines pass over Gruissan before heading out to sea. Gruissan has been called the "little Camargue" but according to a warden it is even better than the Camargue during both migration periods. Certainly there is a similar range of habitats: saltworks, saline lagoons, saltmarsh, reed-beds, pines and garrigue and many of the same species can be found here as in the Camargue: **Flamingos**, many duck species, **Grebes** and **Golden Plover** in winter, waders during migration; **Little Bittern**, **Black-winged Stilt**, **Spoonbill**, **Purple Heron**, **Great Reed** and **Moustached Warblers** breed in the reedbeds in summer, **Little Tern** and **Kentish Plover** in the dunes, **Black-winged Stilt** and **Avocet** in the salt marsh. **Eleanor's Falcon** and **Lesser Spotted Eagle** are seen here annually; **Osprey** stop over during migration.

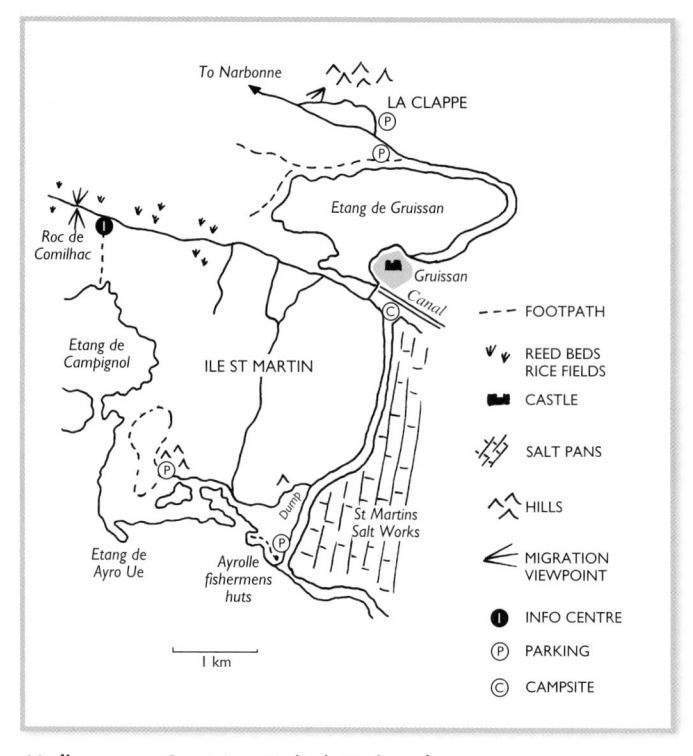

Mediterranean Coast Area 3 site i. Gruissan lagoons

Cory's Shearwater

Site i.
Leave the A8 motorway at exit 37 Narbonne Est/Centre and follow the signs for Gruissan and Narbonne-Plage. Zero the trip metre at the tollbooth. At 11.7 km turn right. Cross the canal at 12 km. Within 300 metres turn right towards Gruissan village and right again towards the Camping Municipal and les Salines. The road follows the edge of the lake with plenty of stopping places. At 13.3 km turn right over the bridge, then immediately left in the direction of Les Salines. You will see the salt works on your left. (Visits are organised in summer to see breeding terns, **Black-winged Stilts** and **Avocets**. Ask at the office). Carry on for another 3 km until the tarmac ends by the canal and some fishermens' huts. This area is good for terns and gulls – mainly **Yellow-legged** and **Black-headed** but check for **Mediterranean** – and waders during migration. There is always **Black Redstart** around the huts. **Kentish Plover** and **Little Tern** breed nearby. Look out for **Audouin's Gull** in spring.

After spending time here, retrace your steps but turn left after 0.8 km towards the rubbish dump. Look for **Blue Rock Thrush** at the little quarry opposite the dump and check the *garrigue* for warblers. Follow this road until the tarmac ends, near another inlet of the lagoon. where there are often **Flamingos**. It may be productive to walk along the dirt tracks around the vineyards and climb the little hills looking for *Sylvia* warblers and **Black-eared Wheatear**. **Great Spotted Cuckoo** can be found here in early spring. Listen for its harsh calls or watch for agitated magpies.

Return past the salt works but at the bridge junction continue straight on following the sign "Migration des Oiseaux". 3.3 km from the junction LPO Aude has an Information Centre in a small house on the left of the road, just below a small hill. Here you can obtain up-to-date information about species and locations. The LPO volunteers manning the centre are very helpful and the small, rocky hill, the Roc de Conilac, is the place to watch migration.

Thousands of **Honey Buzzard, Black Kite, Short-toed Eagle**, harriers and storks and pass overhead during the post-nuptial migration. The very end of August and the first week in September are the best period for maximum numbers. Sea watching at this period can also be good with sightings of **Pomarine** among the **Great Skuas** and **Cory's Shearwaters** in September. A path beside the centre leads to the Campignol lagoon while beyond the centre, as far as the Domaine de Mandirac, there are reedbeds and rice-fields on both sides of the road. Both the mud flats of the lagoon and the fields can be full of waders and herons during migration. **Purple Heron, Bittern** and **Moustached Warbler** can be found in the reeds. While September, April or early May are probably the best months to visit this side of Gruissan, winter can produce flamingos, duck, egrets, **Reed** and **Corn Buntings, Moustached Warbler, Penduline and Bearded Tits.**

Site ii.
LA CLAPE is a noted wine region; a low limestone mountain of some 15,000 hectares rising directly behind the coast, it was an island in Roman times. Besides the vineyards, there are Aleppo pinewoods on the slopes and garrigue (rosemary, juniper, thyme, lavender) higher up, as well as many sheer cliffs. This variety ensures it is also an important birding area where a pair of **Bonelli's Eagle** breed, as well as a couple of pairs of **Eagle Owl** and **Short-toed Eagle**. In addition the highest points are, like the Roc de Conilac, an excellent place to watch migration. **European Nightjar, Short-toed lark, Ortolan Bunting and Spectacled Warbler** are among other breeding species.

ACCESS: Road access is limited and anyway it is probably better to walk. There are a series of well-marked footpaths but it is possible to drive to two high points and start birding from there. From the D32 Narbonne-Gruissan road there is a minor crossroads signed ZAC Bonne Source to the west (away from la Clape) and the narrow road opposite climbs steeply to an Orientation Table on an open shoulder, with cliffs behind. This is a good place from where to watch migrating raptors. In addition, look out for the **Bonelli's Eagles**. They often fly in pairs low along the hillsides and frequently at mid-day. In winter they can be seen hunting over the lagoons. If you wait here until dusk, you may hear **Nightjars** or **Eagle Owls** calling and be lucky enough to see them fly over. **Spectacled Warbler** is found in the lowest, most sparse areas of scrub (often recently burnt areas) and **Orphean Warbler** likes the evergreen oaks. **Ortolan Bunting** prefers the open ground between large boulders, so does **Tawny Pipit**. This is another site for **Great Spotted Cuckoo, Blue Rock Thrush** and **Black-eared Wheatear.**

Nearer Gruissan, another minor road is signed Chapelle des Auzils. There is a parking areas with map just off the road but it is possible to drive to second car park just below the chapel and from there climb up to another good viewpoint or walk a circular, well marked route around the summit. At both car parks make sure nothing of value is left in your car whilst you walk.

Site iii.
The coast road running north from GRUISSAN passes through NARBONNE-PLAGE and turns inland at ST-PIERRE-LA-MER. Before the road swings left and starts climbing through new holiday homes, the lagoon of **PISSEVACHE** can be seen straight ahead. Take the minor road right towards it and you will reach the "Site privée de l'Oustalet" where several sandy walking tracks lead over salt marsh towards the water. The same birds can be found here as around Gruissan but it has also turned up many rarities in the past (Terek's Sandpiper, Pectoral Sandpiper (in autumn), Broad-billed Sandpiper, Marsh Sandpiper). **Fan-tailed Warblers** "zit" over the *salicornica*, where **Crested Larks** can be found. The **Yellow Wagtails** here seem to be *cinereocapilla x iberiae* hybrids but **Citrine** has turned up. **Black** and **White-winged Black Terns** hawk over the water in spring and there is a very good chance of seeing **Audouin's Gull** on the lagoon, as it occurs frequently here. Search the poplars and willows at night for **Scops Owl**.

Fan-tailed Warbler

Returning from the lagoon, and continuing towards FLEURY, the road passes through rocky garrigue-covered hills – a low outcrop of la Clape. Stop below the first cliff on the right. **Blue Rock Thrush** can be found here (as it can on most of the rocky outcrops) and there are Mediterranean warblers in the trees and scrub.

Site iv.
Some 30 km inland, north-west of Narbonne, the old hilltop town of **MINERVE** is worth a visit. Take the D607, then the D907 to la Caunette. The D10 running west from here to Minerve is surrounded by good habitat, so is the D182 leading west from Minerve and the minor road to Azillanet running south from the town. The cliffs on which the town is built have breeding **Raven, Alpine Swift, Crag Martin** and **Rock Sparrow** while in winter **Wallcreeper** can sometimes be found here. The *garrigue* landscape surrounding the town holds the usual Mediterranean warblers: **Orphean, Dartford, Subalpine** and **Sardinian** as well as **Southern Grey, Woodchat** and **Red-backed Shrike, Black-eared Wheatear, Cirl** and **Ortolan Buntings**. Park along any of the minor roads mentioned above and walk a short distance along and off the road.

Other fauna and flora: One of the best botanical areas in France, especially in the limestone hills where flowers are much the same of those found in the *causses* region (see below). More than 20 species of orchids can be found in spring. La Clape Centaury is endemic. The Montpellier snake and Ocellated

Lizard are two reptiles easy to see on la Clape. There is a rich maritime flora around the lagoons; most striking is the large purple *Limoniastrum monopetalum*. Mediterranean butterflies are abundant.

<u>Accommodation:</u> This is a very popular tourist area, well-provided with hotels and campsites in Gruissan –Plage and Port as well as Narbonne-Plage.

Area 4 **CORBIÈRES**

The hills of the Corbières extend for well over 100,000 hectares. It is an important wine area and much of the valley floors and lower slopes are covered with neat vinyards. There are areas of *garrigue* scrub, good for such Mediterranean warblers as **Dartford, Sub-alpine** and **Sardinian**. Slightly higher, on the boulder-strewn hillsides, **Ortolan Bunting** and, if lucky, **Thekla Lark** can be found. Dramatic limestone cliffs and gorges are riddled with caves and ledges where **Eagle Owl, Peregrine Falcon** and a pair of **Bonelli's Eagle** breed.

Site i.

The village of TAUTAVEL used to be a certain site for **Bonelli's Eagle**. Tautavel is better known as prehistoric site where the remains of the oldest human discovered in Europe was found. They are now in the pre-historic museum. French birders, however, know it as the place where conservationists fought to preserve a Bonelli's Eagle nesting site from being destroyed by quarrying. The quarry owners won and the site has been destroyed but the eagles can still sometimes be seen from the village.

ACCESS: To reach TAUTAVEL, leave the A9 motorway or the N9 at RIVESALTES (the first town north of Perpignan) and take the D12, clearly signed TAUTAVEL and VINGRAU. At this latter village, turn onto the D9, heading south in the direction of Tautavel. You will see some cliffs with a radio mast on your left just before you reach the village. Narrow tracks lead up through the vinyards to the foot of the cliffs. You can scan these for the eagle or listen here at dusk in January and February for **Eagle Owl**, which calls and starts breeding very early in the year. A better spot with all-round views to watch raptors is beside the river in the village. Turn right in the village centre towards Estagle, right again and watch from above the footbridge. The quarry can be seen from here. There are always birds to watch along the river even if no raptors fly: **Kingfisher, Black Redstart, White Wagtail, Moorhen, Grey Heron, Cetti's Warbler and Reed Warbler** (in summer).

The road D59 leading out of Tautavel towards Cases-de-Pène climbs up steeply from the river with cliffs on the right towards the quarry entrance. Park wherever there is a lay-by and listen for *Sylvia* warblers: **Dartford** in the lowest scrub and **Sub-alpine** and **Sardinian** in the higher bushes. Check for **Rock Sparrow** around the castle ruins.

Site ii.
The small airfield for light aircraft at **LEZIGNAN-CORBIÈRES** is an important site for **Calandra** and **Short-toed Larks** and **Stone Curlew** with even a few **Little Bustard** remaining.

ACCESS: The airfield lies about 4 km south of the town of Lézignan-Corbières, just to the west of the D611 which here runs between the A61 motorway (from Toulouse to the coast) and the N113. If you leave the motorway at junction 25, 38 km east of Carcassone, the sliproad emerges almost opposite the airfield. Some 100 m after the D611 crosses the motorway a gravel track by a concrete pylon leads past the airfield. It is easy to drive around the small dirt tracks circling the airfield (keep off the signed areas), stopping and searching for birds.

Area 5 THE CAMARGUE

The Camargue is still one of the greatest wetlands in Western Europe; increased tourism, agricultural intensification and ever-expanding rice paddies have not yet destroyed a superb birding area, although those who first visited it a decade or two ago may find it changed for the worst. Besides the impressive number of wintering, passage and breeding birds, rarities constantly turn up. 345 species have been recorded in the Camargue and a few days in spring in the Camaargue, the Crau and the Alpilles hills inland should certainly give you a checklist of 150-plus species.

The Camargue is huge. The Regional Park south of Arles lying between the two arms of the Rhône covers some 850 square kilometres and comprises a variety of habitats: beach, dunes, saltworks, saline, brackish and freshwater lagoons (étangs), marshes, vast reed beds, riverine woodland, vineyards, market gardens and rice paddies surrounding the vast, shallow Etang de Vaccares (6,500 hectares), a National Nature Reserve. There are more marshes and an excellent Reserve on the east bank of the Rhône as well as the Crau, the old delta of the River Durance, now a stony near-desert covering some 110 square kilometres south-east of Arles. The sites east of the Rhône are treated as a separate area (6).

WHEN TO VISIT: The Camargue has something to offer at most seasons. April and May will perhaps give you the largest species list as many of the wintering waders will have returned north but there will still be some stragglers and plenty of passage migrants. Mid-September-October is another productive period, although most breeding birds will have left. All the winter months, from November until March, can be interesting and the weather is often warm, if the Mistral is not blowing. Only the hot summer months, when the tourist season is in full swing, should be avoided at all costs, as should the gypsies' annual pilgrimages to les Saintes-Maries in the second half of May and

October. **NEVER LEAVE ANYTHING IN THE CAR ANYWHERE IN THE AREA.** Remove your radio and even leave the glove-box open to show that it is empty. If your car has bird association stickers, it is even more likely to be broken into. Car thieves are endemic everywhere in the south of France.

It would certainly take a week or more to cover the whole area reasonably thoroughly but three or four days will allow you to visit the most important areas and give you a taste of the region. Each of the following sites are presented in the form of one or more itineraries that can be covered by car in a day or less, although it might be better to spend at least two days on iii). If pushed for time, this is the itinerary to choose.

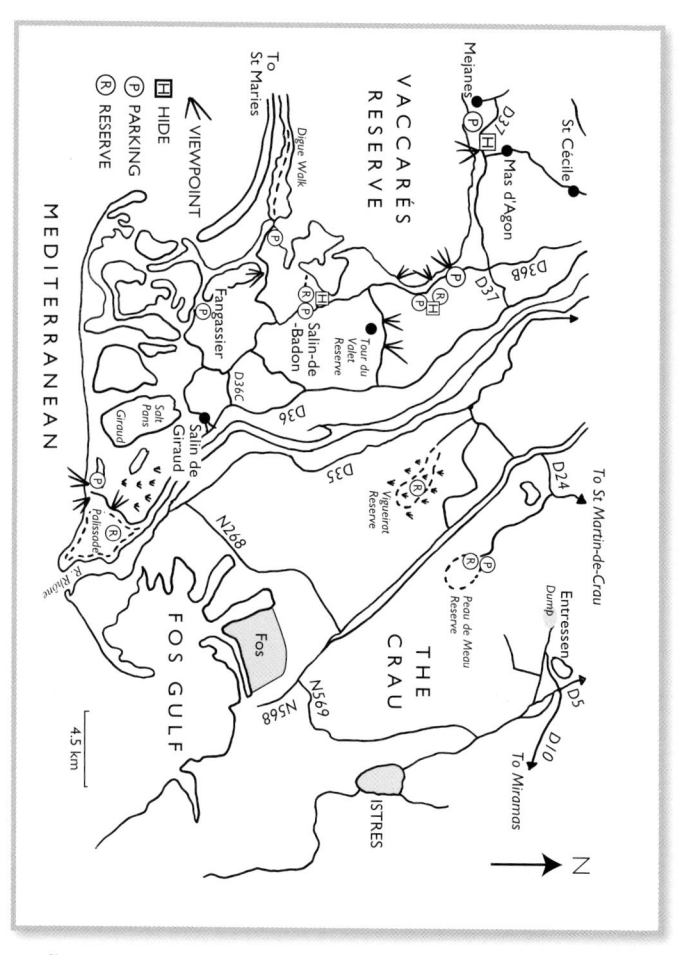

Mediterranean Coast Areas 5 and 6 The Camargue and Crau

Itinerary i.   **The Petite Camargue around Aigues Mortes**
Itinerary ii.   **The east side of the Etang de Vaccares, from les Saintes-Maries to Albaron**
Itinerary iii. **The west side of the National Reserve from Albaron to la Capillière south to the salt pans and mouth of the Rhone.**

Maps and guide books: IGN 303 1:50,000 Parc National Regional de Camargue or IGN 66 1:100,000 Avignon, Montpellier. Sketch maps and leaflets showing reserves and footpaths are available free from Park Information Centres. Also on sale is "Les Oiseaux de Camargue" (J. Boutin. Lynx) which gives the status as well as when and where to look for every bird ever recorded in the area.

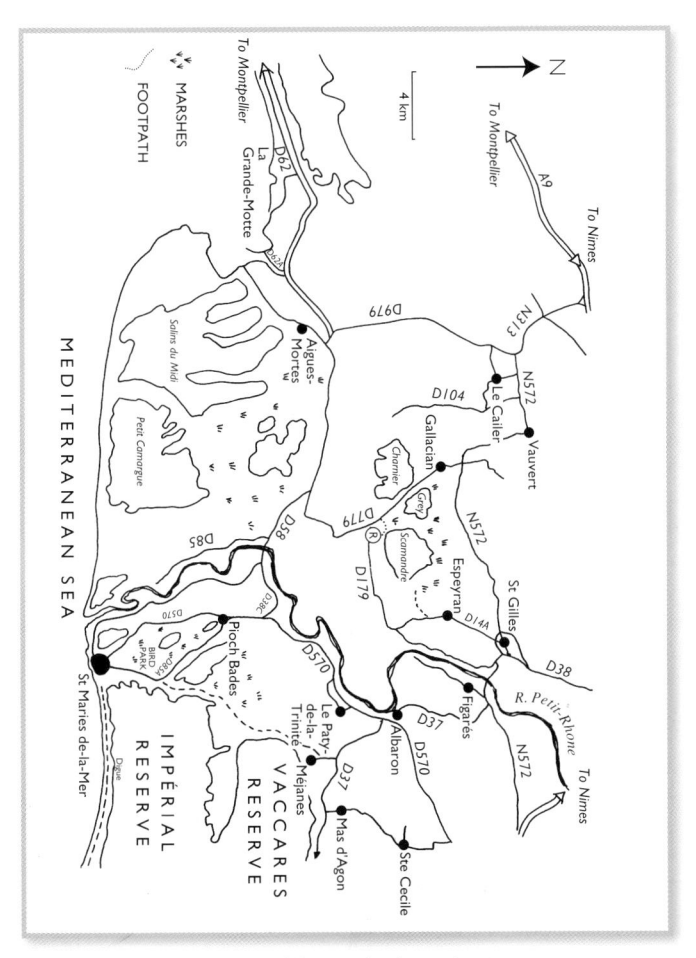

Mediterranean Coast Area 5 itinerary i. The Petite Camargue

Itinerary i.
The "**PETITE CAMARGUE**" is the name given to the area surrounding the western arm of the Rhône, the "Petit Rhône". Access is difficult to much of the marshland south of the medieval walled town of AIGUES MORTES, (which is certainly worth a walk around the walls) but there are frequently **Mediterranean Gulls** (especially in winter) around the little port on the canal. North of the town, the large étangs of CHARNIER and SCAMANDRE are largely hidden by extensive reedbeds (the largest in France). The road D779 running along the canal between them often gives good views of **Great Reed Warbler, Reed** and even **Moustached** (easier in winter) while gaps in the reeds allow views of water birds, including **Red Crested Pochard**. **Purple Herons** frequently fly over the reeds and **Bittern** can be heard booming in spring. There is now a small Reserve, the *Reserve Naturelle Volontaire du Scamandre*, at the junction of the D179 and the D779, from where better views over the lagoon and reeds can be obtained. The Exhibition Centre is open Wednesday to Saturday and there are guided visits throughout the year on Wednesday and Saturday at 10.00 and 14.30. Telephone 04 66 73 52 05 to book in advance.

Part of the marshes to the west of Scamandre can be reached from ESPEYREN and it is possible to walk for some way along a gravel track overlooking marshes both sides.

ACCESS: From St. GILLES take the minor D14a signed to Chateau d'Espeyren both from the centre of the town and from the bypass. At the chateau entrance bear left along its boundary, cross the bridge over the canal and park near the building on the left. Walk down the right-hand track, which bears right alongside a small stream. It runs parallel to the private road signed to the Domaine d'Espeyren -La Briqueterie. This is a good area for marsh terns in spring, **Black** and often **White-winged Black Terns** can be found here as well as waders on passage. **Night Herons** roost in the trees overhanging the stream; look along the stream before you start walking. **Purple Herons** and egrets are plentiful, check them for **Great White Egrets. Glossy Ibis** and even a **Western Reef Heron** have turned up here. **Little Bittern** can sometimes be seen flying over the reeds. There are often **Flamingos** feeding in the stretches of open water. The hedges and brambles lining the stream are good for warblers. (The area is too much hunted over in winter to be any good at this season).

The minor D104 (access between Vauvert and le Cailar) is a good road to drive slowly along, stopping at intervals. There is a **Bee-eater** colony here. The road crosses the Sete canal just south of the Etang de Charnier. The bridge is a good viewpoint. Park at the Mas de Guard and walk a little way west along the lagoon. Among the terns, herons and egrets, you may spot **Bittern** flying. **Great Spotted Cuckoo** has been seen here in April.

Slightly further east is another good spot. Take the N572 south-east from St. GILLES. After 2 km it crosses the Petit Rhone and just under 1 km later a minor road forks back right. Take this and then take the next turn right

Black and Whiskered Terns

towards FIGARÈS. Park and walk along the footpath. **Golden Oriole, Cirl Bunting** and **Woodchat Shrike** have all been seen here and many of the species listed above. The area is excellent for **Black and Whiskered Tern** in April and May.

From Aigues Mortes the D58 through MONTCALM crosses the Petit Rhône. Turn right onto the D38 (avoid the D85 just before the river as you have to take a ferry later and there are often delays) and drive south to SAINTES MARIES-DE-LA-MER, the starting point for the next itinerary. Just before the town, at the mouth of the Petit Rhône, find a track leading down to the water and look out to sea. It can be good for divers and sea duck in winter when the wind is blowing on-shore.

Itinerary ii.
SAINTES MARIES-DE-LA-MER is one starting point for the 12 km walk along the Digue sea wall. Drive east through the town along the beach road and then as far as you can along the rough track to the barrier. There may be a toll in summer. Park the car and walk as far as you wish along the Digue. There are views over the lagoons and out to sea. **Mediterranean and Slender-billed Gulls** may be seen, **Sandwich, Common, Little** and (in spring and summer) **Gull-billed Terns, Avocets and Black-winged Stilt**. There are excellent views of **Flamingos** at any time of the year and ducks in winter and spring usually include **Red-crested Pochard, Common Shelduck and Red-breasted Merganser**. Small flocks of **Black-necked Grebe** (in full breeding plumage March-April) can be seen on passage and often in winter (a few breed). **Spectacled Warbler** can be found in the salicornia bushes and between March and May, there may be spectacular falls of migrant passerines in the tamarisk bushes along the path. It is possible to walk the whole length of the Digue to the east but that means leaving a car

there in advance, otherwise walk only a few kilometres and then return to Les Saintes-Maries.

After walking the Digue, take the D570 north from Saintes-Maries to the PONT DE GAU PARC ORNITHOLOGIQUE. You have to pay. Do not be put off by the fact that the first part of the park contains caged owls, raptors and water birds (most are rescued, injured birds as this has been a Centre de Recuperation since 1974). The food put out for the wildfowl collection also attracts wild birds. Beyond this first section is a stretch of marsh with several kilometres of good footpaths and well placed hides. It is excellent for **Bearded Tit, Marsh Harrier**, ducks and waders in winter and spring. Avoid weekends if possible. There is an information centre next door to the Parc and a convenient restaurant.

At PIOCH BADET, 4 km further north, the D85a loops back towards SAINTES-MARIES. If you have time, it can be rewarding to drive slowly, with frequent stops, around the marshes, especially where the Reserve Imperiaux appears on the left. Otherwise drive up the D570, through PATY DE LA TRINITÉ, to ALBARON, the start of the next itinerary. This route gives a good impression of the "typical" Camargue – vast skies above marshes with white horses and black bulls splashing through them. Try driving it at sunset.

Itinerary iii.

From ALBARON, drive half a kilometre back towards PATY DE LA TRINITÉ on the D570 and then turn left onto the D37 towards MÉJANES. Stop anywhere you can along this road. The marshes both sides are excellent for **Black** and rarer **White-winged Black Terns** in spring. **Bitterns** can be heard (and often seen) on the right, as can **Little Bittern** and **Night Heron**. In winter the shallow water holds large numbers of dabbling ducks and **Bewick's Swans**. After 4 kilometres the road wings to the left. Here a minor road carries straight on towards Domaine de Méjanes. After a few hundred metres a dirt track leads of to the right at the entrance to the bullring and small tourist railway line. Take this track and bird at any likely looking place, continue and park by the bar/ restaurant. This spot gives excellent views over the west side of the Etang de Vaccares and at any season gives good sightings of duck, waders, egrets and heron. It is one place where **Caspian Tern** are often seen and if the regular **Spotted Eagle** is wintering in the Camargue, one can often be seen flying over the étang from here. The bushes around are good for warblers in spring and a few **Pratincoles** nest (in ever decreasing numbers) in the fields behind. Beyond the restaurant a rough track (best to walk it if wet) leads south towards Saintes-Maries. **Gull-billed Tern** and **Moustached Warbler** are two species that breed within the first three kilometres.

Return to the junction with the D37 and turn right. Although somewhat distant, good birds can be seen just after the junction looking north. Park, completely off the road, by the lone tree and scan with a telescope. Stop at the viewing platform a little further on and spend a little more time scanning. Check the reeds for warblers. **Collared Pratincoles** and **Black-winged**

Stilt nest nearby. The minor road to MAS D'AGON and STE. CECILE, some 3.5 km from the junction, can also be good for the two last-named species. If you have time, drive (or walk) as far as STE. CECILE and then return to the D37 as far as VILLENEUVE. At the junction turn right onto the D36b towards LA CAPELIÈRE, where there is an Information Centre and two hides overlooking a small marsh. Both **Penduline** and **Bearded Tits** can often be seen from the hide opposite the Visitors' Centre, especially in winter and early spring. Later in the year, the walk along the footpaths through the reedbeds can be good for many warbler species, including **Moustached** and **Melodious**. The Centre is closed on Sundays and from 12 to 2. Whilst a list of current rarities is not usually on show at the Centre, do ask what birds are about (use the scientific name for ease of communication). The attendants are usually very helpful and will tell you, for example, where and when you are most likely to see **Spotted Eagle** in winter. Access to a newer reserve, the SALIN DE BADON (some 8 km down the road) also has to be booked from here. Visitors are only allowed in this old salt marsh with its footpaths and three hides early morning and late afternoon, so it is worth arriving at la Capelière in the morning and booking an afternoon visit for the Salin de Badon. This will give you time to drive south to the beach and salt pans before returning to the reserve on your way home.

From la Capelière continue south. There are several lay-byes along the D36b with views over the Etang de Vaccares. After about 4 km take the first road to the left towards the Centre d'Ecologie de la Tour du Valat (a research station closed to the public). There is a heron roost in the woods immediately on the right at the corner. The marsh on the left a little further on is good for terns in spring and **Great White Egret** in winter. **Bee-eaters** are also found here during the summer and the verges are good for orchids.

Return to the D36b. You will pass the entrance to the Salin de Badon. The small copse just south of the reserve is where **Spotted Eagle** frequently roosts in winter. 1.5 km from here is a sharp right-hand bend. This is marked as le Paradis on maps; just beyond it the road divides. Keep straight on to the Etang de Fangassier, the breeding site of up to 10,000 pairs of flamingos. During the breeding season, the colony is wardened. There is a viewpoint and information centre at Mon-de Garde digue but you will need a telescope to see the nesting birds well. The track continues and eventually leads to the eastern end of the Digue (follow signs for Phare de Gacholle), where you can park the car and walk along the sea wall. **Kentish Plover, Avocet, Black-winged Stilt** and **Slender-billed Gull** all breed in or near the salt lagoons to the south. Fangassier can also be reached by a track leading from the town further south, the Salin de Giraud. Both these rough, dirt tracks are only driveable in dry conditions. A footpath links the two tracks. **Terns, waders, egrets, Night Heron, Little Bittern, Avocet** are some of the species that can be seen in this area. **Tawny Pipit** can be found in dry areas and **Spectacled Warbler** among the low, scattered bushes of *salicornia*.

In a car you will need to return to le Paradis. Take the right turn that leads eventually to the D36 and SALIN DE GIRAUD. Follow this road which has become the D36d and runs south on the edge of Salin de Giraud . The Rhône will be on your left and you will soon see the saltworks on your right. The road continues for some distance, then swings to the right and leads eventually to the sea. The saltpans and marshes on the right are very good for waders, gulls and terns at any season. There are several lay-byes from where you can scan the salt-pans. During migration there may be a fall of passerines in the scrub. Here, as elsewhere in the Camargue, any large areas of *salicornia* bushes hold **Spectacled Warbler** from mid-March to the end of September. Where the road swings right, the *Conservatoire du Littoral* has a reserve, la Palissade, on the opposite side of the road to the salt-pans. There are nature trails, hides and guided visits through the salt-marsh but it is possible to scan a good part of the reserve from the road-side.

Retrace you steps towards the Salin de Badon if you have booked an evening visit. It will be quicker to drive north straight up the D36 to the Tour de Valat turning, rather than taking the twisting D36b.

Other fauna and flora: The most conspicuous mammal in the Camargue is the introduced large rodent, the Coypu. European Pond Terrapin, Marsh and Stripeless Tree Frogs *Hyla meridionalis* are widespread, including some blue individuals of the last-named species. It is naturally a good area for dragonflies. The Giant Orchid *Barlia robertiana* flowers near Tour de Valat in February. Later in the year Marsh Orchids *Dactylorhiza palustris, D. incarnata* and Summer Lady's Tresses *Spiranthes aestivalis* grow in many areas, often in association with Pale Butterwort *Pinguicula lusitanica.*

<u>Accommodation:</u> There are several hotels (all classes) in Aigues Mortes and Saintes-Maries. There are also some expensive tourist hotels on the roads leading from the latter, as well as two campsites. The *Logis* Flamant Rose in Albaron is central and more reasonably priced. On the east the Salin de Giraud has two small hotels. Many visitors prefer to stay outside the Camargue for easier access to the Crau and les Alpilles. If you wish to avoid large towns like Arles, or smaller ones like Tarascon-Beaucaire, the isolated Hotel Robinson, a *Logis de France*, on the D986 Route de Remoulds, just north-west of Beaucaire has good food, safe overnight parking and birding nearby. Many hotels in the Camargue will be closed in winter. Pre-booking is vital over Easter or any holiday season

Area 6 THE CRAU, MARSHES AND LAGOONS EAST OF THE RIVER RHÔNE

The **CRAU**, that unique, stony semi-desert is, like much of the Camargue, being tamed, irrigated and cultivated. Every year shelter belts are planted and more and more areas turned over to fruit farming. The military also use large stretches of the best habitat; many species of birds appreciate the protection this gives them but it also makes it difficult for bird watchers. In the south around Istres much of the land is owned by the Marseilles Port Authorities and will soon disappear beneath warehouses and factories. The *coussous*, the local name for the stone-covered plain that used to cover 60,000 hectares stretching from the Camargue to les Alpilles to the Etang de Berre in the south, has shrunk to under 11,500 hectares.

This windswept and arid land, scorched by the sun in summer and grazed by thousands of sheep, is unique in Western Europe. It most resembles some of the stony deserts of North Africa. The rounded stones that cover its surface were carried there from the Alps over millions of years by the River Durance before it changed course after the ice ages. During the Second World War the Nazis had stones collected into piles to stop allied aircraft landing. These little pyramids still dot the Crau, providing breeding sites for **Hoopoes, Lesser Kestrels** and lizards; they are one of the most characteristic features of the *coussous*.

The Crau is the only place in France to find **Pintailed Sandgrouse** and **Lesser Kestrel** as well as the best area for **Little Bustard** (there are some 300 males, 30% of the French population and in winter flocks of some 1000 birds congregate in the northern part of the Crau), **Stone Curlew, Calandra** (under 100 pairs now found mainly in the military zones near Istres) and **Short-toed Larks, Roller** (50 pairs) and **Lesser Grey Shrike**. There are also **Southern Grey** and **Woodchat Shrikes**. **Tawny Pipit, Black-eared Wheatear, Corn Bunting, Little Owl** and **Hoopoe** are other typical birds of the Crau. There are enormous numbers of Magpies on the Crau but you will be lucky to see the increasingly rare **Great Spotted Cuckoo**, which parasitises them. It arrives as early as February and leaves by June and its favourite haunt is around the few remaining old Almond plantations. **Red-legged Partridge** is a fairly common Crau bird, though much hunted in winter. A few pairs of **Montagu's Harriers** breed in the Crau. **Red-footed Falcon** pass through the Camargue regularly during their pre-nuptial migration in late April or early May and the Crau is the best place to look for them, often perched on wires along the roadsides. Immature **Bonelli's Eagles** may be seen hunting over the Crau at any time of the year.

WHEN TO VISIT: March to June or possibly September are the best months. There is little to see in winter when both the bustards and the sandgrouse flock mainly in the northern part of the Crau and the wind is bitter and very strong. It is extremely hot in July and August and the area is very crowded with tourists. **Stone Curlew** only arrives in March and leaves in October or November; **Lesser Kestrel** and **Lesser Grey Shrike** arrive later and leave even earlier. In September both **Little Bustard** and **Stone Curlew** may have started to flock but many breeding birds will have left.

Site i.

As so much of the remaining *coussous* is privately owned and out of bounds, there are only a few scattered areas where it is possible to walk and look for steppe birds. One good area is the **PEAU DE MEAU RESERVE**, for which a permit is needed. This can be obtained from the Crau Ecomuseum (open daily 9-12 and 16-18 except on Bank Holidays Tel: 04 90 47 02 01 Fax: 04 90 47 05 28) in SAINT MARTIN-DE-CRAU. Permits, valid for two days, currently cost 15 F per person and the money goes towards the maintenance of the reserve. Three-hour guided visits for groups cost 25 F each (or 35 F for less than 10 people) and must be booked in advance. The Museum, a converted sheepbarn, is situated in the Boulevard de Provence, right beside the N113 from Arles, at the Arles end of St. MARTIN. The turning to it is at the traffic lights by the Church, which is opposite the "Hotel de la Crau". There is a large parking space in front of the museum, which also contains interesting exhibitions on the wildlife, geology and social history of the Crau as well as an excellent small bookshop with local maps. The staff will be happy to answer any queries.

ACCESS: Your permit will give you instructions and a sketchmap to reach the reserve, which lies east of the main N568 running from the N113 to the coast at Fos. To reach the Peau de Meau from St. MARTIN-DE-CRAU take the D24 which crosses the N113 dual-carriage way and runs towards the N568. 4 km from the village, turn left at the sign *Etang des Aulnes*. Drive past the étang (see site ii) and continue for just over 3 km bearing left and then right at the entrance to the Chateau de Vergières. In another 2 km there is a parking area on the left and a marked footpath leading off along the canal. The trees on the far side of the canal are good for **Roller, Golden Oriole, Turtle Dove, Red** and **Black Kites**. Check the brambles for **warblers**, especially **Sardinian** and **Melodious**. **Lesser Grey Shrike** may be perched here or nearer the sheepbarn. 28 species of dragonfly have been counted along the canal. The marked trail turns over the steppe area and leads to a sheepbarn where a hide has been constructed on the first floor. You may well have seen **Hoopoe, Little Bustard** and **Lesser Grey Shrike** on your walk here, otherwise the height of the hide helps considerably when scanning the surrounding area for them, **Pin-tailed Sandgrouse** and **Stone Curlew.** **Lesser Kestrel** nest nearby and may be seen from the hide as they hunt over the steppe. An **Egyptian Vulture** is also often seen in flight on its way to or from Entressen rubbish dump (see site iii) and **Short-toed Eagles** hunt over the Crau. A **Little Owl** sometimes perches on the well near the barn. Most

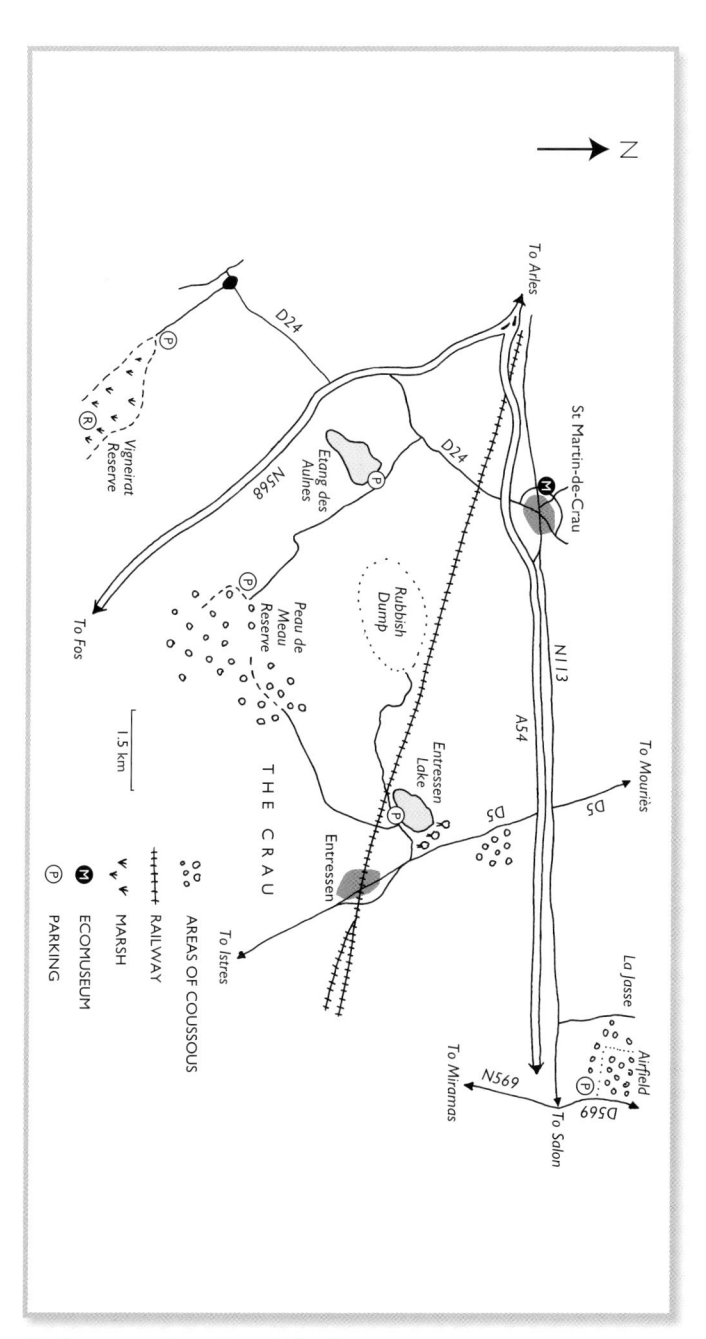

Mediterranean Coast Area 6 The Crau

larks will be **Skylarks** or **Short-toed** (the latter often perch on the piles of stones) but watch out for a large, heavy lark with noticeable white trailing edges to its wings – the rare **Calandra Lark**. **Tawny Pipit** is relatively common.

As the Peau de Meau permits last for two days, it is worth returning the next day at a different time if you failed to find some species on your first visit. Very early in the morning or towards dusk are good times for **Little Bustard** and **Stone Curlew**, which may call or display at these times while the sandgrouse fly to drink morning and evening.

Golden Oriole

Site ii.
Driving (or cycling) back from Peau de Meau, the **AULNES** Lake is worth a visit. There is a car park with maps showing walks some 300 m from the junction of the Peau de Meau road with the D24. The advantage of this lake is that it is possible to walk to the far side – where the birds always are! Swimming and water sports are prohibited, so the wildlife is relatively undisturbed. In winter there are very large numbers of **Great Crested Grebe** on this lake and most of the duck species you would find in the Camargue, including **Red-crested Pochard**. In fact, most species found in the Camargue could turn up here. The reedbeds on the far side hold breeding **Reed** and **Great Reed Warblers**. The woods and scrubby areas near the carpark area can be productive for passerines, **Golden Oriole** and **Turtle Dove**. There are large roosts of **Jackdaws** and **Little Egrets** here in winter. In spring **Stone Curlew** can be found in the grassland around the lake. Coypu are here as everywhere in the Camargue.

Site iii.
The **ETANG D'ENTRESSEN** is known as the "wet Crau". Its reedbeds and surrounding riparian woodland can be interesting. There are some areas of *coussous* on the suggested itinerary which takes in the famous rubbish dump! ACCESS: Take the N113 from St. MARTIN-DE-CRAU eastwards towards SALON (do not get onto the A54 motorway just outside St. Martin). 9 km from the centre of St. MARTIN turn right (south) onto the D 5 towards ISTRES. On the first stretch of open *coussous* on the left, after blue gas buildings and some cultivated land, look for **Calandra Lark** flying. It is possible to park by a small building some 2.5 km from the turning. This used to be a good area for **Little Bustard** and **Stone Curlew** but to find them it is necessary to walk over it and this is now discouraged. However, one can scan from the edge and hope the birds will fly. In winter they are often

disturbed by hunters. At the roundabout in 4.2 km turn right for ENTRESSEN Lake (signed). Park at the lakeside in just over a kilometre. It may be worth stopping before this to look for **Black Kite** and **Roller** in the woods. About halfway between the roundabout and the lake, a footpath on the right leads to the *Tour d'Entressen* and then continues left towards the lake. *Acrocephalus* warblers breed in the reeds. At night **Scops Owl** may be heard near the lake but there is not usually much to see on the water besides **Great Crested Grebe, Coot** and **Moorhen**. In winter especially, huge numbers of seagulls rest on the lake, waiting for the next load of rubbish to arrive at the dump. **Black-headed** and **Yellow-legged Gulls** are the most numerous but there are usually a few **Lesser Black-backed**, **Common** and **Mediterranean Gulls**. The long, low hill on the opposite side of the lake is Marseilles' rubbish dump and trainloads of waste arrive constantly. Besides the thousands of gulls in the air, there are always kites (predominantly Red in winter and Black in summer), corvids and buzzards around the dump. In summer too, one or two **Egyptian Vultures** can usually be seen there. If you want a closer look for these species, follow the lane that runs along the lakeside, turn left under the low railway bridge and then immediately right. Follow the trail of plastic bags covering the trees and bushes! Some 3 km from the lake is an entrance to the dump where you can park and observe, provided you can stand the smell! (The dump or *Déchetterie* is also signed from ENTRESSEN village.)

Return the three kilometres to the start of the lake if you want to explore another area of stony steppe.

Take the turning opposite the first building on the lakeside. The lane is signed *Chemin de Mas Pointu*. Zero here. Keep straight on, or left, at the fork, past the *Petit Mas*. At 2.5 km there is a small wood with a stream on the left. It is worth stopping and walking a short way into it. **Nightingale, Green Woodpecker** and **Black Redstart** can be found here and both **Roller** and **Great Spotted Cuckoo** have been seen on the next stretch of the route. At 4.6 km the tarmac ends and the Crau proper begins. **Crested, Sky** and **Short-toed Larks** are abundant. At 4.8 km there is a place to park and walk over some of the *coussous*. This stretch of Crau leads up to the N568 and the Peau de Meau Reserve. **Montagu's Harriers** sometimes fly over this stretch of the Crau and both **Little Bustard** and **Stone Curlew** can be found here; indeed, all the species listed under the Peau de Meau Reserve. The track, though rough, continues to the N568, where it is possible to turn right in the direction of Arles. It is best to stay in the car and use it as a hide, since some of this land is private and walking over it discouraged.

There is a further *coussous* area just beyond ENTRESSEN village. To explore it, it is necessary to take the D5 which now bypasses the village. South of the village, just where the old main road meets the by-pass, there is an open stony plain on the right (west) side of the road; further south is a restricted military area. It is possible to park just at the edge of the village by an electricity transformer and walk around the first stretch, down to the military area. **Skylark** and **Short-toed Lark** are everywhere; **Southern Grey, Lesser**

Grey and **Woodchat Shrikes** can be found near the wood at the back and **Hoopoe** and **Little Owl** are often near the old sheepbarns. Check all kestrels carefully, in case they are **Lesser Kestrel**. **Little Bustard, Pin-tailed Sandgrouse** and **Stone Curlew** are most likely to be seen flying or calling very early in the morning or late evening, possibly from the military area. Sandgrouse often flock here in winter. **Black Kite** is common here and **Great Spotted Cuckoo** has been seen.

Site iv.
The Crau north of the N113 between St. MARTIN-DE-CRAU and SALON is now nearly all irrigated and cultivated. However there are one or two remaining areas of *coussous* that may be worth searching for flocks of **Little Bustard** and sandgrouse, especially in winter. One of these is the small airfield to the west of the D569, south of EYGUIÈRES village. It is possible to pull off the road and park in the entrance to the Karting area just south of the airfield, from where you can scan the airfield and the grassland to the south. There are also some useful fields a little further north between the airfield and EYGUIÈRES. Another good remnant of Crau in the same area is around LE JASSE. Take the farm track signed to Le Jasse that runs north off the N113 roughly halfway between the D5 and D569 turnings. The area is private but it is possible to park just before the gate and scan some of the plain.

Site v.
The thousand hectares of **VIGUEIRAT MARSHES** are a mosaic of typical Camargue habitats (reedbeds, lagoons, saltmarsh) included here as they lie on the east bank of the River Rhône, right next to the Crau. The Reserve is owned by the *Conservatoire du Littoral*, the largest area of land that this organisation owns in the Camargue and is managed by the Tour de Valat research station. Do not just turn up at the reserve hoping to walk around. The only way to see the marshes is to pay for a guided visit and it is necessary to book this in advance. This is one of the few places in the Camargue where one can walk for any distance through a variety of habitats, with hides and observation towers to get close to the birds, so it is well worth it. For individuals a 4 or 6 hour guided walk (maximum 25 people) costs 55 F per adult. Groups (minimum number 10) pay 45 for a walk of similar length. Guided visits are available all year round. Telephone the reserve at 04 90 98 77 43 or fax 04 90 98 72 54. Individuals may book at the Arles Tourist Office: 04 90 18 41 20.

276 species of birds have been recorded on the reserve and those likely to be seen in spring include **Bittern, Night Heron, Great White Egret, Purple Heron, White Stork, Flamingo, Greylag**, seven duck species, many **waders, Black Kite, Osprey** (on passage), **Black-winged Stilt, Black Tern, Bearded Tit, Fan-tailed Warbler (Zitting Cisticola), Black Redstart** and **Crested Lark**. In winter there will be up to twenty-five thousand duck, **Flamingo, Lapwing, Golden Plover, Greylag, Egrets** and **Grey Heron**.

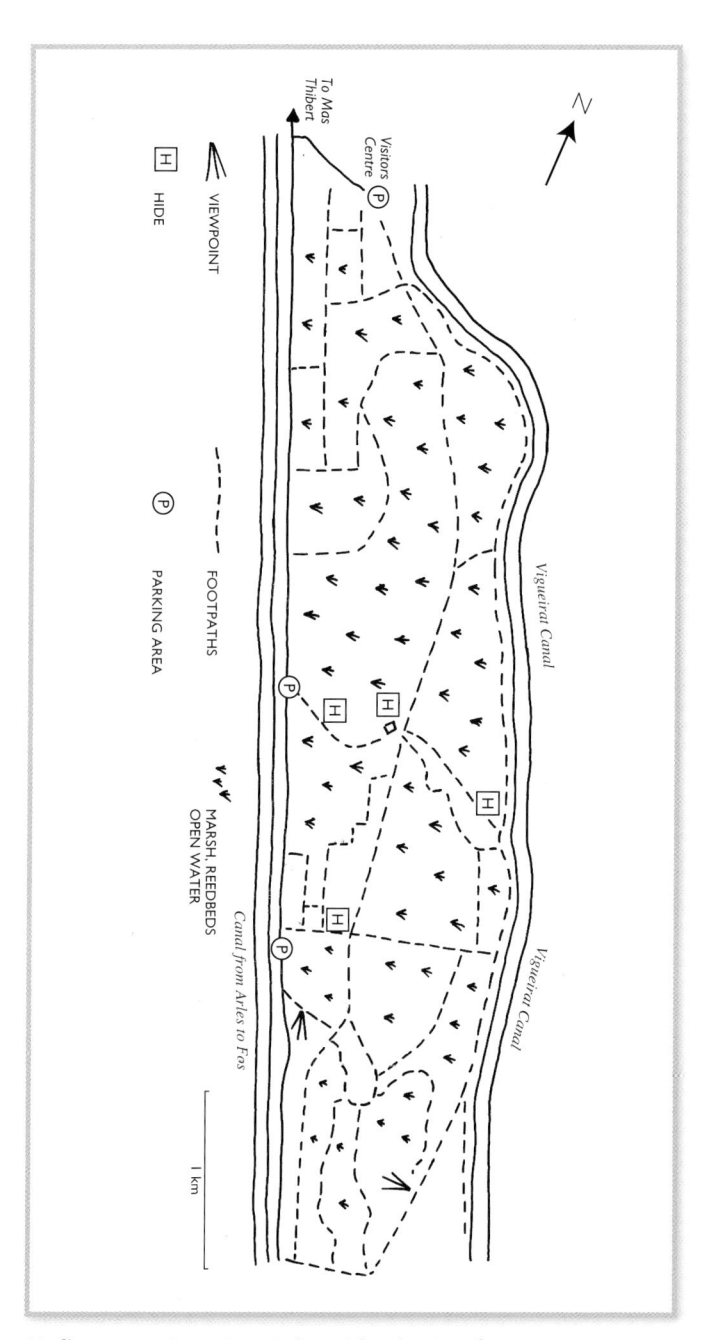

Mediterranean Coast Area 6 site v. Vigueirat Marshes

ACCESS: The Vigueirat Marshes lie 3.6 km south-east of the village of MAS THIBERT on the east bank of the Rhone. Turn south off the N568 1.5 km after the St. Martin turning. In the centre of MAS THIBERT the reserve is clearly signed from the D24 down *Avenue Alain Guigue*. It is signed again on the outskirts of the village after the new housing development. Follow the signs to the Visitors' Centre – *Accueil*, where there is parking in front of the buildings. Please shut any gates behind you, there are both Camargue black bulls and white horses in the fields here. The minor roads, including D83d which turns north off the D24 north of MAS Thibert and runs parallel to the N568, as well as the roads and tracks branching off it are worth exploring for **Roller**. They are frequently seen on posts and wires here.

Other fauna and flora: The Crau is a paradise for insects and invertebrates! There are many semi-desert species amongst the ants and beetles. A Tarantula *Lycosa narbonnensis* can be found under the stones, as well as the (now rare) Yellow Scorpion *Buthus occitanus*. The large, flightless cricket *Prionotropis rhodanica* is endemic; there are three species of Praying Mantis, butterflies are numerous and there are even dragonflies along the irrigation canals. Ocellated Lizards make their homes in the piles of stones. The Crau has a unique low-growing flora with Thyme, *Galectites* thistles and *Eringiums*, *Euphorbia cyparissias* and *E. segueniana*. *Asphodelus fistulosus* covers the southern *coussous* with white in April but Lavender is the predominant *coussous* plant in the northeast. *Scilla autumnalis* flowers in the autumn.

<u>Accommodation:</u> There area two small hotels, one a *Logis*, and a campsite in St. Martin-de-Crau. The nearby villages of Maussane and Mouriès also have hotels. The Crau Ecomuseum in St. Martin can supply a list of local gîtes and chambres d'hôtes and help with the hire of bicycles. This is a good, flat area to cycle around.

Area 7 LES ALPILLES and PETIT LUBERON

The limestone hills of the Alpilles, visible from the Camargue and the Crau, offer wonderful views, an interesting flora and some excellent birding almost anywhere along their length. The limestone plateau of the Luberon lies north and east, on the opposite bank of the River Durance, which forms the southern boundary of the Luberon Regional Park.

In the **ALPILLES**, two sites in particular are the most visited by birders.

<u>Site i.</u>
Site i is the old hilltop town of **LES BAUX**, 20 km northeast of Arles. Although a tourist trap, it is a good place to find **Blue Rock Thrush, Black Redstart** (all year round) and **Alpine Swift** (in summer). Park and walk

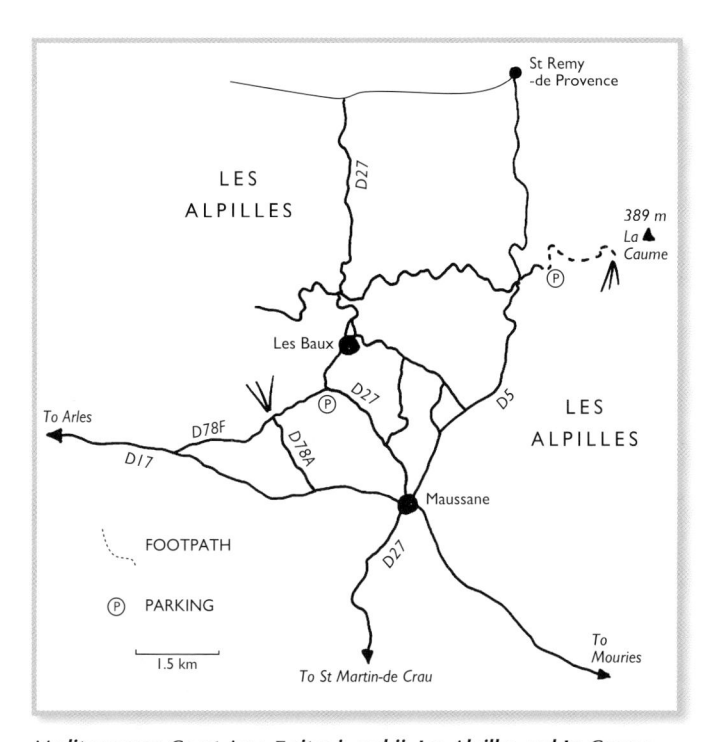

Mediterranean Coast Area 7 sites i. and ii. Les Alpilles and La Caume

around below the cliffs on which the town is built, searching for the above species. In winter, **Wallcreeper** can be found on these cliffs and **Sardinian** and **Dartford Warblers** can be found in the scrub. In spring and summer there is also **Sub-alpine Warbler.** In winter, it is worth walking up through the town and paying to enter the ruins at the top. At this season **Wallcreeper** can often be seen on the buildings and **Alpine Accentor** is regularly in the squares. If you are there at dusk, **Eagle Owl** can sometimes be seen hunting beyond the town.

However just outside Les Baux is a better site for this species. Take the minor D78f south-west from the town for about 3 km. On your right, just before the junction with the D78a to Maussane, is a three-star hotel, the Mas de l'Oulivié. Immediately past it, on the right, is a narrow road. After a couple of hundred metres, there is chain across the road where the tarmac ends. Wait here until dusk, scanning the cliffs ahead. Look particularly at all caves and ledges, since the owls often sit outside just before flying. While you are waiting, listen to the **Nightingales** and look out for **Alpine Swift** and **Peregrine.** In winter, **Wallcreeper** may be found on the cliffs here.

Site ii.
LA CAUME is a radio relay station northeast of les Baux, east of the D5

between ST-REMY and MAUSSANE. The dirt track to the summit (4 km south of St. Remy) is usually closed to cars, but it is an interesting walk of about 3 km, with **Crested Tit** in the pines and **Dartford** and **Sub-alpine Warblers** in the garrigue scrub. The best place to see **Bonelli's** and **Short-toed Eagles**, **Egyptian Vulture**, **Alpine Swift**, **Crag Martin** and **Blue Rock Thrush** is from the top, beside the radio mast, when you can often look down on them. There is an LPO information centre open between April and August. In winter and early spring it is also possible to see **Wallcreeper** and **Alpine Accentor** at the top and very occasionally **Snow Finch**. Listen for **Eagle Owl** calling at dusk, they are quite numerous in the Alpilles. It is worth listening at any suitable low cliff. Two more roads to try are the D24 between MOURIES and EYGALIERES and the D25 that leads east from the D24.

The **LUBERON** plateau is divided by the River Aigue Brun and the D943 into Petit Luberon on the west and Grand Luberon on the east. Other roads are very few and most of the Luberon can only be explored on foot. The Petit Luberon is slightly more accessible and is a possible place to see **Bonelli's Eagle**.

Site iii.
The **GORGE DE REGALON** is an extremely narrow gorge leading up to the top of the plateau of the Petit Luberon. It will probably take about two hours to climb up the stony track and in places it is necessary to scramble over boulders, but you should see a good number of bird species: **Sparrowhawk**, **Alpine Swift**, **Blue Rock Thrush**, **Red-billed Chough**, **Dartford** and **Sardinian Warblers** and hopefully both **Short-toed** and **Bonelli's Eagle** and **Egyptian Vulture** overhead. **Eagle Owl** may be heard at dusk.

ACCESS: Take the D973 from CAVAILLON through CHEVAL-BLANC. 9 km from this village the Gorge is clearly signed on the left (north). There is a large car-park. The path towards the gorge leads through pine and Holm oak woods and olive groves, all good habitats. Views of the cliffs above are best near the opening of the gorge and it is worth scanning the top before starting to walk up. Here you are also likely to see **Blue Rock Thrush** and Mediterranean warblers in the scrub. Different views of the cliffs open up as you climb. It is best to start early in the morning before the crowds arrive. The path can become dangerous during wet weather, so do not attempt it if a thunderstorm is brewing. At the top it is possible to join up with the GR footpath which runs along the plateau for a longer walk.

Site iv.
FONT D'ORME is another site further west that also gives views of the cliffs; the walk is slightly easier but longer.

ACCESS: Continue east along the D973 from the Gorge de Régalon for 2 km. On the right (south) is the D32 turning. Just after it there are two minor roads leading off left (north). Ignore the first, which is a dead-end to Champeau, but

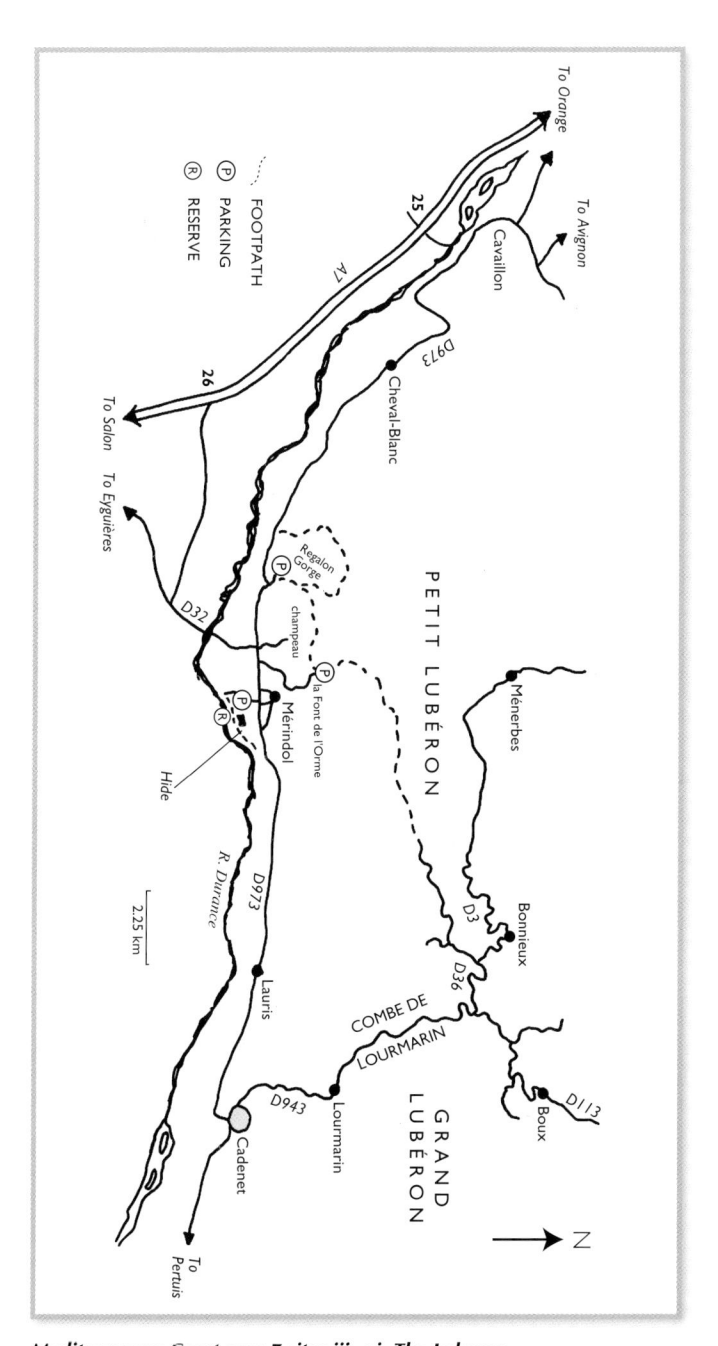

Mediterranean Coast area 7 sites iii.–vi. The Luberon

take the second which is about 350 metres beyond the D32 junction. It is signed *Route de la Font d'Orme* but it is difficult to see this sign until after you have turned. (If you are coming from the east it is 1.5 km after the roundabout at MÉRINDOL village). The track winds upwards for 3.5 km, after about a kilometre there are some good views of the cliffs of the Luberon plateau, and ends at a large car-park by the Font d'Orme arboretum. Signed footpaths lead from here. Take the 1 km one towards the Combe del'Yeuse. The GR 97 also runs along here and it is possible to walk back towards Régalon or east to the heart of the Luberon.

Site v.

The **COMBE DE LOURMARIN** divides the two parts of the Luberon. Anyone unable to walk far might like to take the D943 which runs north through it from LOURMARIN. In 6 km branch left towards BONNIEUX. A minor road runs west into the Petit Luberon 1.5 km before the village, as does the D3 from the centre. Stopping anywhere along these roads will give you a chance to see many Luberon species. Alternatively fork right from the D943 at the Bonnieux junction and right again after 2 km for BUOUX.

Site vi.

THE DURANCE BIRD OBSERVATORY is a hide overlooking a dammed stretch of the Durance River south of MÉRINDOL village. The turning to the Observatory is signed from the roundabout on the D973 just 1.5 km east of the Font d'Orme turning. Follow the signs in the opposite direction from the village, cross a railway line at 0.9 km and turn left. There is a small car-park for the Observatory at 1.4 km. The path that leads to the hide continues along the embankment of the river and it is possible to walk left for some way. It overlooks reeds in one direction and damp woodland on the other. The hide has probably been mainly erected for beavers, which have one of their last strongholds in the River Durance but could also be very good for birds during migration periods, when **Purple Heron, Little Bittern, Marsh Harrier, Black Kite, Night Heron**, and many terns and warblers are likely to be seen, including **Great Reed Warbler**. In winter there are the common duck species (**Mallard, Pochard, Tufted**) as well as **Coot, Cormorant, Black-necked, Little** and **Great Crested Grebes**.

Other fauna and flora: Both the Alpilles and Luberon have a rich Mediterranean *maquis* and *garrigue* vegetation, at its best in spring when blue *Aphyllanthes monspeliensis* and pink Rock Soapwort *Saponaria ocymoides* flower along the rocky verges. The Lady Orchid *Orchis purpurea* is common; *Ophrys bertolonii* grows among lavender and cistus scrub. Look for the saprophytic Violet Birds-nest Orchid *Limodorum abortivum* in clearings in the pinewoods in May. The whole area is good for butterflies: over 150 typically Mediterranean species being found here including Southern White Admiral and Provençal Fritillary. Both Ocellated and Green Lizards are quite common. The Beavers in the River Durance are a relict population of the almost extinct European Beaver. They are difficult to see, being mainly nocturnal, but you might see one swimming a dusk if you are very lucky. They live in riverbank burrows with the entrances under water.

Accommodation: There are several (expensive) hotels near les Baux and Arles is not far away. Many people choose to stay nearer the Camargue or at St. Martin-de-Crau and make a day visit to the Alpilles. Lourmarin, Lauris and Apt all have small hotels and are convenient for the Luberon.

Area 8 PROVENCE – MONT VENTOUX AND THE DENTELLES DE MONTMIRAIL

Site i.
MONT VENTOUX, a famous hill-climb on the Tour de France cycle race, rises to just over 1900 m, and is included as a site because it enables anyone birding the Camargue to observe mountain species that would otherwise entail a long drive towards the Alps or Pyrenees. **Subalpine Warbler, Crested Tit, Citril Finch, Crossbill, Bonelli's Warbler, Rock Bunting** can be found on the lower, scrubby or wooded slopes and **Rock Thrush** and **Alpine Accentor** may be around the observatory at the top. In winter **Snow Finch** can usually be found on Mont Ventoux.

ACCESS: Mont Ventoux is reached by taking the D942 from AVIGNON to CARPENTRAS. Then the D938 north towards MALAUCÈNE. The winding D974 makes a circuit around the mountain, starting in the west at MALAUCÈNE before climbing up to the observatory at the top, then dropping down to CHATEAU-REYNARD on its east slope, where it meets the D164 from SAULT, before turning back west to BÉDOIN and the D938 3 km south of MALAUCÈNE. (Alternatively, take the D974 from CARPENTRAS to BÉDOIN where you fork east, still keeping on the D974 which runs to le CHATEAU-REYNARD and then up to the observatory at the peak to make the circuit in the opposite direction). Note that in winter and early spring the road may be closed beyond Chateau-Reynard and the Mt. Serein junction.

If starting from MALAUCÈNE, check the low cliff on the left just beyond the town for **Blue Rock Thrush**. Stop at the Bar Liotard by the Mt. Serein junction. **Crossbill** and **Citril Finch** are often around here and in winter **Snow Finch** is possible. If the road is open, drive on to the top and spend some time walking around the observatory, checking the scree for **Alpine Accentor** and raptor watching before starting down the east side.

Stop at CHATEAU-REYNARD and bird around the buildings and open woodland here as it is the best place to find many of the above mentioned species. **Black Redstart** is usually around the buildings and **Rock Bunting** on the rocks beside the path leading up into the meadows above where **Northern Wheatear** and **Water Pipit** abound. In winter there are nearly always small flocks of **Snow Finch,** sometimes in the carpark! Woodland species, including **Citril Finch,** can be found around the edge of the trees on the opposite side of the road. Walk into the woods a little way or stop in the conifer woods slightly lower down. **Black Woodpecker** and **Bonelli's Warbler** occur here. Other species you can expect to see if making the circuit around Mont Ventoux are **Raven, Crag Martin, Buzzard, Sparrowhawk** and **Black Kite** as well as **Southern Grey, Red-backed** and **Woodchat Shrikes** as well as a chance of **Lesser Grey.** Birding is good all along the D974 circuit. Stop where it is possible to park safely, walk along the road or off into the wood or scrub where you can.

Red-backed Shrike

The spectacular **GORGES DE LA NESQUE**, on the D942 southwest of SAULT, is good for **Alpine Swift**, **Egyptian Vulture** and **Short-toed Eagle**, among other raptors. These could include **Bonelli's Eagle**. From CHATEAU-REYNARD take the D164 to SAULT, if you wish to drive along the gorge.

Flora: Alpine plants can be found in the scree at the summit of Mt. Ventoux: *Vitaliana primuliflora,* Purple Saxifrage *Saxifraga oppositifolia, Draba aizoides, Androsace villosa, Globularia repens* and *Papaver rhaeticum* all flower at the beginning of June. As you descend the plants become an interesting mixture of Mediterranean and Alpine.

Site ii.

The **DENTELLES DE MONTMIRAIL**, jagged limestone ridges rising above wooded slopes, lie at the western foot of Mt. Ventoux. In spite of increasing disturbance by climbers, it is still a good site, offering a contrast to Mt. Ventoux, as the birdlife is typically Mediterranean. **Sardinian, Subalpine** and **Dartford Warblers** can be found in the maquis, **Orphean Warbler** in the taller trees and orchards, while **Bonelli's Warbler** occurs in the pinewoods. **Crag Martin** and **Alpine Swift** may be seen flying around the cliffs (where **Wallcreeper** can sometimes be found in winter) as well as **Raven** and **Short-toed Eagle. Blue Rock Thrush, Southern Grey** and **Woodchat Shrikes** are relatively common. **Eagle Owl** breeds in the area and **Scop's Owl** can be heard near the villages of Malaucène, Lafare and Suzette in summer.

ACCESS: A road runs from GIGONDAS, over the Col du Cayron (396 m) down to LAFARE on the D90, which in turn runs north to SUZETTE and on to MALAUCÈNE. From the pass marked footpaths lead to the foot of the cliffs above. If starting from the west, take the first left fork after GIGONDAS

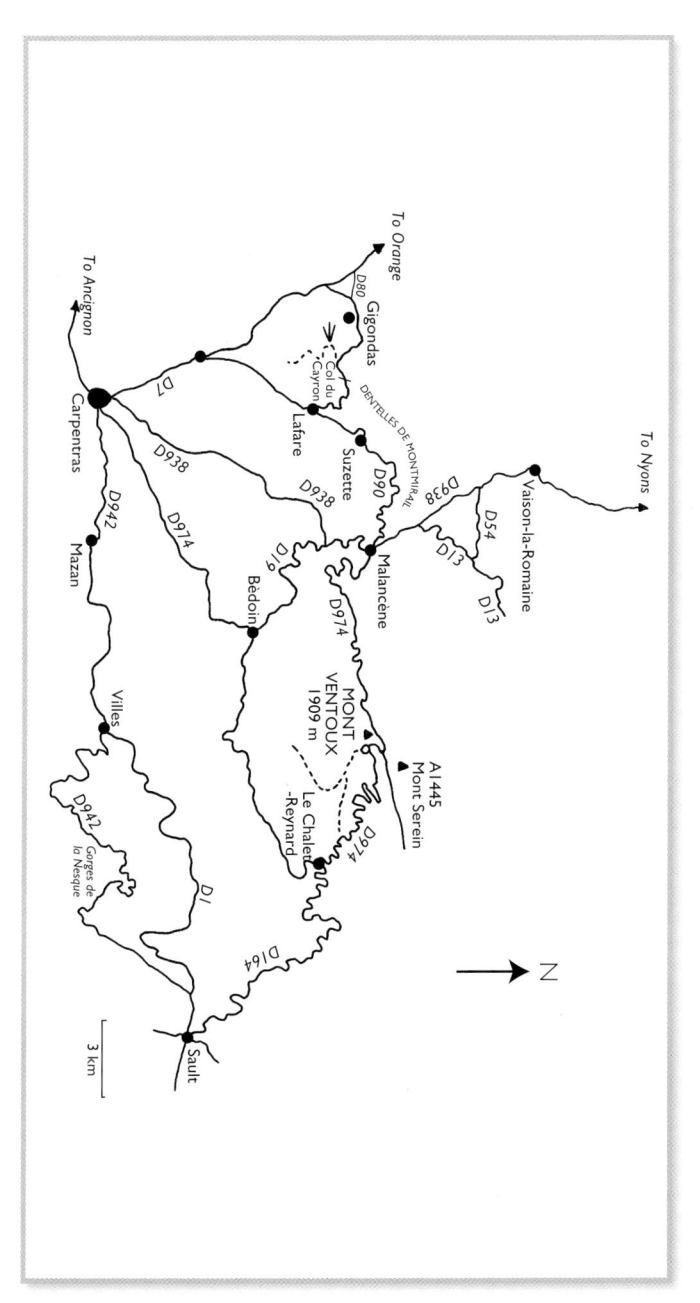

Mediterranean Coast Area 8 sites i. and ii Mont Ventoux and the Dentelles de Montmirail

village, signed to *Les Dentelles*. 1.5 km from this fork there is an open space. Take the left-hand (30 k speed limit) road, the *Chemin d'access aux Dentelles*. The Col du Cayron car-park is 700m up this dirt track, which could be difficult in bad weather. From the car-park follow the path marked with blue dots towards the cliffs and/or walk along the right hand path which leads through some areas of pines. Returning to the car again, take the left-hand track down from the pass towards LAFARE. It soon become hard surfaced. 2 km from LAFARE village there is a good view over some lower cliffs. Listen for **Eagle Owl** from here at dusk. (If starting from Lafare, the road out of the village is also signed to *Les Dentelles*).

Area 9 **HYÈRES, THE ILES D'HYÈRES and THE MAURES HILLS**

This area is the start of the most developed and touristy stretch of the French Mediterranean coast. It is surprising that any bird life remains but, though not as good as some sites further west, Hyères has much to offer a visiting birder, outside the peak summer season.

South of the town of Hyères two sandbars link the ancient island of GIENS to the mainland and enclose marshland, the Pesquiers lagoon and saltpans (disused since 1995). Recently parts of the marsh and lagoon have been made a reserve. **Flamingos** are the star birds, with numbers peaking in September. Giens is also an important wintering site for this species. Ringing has shown than 10% of the Camargue flamingos feed and rest here, especially when it is freezing in the Camargue. **Kentish Plover** are common in the pans in winter, together with a few **Little Stint** as well as gulls, egrets and cormorants. Occasionally **Short-eared Owl** and **Montagu's Harrier** winter here. In April and May, the pans are full of passage waders and terns, especially **Black Tern**. **Kentish Plover**, **Avocets**, **Black-winged Stilt**, **Little Tern**, **Bee-eater and Shelduck** nest here, as well as a few **Little Bittern, Purple Heron** and **Moustached Warbler**.

A footpath runs along the west sandbar, following the old saltworks road, giving good views over the water. The D97 runs down the east side through LA CAPTE where there is an Ecomuseum in the old salt works and the LPO organise guided visits in spring and summer. It is closed in winter but phone the LPO for more information. There are one or two places where you can pull off the D97 to look over the pans and water but mostly the view is blocked by trees.

Site i **PESQUIERS SALTPANS AND LAGOON**

ACCESS: Turn off the A570 (dual-carriageway) in Hyères following the signs towards Presqu'île Giens, Les Iles, le Port through the town. At the roundabout 4.2 km from the junction, turn right with a stretch of marsh on your right (it is worth pulling onto the verge and checking it). Turn right again at the second roundabout onto the D42 in the direction of Toulon *(par le côte)* and Carqueiranne (there is now marsh on both sides of the road). At the roundabout in 6.2 km turn left towards Giens. Signed to *Tombolo ouest de la Presqu'île de Giens*. "Tombolo" is the name for a sandbar. There is a large carpark on the left beside a bar. The footpath starts here, running between the marsh and the sea. You can walk for almost 5 km, looking over the pans and later the lagoon. As you are looking east, it is best in the afternoon when the sun is behind you. (Ignore signs to *Mont des Oiseaux* – this is a smart housing estate!)

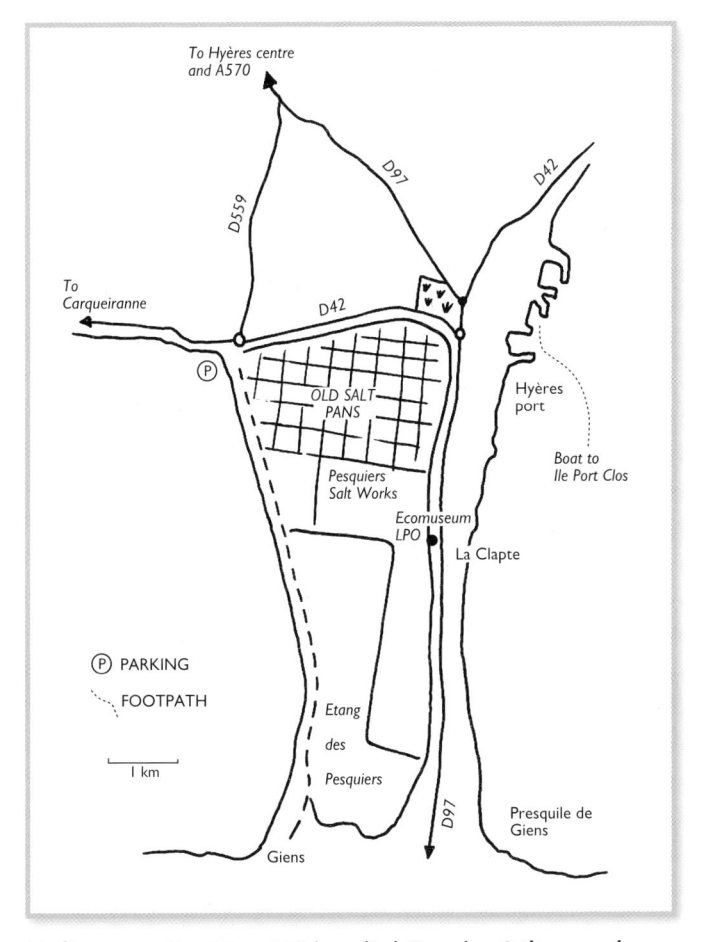

Mediterranean Coast Area 9 Hyères site i. Pesquiers Satltpans and Lagoon

Site ii.
The Iles d'Hyères are three small, rocky, tree covered islands just off the coast. **ILE DE PORT-CROS**, the smallest (685 hectares) is a National Park. About 200 each of **Cory's** and **Yelkouan Shearwaters** breed here and **Eleanora's Falcon** is regularly seen on passage in May and August-September. They may even have attempted to breed. There are colonies of both **Alpine** and **Pallid Swift**, good numbers of **Nightjars**, **Scops Owl** and **Blue Rock Thrush** and, of course, plenty of **Yellow-legged Gulls**.

The Park's information centre is a La Pointe Nord on the quay of the only village on the island, which can be reached by boat from the Port d'Hyères (and in summer from other ports along the coast). It runs daily in summer and Monday, Wednesday, Friday, Saturday in winter (also Sunday in March and October) leaving Port d'Hyères at 9.30 (8.15 July and August), arriving at Port-Cros an hour later and leaving the island at 15.45 in winter and 17.00 the rest of the year, so giving reasonable time to explore the island. The current fare is 115 F. Most visitors go there for the snorkelling, and there is also a glass-bottomed boat, the Aquascope, which runs regularly from Port-Cros and could enable you to see bird as well as marine life.

Other fauna and flora: There are many Orchid species in spring and salt-tolerant plants such as Yellow Horned Poppy, Thrift and Tree Spurge *Euphorbia dendroides*. The rare Leaf-toed Gecko *Phyllodactylus europeaus* and the Tyrrhenian Painted Frog *Discoglossus sardus* are found on Port-Cros (and nowhere else in France except Corsica). The Western Spadefoot Toad *Pelobates cultripes*, which buries in the sand, occurs on the mainland. Two-tailed Pasha Butterflies fly in June in *maquis* where the Strawberry Tree *Arbutus unedo* is growing; they can be found around the only hotel.

Accommodation: There is only one hotel in Port Cros but there is also the possibility of renting a flat or a room; make enquiries at the National Park office on the quay.

Site iii.
The **Massif des Maures** rises up behind the coast from Hyères to Frejus. A comparatively low range of hills (the highest point is La Sauvette 779 m) covered with *maquis*, Cork Oaks on the southern slopes and Sweet

Hoopoe

ATLANTIC COAST Mudflats at Arcachon Bay, a migration and wintering site for tens of thousands of waders and wildfowl.

PYRENEES Autumn migration at Organbidexka in the western Pyrenees. Tens of thousands of Black Kites and Honey Buzzards cross this pass at the end of summer, followed later by Cranes.

PYRENEES The higher peaks of the National Park at Néouvielle. Snow Finch, Alpine Accentor and Ptarmigan breed in the highest scree areas, Citril Finch, Capercaillie and Black Woodpecker in the pines.

MEDITERRANEAN COAST Vigueirat Marshes, Camargue, in winter. The Camargue is the only Greater Flamingo breeding site in France.

MEDITERRANEAN COAST The Crau, a 'stony desert'. The only place in France to find Pin-tailed Sandgrouse and Lesser Kestrel as well as Little Bustard, Stone Curlew, Roller, Lesser Grey Shrike and Short-toed Lark. This is Peau de Meau Reserve with a hide in the distant sheepbarn.

MEDITERANNEAN COAST There is excellent birding in the limestone ranges just inland. This is the Mount Sainte Victoire, a breeding site for Bonelli's Eagle, north of Marseille.

MARITIME ALPS Mercantour National Park in winter when many mountain species are found at lower levels.

HAUTE ALPS Ecrin National Park in summer. Snow Finch are easy to find around Lauteret pass.

HAUTE SAVOIE The Haute Griffe, the only place in France where Black Grouse, Capercaillie, Ptarmigan, Hazelhen and Rock Partridge occur together.

CENTRE Branconne forest near Angoulême. A typical oak-beech forest of central France. Black, Grey-headed, Green, Great, Middle and Lesser Spotted Woodpeckers breed here as well as many raptors.

CÉVENNES Re-introduced Griffon and Monk Vultures fly over these gorges, which are also good for watching raptor migration.

CÉVENNES The limestone plateaux or *causses* hold many good birds, notably shrikes, buntings, pipits and larks.

DOMBES near LYON Like the Brenne, an area with a thousand small lakes that attract large numbers of waterbirds including breeding Night Heron and Black-necked Grebe.

CORSICA The low maquis on the cliffs south of Bonifacio where Marmora's Warbler breeds. Alpine and Pallid Swifts fly below the town and a few Cory's Shearwater nest on the rock stacks and offshore islets.

CORSICA Corsican Pine forest at the Vergio pass, 1500 m. The endemic Nuthatch, Crossbill and Citril Finch all occur near here.

CORSICA The west coast. Ospreys breed on cliffs in Scandola Reserve together with Alpine Swift, Crag Martin and Blue Rock Thrush. The tall *maquis* holds many warblers including Sub-alpine and Sardinian.

Chestnuts on the north side, it holds the usual woodland and Mediterranean bird species, including **Dartford** and **Sardinian Warblers** in the scrub. **Serin, Cirl Bunting, Golden Oriole** and **Melodious Warbler** occur in more open woodland on the lower slopes.

Of perhaps more interest is the area of Mediterranean heathland to the north of the range, east of GONFARON and the A57 motorway where **Bee-eater, Hoopoe, Roller, Ortolan Bunting** and three shrike species, **Southern Grey, Red-backed** and **Woodchat Shrike** can be found. Listen out for **Scops Owl** near the villages.

Ortolan Bunting

ACCESS: Gonfaron lies on the N97 some 40 km north of Hyères, just west of the A57 motorway. To reach the heathland take the D75 from the east of the village; it very soon crosses the motorway. In a couple of kilometres you will come to the "Tortoise Village" on the right (see below). The best heathland, interspersed with vineyards, with scattered pines and Cork Oaks starts immediately beyond this. There are several places where it is possible to walk over the heath away from the road for some way. There is a small wetland just before the junction with the D558. Turn left at this junction and in 1.5 km right onto the D48. Here the heathland is rockier with Tree Heath, Cistus and Stone Pines.

Good roads across the Maures hills are the D39 from Gonfaron to Collobrières crossing the Col des Fourches (681 m) and the D41 from west of Collobrières over the Babaou pass 414 m down to the coast at le Lavendou. There are plenty of places to park and walk along the marked footpaths.

Other fauna and flora: The endangered Hermann's Tortoise *Testudo hermanni* has its last stronghold in France in these hills. There is a 2-hectare "Tortoise Village" (*Village des Tortues*) beside the D75 east of Gonfaron where captive-bred animals are released into the wild and injured ones cared for. It is open every day from 9.00–19.00 March to November. Ocellated Lizard and Ladder Snake are among other reptiles found in the heathland. Butterflies are numerous. This is another exceptional area for orchids and May-early June are the best months for these. They include various species of Tongue Orchids, Violet Birds-nest and Red Helleborine *Cephalanthera rubra*.

Area 10 **THE EASTERN MEDITERRANEAN – VAR RIVER MOUTH, NICE**

The *Côte d'Azur* has been the *Côte de Ciment* for a long time now; motorways, roads and heavy tourist development have left almost no wetlands for birds. One exception is the mouth of the River Var, called locally, and rather confusingly, the *petite Camargue*. Although Nice's airport, France's second busiest, borders it to the east, a large commercial centre has been built on the west bank and the N98, N7, A8 motorway and TGV rail line cross it, it still manages to provide habitat for large number so waders, gulls, herons and duck. The Var is certainly not a site of major importance, but worth visiting if in the area, especially in winter and spring.

ACCESS: To reach the river mouth, do not use the A8 motorway, which runs inland at this point along the east bank of the river, but take the N98 coastal road to St. LAURENT-DU-VAR on the west bank. The *centre commercial* is sited right beside the river, looking across to the airport on the opposite shore. Park in one of the carparks for the commercial centre from where it is possible to walk towards the sea and the river mouth. Scan the mouth and the gravel and reed or scrub-covered islands in the river. In winter **Yelkouan Shearwater, Razorbill, Gannet** and terns may be seen over the bay where there are sometimes **Red-throated Diver, Slavonian Grebe** and **Eider** out at sea. There is a sewage farm (*station d'épuration*) nearer the sea and so are always large number of gulls around; not just **Black-headed** but also **Mediterranean**, which winter here in reasonable numbers, and **Yellow-legged. Common** and **Sandwich Tern** also occur. From the point you can

Little Ringed Plover

walk upstream along an embankment to the Napoleon III bridge (where a few **Crag Martin** nest), stopping to scan wherever there are islands or reedbeds. There is a colony of **Common Tern** beyond the bridge. **Sardinian, Melodious, Cetti's, Great** and **Great Reed Warbler** breed in the reeds or brambles and scrub nearby. **Little Ringed Plover** and **Common Sandpiper** breed on the gravel spits and many other species of waders can be found on the islands during migration periods and in winter as well as **Little Egret, Night Heron, Black-winged Stilt and Avocets** in spring.

Some 11 km upstream, the hydroelectric dams near the industrial zone of CARROS have formed the River Var into small lakes. Many duck species, **Coot, Little Grebe, Cormorant** and **Dipper** are some of the birds that winter here. Often there are only gulls to see, but it is worth checking if in the area and could be very good at migration times. The N202 runs upstream along the east bank but there are no views from this side. Take the bridge across the river towards Carros and turn right onto the riverside road (1st Avenue) signed to the industrial estate. There is a dirt track running between the river and the road from where one can park and look over the lakes. It is only worth going upstream for about 2 km. You can look downstream from the bridge.

CORSICA

Area 1	**The east coast: Lakes Biguglia, Urbino and Diane**
	Site i. Lake Bigulia
	Site ii. Lakes Urbino and Diane
Area 2	**The southern mountains – Zonza and the Bavella Pass**
Area 3	**The south around Bonifacio**
Area 4	**The west coast – Ajaccio to Porto**
Area 5	**Porto to Galeria and Scandola Reserve**
	Site i. Porto
	Site ii. Scandola Reserve
	Site iii. North of Porto and Galeria
Area 6	**The northwest – Calvi and the Regino valley**
Area 7	**Evisa, Aitone Forest and Col de Vergio**
Area 8	**Corte and the central valleys**
	Site i. Asco valley
	Site ii. Restonica valley
	Site iii. Verghello valley
	Site iv. Vivario and the Col d'Erbajo
	Site v. Col de Sorba area
Area 9	**The north – Cap Corse – a migration site.**
Area 10	**The offshore island reserves**

Corsica, France's *Ile de Beauté*, is the fourth largest Mediterranean island. It measures 183 km from north to south, 83 km from west to east and has 1047 km of coastline. Except for the central eastern coastal plain most of the island is rocky and mountainous, mainly granite except for a small limestone area around Bonifacio in the south. The sheer cliffs, precipitous headlands and numerous rocky islets of the remaining coastline support not just seabird colonies but many other bird species. In the central mountain chain, Mount Cinto at 2706 m is the highest peak but there are twenty more rising to over 2000 m. Shrubby, aromatic *maquis* (from the Corsican word for Cistus – "macchia") covers 43% of the island, giving Corsica its reputation as "the scented isle". Forest covers another 27%; main tree species are Holm and Cork Oak, Maritime and Corsican Pine, Sweet Chestnut and Beech. Some 2000 species of plant have been identified on Corsica, of which almost 8% are endemic to Corsica and Sardinia.

In some ways Corsica is a southern France in miniature, with vegetation zones rising from Mediterranean to Alpine. However, lying as it does some 160 km from the French coast but only half that from Italy and 12 km from Sardinia, it is not surprising that Corsica has more in common with the latter and that both bird and plant species often differ from mainland ones.

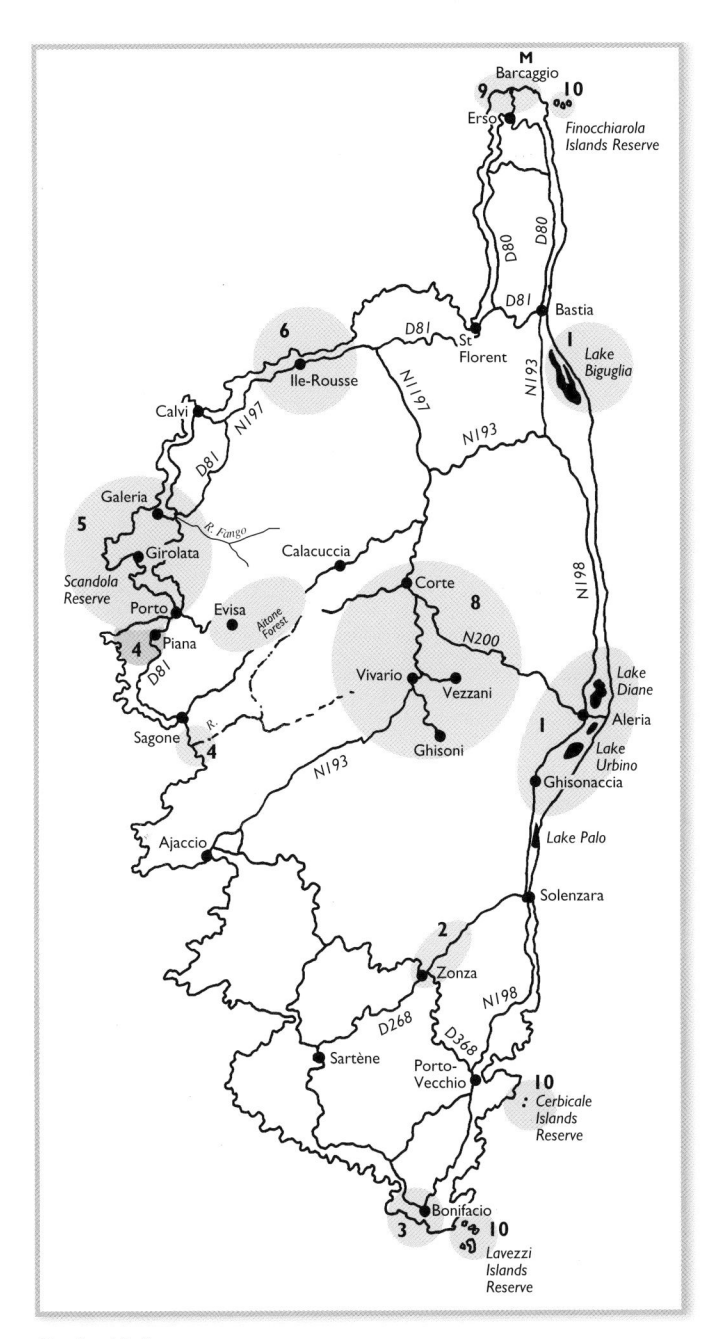

Corsica birding areas

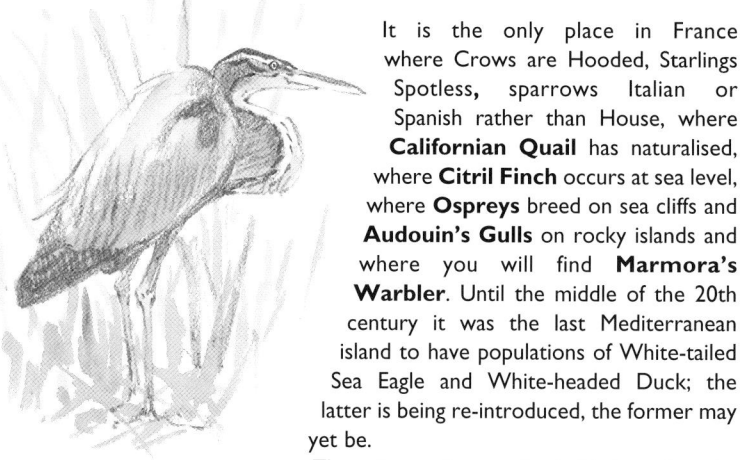

It is the only place in France where Crows are Hooded, Starlings Spotless, sparrows Italian or Spanish rather than House, where **Californian Quail** has naturalised, where **Citril Finch** occurs at sea level, where **Ospreys** breed on sea cliffs and **Audouin's Gulls** on rocky islands and where you will find **Marmora's Warbler**. Until the middle of the 20th century it was the last Mediterranean island to have populations of White-tailed Sea Eagle and White-headed Duck; the latter is being re-introduced, the former may yet be.

Purple Heron

There is one true endemic bird species, the near-threatened **Corsican Nuthatch**, but several woodland species have endemic forms, usually shared with Sardinia and sometimes other Mediterranean Islands. The most striking of these is the **Citril Finch** subspecies *corsicana*, whose mantle and back are streaky brown (like a juvenile *citrinella* instead of that adult's plain grey-green) and face and underparts brighter yellow. Unlike mainland birds, which occur only in higher mountainous regions, it can be found from sea-level upwards. The **Crossbill** ssp. *corsicana* has as stout a bill as the Scottish Crossbill; like the Nuthatch it is confined to Corsican Pine forests. **Marmora's Warbler** is found only on Corsica, Sardinia and the Balearic Islands (where the ssp. is paler). The only Treecreeper is the Common or Eurasian species and it is an endemic form, as is Woodchat Shrike (ssp. *badius* lacking white wing bars). Jay, Coal, Blue and Great Tits, Goldfinch, Wren, Great Spotted Woodpecker, Goshawk and Sparrowhawk, Spotted Flycatcher and a few other species are all endemic races. **California Quail** has established a small but stable feral population on the eastern coastal plain and **White-headed Duck**, recently extirpated, is starting to be re-introduced on Lake Biguglia.

In addition to endemic and rare species, typical Mediterranean birds such as **Purple Heron, Scops Owl, Hoopoe, Tawny Pipit, Red-rumped Swallow, Sardinian, Spectacled** and **Subalpine Warblers, Great Reed Warbler, Blue Rock Thrush** and **Rock Sparrow** all occur while mountain species include **Lammergeier, Golden Eagle, Rock Thrush, Crag Martin, Alpine Chough, Crossbill, Alpine Accentor, Snow Finch** and **Wallcreeper.**

With its long, rocky coastline, Corsica has several breeding seabirds: **Audouin's Gull**, (**Slender-billed** and **Mediterranean** are passage migrants or winter visitors), **Cory's** and **Yelkouan Shearwaters, European Storm Petrel** and **Shag** while many other species are seen around the coast on passage and in winter. About 25 pairs of **Osprey** nest on sea cliffs in the north-west of the island and **Alpine, Pallid** and **Common Swifts** may be seen over the cliffs, which are also home to **Peregrine Falcon, Rock Dove, Blue Rock Thrush** and wintering **Wallcreepers**.

There are some unexpected gaps in the island's bird list: House Sparrows and Magpies are no great loss but the only Buntings are Cirl and Corn; Black Woodpeckers and Crested Tits are unknown in spite of all the pine forests; there are no Garden Warblers, Dunnocks, Bullfinches, Red-billed Choughs, Jackdaws or Black Kites. For more information about Corsican species, refer to the "Special species" section at the end of the book.

TRAVEL: There are regular scheduled and charter flights to Ajaccio and Bastia from both London and other airports in Great Britain as well as daily flights from many parts of mainland France. There are also airports at Calvi and Figari, north of Bonifacio. All the well-known car hire firms have offices at all these airports. Travel around the island except by car is fairly difficult and time consuming. However, the mountain roads are not for nervous drivers or those suffering from vertigo. They are very narrow, often only single track with few passing places, and many stretches have no safety-barrier between the edge of the road and a very long drop! There are regular bus services between the main towns, more frequent in summer, and a single railway line running between Bastia, Calvi and Ajaccio.

Car ferry companies run daily and overnight services from Marseille, Toulon and Nice. CMN and SNCM, two of the main operators, run several ferries daily from the old *Gare Maritime* docks in Marseilles, conveniently situated at the end of the A 55. Return fare for a car and two passengers travelling overnight in a cabin is approximately 2500 F. Overnight boats leave at 19.00 or 20.00 and arrive at 7.00 or 8.00. Daytime sailings are somewhat quicker. It is probably only necessary to book in advance during holiday periods; any travel agency can arrange this. Both companies have ticket offices on the docks.

Books and maps: The island is well covered by both Michelin and IGN (various scales). A variety of maps are available on the ferries, at airport bookstalls or newspaper shops in the larger towns. Michelin's annual book *Atlas Routier et Touristique* (1 cm = 2 km) covers it adequately for touring purposes. Note that while many road signs are in both French and Corsican, some are only in Corsican and spellings may differ from those on the maps (a "u" at the end rather than "o" is common).

There are a number of tourist guides to the island, including both Lonely Planet and Rough Guides. The *Fédération Française de la Randonnée Pedestre* (FRPP) produces a book with maps on walks in the Natural Regional Park and there are many other illustrated guides in French, all available from the sources given above. Anyone seriously birding the island will need the BOU Checklist "The Birds of Corsica", while anyone interested in plants will find the excellent colour photographs in *La Flore endémique de la Corse* published by Edisud very helpful.

WHEN TO VISIT: Like all Mediterranean sites, Corsica will give you the longest species list in April or May but some of the highest roads may still be snow-covered in April. June is not too late and better for the higher areas where breeding starts later; it is also a good month for butterflies. The end of September and October, when most tourists have left, can also be a good time. Winter can be rewarding, as it is, of course, possible to see resident species all through the year and **Corsican Nuthatch** and **Citril Finch** are probably easier to find in winter, when they flock or join foraging parties. **Marmora's Warbler** is also easy to locate on bright winter days. Fares are normally cheaper in winter, the roads are quieter but the highest mountain areas will be impassable and many hotels will be closed.

Area 1 THE EAST COAST

Site i. LAKE BIGUGLIA

LAKE BIGUGLIA is the largest lake on Corsica. A coastal lagoon just south of BASTIA, it is some 11 km long from north to south and 2.5 km at its widest point. It has been a protected Ramsar site since 1990 for its importance as a site for wintering and migrating birds, but the extension of Bastia airport on its west bank, the growing industrial sprawl of Bastia southwards, as well as tourist development along the seaward side has reduced its significance. Additionally hunting is still allowed along a stretch of the north-west shore. There is a narrow outlet to the sea at the north end, which is therefore brackish but the lake is fed by several rivers so the southern end becomes increasingly fresh. Most birds are found in the south but unfortunately both access and visibility are very limited. It is a great pity that one or two simple tower hides have not been erected beside the cycle track that runs along the east bank. In spite of the foregoing caveats, there is still plenty of birdlife. Thousands of duck (mainly **Pochard** and **Tufted** but also **Wigeon, Pintail** and **Red-crested Pochard** – a few of which breed) winter there and tens of thousands of **Coot**. Among them can be found **Great Crested, Black-necked** and **Little Grebes**. The odd **Great White Egret** is seen most winters among the **Grey Herons** and **Little Egret**s and a few **Purple Heron** breed but more are seen on passage. **Marsh Harrier, Kingfisher, Chiffchaff, Sardinian, Cetti's, Fan-tailed** and **Moustached Warbler** can be found all year round (though Moustached is more likely in winter). In summer these are joined by **Reed, Great Reed** and **Melodious Warblers**. The latter in the scrub surrounding the lake, where **Woodchat** and **Red-backed Shrikes** can also be found. **Red-footed Falcon** is regularly seen on passage around Lake Biguglia, most in the first two week of May. **Slender-billed Gull** is a passage migrant in April and so is **Black Tern**, though there are more of this latter species in August. **Ruff** and **Gargany** are two other regular passage birds. **White-headed Duck** figures prominently on all the reserve signs. The last one was sighted in 1966 but they are now being re-introduced from the Spanish population (see notes under "Special Species").

ACCESS: The east side of the lake is reached quite easily from the D107 which runs its full length, crossing the outlet to the sea in the north and joining the dual-carriageway N193 5 km south of Bastia. Coming from the south

Short-toed Lark

leave the N193 at the airport roundabout and turn immediately right onto the D107 (do not take the airport road). It is signed *Lido de Marana-Hotels*. In 3.2 km the D107 swings left, continue following the signs to Lido de Marana. After la Canonica the road runs alongside the River Golo for a short stretch. It can be worth spending a short time here. At 11.7 km from the roundabout there is a small estate of new houses on the left, the Hameau de Potella. It is possible to drive to the end of the development, park and walk along some of the tracks through the Cistus, Tree Heath and bramble scrub towards the lake. **Stonechat, Sardinian** and (in summer) **Melodious Warbler** can be found in the scrub. Trees and reeds block most views of the water, but this is probably as close as you will get to the south end of the lake. 1.5 km further north of the Hameau the road runs close to the lake and it possible to park on the verge. The trees and scrub on the seaward side are good habitat. As you continue northwards a cycle track runs alongside the lake, along which you can walk and look at the lake wherever there are views. Unfortunately tourist development also starts on the seaward side. Some 5 km after the Hameau (roughly the centre of the lake) there is a track leading to a peninsular jutting out into the lake. It is possible to walk or drive along it with views both sides over marsh and reeds. The number of bird species on the water decreases after this point until 6 km further on the road swings left and crosses the mouth of the lake with the sea on the east. There is a car-park here with views over the lake and the beach (early in the morning) might be worth walking along. There is a chance of **Short-toed Lark**.

A short stretch of the south-west side of the lake can be reached. To get to this side take the next turning east off the N193 north of the airport roundabout. It is signed *Gare de Borgo – Hotel des Postes – Gendarmarie*. Drive past the housing estate on the left and in 0.5 km go straight across at the railway crossroads. There follows a stretch with orchards on the right of the road. At the T-junction turn left and immediately right by a yellow post box. Some 2.3 km from the beginning of the road, fork right by a yellow house and continue for just over a kilometre to signs marking the reserve, where the road turns right over a canal, beside a rubbish dump. Leave the car here and walk down to the lake on the left bank of the canal. The canal looks good for Crakes on passage but at the beginning of 2000 it was unfortunately full of dead fish and rubbish from the uncontrolled dumping alongside. **Marsh Harrier, Fan-tailed Warbler (Zitting Cisticola), Cetti's** and **Moustached Warbler**s (more likely in winter), **Cirl** and **Corn Buntings** can be found winter and summer and many warblers on passage as well as **Hobby** and **Red-footed Falcon**. It is possible to walk down the right-hand bank of the canal and then turn south along the lakeside for a kilometre or so. The gate is wired-up to stop cattle roaming but the land is part of the reserve and does not seem to be private. Inquisitive bullocks are probably the greatest danger! The reeds here are good for **Great Reed Warbler** in summer and **Purple Heron** is possible. Although the reedbed is dense, there are one or two places where it is possible to scope the open water.

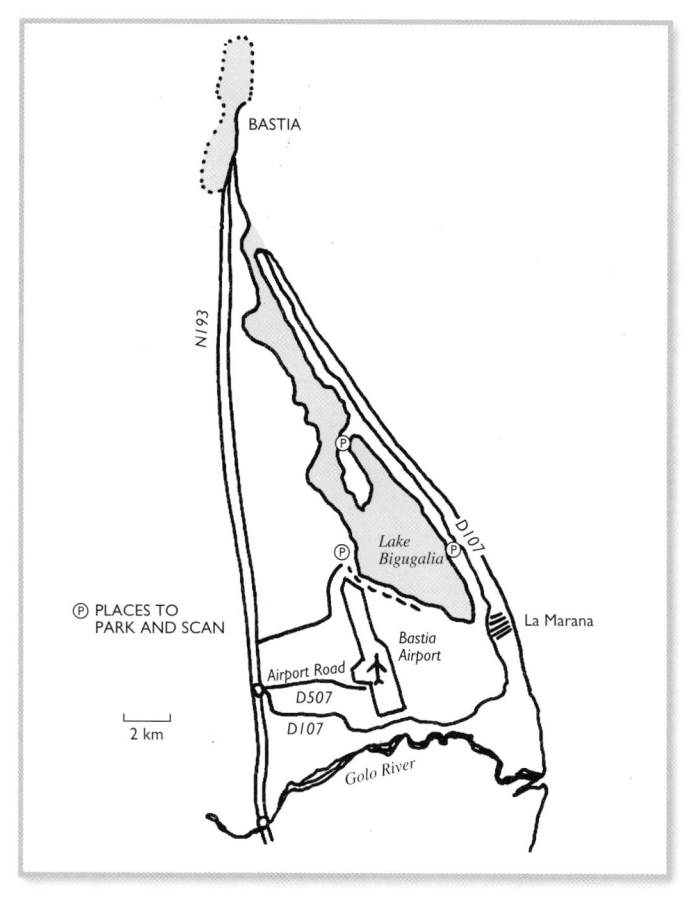

Corsica Area 1 site i. Lake Bigulia

Site 1. **LAKE URBINO**

LAKE URBINO lies half-way down the east coast, south of ALERIA and **LAKE DIANE** just north of this town, between the N198 main coastal road and the sea. Neither are major sites but both are worth a short visit as some species rare elsewhere on the island can be found around them. Both lakes are signed from the N198, which is a straight, fast road.

LAKE URBINO lies 2.6 km east of the N198. After turning off the N198 a view of the lake can be obtained in 2 km. Stop and scan from here; a telescope is needed. Among the numerous wintering ducks, **Coots** and **Cormorants**, all three **Grebes** can be found and there is sometimes a **Great White Egret** with the **Little Egrets** and **Grey Herons**. **Lapwings** are numerous in the fields around the lake and occasionally in winter an **Osprey** can be seen perched nearby. **Marsh Harriers** may be seen all through the year. In late spring or summer the surrounding fields may be of more interest. Both **Short-toed Lark** and **Tawny Pipits** may be found in the short, grazed grassland; it is one place in the island with suitable habitat for them. With a lot of luck, **Californian Quail** may be heard or seen; they live in cultivated fields with some low-growing scrub or low maquis to hide in. **Woodlark** and **Red-backed Shrike** are other breeding birds. Look for **Rock Sparrow** among the **Italian Sparrows** near the farm buildings. **Spotless Starlings** and **Hooded Crows** are very numerous around here. The road to the lake ends by the buildings of some shellfish producers, from where there is another view over the water.

LAKE DIANE is also signed from the N198 because it too is used by shellfish producers. Much the same species can be found on the water. In summer **Woodchat Shrikes** can be found nearby as well as **Bee-eaters**. **Rock Sparrows** are often found around Bee-eater colonies as they sometimes use the old holes.

(South of GHISONACCIA there are two more coastal lakes between the N198 and the sea. Lake CANNA GRADUGINE is signed as a reserve and no cars are allowed up the track to it. Lake PALO lies closer to the N198 some 5 km further south. Neither lake seems to have many birds but are possibly worth checking in spring).

Area 2 THE SOUTHERN MOUNTAINS – ZONZA and the BAVELLA PASS

The **BAVELLA PASS** on the D268 30 km above SOLENZARA can also be reached from the D368 from PORTO-VECCHIO or the D69/D268 from

SARTENE. Both meet at ZONZA and the Bavella pass is 9 km east of this village. The final stretches of the D368 before Zonza run through good forest habitat. The forest here, like the higher parts of the Zonza forest, is composed mainly of Corsican Pine, home of the **Corsican Nuthatch**. This endemic species may be found in any strand of mature pines along the higher stretches of these roads or at the pass itself. It is not even necessary to walk far into the forest since the Nuthatch is found around clearings and forest edges and roads make good clearings! Stop anywhere where there are belts of mature trees and listen. When disturbed it utters a harsh almost Jay-like call, astounding for so small a bird. In winter it flocks with foraging parties of Coal Tits, Goldcrests and Treecreepers. If you cannot find it around the top of the pass, then stop in just over 1 km from the pass on the downward slope towards SOLENTARA. After passing the small summer cottages park beside the "Alta Roca Welcome" sign. Nuthatches are often on the opposite side of the road by the bend among the mature trees there. At the pass check the impressive jagged ridge to the north, the Aiguilles, for **Golden Eagle** or even **Lammergeier** flying along them. **Crossbills** and **Citril Finch** are often in the pines at the pass and small flocks of **Alpine Chough** can also be seen over the higher peaks along this road.

Area 3 **BONIFACIO**

The historic town of Bonifacio perches on high limestone cliffs in the south of the island. South of the town the clifftop is covered with low-growing *maquis* (predominantly Rosemary, Juniper and Lentisc) and criss-crossed with paths leading to the signal station and lighthouse. In the *maquis* can be found **Sardinian, Dartford** and **Marmora's Warblers**. This southernmost peninsula is the only part of Corsica that is limestone; it is also the only part where **Spanish Sparrow** may be found. Check all **Italian Sparrows** around Bonifacio carefully. **Black Redstart** and **Corsican Citril Finch** may be found around the ruined buildings that dot the plateau. Both **Pallid** and **Alpine Swifts** can be seen in summer flying around the cliffs below the town while **Shag, Yellow-legged Gull, Cory's** and **Yelkouan Shearwater** may be see out to sea.

ACCESS: Leave the N196 below the old part of the town and take the D58 signed to PIANTARELLA past the hospital and shortly turn right, still signed Piantarella. In just under 1 km there is a good stop on the clifftop. It is possible to pull off the road beside a sign "Domaine de Licetto" and walk towards the sea. A combination of very low-growing *maquis* and a high concentration of **Marmora's** and **Sardinian Warblers** means that Marmora's are likely to be seen well. From the cliff top there are excellent views of the cliffs below Bonifacio where **Rock Dove, Blue Rock Thrush**, and both **Pallid** and

Alpine Swifts may be seen. Look out or listen for **Cory's Shearwater** at dusk; a few still fly in to the rock stacks below the town.

Having explored this area thoroughly, move on. In another half kilometre fork right onto the D260 signed Pertuasi (Pertusato). In a kilometre there is a large ruined building beside the road on the right. Check around here for **Citril Finch**. It is half a kilometre from here to the signal station, which is as far as a car can go. From the station area more sea and cliff watching can be done or you can walk to the lighthouse on the southernmost promontory. All the *maquis* here provides good habitat for warblers. **Cory's Shearwater, Shag** and a few pairs of **Storm Petrel** breed on the Lavezzi Islets (a reserve) between here and Sardinia, so can sometimes be seen flying offshore.

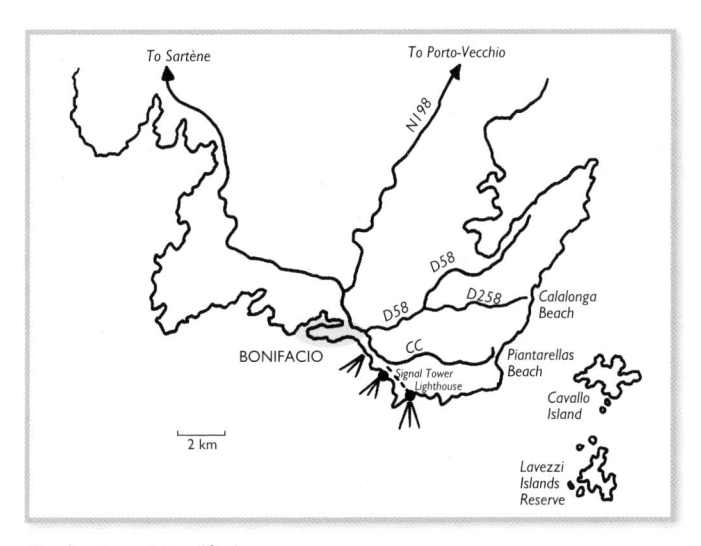

Corsica Area 3 Bonifacio

Area 4 **THE WEST COAST**

There is some good habitat each side of the main road N196 north from BONIFACIO to AJACCIO, but no one special site that can be described as outstanding. There are many areas where the *maquis* holds Mediterranean warblers and one or two where **Marmora's** may be found, especially just north of Bonifacio. **Cirl** and **Corn Buntings, Woodchat Shrike, Blue Rock Thrush, Spotless Starling, Rock** and **Italian Sparrows** are all likely to be seen along this road. A stop almost anywhere near woodland, farmland or slopes covered in *maquis* will produce some good birding, especially early in the morning.

30 km north of AJACCIO the D81 crosses the mouth of the **RIVER**

LIAMONE. It is worth stopping near the bridge and walking a short way up stream. **Nightingale, Cetti's, Sardinian**, and with some searching **Marmora's Warbler**s, all occur in the riverside scrub or *maquis*. Both **Corn** and **Cirl Buntings, Tawny Pipit, Turtle Dove, Stonechat, Bee-eater** and **Woodchat Shrike** are among the species that can be found nearby. A **Red Kite** is often overhead and there could even be an **Osprey** near the bridge.

The D81 turns inland soon after Cargèse but returns to the coast after Piana. Between PIANA and PORTO, LES CALANCHE are spectacular, eroded rock formations of beautiful rose granite. **Crag Martin, Blue Rock Thrush** and **Rock Dove** can all be seen around the cliffs; **Citril Finch, Firecrest, Cirl Bunting, Sardinian** and **Sub-alpine Warblers** in the pines and shrubs nearby. Explore the D624 north-west of PIANA. It is also worth walking along the D81 where the cliffs are just above the road, even though the road is narrow and the traffic can be heavy in summer. Nearer to Porto on the D81, stop at the small parking space by the *Tête de Chien* rock and take the marked footpath towards the sea; it passes through some good habitat and gives views over the cliffs.

Area 5

The small resort of **PORTO** is a convenient centre from which to visit the SCANDOLA RESERVE by boat and to explore the coast further north around GALERIA as well as inland to Evisa and the Vergio and Sevi passes. The D84 runs from Porto to Evisa and then to the central valley, north of Corté.

Site i.

In the immediate surroundings of PORTO and nearby Bussaglia beach (first turning off the D81 4 km north) **Italian Sparrow, Blue Rock Thrush, Rock Dove, Crag Martin, Spotless Starling** and **Raven** can all be seen. An **Audouin's Gull** is often among the **Yellow-legged Gulls** in the bay where **Shag** may be seen fishing.

Site ii.

In the spring and summer several boats sail from PORTO around the **SCANDOLA RESERVE**, a three-hour trip, usually with a short stop at Girolata, a village that can only be reached by sea. Ask for details at the Tourist Office on the quay, in front of the Hotel les Flots Bleus. Most of the hotels and bars have information on boat trips and sell tickets. Morning trips normally leave at 9.00, afternoon ones after lunch. Warning: most of the boats are small and sailings are likely to be cancelled if the sea is rough so if you are very keen to do this trip, allow more than one day.

The Scandola peninsula is part of a collapsed volcano; not only is the coastal scenery very impressive but it is interesting geologically. Virtually the only way to see it is from the sea; although there are long-distance footpaths from Galéria to Girolata, none go near the Scandola cliffs. This protects the **Ospreys** that nest on rock stacks and ridges. **Shag, Peregrine, Kestrel,**

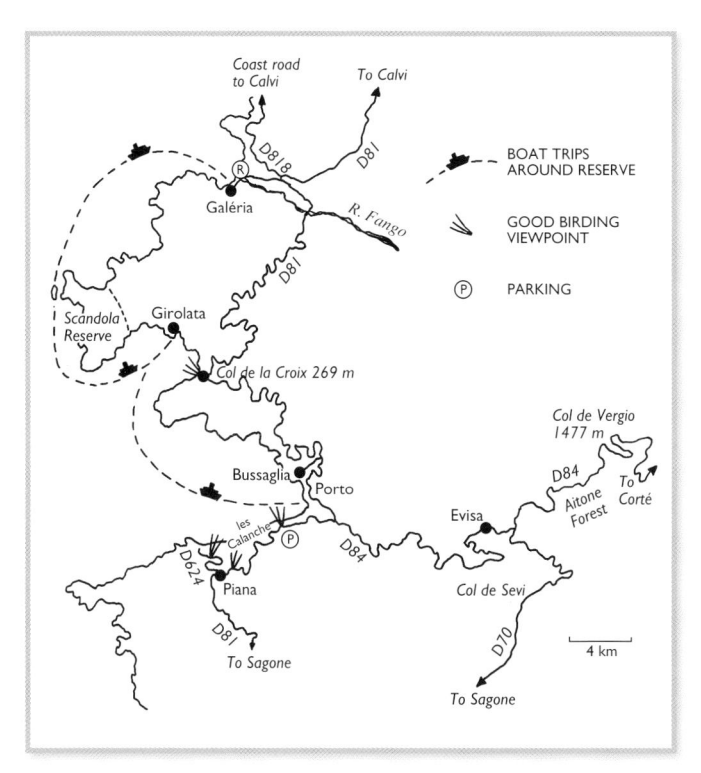

Corsica Areas 5 and 6 Porto, Scandola, Aitone Forest and Vergio Pass

Blue Rock Thrush, Rock Dove, Crag Martin, Alpine and Pallid Swifts are other species to be seen during the boat trip. A short walk inland from GIROLATA should produce **Marmora's, Dartford and Sardinian Warbler.**

All-day boat trips to the Reserve also leave from Calvi and the Regional Park has an office and boat at Galéria.

Site iii.
The D81 north of Porto winds and twists through tall *maquis*, composed mainly of Strawberry Tree, Lentisc and Tree Heath. 22 km north of Porto, the viewpoint at **COL DE LA CROIX** or *Bocca de la Crocci*, is worth a stop. Walking up to the cross on top, with views over the bay to Girolata, you should see **Crag Martin, Citril Finch, Sardinian** and **Sub-alpine Warblers and Cirl Bunting.** A scan out to sea might produce **Osprey** or **Shag**. A footpath runs from here to Girolata, a walk of some three hours.

24.5 km further north stop at the bridge over the River Fango just beyond the junction of the D351 leading to **GALERIA** before taking the road towards Galeria. Besides the views downstream, there is low *maquis* around the gravel bed of the river, good habitat for warblers. Before reaching the village of GALERIA, there is a protected area of shoreline at the river mouth belonging to the *Conservatoire du Littoral*, with a large car-park just beyond it. It is signed RICINICCIA. Walk back towards the old building. **Citril Finch, Stonechat, Blue Rock Thrush, Dartford, Marmora's** and **Sardinian Warblers, Blackcap** and **Crag Martin** can all be found in the *maquis* here or near the bridge. **Moorhen** and **Grey Heron** may be seen in the river; **Osprey** sometimes fish near here and **Red Kite** is seen frequently, as are **Raven** and **Hooded Crow. Shag** may be seen out to sea and during the right conditions shearwaters fly past.

Area 6

The **REGINO VALLEY** follows the river of the same name from south of L'ILE-ROUSSE to its mouth north-east of the town. There are vineyards, grassland, slopes covered with *maquis*, young oak and a little riparian woodland and the river has been dammed at one place to form a lake. High peaks rise to the south. It is certainly the easiest place to see **Red Kite**; this valley holds the highest concentration in Corsica. **Golden Eagle** may be glimpsed over the mountains. **Rock Sparrow, Woodlark, Tawny Pipit, Bee-eater, Cirl Bunting, Corn Bunting** and **Spotless Starling** are all common or very common. **Sardinian** and **Marmora's Warblers** can be found in the *maquis*, the latter in some of the recently burnt areas; **Blue Rock Thrush** on the cliffs near the coast.

ACCESS: One possible circuit through a variety of habitats takes the D13 south from L'ILE-ROUSSE, towards STA. REPERATA. Continue south on the same road in the direction of FELICETO. Check around the Domaine Clos Regino vineyards for **Woodlark, Tawny Pipit** and **Rock Sparrow**. At the junction with the D113, some 6 km from Sta.Reperata, turn left onto the D113 signed to SPELONCATTO, MONTICELLO. This stretch runs through some good *maquis* on the slopes (**Tawny Pipit** can be found in the newly burn areas) and past the lake, which is worth a stop. Check both the low *maquis* around the lakeside for **Marmora's Warbler**, as well as looking for birds on the water – they may be only gulls and grebes but certainly in spring could be more interesting. At the junction with the D63, turn right towards Speloncatto and in 0.5 km left, (signed to Regino Golf Course). This minor road passes the golf course and then follows the river to the main coast road.

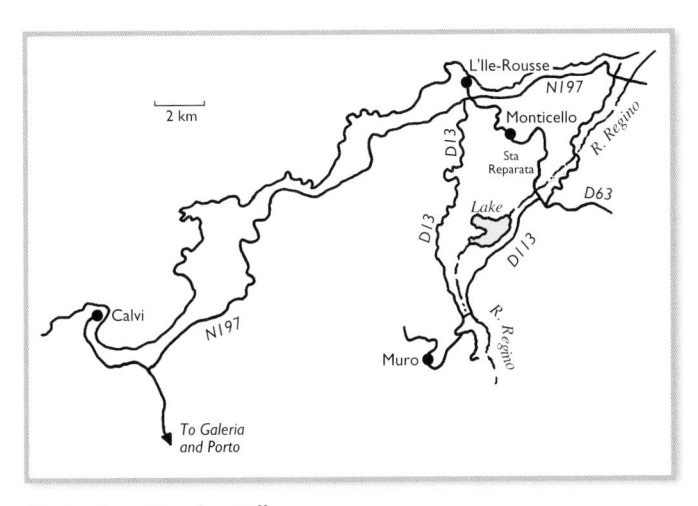

Corsica Area 6 Regino Valley

Area 7 EVISA, AITONE FOREST and COL DE VERGIO

The D84 leads from PORTO to EVISA. Birding anywhere in appropriate habitat along this road should give you views of **Citril Finch, Raven, Peregrine, Crag Martin** and **Spotted Flycatcher**. Above EVISA it is worth turning onto the D70 to CRISTINACCA for a detour to the **COL de SEVI**, just over 7 km away, as this is a good site for **Marmora's Warbler, Red-backed Shrike** and **Citril Finch**. (If returning to Porto you can make a circuit by continuing down the D70 to Sagone on the coast and then back via Cargèse and Piana). If driving to CORTÉ and the centre of the island, return to EVISA and continue on the D84. **AITONE FOREST** starts soon after the village and the D84 runs through pine and fir woods up to the pass at 1467 m, the **COL DE VERGIO**. **Crossbill, Treecreeper, Goldcrest, Firecrest** and **Corsican Nuthatch** can all be found here. Roughly 3 km from the D70 junction and 7 km below the pass there is an actual *Sentier de la Sitelle*, a special Nuthatch footpath marked with pink nuthatches, leading off from the north side of the road. This track is also good for woodland plants, especially Cyclamen. There is a good density of Nuthatches just below the pass, where large trees are growing close to the road. At the top of the pass, look for raptors along the ridges; both **Golden Eagle** and **Lammergeier** can be spotted here. There are **Crossbills, Goldcrest, Treecreeper** and **Coal Tit** in the pines at the pass and **Corsican Citril Finch** around the ski-station on the east side, especially early in the year.

There is more forest on the east slope; another good spot for **Nuthatch** and other forest species is 7.3 km east from the pass at a viewpoint with a large parking space. It is almost 24 km from the pass to the village of CALACUCCIA. There is varied habitat around the village; **Citril Finch, Linnet** and **Corn Bunting** are among the species to be found here. From Calacuccia the D84 follows the Golo River for 15 km to the junction with the D18, which takes you south into CORTÉ or continue to the junction with the main N193, if you wish to go north to the ASCO valley (see site below).

Area 8 **CORTÉ**

CORTÉ is situated in Corsica's broad, central valley with mountain ranges rising east and west. It is a good centre from which to explore several of the higher valleys that branch off into the mountains. Both **Lammergeier** and **Golden Eagle** can often be seen from the head of these valleys and **Dipper** can be found in most of the mountain streams.

Site i.
26 km north of Corte, and 11 km north of the D84 junction from Evisa, the D47 and D147 lead up the **ASCO** valley and gorge. There is some good protected *maquis* habitat around the "Tortoise Village" of the Regional Park authority along the D47. 20 km up the gorge is ASCO village (look for **Cirl Bunting** around it) and 7 km above the village is some good forest for **Corsican Nuthatch**. The road continues to the Haut Asco ski station on the slopes of Mt. Cinto, an area for high-mountain birds but the road is bad until late in spring. The pine forest is less dense in the upper reaches of this valley and the trees grow in scattered groves over the slopes.

Site ii.
On the southern edge of CORTÉ, the **RESTONICA VALLEY** runs south-west. There are several hotels at the start of the valley where **Dipper** and **Grey Wagtail** can be seen in the river and **Scop's Owl** heard. Above the hotels a narrow and tortuous road climbs for 14 km to an upper car park at the Bergeries de Grotelle (only the first few kilometres will be open in winter and early spring). From the car park there are footpaths to a mountain refuge and a couple of small mountain lakes. Even a short walk up here should enable you to see such typical upland birds as **Water Pipit, Northern Wheatear** and **Alpine Chough**. This is one of the best valleys for **Lammergeier**; check the peaks to the north. Look for **Rock Thrush** on the scree slopes.

Site iii.
The **VERGHELLO** valley runs west from the Vecchio bridge at the Col de Morello 17 km south of Corté. It is surrounded on three sides for tall peaks of which Mt. Rotondo 2622 m, lying between the Verghello and Restonica valleys, is the highest. If coming from Corté on the N193, turn right (west)

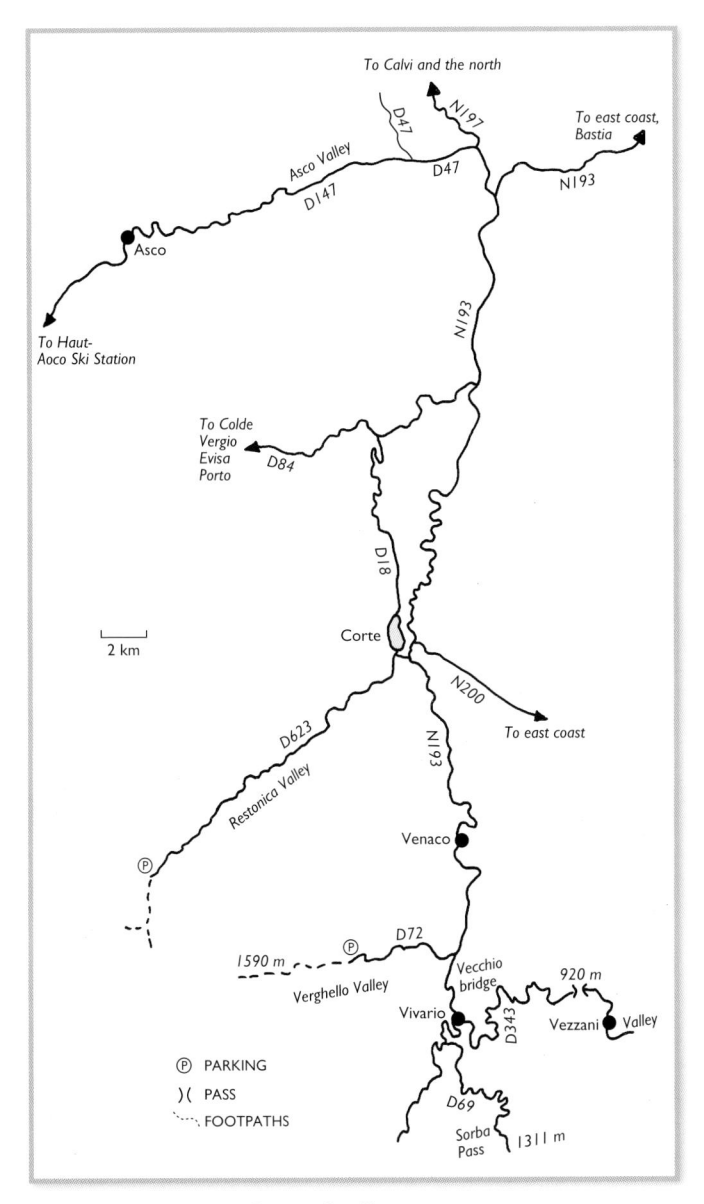

Corsica Area 8 Corté and Central Valleys

immediately before the new road bridge. The D723 crosses the railway just above the old rail-bridge. It is possible to drive some way up this narrow road or park near the beginning and walk. A compromise, if short of time, might be to drive to the bridge 5 km up the valley and then walk. It is another 5 km to the pass and quite steep in places. Like the Restonica valley, Verghello rises through different vegetation zones: upper Mediterranean, montane and sub-alpine – *maquis*, Maritime Pine and Corsican Pine. Birds in the lower reaches include **Marmora's**, **Subalpine** and **Sardinian Warblers** and **Cirl Bunting**. **Coal** and **Long-tailed Tits, Firecrest** and **Great Spotted Woodpecker** can be found in the pine forest. Once the zone of Corsican Pine has been reached, after the bridge, **Corsican Nuthatch** should be heard. **Alpine Swift** is often seen overhead. Check the peaks to the north for **Lammergeier** and **Golden Eagle**.

Site iv.

From the Vecchio bridge the N193 climbs a few kilometres to the village of VIVARIO. In the village turn left (east) onto the D343 just after a statue of female and child. It is signed to VEZZANI. The road runs through some open areas where **Citril Finch** may be found before the forest closes in again. At 10 km from Vivario there is a picnic site surrounded by good mature pines. **Corsican Nuthatch** is often seen close to the road here or there is a forestry track running parallel to the road if you wish to walk. Half a kilometre before the Col d'Erbajo (920) m there is another forestry road running steeply up to the right. Walk up here to the tree limit for more Nuthatches and **Citril Finch. Goshawk** is another forest species that may be found here.

Site v.

Another site for **Corsican Nuthatch** is along the D69 COL DE SORBA road. Turn left (east) at the top of the pass beside two roadside restaurants 2 km south of VIVARIO. It is signed to GHISONI. From here it is only 3.2 km to an area of Corsican Pine where the Nuthatch may be seen. Other species to be found along this stretch of road include **Marmora's** and **Subalpine Warbler, Wood Lark** and **Cirl Bunting**. There is also some good *maquis* on the opposite side of the road to the restaurants.

Area 9

CAP CORSE – a migration site. Spring migration has been studied for over 20 years at BARCAGGIO, the northern tip of Corsica, where the small river Acqua Tignese flows into the sea and there are ponds and sandy beaches nearby. Most spring passage is along the coast, as the inland mountains are still snow-covered. The end of March to the end of May is the best time here, though there are certainly birds to be seen in other months. However, it is a long slow drive and outside the migration period you will probably see little that cannot be found elsewhere. However, Cap Corse is the best place to find **Audouin's Gull**. (See area 10 below). Among the 170 or so species that have been recorded on migration are **Black** and **White Storks, Little** and

Red-rumped Swallows

Spotted Crakes, Alpine Swift, Red-rumped Swallow, many waders and warblers, including **Icterine, Ring Ouzel, Red-throated Pipit** and **Short-toed Lark** (some of the latter breed here).

ACCESS: Take the D80 north from either Bastia or Patrimonia, north of L'Ile-Rousse. At ERSA turn onto the D253. It is 7 km to BARCAGGIO. There is a track to the river before you reach the village and other paths lead east past the dunes and ponds to Agnello Point and tower (*tour*), some 3 km from the river, which is a good place to watch for migrating raptors, especially **Honey Buzzard** and **Montagu's Harriers** or seawatch for **Shag, Shearwaters** and **Audouin's Gull**.

Area 10 ISLAND RESERVES

Several of Corsica's reserves are on offshore islands and permission is needed to visit them. It can be obtained from 3 rue Luce de Casabianca, 20200 Bastia. Tel: 95 32 38 14. No landings are allowed during the breeding season; overnight camping is forbidden and it is usually better to take one of the regular boat trips which run from the nearest port.

The **ILES FINOCCHIAROLA** lie off the north-east of Cap Corse. Varying numbers of **Audouin's Gull** (between 20 to 100 pairs) breed there, as well as smaller numbers of **Shag** and both **Cory's** and **Yelkouan Shearwaters**. Pleasure boats from nearby ports have caused considerable disturbance to breeding birds in the past and the islands are wardened during the breeding season and no landings allowed. There are footpaths to the headlands opposite the islands from where you can watch out for Audouin's

Gulls flying past. They arrive at the breeding sites from mid-March and leave during the first week of August.

The **ILES LAVEZZI** lie between the southern tip of Corsica and Sardinia. Over 300 pairs of **Cory's Shearwater**, a few **Storm Petrel** and several hundred **Shag** breed here. The shearwaters are present on Lavezzi from mid-February to October, leaving to feed at sea at dawn and flying back to their nest sites at dusk. There are some boat trips to the islands from Bonifacio in summer.

The **ILES CERBICALE** lie a couple of kilometres or so off the south-east coast of the Porto-Vecchio peninsula and boat trips to the islands can be arranged from Port Vecchio. Up to a hundred pairs of **Cory's Shearwater** breed on the various small islands, as well as **Storm Petrel, Shag** and occasionally **Audouin's Gull**. Birds flying past can be watched from the cliffs at Point Cerbicale, reached from the minor road that circles the peninsular.

Other fauna and flora: Corsica has several endemic butterflies: Corsican Swallowtail, Fritillary, Grayling, Dappled White and Heath are local but should all be found quite easily, in suitable habitat around 1000 m in altitude. Mediterranean Skipper is found on Corsica but nowhere else in France. Of the 50 or so butterfly species that occur on the island, some of the more striking are Scarce Swallowtail, Two-tailed Pasha (around Strawberry Trees), Cardinal, Southern Comma and Southern White Admiral. Mammals include Sardinian Moufflon while several species of whales and dolphins are found off the west coast, including Fin Whale. They may sometimes be seen from boats around Scandola Reserve. Recently, special whale-watching boat trips have also been organised. Among reptiles and amphibians to be found on the island, the Corsican Brook Salamander *Euproctus montanus* is endemic, occurring in or near running water up to 2100 m but most abundant at lower altitudes. Fire Salamander is also found on the island. Italian Wall Lizard *Podarcis sicula* is widespread and so is Tyrrhenian Wall Lizard *Podarcis tiliguerta*, another Corsican-Sardinian endemic species as is Bedriaga's Rock Lizard *Lacerta bedriagae*, which is a mountain lizard usually found on rocky surfaces. Tyrrhenian Painted Frog *Discoglossus sardus* and the rare Leaf-toed Gecko *Phyllodactylus europeaus* occur in suitable habitat in several areas. Both Turkish and Moorish Geckos are also found on Corsica. A very small lizard, the Pygmy Algyroides *Algyroides fitzingeri* is restricted to Corsica and Sardinia. The endangered Hermann's Tortoise occurs in Corsica and the Regional Park authority has a "Tortoise Village" near the beginning of Asco valley, beside the D147, and protects its habitat there.

The Corsican-Sardinian flora also includes several endemics: One of the showiest is the Sea Daffodil *Pancratium illyricum* which in Corsica can grow in the mountains but always in very damp places; *Saxifrage corsica* also likes damp; it is found in crevices in cliff faces; the endemic Butterwort *Pinguicula corsica* and *Crocus corsicus* also grow in very wet areas, beside streams for the former and sodden snow fields for the latter; *Erodium corsicum* and *Morisia monanthos* grown near Bonifacio in the south. *Cyclamen repandum* grows in light woodland together with lime-green, winter-flowering *Helleborus corsicus* at all but the highest levels, as does the rarer *Brimeura fastigiata*. Other bulbous plants include several species of Sand Crocus or Romulea, Allium and Anemone, *Narcissus tazetta* and *Leucojum longifolium*. Another endemic is the bright blue *Sedum caerulea* to be found on west-coast rocks. The *maquis* includes typically Mediterranean species such as Brooms, Cistus, Asphodels, Junipers, Spurges, Lavender and Rosemary. The taller parts are dominated by Strawberry Tree *Arbutus unedo,* Tree Heath and Holm Oak. Orchids (mainly found around Bonifacio in the south) include Elder-flowered *Dactylorhiza sambucina*, Man *Aceras anthropophorum*, an abundance of Tongue or *Serapias* orchids, many "Bee" or *Ophrys* species as well as *Orchis mascula, morio, longicornu, purpurea, lactea* and *papilionacea* and the rarer *O. tridentata* and *Dactylorhiza sambucina insularis*. Most of the above plants and orchids are in flower between April-June, depending on altitude and weather.

Roller

THE ALPS

The French Alps, straddling the Italian and Swiss frontiers from the Mediterranean to Lake Geneva, comprise four main ranges from south to north:

Area 1	**THE MARITIME AND HAUTE PROVENCE ALPS** in the **Mercantour National Park**	
	Site i. Vésubie Valley	
	Site ii. Cayolle and Bonette Passes south of Barcelonette	
Area 2	**THE HIGH ALPS (Hautes Alpes)**	
	Site i. Lautaret Pass	
	Site ii. Ecrins National Park – central region	
	Site iii. Bois des Ayes	
	Site iv. Izoard Pass	
Area 3	**QUEYRAS REGIONAL PARK** on the Italian frontier	
Area 4	**THE SAVOY ALPS (Haute Savoie) Chamonix-Samoëns area**	
	Site i. Vall Reposoir	
	Site ii. Aravis	
	Site iii. Haut Giffre-Sixt-Fer-a-Cheval	
	Site iv. Loex Plateau	
	Site v. Bellevaux Forest	
Area 5	**THE JURA MOUNTAINS**	
	Site i. The southern end of the Haut-Jura around Collonges	
	Site ii. l'Ecluse gorge	
	Site iii. Bugey marsh	

The northern foothills of the Alps merge into the southern Jura Mountains south of Geneva. The highest and most spectacular parts of the alpine ranges have been designated National or Regional Parks; each has a subtly different appearance, based on rock formation and vegetation but share very similar habitats and therefore broadly similar species of birds. Some of the country's most sought-after species are the birds of these mountain forests and peaks: **Ptarmigan, Capercaillie, Black Grouse, Hazelhen, Rock Partridge, Nutcracker, Snow Finch, Rock Thrush, Wallcreeper, Pygmy Owl, Tengmalm's Owl, Three-toed Woodpecker...** but be warned, they are not at all easy to see without considerable luck, patience and effort. Haut Griffre, in the Haute Savoie is the only place in France where all four mountain game birds can be found together. Furthermore the Alps are a very popular winter sports area; ski stations with all their attendant infrastructure cause considerable disturbance to wildlife, as does the rapidly growing number of tourists holidaying in the mountains in the summer and the increasing

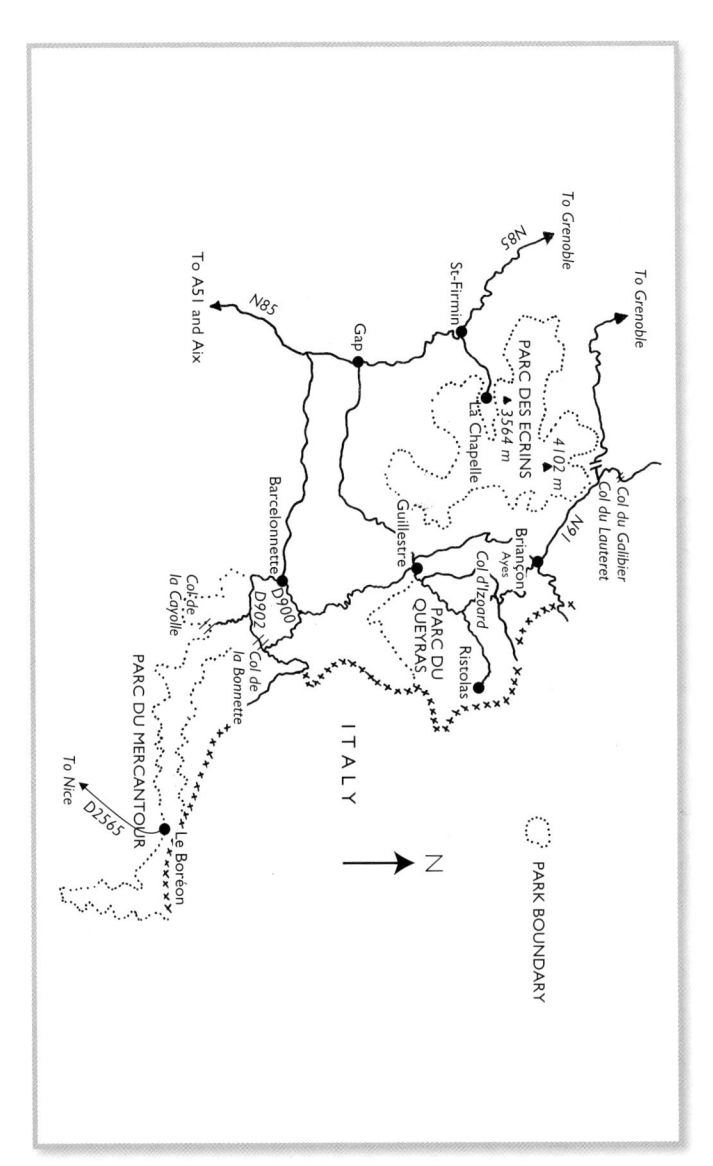

The Alps – National Parks and birding areas described in text

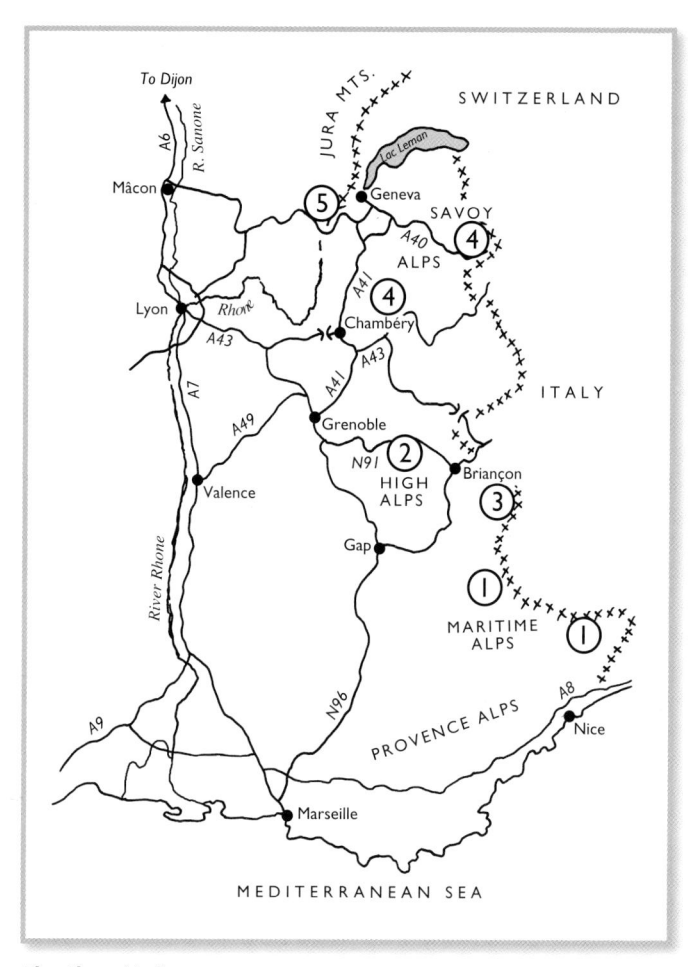

The Alps – birding areas

popularity of "adventure sports" such as hang-gliding, abseiling, canyoning, white-water rafting, etc. The recent development of many parts of the French Alps is one reason why there are comparatively few sites described. Areas that look ideal on the map, with access to high altitude ski resorts, often prove to be poor for birdlife. The more inaccessible areas where mountain birds still occur really <u>are</u> inaccessible without a very long hike up steep mountain slopes. Any keen walker/climber will probably see many of the above species on a trek lasting two or more days but the touring birdwatcher with less time or inclination to struggle up near-vertical faces will find high-mountain species much more difficult to locate. Woodland birds are even more elusive as the forest areas here are huge with little access.

WHEN TO VISIT: Most of the sites in this region are at high altitudes and snow lies late, so mid-June to September is not too late for birding here, though the end of May to mid-June may be the best time. Additionally, minor roads over high passes will be closed until late spring. If birding in mid-summer it is probably best to start your observations as soon as it is light, if you wish to find game birds and avoid crowds of people. Remember, in the mountains all locations are signed by the length of time it takes to reach them, rather than the distance in kilometres. Walking at birding pace, you should double the times given! If you are skiing in this area, several species such as Yellow-billed Chough, Alpine Accentor and even Snow Finch may be observed around ski stations. Additionally some of the following sites can be rewarding in winter, but snowshoes or cross-country skis may be needed.

Maps and guide books: IGN 54 1:100,000 covers the Ecrins and Queyras Parks, IGN 61 (same scale) Mercantour. You need four 1:25,000 scale maps to cover Ecrins, another four for Mercantour and two for Queyras. They are not worth buying unless you plan on doing a lot of walking. All Park headquarters and Offices (at Lautaret, la Chapelle, above Ristolas and Barcelonnette) stock these maps as well as leaflets, sketchmaps and books on each Park. Some leaflets are free; others range from a few Euros up to expensive, full-colour books. Most Park staff will be happy to answer your queries as to the best places to find different species but not all are naturalists. The Parks organise many walking or skiing tours, varying in length and difficulty.

Area 1 THE MARITIME AND PROVENCE ALPS

The Maritime Alps that make up most of MERCANTOUR NATIONAL PARK stretch from the Mediterranean foothills to the high Alps; its northern boundary is only some 24 kilometres from the high mountains of Queyras (Alps area 3). Most of its eastern boundary runs parallel to the Italian frontier. Only a couple of minor roads cross the Park, although there are footpaths, including the GR 5, 52 and 56. Wolves from Italy or further east have settled in the Park in recent years, fuelling more controversy between conservationists and local farmers, already at loggerheads over the opposing claims of wildlife and livestock. In the 1970's, Lammergeiers were regularly seen here, possibly ones coming from the small population on Corsica. For that reason, captive-bred Lammergeiers have been released here and in the adjoining National Park in Italy over the past few years. The north-west of the Park is where they are most likely to be seen, with luck from the Bonette or Cayolle passes.

Site i.
Easily reached from the Mediterranean coast at Nice, the **VÉSUBIE GORGES** run north-east from the N202, (24 km north of Nice) to the village of St. MARTIN-VÉSUBIE, a distance of 35 km along the D2565. Above St. MARTIN the minor D89 road continues to climb to the small Nordic/cross country ski station of BORÉON, the D94 to MADONE DE FENESTRE. Both these higher areas have plenty of marked walking trails to explore the forests and the high mountains to the north. **Black Woodpecker, Nutcracker, Crossbill, Crested** and **Coal Tits, Firecrest** can be found in the conifer forests, **Citril Finch** where the tree thin out and **Alpine Accentor** and **Ptarmigan** on the higher scree slopes. **Golden Eagle, Raven** and both **Choughs** fly over the ridges. **Dipper** can be found in the river.

From BORÉON, continue past the second hotel and the ski centre and take the road that bends left, signed up to Mollière and the Vachéries de Salese. (In winter and spring this road may be blocked by snow after a kilometre or so). Marked footpaths lead off through the forest towards different vachéries (high alpine pastures for cows in summer) as well as the GR 52 long-distance footpath which runs through the Park. The ones on the right about 2 km above Boréon are good for forest species or take the longer (3 hours or more) path to the Col de Cerise 2543 m, on the Italian frontier, an area with superb alpine flowers. In early spring when the paths are snow-covered and snowshoes or skis are needs, good birds can be found by just walking up the road. Alpine Accentor are often on the road just above the village and Black Woodpecker can be heard and seen in the woods behind the hotel and below the road.

Turning eastwards above Boréon the track leads to a parking place at the Vachérie du Boréon and from here a path leads towards the Alpine climbers' hut at Cougourde 2090 m, at first through forest and later alpine meadows and scree.

The D94 from St. Martin to the church and refuge of LA MADONE DE FENESTRE also runs through good forest, where it is worth stopping and listening for woodland species, before opening out into meadows at the top. Footpaths (including the GR52) lead from the church towards the peaks above.

Other fauna and flora: Chamois are numerous and quite easy to spot on the slopes above Boréon, as are Marmots. There are also Mouflon and Ibex near the higher peaks. The alpine flora is exceptional (crocus, gentians, primula and viola species, *Soldanella,* etc) and includes the emblem of the park, the Ancient King *Saxifraga florulenta.*

<u>Accommodation:</u> There are several reasonably priced hotels in St. Martin and two in Boréon, both open throughout the year.

Site ii.
THE CAYOLLE AND BONETTE PASSES are two high mountain

passes in the north of the Park, south and south-east of BARCELONETTE respectively. Both passes are closed in winter and may be blocked by snow until June but in summer give access to high alpine areas without hours of climbing. There are Park Information centres at both passes and reasonably easy walking paths leading from them. **Golden Eagle, Short-toed Eagle, Raven, Red** and **Yellow-billed Chough** should all be seen over the ridges. **Alpine Accentor** and even **Snow Finch** and **Ptarmigan** could be found if you walk high enough, **Rock Thrush** and **Black Redstart** are easier to find. **Water Pipit** and **Northern Wheatear** are the commonest birds of the alpine grassland. **Crested Tit, Crossbill** and **Black Woodpecker** occur in the pine forests. **Tree Pipit, Ring Ouzel** and **Citril Finch** can be found where there are scattered larches, **Rock Bunting** and **Lesser Whitethroat** on sunny, south-facing slopes with bushes. There are quite large flocks of **Fieldfare** in winter.

ACCESS: For the CAYOLLE pass take the D902 from Barcelonette. In 4.5 km you will pass through UVERNET village and soon afterwards the road enters the Bachelard Gorge. This is a site for **Wallcreeper** so it is worth spending some time searching the cliff faces. There are places to pull off the road near the bridges. **Dipper** occurs in the river. From the second bridge it is possible to walk a short way into the Spruce forest for woodland species. The road continues up and through the gorge. Check the south-facing slopes beyond the village of VILLARD D'ABAT for **Rock Bunting** and keep watching the skyline for raptors and corvids. Where the slopes are rocky and the trees thin out, look for **Citril Finch** and **Ring Ouzel** (the local subspecies *alpestris* have pale wings and white feather fringes on their underparts and look much greyer than northern birds). In about 14 km from Villard, a kilometre before the pass, there is a car-park by the Cayolle refuge at 2296 m. Walk around here for high-altitude birds or take the signed walking track towards the lake. **Golden Eagle** is often seen here (If you continue down the southern side of the pass, through ESTENC, ENTRAUNES and St. MARTIN to GUILLAUMES, it is possible to reach site i, the Vésubie valley, by driving east along the D28, D30 and D2565 over some lower passes. All the birds listed above can be seen in similar habitat).

To reach the BONETTE pass, at 2802 m the highest hard-surfaced road in France, take the D900 for 9 km east of Barcelonette and turn onto the D64 at JAUSIERS. On the road up to the pass there are similar habitats and bird species to those given for Cayolle. Bonette is certainly the easiest place to find high-altitude species and, with a lot of luck, one of the newly released **Lammergeier**s might be spotted from here. The D64 joins the D2205 some 20 kms south of the pass and this is another way of reaching the Vésubie valley through magnificent scenery.

Other fauna and flora: Marmots are common, especially around Bonette; Chamois and Ibex are also likely to be seen. This is another excellent area for alpine flowers and butterflies.

Accommodation: Barcelonette has several hotels and camp sites and there are hotels at St. Martin d'Entraunes and Guillaumes south of Cayolle and several of the villages south of Bonette pass.

Area 2 THE HIGH ALPS

The ECRINS NATIONAL PARK covers a huge area between Gap, Grenoble and Briançon. There are more than one hundred peaks over 3000 m in height and 17,9000 hectares of glaciers. 210 species of birds, 64 mammals and 140 butterflies have been recorded in the park and the alpine flora is outstanding. Although 700 hectares in the north-west (the Lauvitel Reserve) are totally protected from human disturbance, the remainder of the Park is understandably popular with walkers, climbers and the general public, but even at the most "touristy" spots some good birds can be found.

Site i.

One of these, the **COL DE LAUTARET** (2057 m), lies just outside the north boundary of the Park but footpaths lead into it. The advantage of this site is that it is possible to reach the pass by car or bus on the N91 from

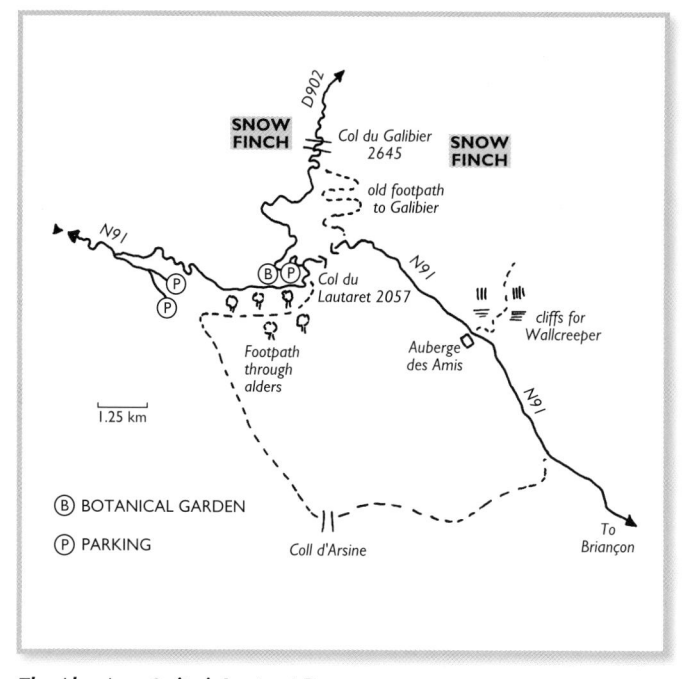

The Alps Area 2 site i. Lauteret Pass

Grenoble or Briançon, there is plenty of parking and an easy, relatively level footpath through some good birding areas. The disadvantage is that it is very popular in summer. Try and start walking at daybreak. Take the track that starts on the west (Grenoble) side of the pass by a carpark and a "Les Ecrins Park" sign and turn right over the small bridge following the signs towards the Alpe de Villar d'Arene (2h) and the Col d'Arsine (3h30). You may well have to walk almost to the pass to find **Ptarmigan** and **Alpine Accentor** but many other species will be seen within the first hour – walking at birding speed!

This footpath at first runs through a damp area of shrubby Green Alder *Alnus viridis*. Breeding birds here include **Redpoll** (numerous), **Marsh Warbler, Lesser Whitethroat, Tree Pipit, Ring Ouzel and Whinchat** – all very easy to see. **Black Grouse** skulk under the bushes and are only likely to be seen or heard very early in the morning. Marmots are numerous; look for Chamois and Roe Deer on the slopes above. **Golden Eagle** can suddenly appear over the ridges; the Ecrins Park has a healthy population (37 pairs) of this species, as well as both **Red and Yellow-billed Choughs**. After the alder bushes thin out, there is a stretch across bare alpine meadow, with plenty of **Water Pipits** and **Northern Wheatear**, until you reach a viewpoint overlooking the Lautaret glacier and the valley of the Romanche river. From now on the track runs up through rock and scree. **Alpine Accentors** and later **Snow Finch** may be seen but it will need a long, and not very rewarding walk as far as birds are concerned but through breathtaking scenery.

An easier alternative to find the latter species is to return to the COL DE LAUTARET and take the D902 road for 8 km up to the COL DE GALIBIER, some 500 m higher. Do not be put off by the number of cars and cyclists also going up; Snowfinch seem unbothered by tourists. Drive first to the top of the pass; it looks as rocky and barren as Lautaret was grassy and green but interesting alpine plants (Primula, Ranunculus, Anemone and Androsace species) grow among the scree. The pass is usually just too crowded with people for birds but check while admiring the view; on a clear day you can see as far as Mont Blanc. Drive down back towards Lautaret and park beside a large building named "Chalet de Galibier". From beyond the car-park you can walk a little way towards the cliffs, which still have snow patches beneath them in July. **Snow Finch** are often flying and feeding around these, sometimes together with **Black Redstart** and **Alpine Accentor** while **Alpine (or Yellow-billed) Chough** wheel above. Two kilometres further down there is another place to pull off the road. Checks the rocks on the right bank for **Snowfinch** and the cliff faces on the left for **Wallcreeper** (though there are often too many climbers). It is also possible to walk the old track to the Galibier Pass, starting from just below the avalanche tunnel on the Briançon side of the Lautaret Pass. It leads upwards to these cliffs and all the same birds can be seen, with the addition of **Rock Bunting** and **Grey Wagtail**. Again, early morning is best, before the climbers arrive.

Some 7 km from the top of the Lautaret Pass, going down towards Briançon, there is a track climbing steeply north towards some more cliffs opposite the "Auberge les Amis" on the right. You will recognise the place by the cars parked on both sides of the road and the "Via Ferrata" sign, which means that it is a climbing trail. **Wallcreeper** have been found on the rock faces here but they are also very popular with climbers. **Crag Martins** can also be seen here.

Site ii.

Near the centre of **ECRINS NATIONAL PARK** is the village of **LA CHAPELLE**, a good centre from which to explore this part of the Park.

ACCESS: To reach LA CHAPELLE, take the N85 from GAP and turn onto the D985a at St. FIRMIN. La Chapelle, in the centre of a valley that penetrates deep into the heart of the park, is understandably popular with walkers and climbers. The species mentioned above can all be found near here, but with more effort.

From the centre of LA CHAPELLE a very minor road is signed to LES PORTES (1280 m). It climbs uphill through woods **(Green Woodpecker, Crossbill, Bonelli's Warbler)** to a small carpark. Walk into the centre of the village where a footpath signed to the PÉTAREL lakes leads steeply uphill on the right. It is a long, hard slog through the woods for several kilometres. At the first large clearing **Nutcracker** can often be heard and may be seen flying into the top of pines. Even in late spring it should be possible to reach the area knows as the Belvedere du Châtelard (1572 m) by a track leading off to the left after some 1.5 km. This is a good place to listen out for both **Rock Partridge** and **Black Grouse**. To find **Alpine Accentor** and **Ptarmigan**, it will be necessary to continue climbing through the forest for another couple of hours at least, until you emerge onto the scree and rocks which lead up to the lakes. This area is likely to be snow-covered until mid-summer.

Alternatively, if you do not want to climb, you can take the track following the river beyond the village of les Portes and scan the slopes on the right hand side early in the morning in the hopes of sighting **Rock Partridge** and **Black Grouse**. **Golden Eagle** can also be seen above the ridges.

The road from la Chapelle continues to and ends at GIOBERNEY, where there is a hotel and restaurant. It is a beautiful glacial cirque but too full of walkers to be good for birds, other than Choughs and the occasional raptor. Early in the morning, the scree slopes on the right-hand (south) side between la Chapelle and Gioberney may be worth searching for **Black Grouse**. There are several places to park overlooking the opposite slope.

Site iii.

The Ecrins National Park and the Queyras Regional Park are separated by the wide Durance valley. On the east bank of the Durance, just south of BRIANÇON, is a site known as the **BOIS DES AYES** (Ayes Wood). It is included in the list of "Important Bird Areas" of France because it contains several pairs of **Pygmy Owl**, besides **Nutcracker, Crossbill, Willow Tit,**

Black Woodpecker and (higher up) **Black Grouse, Ring Ouzel** and **Alpine Accentor.**

ACCESS: The starting point is the village of VILLARD-ST-PANCRACE which can be reached from minor roads leading off the N94 south of Briançon or from the main junction into the town centre. Turn into the town at the traffic lights on the N94, following the signs to the station (gare SNCF). From the station VILLARD-ST-PANCRACE is signed. In the village the D236t leads towards the summer chalets of Ayes and the small lake above it. Several forest tracks lead off this road and wind through the forest. It is well signed from Villard; follow the signs for "Les Ayes" through the village and after one kilometre the road forks. The left-hand (rough) track follows a gorge to Ayes and the lake, some 10 km higher up, or take the right-hand road and then the first turning to the left. This road eventually joins up with the gorge road. The forest between the two roads contains at least one pair of **Pygmy Owl**. Drive approximately half way along either track (about 2 km) and listen. **Pygmy Owl** usually starts calling and hunting a couple of hours before dusk throughout the year; this is the best way of locating them.

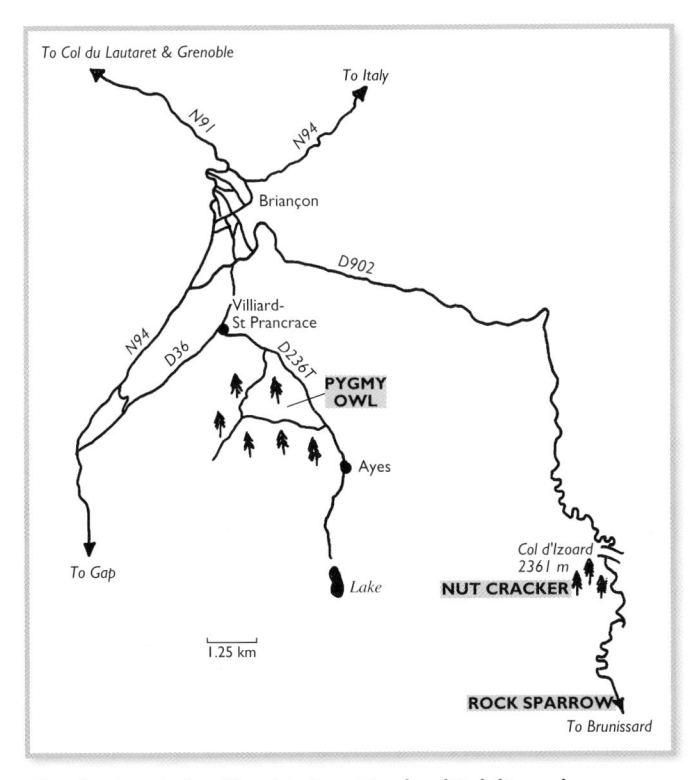

The Alps Area 2 sites iii and iv Ayes Wood and Col d'Izoard

Site iv.
The **IZOARD PASS** (2361 m) is clearly signed from the traffic lights at the Briançon-N94 junction. Follow the D902 south-east. There is **Rock Bunting** on the north side but the best birding is on the south side of the pass, where the D902 enters the Park. Listen for **Nutcracker** calling as they fly among the scattered pines. The usual alpine species can be found here, including both **Choughs, Crested Tit** and **Citril Finch**. Stop at any suitable habitat during the next few kilometres; **Nutcracker** and **Crossbill** may be found in any group of pines. There are some good cliff faces for **Wallcreeper** in the section known as the *Casse-déserte* (Landslide Desert) where jagged pinnacles rise out of bare scree. In BRUNISSARD the first village after the pass, **Rock Sparrows** can be found among the House Sparrows and **Alpine Swift** among the Common Swifts.

Accommodation: There is a small hotel at the Lautaret pass and plenty of hotels at all price ranges in Briançon. A pleasanter alternative for this region is to stay in one of the many hotels in the small skiing villages along the N91. Outside the winter season and August, advance booking should not be necessary.

La Chapelle has two hotels, several "Chambres d'hôtes" (bed and breakfast) and large campsites. The hotels are likely to be full in summer.

Area 3 **QUEYRAS NATIONAL PARK**

ACCESS: From the IZOARD PASS continue south along the D902 until it divides south of ARVIEUX. Turn left onto the D947 that runs alongside the River Guil through CHATEAU-QUEYRAS and AIGUILLES. The top of the Guil valley, the most eastern part of Queyras, forms a "finger" jutting into Italy. The village of **RISTOLAS** is the nearest centre from which to bird this region. Above Ristolas the road continues for some 6 km and finishes at a large car-park, beyond which the road is barred. Well-marked tracks lead from here through larch and pine woods to the Italian frontier and Mt. Viso (3848 m). There is a park office beside the car-park where leaflets and maps of the various trails can be obtained. **Nutcracker** can be seen near the car-park; check the top of the Arolla pines. As you follow the Guil river, you gradually climb onto more open moorland. There are **Marsh Warbler** near the river, **Crossbill** and **Crested Tit** in the conifers. **Tengmalm's Owl** is far more common than Pygmy in these woods but can usually only be heard calling in winter. They rarely appear before it is fully dark. **Black Grouse** have been studied and protected here for some years. Scan the moorland and clearings on the steep southern slopes.

Rock Partridge prefer the drier, sunny slopes opposite RISTOLAS village, which are also a good spot to see **Red-backed Shrike**. **Eagle Owl** breed in the gorge above GUILLESTRE, on the extreme west of the Park. **Dipper** can be found in the river here.

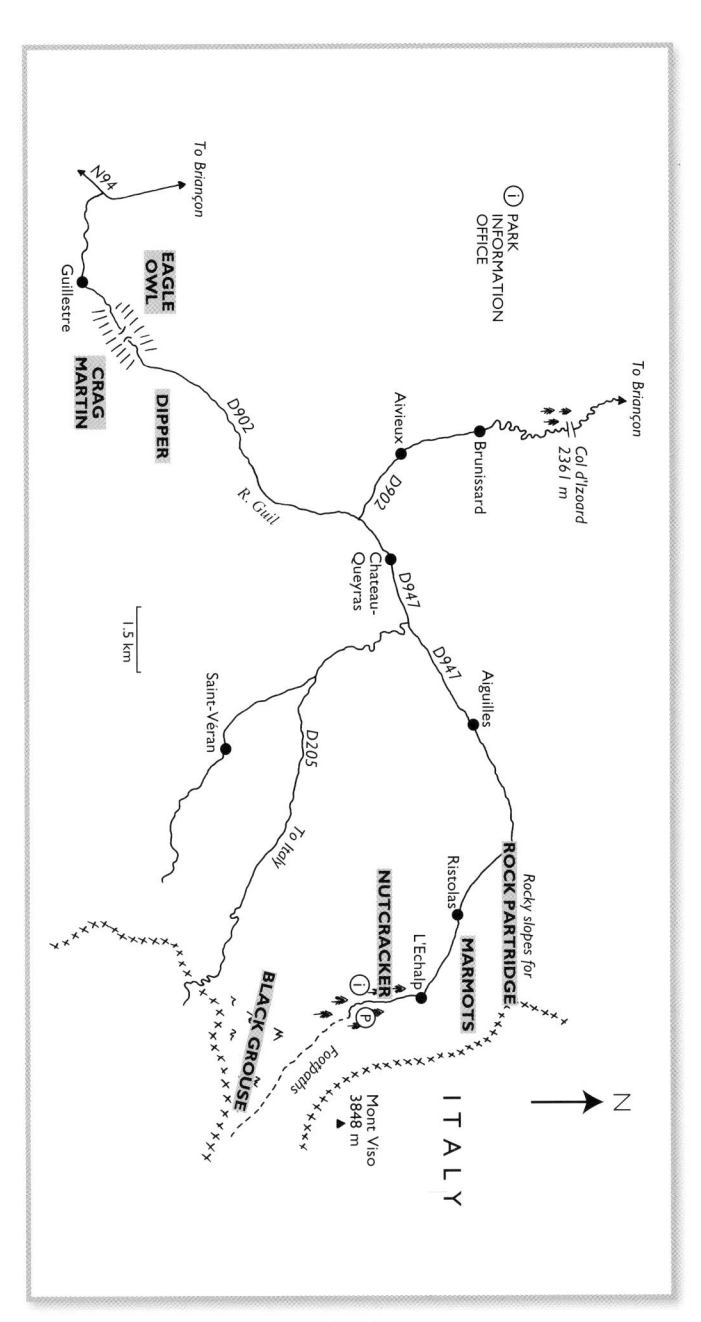

The Alps Area 3 Queyras National Park

Other fauna and flora: Marmots are numerous in both Ecrins and Queyras, especially near Ristolas. Learn to recognise their shrill whistling alarm call, which can sound disconcertingly like some unknown bird! Chamois can easily be seen on the highest slopes at both Lautaret and the Mount Viso area. Ibex have been introduced into both parks, most recently in Queyras, but numbers are small, they like the highest, north-facing slopes and so are more difficult to see except in winter when they come lower. Both parks are rich in mountain butterflies. The Apollo is widespread and common from June to August. Other species include several Skippers, including the Large Grizzled and Alpine Grizzled, Black-veined White, Mountain Clouded Yellow, Dark Green Fritillary, Rock Grayling, Dryad, Woodland, Sooty, Water and the rare Larche Ringlet (the latter in Queyras), Baton and Iolas Blue and Silvery Argus. The Spanish Moon Moth *Graellsia isabellae* is found in fir woods in Queyras. It overwinters as a pupa and flies in spring.

There are 40 rare or endangered flower species in the Ecrins and 35 endemic ones. The alpine flora at the Col de Lautaret is spectacular as late as the end of July when the meadows are a blaze of colour with blue *campanula* species, orange Hawkbit *Hieracium aurantiacum* and pink *Dianthus pavonius*, white and yellow *Helianthus* and *Potentilla* species and purple Alpine Aster *Aster alpinus*. Earlier in the summer *Viola calcarata, Vitaliana primuliflora, Dactylorhiza majalis* ssp. *alpestris*, saxifrages and androsaces will be flowering. The famous Alpine Garden at the pass is worth visiting, not only to find out the names of the flowers seen in the meadows but also for the butterflies. At the Col d'Izoard, the most striking flowers are Large-flowered Bellflower *Campanula grandiflora* and the most unobtrusive, Edelweiss. The endemic, if unexciting, *Brassica repanda* and *Thlaspi rotundifolium limosellifolium* can also be found here. Queyras is drier and sunnier so flowers there finish flowering earlier and are at their best in June, except in the highest areas.

<u>Accommodation:</u> Ristolas has two hotels; the larger one, le Queyr' de l'Ours also has dormitories for walkers, is pleasant but fairly basic, the other is a conventional *Logis de France*. Birders have recommended the Hotel L'équipe in Molines-en-Queyras.

Area 4 **THE SAVOY ALPS SAMOËNS AREA – THE MOUNTAIN RESERVES OF THE HAUTE-SAVOIE**

Site i.
The **REPOSOIR VALLEY**, lying between the Bargy and Reposoir mountain ranges south-east of Geneva, was chosen as the first **Lammergeier** release site in the French Alps because it is relatively untouched by skiing or tourism. It can also provide enough food for the birds as there are healthy populations of both Ibex and Chamois, as well as a continuing tradition of pastoralism, with sheep and cows in the alpine meadows. Since 1997 a pair of released birds has been breeding in the wild and the Reposoir Valley is probably the easiest place in the Alps to see **Lammergeier**, as well as other mountain birds such as **Yellow-billed Chough, Rock Thrush, Alpine Accentor** and **Snow Finch.**

ACCESS: Reposoir is reached by leaving the motorway A40 at the CLUSES exit and heading south on the D4, which runs down the valley. Stop in LE REPOSOIR village where in July and August there is an exhibition on the Lammergeier release scheme at the chalet "Le Prariand". Here you will be able to obtain information on recent Lammergeier sightings and breeding success.

7.5 km south of Reposoir village, the **COL DE LA COLOMBIÈRE** (1618 m) is one of the best sites. There is plenty of space to park, a shop, restaurant and maps showing walks leading from the pass. Take one of the paths leading north into the Bargy Mountains which are signed from the map beside the shop/restaurant. The paths to the "grotte Montaiguis" and the "Lac de Peyre" start together. Follow the lake path, past an old chalet where **Black Redstart** are common and **Yellow-billed Chough** can always be seen (if they are not around the carpark). It is an easy walk for most of the way to the lake (1990 m) and from it there are views over the north-west side of the Bargy range – and with luck good views of Lammergeier. Keep looking at the limestone cliffs on the skyline, especially a "square" shaped one. **Lammergeiers** can often be seen flying in front of them, together with **Ravens** and Choughs. **Water Pipit** is the commonest species as you climb higher but **Rock Thrush** is not uncommon and there are even a few **Snow Finches** in the scree around the lake.

If you do not have the time to walk far, it is quite likely that you will sight **Lammergeiers** from the old chalet or even from the carpark. Indeed the grassy slopes on the other side of the pass to the lake walk make a very good viewpoint, as all the cliffs above the pass can be seen from here.

If you want to see woodland species, such as **Crossbill** and **Crested Tit**, try searching any of the clumps of conifers on the east side of the pass or walk down a cow-track which follows a stream running north back to Reposoir down the east side of the road. It runs through conifers, shrubs and marshy patches and should add tits, finches and warblers to your species list.

Site ii.
Lammergeiers can sometimes be seen flying over the **ARAVIS** mountains on the opposite side of the Reposoir valley. Take the N205 from CLUSES to SALLANCHES and then the mountain road leading north-west towards the Chalets de Doran. There is a mountain hut, the Refuge de Doran at 1495 m, open from June to September for meals and overnight accommodation. Walks from here over the alpine meadows up to the scree slopes should enable you to see all the high mountain species, including **Lammergeier**.

Other fauna and flora: Ibex can be seen on the tops of the highest cliffs. Marmots are common among the rocks on the way up to the lake. Both Fire Salamander *Salamandra salamandra* and the all-black Alpine Salamander *Salamandra atra* can be found here, the latter up to 2500-3000 m. There are plenty of high-altitude butterflies, including Apollo and numerous Ringlets and Blues. The grassy slopes of the pass are wonderful for alpine flowers and orchids, including the rare Lady's Slipper Orchid *Cypripedium calceolus* from end-May to August.

<u>Accommodation:</u> There are two small hotels in Reposoir and several more in le Chinaillon and le Grand-Bornand, on the south side of the Col de la Colombière, as these are ski stations. Sallanches has several hotels as well as an interesting information centre on mountain wildlife and geology in the 14th century Château des Rubins, open daily.

Site iii.
The **SIXT FER-À-CHEVAL RESERVE** comprises two glacial *cirques* in one of the most beautiful parts of the Haut-Griffe Mountains right on the Swiss border. There are glaciers, high cliffs with plunging waterfalls, alpine meadows, rivers and woodland. This diversity of habitat and the altitude range from 700 to 3100 m ensures a large number of bird species.

ACCESS: Motorway A40 to CLUSES. Then the D902 to TANINGES, from there the D907 to SAMOËNS and through the town to SIXT (all well signed). The D907 continues through Sixt right up to the Fer-à-Cheval where these is parking, restaurant and visitors' centre. To visit the southern part of the reserve, take the D290 from Sixt to the Chalets de Lignon, from where footpaths lead towards Sales and Anterne.

From the FER-À-CHEVAL visitors centre, a well-signed trail leads to the Fond de la Combe, alongside a river (look out for **Dipper**) and through woodland where you may see seven species of tits, as well as woodpeckers and warblers. Where the cliffs tower up near the path, search all the wetter rock faces for **Wallcreeper**. **Alpine Swift** fly above the cliffs, together with **Crag** and **House Martins**. Keep looking over the mountains at the far end of the path, above the Combe. This is where both **Golden Eagle** and **Lammergeier** can often be seen flying. **Pygmy Owl** occurs in the woods but is very elusive; listen for them calling. From the glaciers at the foot of the Combe, paths lead steeply upwards towards the higher mountains on the Swiss border. **Alpine Accentor, Snow Finch** and with luck, **Ptarmigan**, should be found at the highest altitudes.

Site iv.

Black Grouse occur at the upper limit of the forest, where the trees thin out into alpine meadows but an easier site for this species is the **PLATEAU DE LOEX**, where it can be seen in the damp meadows and clearings within the forest (see notes for this species at end of book).

ACCESS: To reach the LOEX plateau, retrace your route on the D907 from SIXT to TANINGES and turn north onto the D902 leading to LES GETS. In 2.7 km from the junction a very minor road runs off right, directly after a hairpin bend and just before a parking sign. It is signed to the Plateau de Loex but this sign is only clearly visible after you have turned off. Follow this road through the forest. After 5 km there are some footpaths on the left or continue to a no-entry sign after 8.6 km. Check the woodland edges around all the marshy clearings.

Other fauna and flora: This is another good area for alpine flowers and therefore butterflies. Ibex can be seen on the highest rocky slopes and the Mountain Hare, which turns white in winter, is found in the reserve.

Accommodation: There are plenty of hotels and campsites in all the towns and villages named above. This is a popular tourist area both winter and summer.

Site v.

BELLEVAUX FOREST, some 20 km south of Lake Annecy, in the southern part of the Bauges Massif, is included mainly as another **Black Grouse** site. It is a beautiful part of Savoie with lower, more wooded mountains than further north. It is also quieter and much less touristy. The forest is part of the Rèserve National de faune des Banges and no hunting is allowed, so not only game birds but also forest birds and mountain animals do well. **Black Woodpecker** and **Hazelhen** can be found in the woods, together with **Short-toed Treecreeper, Crested Tit** and other tits and warblers. Where the forest thins out at its upper limits **Black Grouse** are quite numerous (though finding them entails a walk of several hours). **Ring Ouzel** can also be found at this level, **Golden Eagle** and **Alpine Chough** fly over the peaks where **Alpine Accentor** occurs. There are **Dippers** in the rivers.

ACCESS: Leave the A41 motorway south of ANNECY at exit 15 and take the D3 south to CUSY, then the D911 towards and through LE CHATELARD. Continue for another 4 km to the small village of ECOLE. Opposite the Mairie in Ecole turn left onto a minor road signed "N.D. de Bellevaux-Carlet". Near the first parking space a road leads up towards the chapel of N.D. de Bellevaux. Walk up here, at the beekeepers cross the bridge and turn left along the walking tracks towards Armene-LePecloz. It will take some six hours to reach these peaks but the woodland on the way to the chapel is good for woodland birds. Alternatively, continue along the Carlet road. It is driveable for just over 6 km from the Ecole turning to the final carpark. Here there is map showing all the walks in the reserve. It will still take several hours to walk through the forest onto the alpine meadows.

Other fauna and flora: Chamois, Mouflon and Marmots are found in the reserve. It is a good area for orchids and a typical Alpine flora grows on the higher slopes.

Area 4 THE HAUT-JURA REGIONAL PARK

Much of the Jura Mountains lie further north, outside the area of this book but the southernmost tip of the Haut-Jura Regional Park, north and east of BELLEGARDE, around COLLONGES, can be included.

Site i.
THE RÉSERVE NATURELLE OF THE HAUTE-CHAÎNE DU JURA covers over 10,000 hectares. It is a long, narrow reserve, running from above GEX in the north down almost to COLLONGES in the south, over 25 km. A long-distance footpath (GR9) runs the length of the ridge but otherwise access is limited to a few forestry roads. The reserve ranges in altitude from 700 m up to some peaks above 1770 m. The slopes are clothed with a mixture of mixed deciduous (oak and beech predominating) and coniferous trees with alpine meadows at the highest level. Birds include **Capercaillie, Hazelhen,**

Redstart

Tengmalm's Owl, Black Woodpecker and a small number of **Three-toed Woodpecker** (but see notes on these species in the "Special Birds" section at end of book). Woodland birds more likely to be seen include six species of Tit including **Crested Tit, Bonelli's Warbler, Jay, Mistle Thrush, Black Redstart.**

ACCESS: The southwest part of the reserve can be reached from the D991, which runs from BELLEGARDE through the village of LANCRANS to CONFORT. In the centre of this village turn right onto the D16 signed Menthières. This minor road climbs for 8 km to the Menthières ski station. However, at 7.2 km take the forestry track on the right by the sign for Menthières. Follow this road, taking the left fork, until it ends in a clearing where the GR yellow and red markings lead to the Crêt de la Goutte or down to Menthières. Another little-used footpath, the "Sentier de Varambon", can be found leading up through the woods on the right some 100 metres past the road fork. It is very narrow and steep in places but useful for getting deep into the forest. The right fork forestry road can only be used in summer but could be worth exploring.

The south-east slopes can be reached from the D89E, which runs north from COLLONGES to the next village of FARGES. In the centre of Farges there is a crossroads with one road leading to the D76A and the opposite one called "Route de Col de Sac". Take this road, keeping left and climbing up for 7.2 km to a mountain hut at PreBouillet (1045 m). The driveable road ends here but a GR footpath continues up to the top ridge.

Alternatively, it is possible to drive around the reserve by going north on the D984 past GEX, crossing the reserve at the Col de la Faucille (1320 m) from where both the GR footpath and more forestry roads lead south down the reserve.

Site ii.

Situated south of the Jura ridge and partly within the reserve, the **ECLUSE GORGE** on the D984 east of BELLEGARDE is a good autumn migration site as it funnels birds flying south to the Rhone valley. Throughout September and October passerines as well as both **Storks, Crane, Honey Buzzard, Buzzard, Kestrel and Sparrowhawk** pass through. In winter, **Wallcreeper** has been seen on the walls of the fort. The migration follows the normal pattern, starting with **Honey Buzzard** in August, closely followed by **Black Kite**, then in September and October come **Buzzard, Osprey**, Accipiters and storks ending with a few Cranes in November. Migrating passerines include a few **Brambling** and **Hawfinch** among the commoner **Chaffinch** and **Greenfinch**. Two forts guard the narrowest part of the gorge. The lower fort is situated just below the tunnel east of LONGERAY village on the D984. A slip-road leads off right just before the entrance to the tunnel if driving east from Bellegarde. There is parking by the entrance. Look for **Crag Martin** flying around the fort and the rocks above. Both the walls of this fort and the higher one can be scanned from the entrance. To reach the higher fort, again if coming from the direction of Bellegarde, there is small road with a "no-through" road sign on the left at the entrance to the village of LONGERAY, called "Route du Fort". It is possible to drive for half a kilometre to a barred gate. From here it is 20 minutes walk to the top fort through good oak woodland with the usual birds (see site above). The top fort is an excellent spot from where to watch migration with spectacular views both up and down stream.

In autumn and winter it may also be worth checking waders, ducks and gulls on the river from the Carnot bridge over the Rhône as they too use the river as a migration route. The bridge can be reached by taking the N206, signed to St. JULIEN-EN-GENEVOIS, which forks off right at the far end of the tunnel. It is possible to park just before the bridge, walk over it and down the narrow, minor road that forks off left immediately after the bridge and follows the left bank of the river upstream, with several openings onto the river.

Other fauna and flora: Woodland butterflies include Arran Brown, Great Banded Grayling, Black Satyr, Brown Argus and Purple Emperor. Apollo is found on the highest meadows. Lynx has returned to the Haut Jura from reintroductions in Switzerland but they are unlikely to be seen. There are also Chamois and Roe Deer.

Accommodation: There are several hotels in Bellegarde and *Logis de France* at both Lancrans and Farges.

Site iii.

CORMARANCHE-EN-BUGEY MARSH lies in the limestone hills of the lower Jura. It is only 30 km from Collonges as a bird flies but much further by road. It is included as it is a breeding site for **Corncrake**, a rare and declining species in France, while **Black Woodpecker** and **Hazelhen** are among the species found in the nearby beech-spruce woodland. The lake holds the commoner water birds such as **Great Crested** and **Little Grebe**, **Grey Heron** and **Water Rail**. **Lapwing** breed in the marsh and **Hen Harrier** may be seen over the fields nearby. **Woodcock** occur in winter.

ACCESS: BUGEY can be reached from BELLEGARDE by taking A40 motorway, leaving it at exit 8 where it joins the A404 and getting on to the D12 at St. Martin-du-Frene. Drive south for 13 km, then turn onto the D8 for HAUTEVILLE-LOMPNES, another 11 km. Take the D21 for TENAY out of this town but on the outskirts turn left onto a minor road for Bugey. It ends at a car-park beside the lake and marsh. An information board shows the walks around the lake and marsh. Walks through the marsh are only allowed from July 1 to September 15. From the information board a path leads along the right hand side of the lake. Near a red seat (after some 150 m) it is possible to walk right up through a corner of a field to the conifer-beech wood where several footpaths meet. Alternatively from the D21 opposite the NANTUY turning (some 2 km from Hauteville) take the Route Forestière de "Dergit" which leads through the wood. Turn left after 500 m and left again to reach the car-park by the lake. Or take the right fork to walk along a dead-end forest road.

Flora: There is an interesting marsh flora, best in spring, which includes Fritillaries, Sundew and Marsh Orchids. There are Common Frogs by the hundreds and Viviparous Lizard around the marsh, Roe Deer and Wild Boar in the woods. The marsh is grazed by wild Konics, small horses of Polish origin, direct descendants of the last Tarpan horses. They help keep the vegetation down.

Accommodation: There are several hotels and campsites in Hauteville.

THE CENTRE

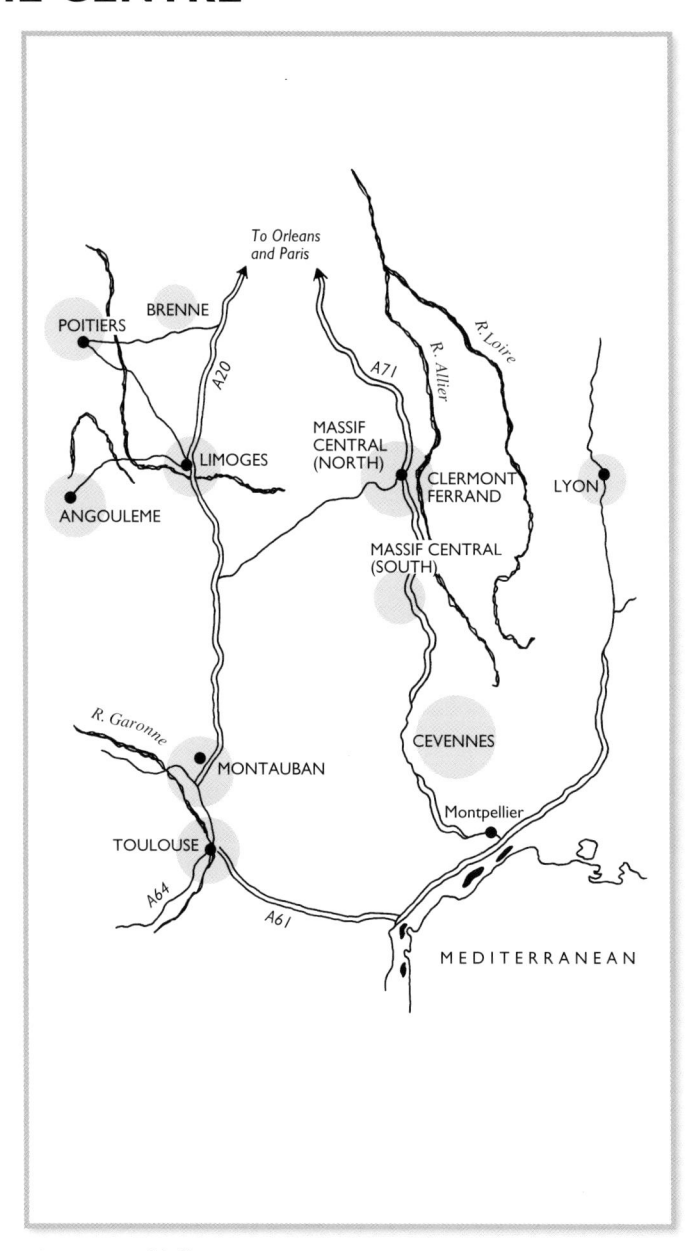

The Centre – birding areas

Area 1	**Angoulême**	
	Site i.	Branconne Forest
	Site ii.	The Touvre river
	Site iii.	The Charentes river
	Site iv.	Combourg Lake
Area 2	**Poitiers**	
	Site i.	Pinail Reserve
	Site ii.	Mouliere Forest
	Site iii.	Plains north west of Poitiers
	Site iv.	Cebron reservoir
Area 3	**The Brenne**	
	Itinerary i.	Chérine/Beauregard/Gabriere/Massé/Foucault/Rosnay
	Itinerary ii.	Lancosme Forest
	Itinerary iii.	Azay-le-Ferron
Area 4	**Limoges**	
	Site i.	Dauges Peatbog
	Site ii.	Millevaches and Longéroux Plateaux
	Site iii.	The Dordogne Gorge
Area 5	**The Northern Massif Central near Clermont-Ferrand**	
	Site i.	Chaudefour Reserve
	Site ii.	Sancy massif near Mont Dore
	Site iii.	Ancient craters of Vache and Lassolas
	Site iv.	Serre migration watchpoint
	Site v.	The Allier river
Area 6	**The Southern Massif Central**	
	Site i.	Monts de Cantal
	Site ii.	Lascols marsh
	Site iii.	The Truyère river
	Site iv.	Gorges de l'Allier
Area 6	**Lyons**	
	Site i.	The Dombes
	Site ii.	Migration watchpoint near Bourg-en-Bresse
	Site iii.	Parc de Miribel-Jonage
	Site iv	The Mont du Lyonais
	Site v.	Etang du Grand-Lemps Reserve
	Site vi.	Lavours marsh
Area 7	**Montauban**	
	Site i.	The Aveyron river and châteaux at Bruniquel and Penne
	Site ii.	Grésigne National Forest
	Site iii.	The Garonne river at Saint-Nicholas-de-la Grave

Area 8	**Toulouse**	
	Site i.	Parc Naturel de Confluent Ariège/Garonne
	Site ii.	Bouconne Forest
	Site iii	Cambounet-sur-le-Sor Bird Reserve
Area 9	**Cévennes National Park**	
	Site i.	Blandas Causse
	Site ii.	Gorges of the Tarn and Jonte
	Site iii.	Méjean Causse
	Site iv.	Mont Lozère
	Site v.	Mont Aigoual
	Site vi.	Dourbie Gorge

The huge area of France named the Centre in this guide does not refer to the region of that name (it includes only the southern part of it) nor is it just the Limousin -Auvergne region, but also covers the northern part of the Midi-Pyrenees, the eastern sides of Aquitaine, Poitou Charentes and Pays de la Loire and the west of Burgundy and the Rhone-Alpes; in fact, all the centre of France south of the River Loire that lies away from the Atlantic and Mediterranean coasts, the Alps and the Pyrenees.

Although this is such a large area much of it (outside the **MASSIF CENTRAL** and the **CÉVENNES**) is intensively farmed and there are very few outstanding sites apart from the **BRENNE** and the **DOMBES** lakes north of Lyon. These are wetland areas and many of the other sites in the centre are near rivers or reservoirs. In addition, some of the largest forests in France lie in this region and in them can be found **Black, Great, Middle and Lesser Spotted, Green and Grey-headed Woodpeckers**. The difficulty here is that the areas covered with woodland are so enormous that finding small parts of them that are accessible, not hunted over, and which hold all the species British birders want to see, is almost impossible. The Brenne, Poitiers and Angloulême areas all contain good woodland sites. The few areas of meadow and moorland that are not intensively cultivated hold rapidly declining populations of **Little Bustard**, as well as **Stone Curlew, Short-toed Lark, Woodchat Shrike** and **Ortolan Bunting. Montagu's Harriers** breed in cereal fields which, increasingly, **Stone Curlew** are also using. **Nightjars** and **Hen Harriers** occur in moorland areas and **Crested Tits** and **Crossbills** in coniferous woodland. **Savi's, Sedge, Reed** and **Great Reed Warblers** breed in reedbeds.

Of course, as a very large percentage of this area is still predominantly agricultural land, a good number of the more common bird species will be found throughout the region: **Crested Larks, Black Redstarts, Corn** and **Cirl Buntings** occur almost everywhere in suitable habitat, **Rock Buntings** in hilly areas; **Golden Orioles** nest in tall poplar groves, especially along rivers, **Buzzards** are very common and **Honey Buzzards** and **Black Kites** relatively so in forest areas, where **Bonelli's Warblers** and **Short-toed Treecreepers** are also widespread. In appropriate habitat so are **Nightingales, Meadow** and **Tree Pipits** and **Red-backed Shrikes**. To help locate some of the best sites, they have been somewhat loosely grouped together around large towns, which make convenient centres, and while some sites are quite close to the towns, others may be 50 or so kilometres away. However, it does mean that if you are staying in an area, you can quickly see what birding sites are within driving or public transport distance.

Area 1 **ANGOULÊME**

Besides the plains area between Angoulême and Niort (described under NIORT – Atlantic Coast site 14), there are two river sites and a good forest very close to the city of Angoulême.

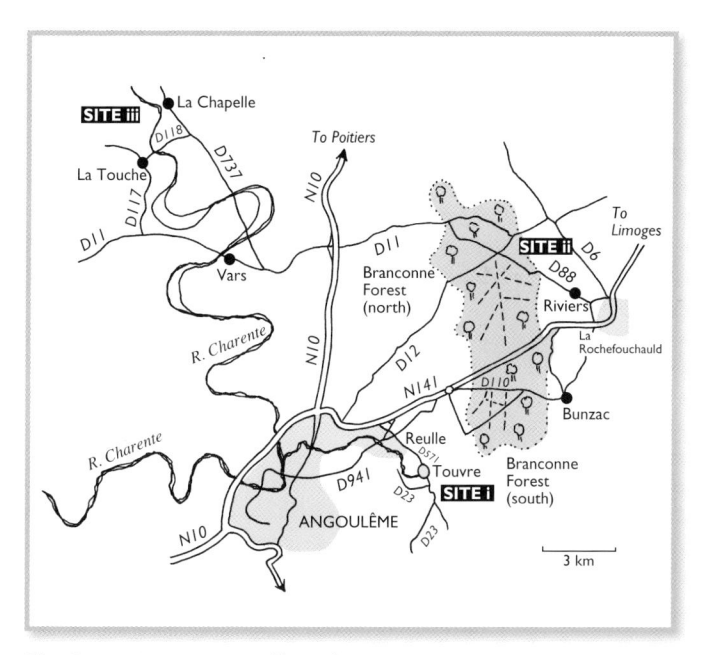

The Centre Area 1 – Angoulême Sites

Site i.
BRANCONNE FOREST lies some 15 km north-east of Angoulême, crossed by the N141 leading to la Rouchefoucauld and eventually Limoges. It

is primarily a woodpecker site, with **Great, Middle** and **Lesser Spotted, Grey-headed, Green** and **Black** (a fairly recent coloniser) all breeding there, so the notes given under these species in the "Special Species" section at the back of the book should be read before setting out to look for them. In addition, raptors breeding in the forest include **Buzzard, Honey Buzzard, Short-toed Eagle, Black Kite, Goshawk, Sparrowhawk, Montagu's** and **Hen Harriers**, the two last in some of the newly-planted and open areas where **Nightjar** can also be found. Three *Phylloscopus* warblers breed: **Bonelli's, Wood,** and **Chiffchaff; Nightingale** and **Redstart** are other summer breeders and tits include **Crested**. Look for **Bonelli's Warbler** and **Crested Tit** in the conifers. **Nuthatch** is very common and **Short-toed Treecreeper** is easy to find.

WHEN TO VISIT: Woodpeckers, though resident, are always easier to locate early in the year. **Hen Harriers** can also be seen year round, even in winter. Spring (April and May especially) is probably the best birding time when all the summer breeders have returned, males are singing and newly-arrived **Montagu's Harriers** and **Honey Buzzards** may be displaying. **Black Kites** arrive earlier.

ACCESS: The south side of the forest is easiest reached from the N141 dual-carriageway from Angoulême. Turn off at the first junction after the Ruelle roundabout, signed to BUNZAC and the Military Camp. Turn right onto the D105 in the direction of Bunzac and Rancogne and then take the first right, (unsigned but with a "*Toutes Directions*" sign pointing in the opposite way) 0.7 km after the junction. Park at the first Forestry dirt track and walk some way into the forest, here mainly composed of Oak with some large trees. **Great** and **Middle Spotted** can be found quite close to the road. This Forestry track turn left and loops back to the tarmac road which finished at a dead end near the Maison Forestier de Rassats.

Return to the D105, continue south and then turn left onto the D110 towards Bunzac. There is a parking area and some good, large trees on the corner. Explore this part of the forest too.

The north side of the forest covers a larger area and can be reached from the D12, which branches off the dual-carriageway N141 at the first junction east of the N10. In 13 km it reaches the cross roads with the D88, the Rond-point de la Combe, a good area for birds with several forestry tracks leading off from here. Alternatively take the D88 from LA ROCHEFOUCAULD towards JAULDES, and in 7.5 km you will arrive at the same cross roads. The Rond-point Limousin and the Forester's house of the same name at the next road junction in the direction (south-east) of La Rochefoucauld, has a notice board with a map of the forest. Walk down the track beyond this board, turn right and right again to make a short triangular walk. This part of the forest is composed mainly of Beech and **Black Woodpecker** has been seen here, as well as **Lesser Spotted Woodpecker**. **Crested Tit** can be found in the conifers near the information board, as well as **Bonelli's Warbler**. Look out for **Hawfinch** near the forester's house in spring. It is also worth walking down the tracks on the opposite side to the information board.

The D88 to the north-west of its junction with the D12 runs through some clearings and nearly planted areas, good for **Hen Harrier** and **Nightjar** and allowing views over the forest for other raptors.

Almost any of the forestry tracks, especially ones that lead through mature trees, are worth exploring. Often it is not necessary to walk very far to hear and see birds; many species prefer woodland fringes to the dense centre, unless there are clearings. If you visit the forest in winter, during the hunting season, make sure that you read the notices near the entrances, giving the days when hunting takes place, usually Friday or weekends. Avoid these days. When Wild Boar or deer are being hunted with dogs, notices are placed along the roadside. It is very dangerous to ignore them and walk beyond these points.

Site ii.

The **RIVER TOUVRE** rises to the surface just south of Angoulême forming a lake before it flows north-west into the Charente. The water is clear and shallow, attracting dozens of **Little Grebe** and **Moorhen**. **Kingfisher, White** and **Grey Wagtails, Lesser Spotted and Green Woodpeckers** can be seen all year round. Check the trees near the car park for **Short-toed Treecreeper**. **Golden Oriole** breed in the surrounding trees in summer and in winter **Siskin** may be seen feeding on the Alders. **Water Rail** is usually found further downstream. In spring many migrants, both waders and passerines, stop over here and the area around the lake is good for commoner passerines at all times of the year.

ACCESS: The "Sources of the Touvre" are well signed from RUELLE. Turn off the N141 into Ruelle and then follow the *"Sources"* signs along the D57 for almost 3 kms to the car park. Walk down to the lake. When you have finished birding this area it is possible to visit some other sites further along the river.

Turn right out of the car park, cross the railway line and immediately right again onto the D408. Turn right onto the D23 at the junction. Continue along the D23 as it bends sharply right towards MAGNAC. Cross the railway line again. Immediately after the level crossing, a narrow lane leads off right towards the *"Pres de la Curée"*. If you can park and walk down here there is a close view of the other side of the lake. Otherwise continue on into Magnac and turn right at the traffic lights onto the D699. Cross the bridge and park either on the right pavement or turn left into a small parking area on the north bank. You can view the river from here (a good spot for Water Rail) or walk back onto the bridge for a view up and down river.

It is also possible to reach the riverbank from the sports ground. Turn back over the bridge in the direction of Ruelle and turn right just before the railway. Continue on this road with the railway running on your left, following the signs for *"Complex sportif"*. There is parking beside the *"Salle Communale"* right beside the river.

Hobby

Site iii.

In Angoulême the **RIVER CHARENTES** turns sharply west to flow to the sea. For a 20 km stretch north of the town, the river, dividing into several channels, loops its way across the plain. There are several places where a minor road crosses it, and some of these afford good birdwatching in spring. The area is important as the endangered and declining **Corncrake** breeds in the water meadows. The birds return in April-May and the male's characteristic "crex-crex" call can be heard at dusk and very early in the morning. **Kingfisher, Golden Oriole** and **Red-backed Shrike** also breed along the river and **Black Kite** and **Honey Buzzard** may be seen overhead. Many species use the river valley during migration periods.

ACCESS: The D11 from JAULDES crosses the river at VARS to PORTAL on the opposite bank and minor roads lead north from these villages close to the river. The D115 runs north to MONTIGNAC, where there are other bridges. From VARS, take the D11 to BASSE and turn north onto the D117, through BIGNAC to LA TOUCHE/le Pontour, where there is another bridge and some wet meadows. There is suitable habitat along this stretch of the D117, although old meadows are being turned over to maize. Cross the bridge at la Touche onto the D118 and in 2 km left onto the D737 to LA CHAPELLE, also on the river.

Site iv.

Another lake, much further north, is included with the Angoulême sites for convenience, although it lies roughly equidistant between Angoulême, Limoges and Poitiers. Anyone going towards either of the two latter towns might like to make a detour to take it in. **COMBOURG LAKE** near

PRESSAC is the largest of several, dotted around an agricultural, wooded area. It has quite a large reedbed but at the far end of the lake, to which access is very difficult if not impossible. However, it can be scoped. **Grey** and **Purple Heron**, **Kingfisher**, **Reed**, **Sedge**, **Cetti's** and **Savi's Warblers** breed there, **Red-backed Shrike**, **Hen** and **Montagu's Harriers** nearby. **Honey Buzzard** and **Black Kite** can often be seen around the lake and the occasional **Osprey** may stop off on migration, as well as marsh terns and waders. In winter there are numerous duck and Cormorants on the lake, flocks of **Lapwing, Corn Bunting, Meadow Pipit** and **Skylark** in surrounding fields. The woods around the lake have several species of warblers and other woodland birds during the breeding season.

ACCESS: PRESSAC is at the junction of the D148 and the D741, 12 kms north-west of CONFOLENS. In Pressac turn north onto the D741, direction Gençay. 2 km from the D741 junction, turn left (west) onto a very minor road with small wooden signs to "Combourg" and Circuit D'oil & D'oc". 200 m from the road take the right fork, signed Combourg. In 2 km you will see a dirt track on the left with the same signs. A 500 metre walk down the track alongside a wood will bring you to the edge of the lake. (The Etang de Ponteil signed nearer to Pressac is normally devoid of birds).

Accommodation: Angoulême has hotels in all price ranges; several of the cheaper ones are situated right beside the N10 alongside the supermarkets just north of the town. La Rochefoucauld, some 20 km to the north-east, is a charming small town with a magnificent chateau and a much pleasanter place to stay as well as being convenient for the sites above. It has a *Logis*, the Vieux Auberge and several restaurants.

Area 2 **POITIERS**

Site i.
Though Poitiers is only some 100 km from the Brenne, a much better birding area, anyone spending some time in this region (or who has left the family at Futuroscope) might like to take in some of the Poitiers sites. Some 20 km to the north-east, **PINAIL RESERVE**, a peat-bog heathland at the northern end of the huge Moulière Forest, is certainly worth visiting as it is one of the best places in central France to watch **Hobbies** hawking dragonflies on summer evenings and **Montagu's** and **Hen Harriers** (some 20 pairs breed here) displaying or passing food to their mates. Additionally, **Dartford Warbler** (some 200 pairs), **Linnet, Stonechat** and **Grasshopper Warbler** may be found among the gorse and heath, **Tree Pipit** around scattered trees, **Short-toed Treecreeper** in the woods and **Short-toed Eagle** hovering overhead. At dusk **Nightjar** start calling from the heath.

During the eighteenth and nineteenth centuries rock for mill-stones was

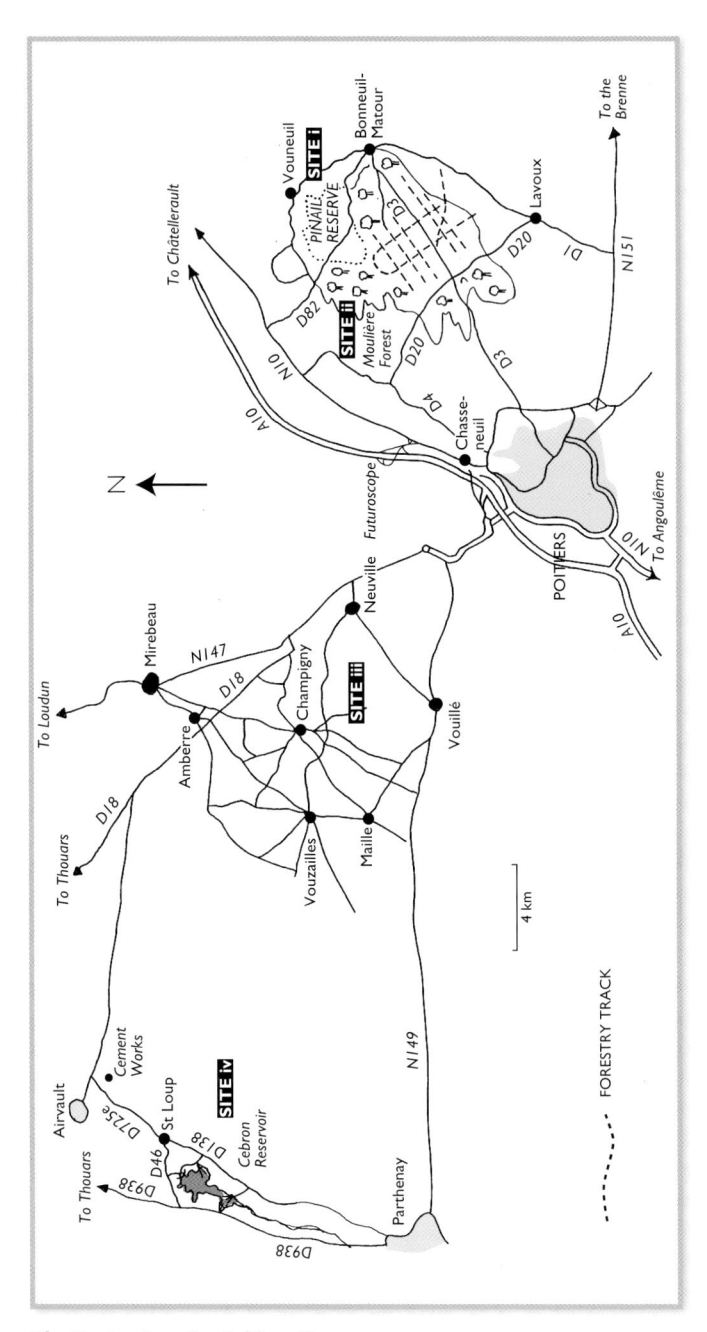

The Centre Area 2 – Poitiers Sites

dug from here, resulting in more than three thousand deep, water-filled craters scattered among the heath and gorse – a unique landscape.

WHEN TO VISIT: This is definitely a spring and summer site. Species numbers are increased by migrants passing through in April-May and at the end of summer.

ACCESS: The nearest village is VOUNEUIL-SUR-VIENNE and from here the Reserve is clearly signed. To reach Vouneuil, take the D3 through Moulière Forest to BONNEUIL-MATOURS. Turn north onto the D1; the Reserve and Vouneuil are signed. Continue following the Reserve signs through Vouneuil village to the car park, a thatched shelter with picnic tables and a large information board showing the three marked trails which vary from a very short one of some 600 m to a long 5 km one. The intermediate *Sentier de la découverte* is recommended for a short visit. It can be very wet underfoot in bad weather and beware of the potholes – they are so deep a horse can disappear if it falls into one.

Other fauna and flora: 48 species of Dragonfly (out of the 90 found in France) occur here. Four-spotted Chaser and Downy Emerald are both common and a favourite prey of Hobbies. Rarer ones include White-faced Dragonfly *Leucorrhinia dubia* and *Leucorrhinia caudalis*, *Sympecma fusca*, *Lestes barbarus*, *Platycnemis pennipes*, *Ceriagrion tenellum*, *Brachytron pratense*. Marbled Newt breeds here and several toads and frogs including Natterjack and Parsley Frog as well as the tree frog *Hyla arborea*. Red Deer can be found feeding here as well as in the forest.

450 species of plants are found in Pinail, including 4 nationally protected ones. Summer Lady's Tresses *Spiranthes aestivalis* is the rarest and there are several carnivorous plants: Sundew *Drosera rotundifolia*, Pale Butterwort *Pinguicula lusitanica*, Bladderworts *Utricularia minor* and *U. australis*. The dominant heath is *Erica scoparia* but there are three other Erica species including Cornish Heath *E. vagans* as well as Heather *Calluna vulgaris* and Dwarf Gorse *Ulex minor*.

Site ii.

MOULIERE FOREST to the south of Pinail is a huge mixed forest of Oak, Beech, Hornbeam and many conifer plantations. **Honey Buzzard** breeds there as does **Buzzard; Black, Great and Lesser Spotted Woodpeckers** can be found in the more mature strands; **Nightjars** occur in the cleared area, on the north side adjoining Pinail and **Cranes** can sometimes be seen in this area in November or early March when on migration. **Nuthatch, Short-toed Treecreeper** and **Long-tailed Tit** are common, **Crested Tit** can be found in the conifer plantations along with a few **Coal Tit, Goldcrest** and **Bonelli's Warbler**.

WHEN TO VISIT: Woodpeckers are always easiest to find in winter or early spring but for most other species April to June, when **Honey Buzzard** may be displaying and **Nightjars** are calling, is probably the best time.

ACCESS: If coming from Pinail on the D15, turn left onto the D85 at BONDILLY, back towards Bonneuil-Matours. This road runs between the southern boundary of Pinail and the forest and there are many open areas. This is where **Cranes** and **Nightjar** may be seen, as well as **Hobby**. Just outside Bonneuil, turn right onto the D3, which leads back south-west into the forest. After 5 km the first of the hard-surfaced foresters' roads crosses the D3. The first is named du Défens and it may be worth parking and walking along it to the right (north-west). More productive normally are the dirt tracks (*sommières*), that lead off these roads, forming a grid. In another 3 km the D20 crosses the D3. Turn right onto the D20 and walk a little way up the *sommières* that lead off it. The Gouffre de Grand Soubis can be a good area as there are old Beech trees growing there. Of course, it is possible to take a longer walk around a complete square of tracks. There are a lot of conifer plantations and younger trees in the north-west sector, so this does not seem to be so good for woodpeckers.

A *Maison de la Forêt* is signed at the D3 and D20 crossroads; it is a short

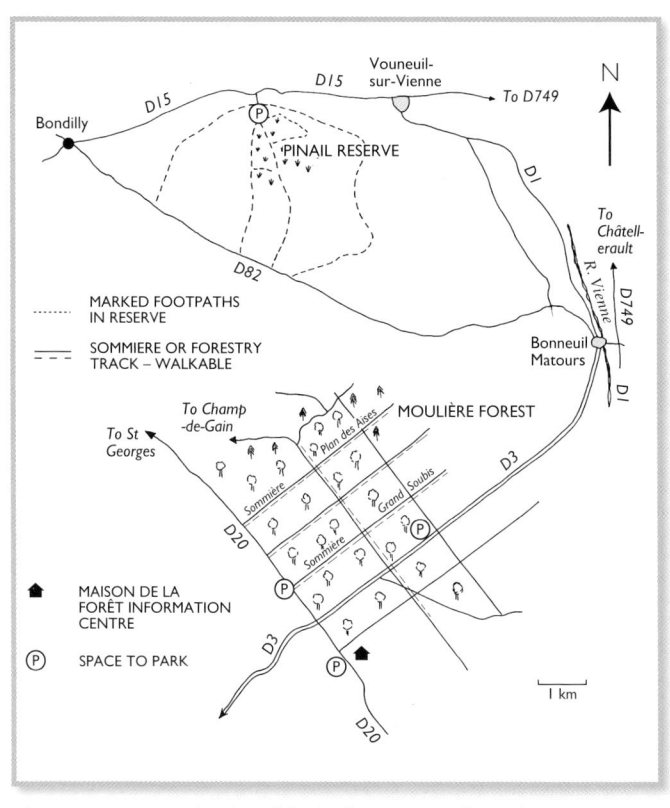

The Centre Area 2 sites i. and ii Pinail Reserve and Mouliere Forest

way down to the left (south-east). It is an information centre and refreshments can be obtained there.

Site iii.

To the north-west of Poitiers is a plains area where **Little Bustard** and **Stone Curl**ew can be looked for in summer. It is also a good area for **Montagu's Harrier** between May and August. As on the Niort plains, the two former species flock here before migrating, so in September and early October there may be flocks of several hundred birds.

ACCESS: Take the N147 out of Poitiers towards NEUVILLE-DE-POITOU (10 km from the outskirts) and MIREBEAU (14 km further north). North of NEUVILLE turn left onto any minor road leading to the villages of le Rochereau, Champigny, Vouzailles, Massognes or Amberre. Drive slowly along the network of narrow roads linking these villages, scanning the cereal fields around. Check the uncultivated patches for **Stone Curlew**. Dusk is the best time as **Little Bustards** often fly then and **Stone Curlew** start calling. South of Amberre, on the D24, is an interesting area for fossils. A marked trail shows not only the rock formations (falun) but skirts some small coppices and vineyards, where woodland birds may be found. Look for **Ortolan Bunting** in the scrubby, rocky areas. **Scops Owl** can be heard at night around the villages where there are trees. In winter there may be large flocks of **Lapwing** and **Golden Plover**, as well as many larks and pipits, in the ploughed fields, if the waders are not all at the next site.

Site iv.

Further north-west still, beyond PARTHENAY, is the last Poitiers site, the **CEBRON RESERVOIR**. This large dammed lake can be particularly good in winter and early spring. There are very often large numbers of **Lapwing** and **Golden Plover** on the banks as well as **Snipe** and other waders during migration periods. Duck species normally include **Mallard, Gadwall, Wigeon, Teal, Pochard** and **Tufted Duck**. **Cormorant, Black-headed** and **Yellow-legged Gull** are other wintering species and **Stone Curlew** may be seen around the edge in spring. **Greylag Geese** may stop off here during their migration north and the hedgerows and bushes around the lake hold good numbers of smaller birds.

ACCESS: From Poitiers, or the plains area described in site iii, take the D18, which runs through the plains west of MIREBEAU, and fork left off it onto the D725 to AIRVAULT (25 km from Mirebeau). On the outskirts of AIRVAULT turn left onto the D725e which runs south past large cement works to St. LOUP. Take the D138 out of this village. In 3 km turn right onto a minor road signed *Barrage du Cebron*. Pull off the road at 0.8 (right beside another *Barrage du Cebron* sign. There is a good view from here over the most productive part of the lake but a 'scope is needed for the far side. The dam is a further 1.4 km along this road. There are parking, toilets and a picnic area by the dam but not always too many water birds! However, it is possible to walk a short way around the lake from here and the area can be good for passerines, especially during migration periods, when wagtails, buntings, chats, redstarts and flycatchers join the resident species. If you wish to view the far side of the lake, drive across the dam, in just over a kilometre turn left onto the D46 and after 1.7 km left again onto the larger D938 (direction PARTHENAY). At the D137 crossroads (signed Oefeuille) in 1.3 km turn left and immediately right onto an unsigned no-through road. This runs down towards the lake for just over a kilometre and ends at the Jinchères lakeside carpark, used by fishermen. In spring this can be a good site for raptors hunting over the lake, especially **Black Kite** but also **Buzzard** and perhaps **Honey Buzzard, Sparrowhawk** and **Kestrel**. **Nightingale** and **Melodious Warbler** are among the species that breed in the bushes nearby.

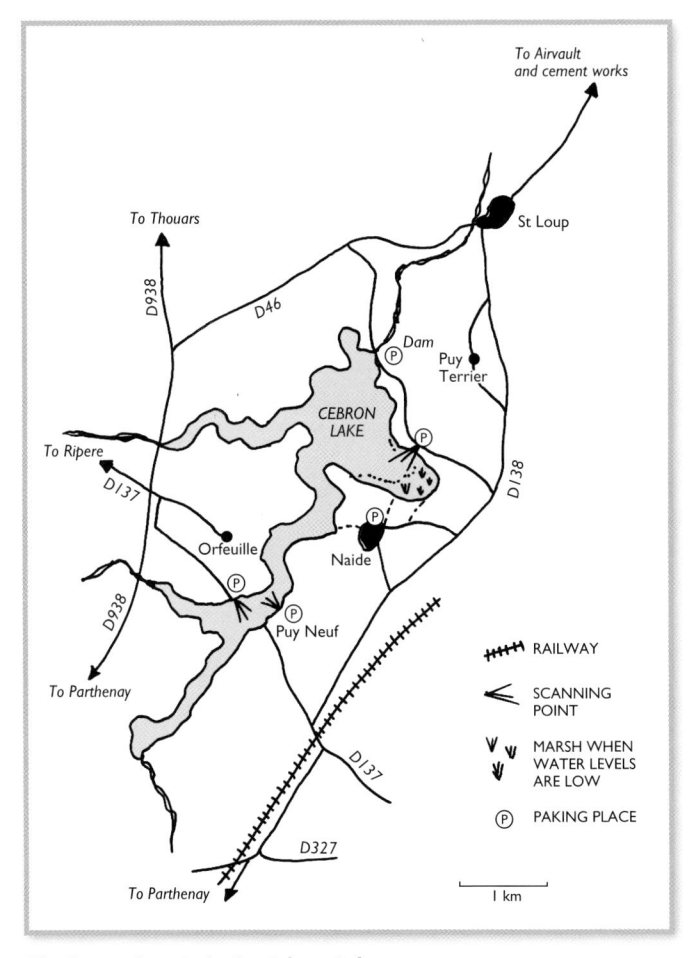

The Centre Area 2 site iv. Cebron Lake

Puy Neuf, another parking area for fishermen, is on the opposite side of the lake to Jinchères. If most birds are on the far side, then it may be worth driving back over the dam, past the first site and turning south when you reach the D138. Take the next turning right (north) after the Naide turnings (though, with a short walk, the lake can be viewed from Naide). Puy Neuf car park is signed.

Accommodation: Several hotels, including cheap ones, can be found near Futuroscope, north of Poitiers between the A10 motorway and the N10, as well as two good ones in the village of Chasseneuil, a little further south. There are a couple of small hotels in Bonneuil-Matours and Vouneuil, handy for Pinail.

Area 3 THE BRENNE

The Parc Natural Régional de la Brenne contains thousands of lakes (over 1200 at the last count) covering some 10,000 hectares. They are all man-made, are used for fishing and fish-farming and continue to increase in number, although water levels are dependent on weather conditions and reed-beds are cleared from existing lakes to increase fish productivity. During long periods of drought (as occurred between 1988 and 1992) many lakes will dry up partially or completely. Currently water-levels are high but any lake varies from season to season and from one year to the next, depending on many factors, so local, up-to-date information is very useful (see below). In addition to the lakes and reedbeds, both large and small, there are a great variety of other habitats: moorland, meadows, cereal fields, woodland and scrub. It is therefore not surprising that bird species recorded there number over 280, mammals 60, reptiles and amphibians 26, dragonflies and butterflies over 60 each and wild flowers, including several rare species, are abundant; 1000 plants, out of the 4672 found in France, grow in the Brenne.

ACCESS: The Brenne lies west of Chateauroux (the nearest railway station 2 hours from Austerlitz, Paris) and east of Poitiers. It is approximately three hours by car from Paris. The best birding areas lie between the villages of MÉZIÈRES-EN-BRENNE and ROSNAY in the north of the Park. Chateauroux is some 45 kms and Poitiers 80 km from here and there is only a very limited daily bus service from these towns to the above villages. If travelling by car, leave the A10 north of Poitiers, take the ring road to the east and exit onto the N151 for le Blanc, which is inside the Park, and finally take the D27 towards Rosnay. Alternatively, get off the A10 at Chatellerault and take the D725 to Azay-le-Ferron and then the D925 to Mézières. From Chateauroux, leave the A20 at Chateauroux centre and go west on the N143 to Buzançais, then towards Mézières on the D926.

The Brenne is an excellent, mainly flat area to explore by bike. Cycles can be hired from the Tourist Office in Mézières-en-Brenne: "Le Moulin", 1 rue du Nord, 36290 MÉZIÈRES Tel: 02 54 38 12 24 as well as in LE BLANC – 75 rue Villebois Mareuil, 36300 le Blanc. Tel: 02 54 37 36 85 and 2 Quai André Liesse, 36300 le Blanc Tel: 02 54 37 19 21.

WHEN TO VISIT: The Brenne is of interest at any time of the year but April to mid-July and the beginning of October to mid-November are the best times, although the autumn is of less interest to British birders. To do the area justice a week's stay is recommended but it is possible to bird the Mézières-Rosnay area in a weekend or even see quite a number of species in one long day of intensive birding.

Maps: The Tourist Offices have an excellent free one of the Park. Recta-foldex 3 (Pays du Loire) covers the whole area and much more. The Maison du Parc produces a very useful book giving information with sketch maps on walks, bike rides, the best lakes to visit, lists of hotels and restaurants etc.

The Park has a resident English naturalist, Tony Williams, who works in the area for the LPO. He can be contacted through the Parc headquarters at Le Bouchet, Rosnay. Tel: 02 54 28 12 13 or by writing to him, c/o PNR de la Brenne, Le Bouchet, 36300 Rosnay. He would be pleased to give information on where to go and what to see. The Maison du Parc, at le Bouchet, lists current bird species and will also give helpful advice. Le Bouchet is a picturesque small village a few kilometres northwest of Rosnay just off the D32. The Maison is well signed and is open everyday from 10 to 18 hrs (longer during the summer). Besides giving up–to-date information on wildlife, the Visitors' Centre has a sales area for local produce and natural history books as well as a bar where local food is served. By the end of 2000 there will be a new visitors' centre at Cherine, especially for naturalists, next to the D6a/D17 crossroads.

The Brenne should be explored following the order of the itineraries given below. If short of time concentrate on the first one (or just part of it).

Itinerary i.
MÉZIÈRES – CHÉRINE RESERVE – BEAUREGARD – GABRIERE AND GABRIAU – MASSÉ – FOUCAULT LAKES – ROSNAY.

Obviously this itinerary can be followed in the reverse order; the hide at Cherine is best in the early morning or early evening and the walk around the new lakes on the west side of the Reserve in late afternoon. If returning to Mézières, start the morning in the Chérine hide and return to the new lakes at the end of the day.

Leave MÉZIÈRES going south taking first the D15 and then after 2.5 km branch right onto the D17. In another kilometre or so you will see the car park for CHÉRINE National Nature Reserve. Cherine has one of the last remaining extensive reedbeds in the Brenne. It is managed (by grazing and creating new scrapes) to encourage as many species as possible to breed and feed there. Park

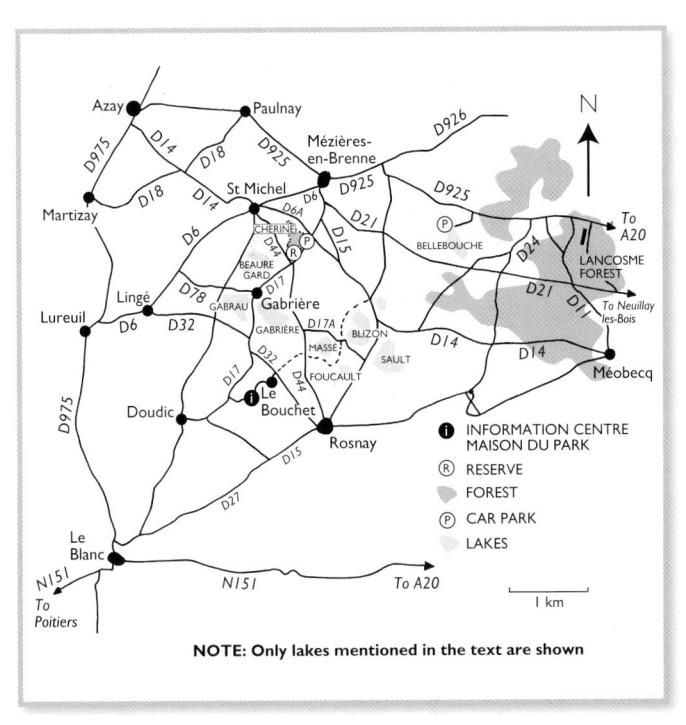

The Centre Area 3 – The Brenne – Sites. Note: only lakes mentioned in text are shown

and walk to the tower hide a short distance away. Early morning is the best time, so start your itinerary here. Chérine is good for **Little Bittern, Bittern, Purple Heron, Marsh Harrier, Savi's** (not rare but rather local) and **Great Reed Warbler** (rarer) in spring and summer. **Bearded Tit** are usually easier to see in autumn and winter. At the latter season it is not unusual to see Wild Boar lying around the lakeside – they presumably know they are safe here! It is also a good spot to see European Pond Terrapins sunning themselves once hibernation is over. **Black Woodpecker** can sometimes be heard in the woods around the car-park.

Having spent as long as wanted at the hide, return to the D17. (If you want to see the new lakes take the next turn right onto the D44 in the direction of ST. MICHEL-EN-BRENNE. Access is from the communal footpath that runs along the Reserve. However this side is better in the afternoon, so it might be best to continue the tour and return to this part of Chérine in the late afternoon.) Continue on the D17 until the BEAUREGARD Lake can be seen on your right. There is a footpath running along the southern side of the lake; this is quite a long walk but it may be worth doing the first part and scoping the lake from a good viewpoint. In spring there may be **Whiskered Tern** as well as

Black-necked Grebe, which breed in the Brenne. There are plenty of duck in winter.

Continue along the D17 to the crossroads with the D78. Turn right and follow the GABRIAU lake for a kilometre or so. Stop wherever there is a lay-by to see what is on the lake. In autumn, there are often waders along the muddy edges. Walk along the road for a stretch before returning to the crossroads. Go straight over, still on the D78. There are several places to park and the walk along the edge of GABRIÈRE lake. When the water-level is right, this can be one of the best lakes. **Black-necked Grebe** are frequent and there may be both **Whiskered** and **Black Tern** in spring, as well as duck in winter.

Continue on the D78 to its junction with the D44. Turn right and after about 2 km left onto the minor D17a. After about 4 km you will come to a sign and small car park for the MASSÉ lake on the right. Walk to the hide, which is about 300 m up the track, follow the arrows. **Bittern** can often be heard, especially on early spring mornings or seen flying in late summer; there are also **Little Bittern, Purple Heron** and **Savi's Warbler**. The large lake on the opposite side of the road, BLIZON, can be scoped from the verge side. Blizon is noted for frogs and dragonflies and has a short nature trail (about 1.5 km) which may be worth walking.

When this minor road meets the D15, turn right towards Rosnay and check the small FOUCAULT lakes from the new hide with wheelchair access, about 250 m up the footpath. They are usually very worthwhile, probably best in the morning but often have **Great White Egret** in the late afternoon (although the best place for this species is Puichevreau north of Blizon). Either continue to ROSNAY (for a visit to NEUF lake) or retrace your steps. The walk around the CHÉRINE Reserve is best undertaken in the afternoon. The birds mentioned from the hide can be seen and there may be **Black-winged Stilt** on the new lakes. Additionally, listen for **Black Woodpecker** in early spring and look out for **Red-backed Shrike** as well as watching the sky for **Short-toed Eagle** or **Marsh Harrier**.

From ROSNAY it is about 5 km to NEUF lake, which also has a hide. Take the D27 towards MIGNÉ for 5 km, then turn right towards MOUTON lake where there is parking. Follow the footpath on the right of Mouton lake for about 400m. This hide is good in the afternoon.

Itinerary ii.
LANCOSME FOREST is a large area of woodland lying east of Rosnay and Mézières. It is a good for woodland birds generally, including **Black** and **Middle-spotted Woodpeckers, Bonelli's Warbler** (in summer), **Crested Tit** and **Short-toed Treecreeper**. The D21 runs through the centre of the wood between MÉZIÈRES and NEUILLAY-LES-BOIS. A stop anywhere in the wood to look and listen can be worthwhile but the area around the old Chapelle St. Sulpice (signed) to the south of the road about 7 km west of Neuillay is one of the better spots. The D14 west from MÉOBECQ also runs through the southern part of the wood and a stop anywhere along this road is another option. There are several walking tracks leading off both roads.

Itinerary iii.
The area around **AZAY-LE-FERRON** is the best (if not the only) site for **Little Bustard**; **Stone Curlew** and **Montagu's Harrier** can also be seen here. Take the D925 from Mézières to PAULNAY and continue along it to Azay-le-Ferron. Little Bustard has been seen from this stretch of road but a more likely site is to turn left (south) onto the D975 and after about a kilometre, left again onto the D14. At the crossroads with the D18 turn left back towards Paulnay to complete the triangle. Keep stopping and scanning from wherever you can park. Mid-April to mid-June is the best time to hear calling males (a far-carrying sound likened to "blowing a raspberry"). When they call, they inflate their striking black and white neck feathers and it is these, sticking up above the grass, that you are likely to spot.

Site iv.
Another lake with hides is **BELLEBOUCHE**. It lies 8 km east of Mézières, off the D925. The turning to the lake on the right is signed. In summer you must pay to park. As Bellebouche has a very popular bathing beach, high season should be avoided. A footpath runs through woods and heathland around the lake, which is surrounded by reeds. There are three hides, marked by arrows. The entire walk of some 6 kms will take at least three hours at birding speed.

Flora and fauna: European Pond Terrapin and Green Lizard are common reptiles. Wild Boar (especially in winter around Chérine), Red and Roe Deer and Red Squirrel are relatively easy to see in the woods, Beech Marten less so. It is an outstanding area for dragonflies and good for butterflies, with over 60 species counted. April-June is the best time to see the maximum number of plant species in flower. The Brenne is especially rich in water plants and orchids, which include Tongue, Loose-flowered, Burnt, Spider and Lizard, all quite easily found.

<u>Accommodation:</u> There is a Logis de France (*Auberge de la Gabrière*) right on the lakeside at la Gabrière (crossroads of D78 and D17) and another at Mézières (*Boeuf Couronné*). The *Auberge St. Hubert* in Migné is central and there is good birding around the village. Going upmarket, there is a charming small chateau hotel, *L'Etape*, between le Blanc and Belabre (Tel: 02 54 37 18 02). These are open all year round. Campsites – Mézières (Bellebouche) and Rosnay have good ones, the former open only from March to November, except for chalets. Rosnay campsite is very central, open all year and good value for money; **Hoopoe, Serin, Melodious Warbler** are among the species that can be seen in the campsite. Reservations are not required but can be made through the Marie 02 54 37 80 17. There are several more municipal campsites. There are also a number of holiday cottages (rural gîtes) (telephone Gîtes de France on 02 54 27 58 61 for details). The Tourist Offices in Mézières (Tel: 02 54 38 12 24) or le Blanc (02 54 37 05 13) (both open all year) will give information on other hotels open.

(Though lying north of the area covered by this book, the **SOLOGNE** in the

Red-crested Pochard

Blois-Orleans area is often described as one of France's most important inland wetlands, second only to the Brenne in the numbers and different species of birds found on and around the thousands of lakes, large and small, that dot the landscape. A brief description is therefore included as any reader driving to or from the Brenne might like to visit this area too. Unfortunately, from a birdwatchers' point of view, nearly all the lakes are private and fenced off, the area is more wooded than the Brenne, access is restricted to a limited number of viewpoints from lay-bys alongside public roads and (very few) footpaths while the area is heavily hunted over in winter.)

ACCESS: The Sologne lies south of Orleans and east of Tours, in a triangle formed by the A10 and A71 motorways and bounded on the south by the D765 from Blois to Romorantin Lanthenay and the D724 from there to the A71 motorway. If you are driving through the region in spring or autumn, it might be worth making a detour to look at some of the best lakes. Some of the easiest to view lie in the area around St. VIÂTRE. Leave the motorway at the Salbris exit and take the D121 westwards towards MARCILLY. Continue through the village and north towards Neung still on the D121 until you can turn right onto a very minor road, the C6, a couple of kilometres beyond Marcilly. This road leads to la FERTE-BEAUHARNAIS and passes between some of the more viewable lakes where it is worth stopping wherever it is possible to pull off the road and scan the lakes.

When the C6 meets the D63, go straight over and continue for some 200 metres. There is a lake, the Etang de Marguilliers, on the left. When you have watched this lake, return to the crossroad, turn left (east) towards St. Viatre, passing the Etangs de Marcilly and Favelle (some of the larger lakes) on your right and in St. Viatre turn right again onto the D49 back towards Marcilly. The Etang de Brosses is close to the road on your right and a track, also on the right, leaves the D49 just before you reach it and enables you to view the other side of the lake.

In spring, look for **Black** and **Whiskered Tern** especially over Marguilliers lake, where **Great Crested, Black-necked and Little Grebes** can also be found. **Marsh Harriers** can be seen over the reedbeds around Brosses lake, where **Reed, Sedge, Grasshopper** and **Savi's Warblers** also breed. **Shoveler, Gadwall, Teal, Pochard** and **Mallard** can be seen all year round. and in hard winters **Merlin, Goldeneye** and sawbills may turn up. Of the migrants, **Cranes** and **Greylag Geese** can sometimes be found in late autumn and **Garganey** are often on Marcilly lake in spring. At this season too **Bittern** can sometimes be heard on Marcilly lake.

The woods in this area have breeding **Grey-headed, Middle-spotted** and **Black Woodpeckers, Woodlark** and **Honey Buzzard**. A good time to find the woodpeckers is early March, when they are calling and drumming and the trees are not yet in leaf. The woods along the C6 have several good places to stop and listen. Look for **Black Woodpecker** in the woods with the largest trees; **Middle-spotted** seems to prefer smaller copses with younger trees, provided there are some mature ones amongst them.

Area 4 LIMOGES

East of Limoges the Limousin countryside is beautiful if undramatic; rolling, thickly-wooded hills of Beech, Oak and Chestnut broken up by cultivated valleys, moorland and, increasingly, large conifer plantations.

The two sites described are both a mixture of woodland and peat-bog moorland. Either or both are worth visiting if in the area or by anybody wanting to explore a relatively unvisited part of France, though Pinail, near Poitiers, is a better site and not very far away.

WHEN TO VISIT: Both are spring and summer sites, though September migration could be rewarding. In winter there is little except solitude!

Site i.
The **DAUGES PEATBOG** or *Tourbière de Dauges* is a small site some 26 kms north-east of Limoges, just east of the A20 motorway. This is as much a woodland site as a moorland one as the peatbog is small and is surrounded by the wooded hills of the Monts d'Ambazac, where **Buzzard, Honey Buzzard**, accipiters, **Great Spotted** and **Black Woodpeckers** may be found as well as many woodland passerines, including **Bonelli's Warbler**. **Rock Bunting** occurs on the scrub covered hillsides and **Stonechat** and **Nightjar** in the heathland.

ACCESS: Drive north from Limoges on the A20 motorway and take either of the exits signed to AMBAZAC and the D914. Keep on this road through the town and some 6 km after Ambazac, turn left (north) onto the minor D28a, signed St. LÉGER. In 2.5 km there is a turning signed *"Tourbière de Dauges"* on

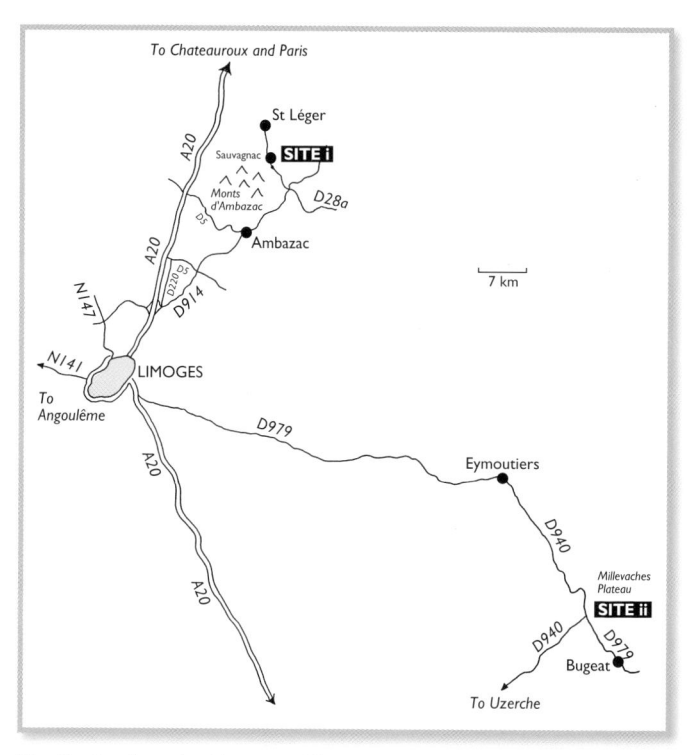

The Centre Area 4 – Limoges – Sites

the left just at the entrance to SAUVAGNAC village. There is another signed lane in the centre of the village. Park here and walk. After 400 metres the track forks left to the peatbog (signed *Tourbière* – the right-hand fork leads to St. Léger). Follow the footpath which is well signed (pink on the ground, red and yellow or orange painted on the trees) for as far as you wish. It is possible to make a circular walk but probably easier to return the same way. Some good woodland for **Black Woodpecker** occurs after another 600 m or so. The source of the Dauges and the bog lie below on the left. Keep scanning this open area for raptors or moorland birds.

Site ii.
MILLEVACHES PLATEAU AND LONGÉROUX PEATBOG is a very much larger site some 75 kms south-east of Limoges. Millevaches Plateau (over 900 m in height) covers a huge area and the itinerary suggested here takes in only a tiny corner of it, around Longéroux peatbog. Most of the heathland is now covered with conifer plantations. Millevaches does not mean a thousand cows as "vaches" comes from the Celtic word *batz*, meaning springs or sources, for several rivers rise on the plateau.

The bird species likely to be seen include the same raptors listed above, with the addition of **Hen** and **Montagu's Harriers, Short-toed Eagl**e and possibly **Red Kite**. **Nightjars** call at dusk from the heath and forest clearings and smaller birds include such moorland species as **Whinchat, Linnet, Tree Pipit, Yellowhammer** and **Rock Bunting**.

ACCESS: Take the D979 from Limoges towards Eymoutiers and continue through BUGEAT towards MEYMAC or if driving north up the A20 towards Limoges take the N89 through Tulle, continue towards Clermont-Ferrand and turn off onto the D979 towards MEYMAC.

Some 5 km beyond MEYMAC the D979 meets the D36 to MILLEVACHES. From Millevaches the D164 runs west to BUGEAT. The peatbog is found within this triangle of roads. Start at the junction of the D979 and D36. The peatbog is signed to the left but a short detour north towards Millevaches may be worthwhile. 2.8 km up the D36 a minor road leads past Puy Pendu (977 m) giving views over the heath and a little further on a footpath runs to Chavanac village. Explore these and then return to the D979 junction and turn right towards BUGEAT. Several walking-forestry tracks lead off this stretch of the road and may be worth walking along for such conifer-loving species as **Coal** and **Crested Tit** and **Goldcrest**. In 3.9 km turn right onto the D109 towards CELLE. 0.4 from the turning there is a good open areas for **Nightjars**. The road leads through the Forest of Longeroux with a good mix of conifers and open broom and heath moorland. Some 100 m after the St. MERD junction (do not take the left hand road into Celle village) an unsigned footpath can be seen on the right, just before a large conifer plantation. It is possible to walk some 2 kms towards the bog up this track (return the same way). The early part leads through coniferous woods. Otherwise continue along the road and a kilometre from Celle junction there is a large information board on the right side of the road. Park here as there are good views across open country on both sides. It is also possible to walk cross-country down towards the bog. In another 400 m a track on the right leads past some old beeches towards the moorland.

The D109 continues on to St. MERD where you can turn left onto the D164 towards Bugeat. This stretch of the road follows the River Vézère through several good, open areas. Look for **Dipper** in the river.

This triangular route only covers a very small part of this area. It would take several days to explore the whole plateau thoroughly. Millevaches is a vast, hilly mosaic of coniferous and deciduous woods, small lakes and heathland.

Other fauna and flora: Otters are reputed to occur in the rivers here. The peatbog is a good area for Golden-ringed Dragonfly and Emperor Moth. Flowers include several *Erica* species, Tongue Orchid *Serapias lingua*, Summer Lady's Tresses *Spiranthes aestivalis* and Bog Rosemary *Andromeda polifolia* (both rare), Marsh Gentian *Gentiana pneumonanthe* and commoner bog plants such as Sundew and Marsh Cinquefoil.

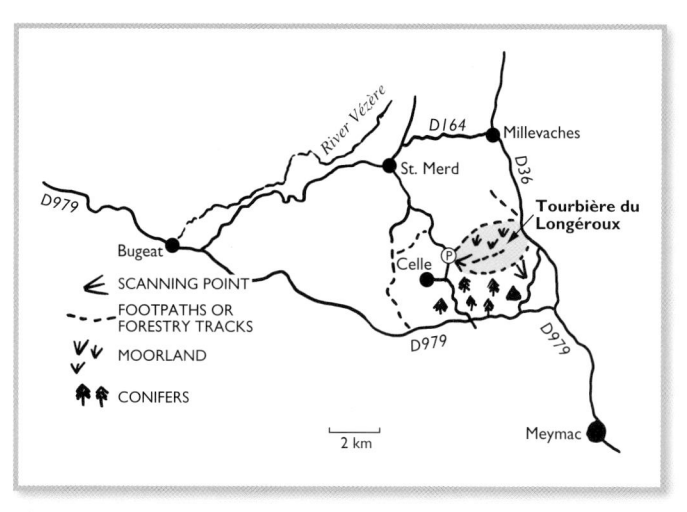

The Centre Area 4 site ii. Millevaches Plateau

Site iii.
Some 25 kms south-east of Meymac the **DORDOGNE GORGE** is an excellent migration corridor and good for raptors at most times of the year as they hunt over the wooded sides and heaths. **Honey Buzzard, Black and Red Kites, Short-toed Eagle, Hen Harrier, Booted Eagle and Peregrine Falcon** are some of the breeding birds. Large numbers of kites and **Honey Buzzards** follow the gorge during migration and **Ospreys** can usually be seen there in September. Anyone continuing east to the sites in the Massif Central might like to make a detour to the gorge on the way.

ACCESS: Several good viewpoints can be reached by road. From MEYMAC return to the N89 and continue in the direction of Clermont-Ferrand, turning off onto the D979 some 7 kms before USSEL. In 5 km turn south onto the minor D168 towards LIGINIAC, after a stretch on the D20 you will pick up the D168 again, continue on it to the BELVEDERE DE GRATTE-BRUYÈRE, about 12 km to the south. This viewpoint is usually good for raptors. It is possible to reach another viewpoint by taking the D20 north from LIGINIAC for some 6 km and then turning south (right) onto a lane leading to the edge of the gorge near the SITE DE St. NAVAIRE, or alternatively return to the D979, turn off onto the D64 and then the D127 signed to another good viewpoint over the St. NAVAIRE area

THE MASSIF CENTRAL

Stretching from north of Clermont-Ferrand to south of Millau, the mountainous heartland of France has several peaks over 1500 m and six major rivers rise there – the Loire, Allier, Dordogne, Creuse, Lot and Tarn, cutting deep gorges through the plateaux. The granite plateau forming the centre is very ancient rock indeed. The limestone plateaux or *causses* lying to the south are far more recent, only some 200 million years old. This is the most sparsely populated and undeveloped part of France and the weather is harsh and changeable, even in summer.

The enormous regional Park des Volcans d'Auvergne covers 3,500 square kilometres and contains most of the sites described below. This volcanic area was active up to 8,000 years ago; the cone-shaped *puys* or peaks and their craters are still obvious, so are the lava-flows and basalt "plugs" such as Le Puy, the dykes or *crêtes* that form sheer cliffs and the "organ pipe" cliffs where the molten magma welled up through the earth's surface.

WHEN TO VISIT: Snow lies late so mid-May through June is possibly the best time to find the rarer species but the autumn migration period is also interesting and there is likely to be something of interest throughout the summer, although there are a great many tourists in August.

Maps: There are several walking maps of the region in IGN (National Geographical Institute) 1:50,000 series. These are available at the visitors' centres mentioned in the text. The IGN 1:100,000 series number 49 covers most of the area described below.

Area 5 THE NORTHERN MASSIF CENTRAL NEAR CLERMONT-FERRAND

Site i.
CHAUDEFOUR RESERVE protects part of the Mount Dore massif, southwest of Clermont-Ferrand. The altitude ranges from about 1000 m to 1885 m at the top of Puy de Sancy. A large part of the reserve is wooded but the rest is composed of alpine meadows on two volcanic *cirques* scraped out by glaciers during the last ice age, with several sheer cliffs.

ACCESS: From the small village of CHAMBON-SUR-LAC on the D996, just after the lake, turn south, signed to the reserve, onto the D637. Watch out for a hidden turn in the centre of the village which is not clearly signed. It is 7 km to the visitors' centre, from where marked trails and walks start. There is parking and a small restaurant just opposite the centre, which sells maps and

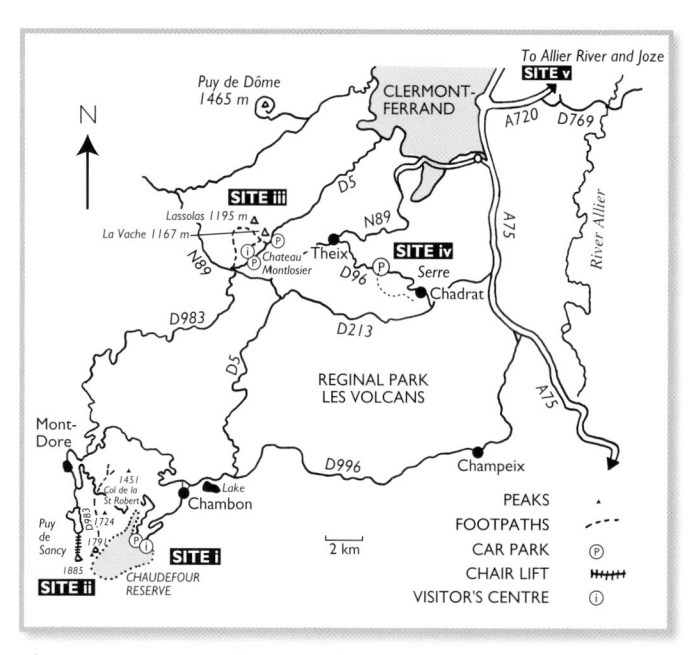

The Centre Area 5 Northern Massif Central near Clermont-Ferrand

books and has a small exhibition on the flora and fauna of Chaudefour.

From the centre it is just 1.5 km to the bottom of the valley through woodland, where **Black Woodpecker, Short-toed Treecreeper, Crested Tit, Goldcrest and Honey Buzzard** can be found among the commoner woodland species. **European Nightjar** are locally quite abundant in suitable habitat such as clearings. The track emerges into alpine pastures and climbs for 7 km towards Puy de Ferrand (1854 m) or a shorter trail continues along the bottom of the valley. In the higher grassland **Skylark** and **Water Pipit** are the most abundant species, **Northern Wheatear** also occurs and there are a few **Rock Thrush** and **Alpine Accentor** in the highest, rocky areas. **Raven, Peregrine** and **Eagle Owl** nest in the crags, where some nest boxes have been erected.

The valley is also a good spot to watch raptor migration; post-nuptial migration starts with **Black Kite** and **Honey Buzzard** during August and continues with **Red Kite, Marsh** and **Hen Harriers, Buzzard, White Stork** and **Osprey** from September, while even **Cranes** pass in October and November. Other migrating species include **Golden Oriole** and **Brambling** among thousands of hirundines and pigeons.

Another good viewpoint is slightly further north. Continue on from the reserve, past the restaurant on the right, following the road to the Col de la Croix St. Robert (1450m). From the pass, footpaths lead off both right and left to some of the peaks nearby, where the birds listed above can be seen. The

Col road continues down to the nearby town of MONT DORE.

Site ii.
Another part of the Sancy massif can be reached from the **MONT DORE** ski station (1325 m). Follow the small valley to the right facing the summit (the Val de Courre). Climb up to the pass (1722 m) from where there is a good view and from here go left in the direction of Puy de Sancy. It is possible to climb to the summit (1885 m). Descend the same way or follow the ski pistes. **Sky Lark, Water Pipit, Tree Pipit** and **Northern Wheatear** are among the species that can be found on the lower slopes, **Rock Thrush** and **Alpine Accentor** on the rocky scree slopes after the pass. **Crag Martin** is present. *Other wildlife and flora*: Corsican Moufflon were released for hunting some time ago and can be seen around the higher peaks, together with Chamois and Marmots. There is an interesting alpine flora; *Androsace carnea rosea* glows on the rocks, white *Pulsatilla alpina* and the yellow subspecies *P. a. apiifolia* grow intermingled and the lower meadows are covered with Wild Daffodils and Poet's Narcissi in spring.

Site iii.
An interesting walk can be made around the ancient craters of **VACHE AND LASSOLAS** (1195 and 1167 m) in the south of the Monts-Dôme chain, which runs west of Clermont-Ferrand.

ACCESS: From MONT DORE take the D983 for some 25 km to the junction with the N89. Cross straight over onto the minor D5. In 1.5 km you will see some impressive buildings on the left; this is Chateau Montlosier, which is now a visitors' centre, with an interesting exhibition on the volcanoes. Local maps can be obtained here. In another 1.5 km is a large car park with a map showing the footpaths through the woods and around the two peaks. Take the one that leads to the "little crater" and continues past it towards the higher peak of Puy de Vaches. Woodland birds include **Short-toed Treecreeper,** both 'crests, **Bonelli's Warbler, Crested Tit, Crossbill, Black Woodpecker, Sparrowhawk, Goshawk** and **Short-toed Eagle** (likely to be seen hunting over open ground). Further woodland walks can be taken by driving on a little further along the D5. There are several other smaller parking areas and many footpaths through the woods.

Site iv.
A migration corridor, which has been studied for over a decade, is the **SERRE** mountain just south of Clermont-Ferrand. The Serre is an ancient lava flow, criss-crossed with footpaths and with a variety of habitats. A minor road, the D96, runs along it between the villages of CHADRAT and THEIX. There are places to park and tracks to walk along the length of this road. The migration observation point is some 1.5 km west of Chadrat; there is a parking space and track leading towards a water-tower. The species to be seen will be similar to those given for the previous two sites. **Black** and **Red Kites** and **Honey Buzzard** are the most numerous migrants with several thousands passing through but harriers, **Booted** and **Short-toed Eagles** also use this

corridor as well as **Osprey**. In October/November up to a thousand **Cranes** fly over as well as large flocks of **Woodpigeon** and **Stock Dove**. Additionally, **Wood Lark, Nightjar** and **Red-backed Shrike** breed there and **Siskin, Crossbill** and **Hawfinch** occur on autumn passage.

ACCESS: From Clermont-Ferrand, drive south on the A75, leave at exit 5 onto the D213 heading west and turn right onto the D96 after 5 km. August to October is the best period for the greatest number of species.

Site v.

The **ALLIER RIVER** has some excellent birding along many of its stretches. The section of river running northeast of Clermont-Ferrand can be viewed from bridges at JOZE, where the D20 crosses the D1093 and east of MARINGUES, where the D223 crosses the river before running south to Lezoux. Both bridges have tracks or very minor roads running alongside the east bank of the river with openings from where it can be viewed. Take the north track at the D223 bridge and the track running south at Joze. **Grey** and **Night Herons, Kingfisher** and **Common Sandpiper** breed along the river, **Black Kite** nearby, **Little Egrets** are always to be seen, especially in autumn. **Sand Martin** is among the many hirundines that hunt over the water. The riverine woodland along the banks is good for warblers, including **Cetti's** as well as **Nightingale** and **Serin. Red-backed Shrike** are quite common nearby and **Turtle Doves** numerous, almost outnumbering the **Collared Doves. Osprey** use the river on migration, especially in spring. However, there is considerable disturbance from fishermen.

Further north a stretch of the Allier River has been made into a reserve. From MONETAY-SUR-ALLIER north to BRESSOLLES (where there is a Bird Centre) almost 20 km of the river is protected. It is an important migration route both in spring and autumn, when waders can be found on the mudbanks, as well as a good wintering site for duck, mainly **Mallard** and **Teal**, and **Cormorants**. In addition **Yellow Wagtail** (Blue-headed race), **Kentish Plover** and **Common Tern** breed on the gravel islands and **Stone Curlew** can sometimes be seen on them at the end of summer. There are also **Sand Martin** colonies. **Grasshopper Warbler** and **Woodlark** are additional breeding species to those listed above. The D9 runs along the west bank of the river and there is access from the villages named above and tracks down to the river at various points. At the village of CHÂTEL DE NEUVRE, 13.5 km south of BRESSOLLES, the D32 crosses the river, affording good views up and down stream.

Accommodation: There are hotels in nearly all the villages mentioned. The Mont Dore area especially is a popular tourist destination with plenty of hotels and campsites, which may be full in August. Clermont-Ferrand has several of the cheaper chain hotels on the outskirts near the A75.

Area 6 **THE SOUTHERN MASSIF CENTRAL**

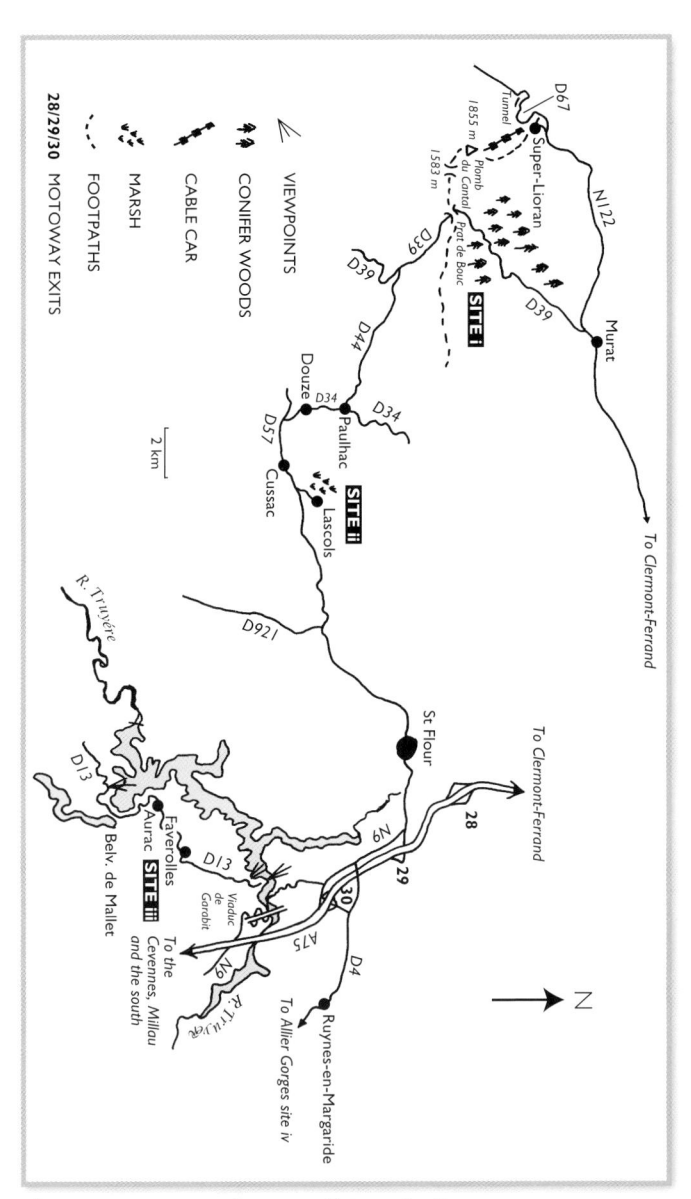

The Centre Area 6 Southern Massif Central – Sites

Site i.

The **MONTS DE CANTAL** site lies just east of the N122. The highest peak, the Plomb de Cantal (1855 m) dominates the southern end of the Park. It is both an impressive viewpoint (on a clear day) and a good birding area. It can be reached either by cable-car from the unattractive ski resort of Le LIORAN or by walking from the Prat de Bouc pass (1392 m) further east.

The N122 runs from AURILLAC to MURAT, passing through VIC-SUR-CÈRE. Le LIORAN is some 18 km north of Vic, by the new tunnel. (If you drive through the tunnel, turn back to the cable-car). It is better to take the old, twisty scenic road and bird on the way. Follow the signs "Circuit de Monts de Cantal". Both **Crossbill** and **Crested Tit** can be found in the pinewoods and even in the conifers around the ski station, while **Alpine Accentor** may feed around the cafés in winter. **Black Redstart** is always around the buildings and watch out for **Crag Martin**.

The cable car runs during the skiing season, when there will be too many skiers to make for good birding, and during July and August. In summer it runs every quarter hour from 9.30 to 5.15 and it is a 10 minute walk from the station to the summit. Birds likely to be seen include **Water Pipit, Northern Wheatear, Rock Thrush, Alpine Accentor** (with luck). It is a two-hour walk (at birding speed) to the pass.

Alternatively, start at the PRAT-DE-BOUC pass and walk towards Plomb du Cantal. To reach the pass, continue on the N122 towards MURAT and turn right onto the D39 at the entrance to MURAT. Follow the signs for "Prat-de-Bouc et migration des oiseaux". You will still be on the "Monts du Cantal" circuit. If you want woodland birds stop in the Murat forest *(Forêt Domaniale de Murat)* by the large map and walk along the tracks for some way.

At the top of the pass (1392m) there is plenty of parking space, a restaurant and marked trails. The Puy de la Jambe (signed up the hill) is an important observation point for the protection of migrating birds. British migrants (among others) pass through this route between the beginning of August and the end of October; thousands of **Chaffinches, Swallows** and **Wood Pigeons** have been counted as well as warblers in August and several hundred **Red Kite** in the middle of October. Other raptors using this pass include **Honey Buzzard, Short-toed Eagle, Black Kite, Sparrowhawk, Montagu's Harrier, Peregrine,** and **Merlin. Ring Ouzels** may also be seen feeding on the slopes during migration, although some also breed nearby.

The footpath to the Plomb du Cantal is clearly marked from the carpark. It is a four-hour round walk at birding pace but walking even a short distance along it towards the nearest ridge will allow you to see many mountain species: **Northern Wheatear, Dunnock, Linnet, Meadow Pipit, Grey** and **White Wagtails,** above all **Rock Thrush,** which can often be seen perching on the green ski marker posts very near the station or on the rocky slopes behind. **Black Redstart** is around the buildings and **Buzzard** overhead.

The D39 road that continues south-east from the pass, runs along high ground and is especially good for observing raptors during migration periods; even in summer **Red Kite, Buzzard, Skylark, Pipits, Stonechat** are common. It also leads to the next site, an unusual high altitude marshy area near LASCOLS village.

Site ii.

To reach **LASCOLS MARSH**, continue along the D39, then after some 3 km take the D44 to PAULAC. Turn right in this village onto the D34, drive through DOUZE and after 2.5 km turn left onto the D57 to CUSSAC (a small village with a pale blue soldier war memorial). Some half a kilometre beyond Cussac, turn left onto the C4 signed LASCOLS. It is one kilometre to the edge of the village where you can park on the grass opposite the cross.

The marsh or "*narse*" lies at 1000m and covers some 100 hectares. It is a large reedbed with open water in the centre, although water levels, mudflats and reed cover vary according to seasons and weather conditions. It lies to the left of the C4, so walk back along the road or out into the marsh if conditions allow. Alternatively, turn left into the marsh down the track which runs in front of the first houses on the left in the village or continue on the hard road through the village and then scan the open water from the slightly higher position just beyond the last houses. Please note that although birding may be best at dawn and dusk, it is forbidden to enter the marsh before 7 a.m. or after 6 p.m. **Lapwing** and **Black-headed Gull** are the commonest species and both breed here, as do **Spotted Crake, Snipe and Curlew** (all at their altitudinal limit in Western Europe). **Spotted Crake** and **Water Rail** can be heard at dusk. **Grey Heron, Whinchat, Coot, Teal, Garganey** and **Mallard** are other breeding birds but the marsh is best visited in spring and autumn when passage birds include many species of duck and waders, **Whiskered** and **Black Terns, Marsh, Hen and Montagu's Harriers**, even **Cranes** and **White Storks**. **Red Kite** and **Buzzard** can be seen here throughout the year.

It is 7 km from CUSSAC to the main road, the D921 and then another 10 to ST. FLOUR.

Flora: In summer the Large Yellow Gentian (*Gentiana lutea*) dominates the rich alpine flora in the higher meadows. A local liquor, Salers, is made from its roots.

Accommodation: There are campsites, hotels and/or pensions at Vic, Lioran, Murat, St. Flour and Albepierre (a small village nearest the Prat-de-Bouc pass).

St. FLOUR makes a convenient starting point from which to visit sites on two gorges. The TRUYÈRE GORGE is mainly a migration route but the upper ALLIER RIVER is good for birding at any time of the year.

Site iii.

The **TRUYÈRE RIVER** south of St. FLOUR has been dammed for hydro-electricity and forms broad lakes surrounded by wooded or broom-covered slopes. Take the new motorway, the A75, south from St. FLOUR and leave at the first exit (30), following the signs for "*Viaduc de Garabit*". This will take you onto the old N9 for about 3 km then by the viaduct turn right onto the D13 following the "*Route des thermes*". Almost immediately the road runs close above the water although this is not the best observation point as this part is so much used by boats, but scan anyway. Go through FAVEROLLES (5.5 km further on) and continue on the D13 in the direction of CHAUDES-AIGUES. After 4 km (soon after passing through the small hamlet of Auriac-de-Faverolles) the D13 runs along the water's edge for several kilometres. There are several observation points before the *Belvedere de Mallet* viewpoint. **Cormorant, Grey Heron, Common Sandpiper, Little Ringed Plover, Yellow-legged** and **Black-headed Gull** can be seen on the banks and islands even in summer and overhead both **Red** and **Black Kites** and **Buzzards** are common. During migration periods they are joined by terns, duck, and many species of raptors including **Osprey**. **Whitethroat** is the commonest breeding warbler on the broom and scrub covered banks and **Green Woodpecker** the most frequently seen 'pecker in the woods. **Grey-headed** and **Middle-spotted** also occur but are much rarer. Return to the motorway by the same route.

Site iv.
The **GORGES DE L'ALLIER** lie east of St. Flour and SAUGUES and southeast of LANGEAC. If you have visited the Truyère Gorges first, then return to the same exit (30) on the A75 but cross the motorway and continue east on the D4 towards RUYNES-EN-MARGERIDE and then the D589 through SAUGUES towards MONISTROL D'ALLIER. This village is the start of the Allier site, and you can either drive or walk along the riverbank to PRADES. It is 17 km by road or 13 along the river footpath. It would be possible to make a circular walk by going one way and returning by the other. The basalt cliff that rears up behind Monistrol has a colony of breeding **Crag** and **House Martins**.

If going by road cross the river and in 0.2 km from the bridge turn left onto the minor road towards PRATCLAUX. In 2 km turn left onto the D301 towards PRADES (15 km). The D301 runs through moorland and woodland high above the river. **Skylark** can be found on the highest heathland, **Woodlark** where there are scattered trees, **Red-backed Shrike** is common, **Great Grey** can be seen in winter. Both **Grey-headed** and **Middle-spotted Woodpeckers** occur in the woods. Look out for **Crested** among the other **Tit** species in the coniferous woods.

In the village of PRADES the river Seuge joins the Allier. Look for **Dipper** here, especially in winter and early spring; they are much harder to find during the breeding season. **Grey Wagtail** and **Common Sandpiper** are other breeding birds. Another "organ pipe" basalt outcrop (the *Rocher de Prades*) dominates the river here; **Crag** and **House Martin** breed on it and a few **Alpine Swift** can always be seen around and over the river in spring and summer. In winter **Wallcreeper** may be found on the cliff face. The wooded valleys that meet at Prades are good for raptors (**Red and Black Kites,**

Short-toed Eagle, Honey and Common Buzzards, Goshawk, Sparrowhawk, Kestrel) and the cliff is a good vantage point. Whitethroat and Blackcap are among the warblers in the trees and bushes below the cliff.

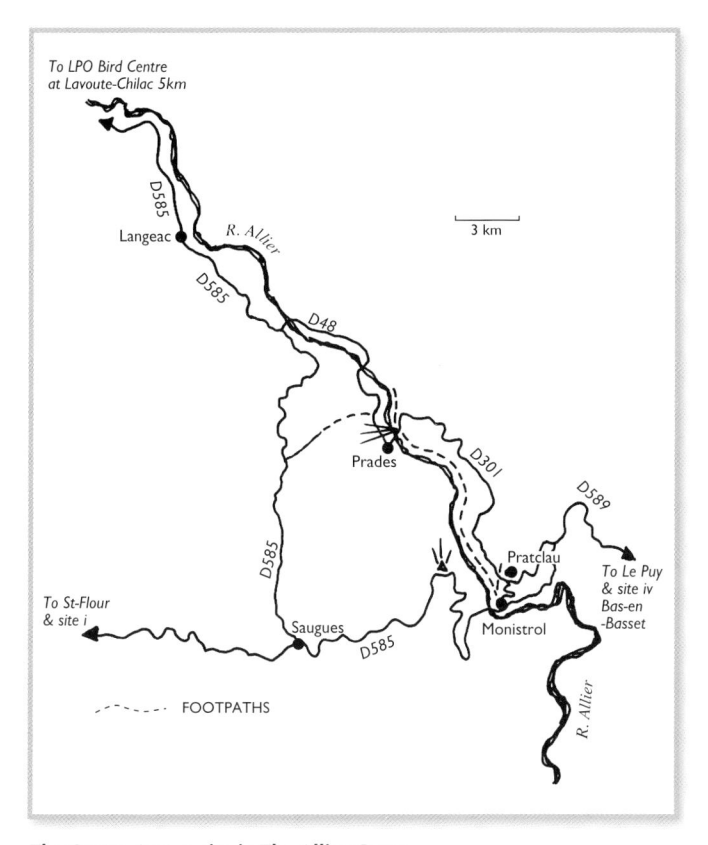

The Centre Area 6 site iv The Allier Gorge

Site v.
Further downstream at **LAVOUTE-CHILHAC** (on the D585 north of Langeac) the LPO has a reserve and a visitors' centre the "*Maison des Oiseaux*" at the old Priory (*Prieuré*). There is a huge diorama of the Allier Gorges with more than 35 lifelike wooden sculptures of the regions' birds. The centre is open to the public from June to September from 2 to 6 p.m. (closed Monday and Tuesday). On Wednesday and Friday mornings in July and August an LPO warden will lead walks along the river. Groups are welcomed from April to October but must book well in advance. (Tel: 04 71 77 43 52). The species to be seen are likely to be the ones listed above.

Site vi.

The gravel pits and River Loire at **BAS-EN-BASSET** Some 60 km northeast of LE PUY, **BAS-EN-BASSET** lies on the D42 which at this point runs alongside the River Loire. It continues north beside the river to AUREC-sur-Loire. Minor roads running east off the D42 cross the river and lead to different observation points along the banks. There are some old gravel-pits and an ox-bow lake where in spring and summer **Common** and **Little Tern, Lapwing, Little Ringed Plover, Sand Martin, Grey** and **Night Herons** can be found. Various duck species occur on migration. This is also a good area for raptors: **Short-toed Eagle, Red** and **Black Kites** and possibly **Hobby** are among the species likely to be seen.

Area 7 **LYON**

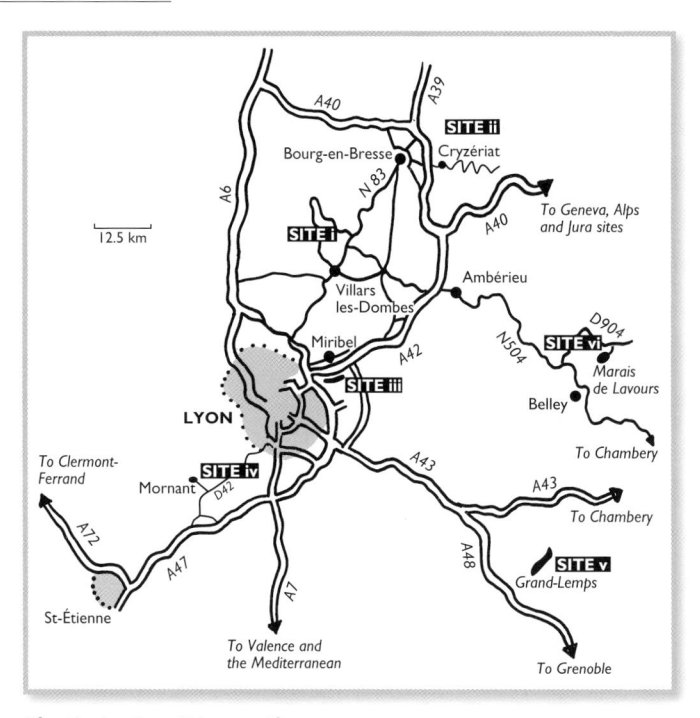

The Centre Area 7 Lyon – Sites

Site i.

The most famous birding site around Lyon is certainly the **DOMBES**, a large area (almost 1000 square kilometres) of small lakes and fishponds situated some 25 km north-east of Lyon and 16 km southwest of Bourg-en-Bresse on a low plateau with an average altitude of 280 m. Although there are over a thousand man-made lakes, many of them extremely ancient, most are on private land without access, they are heavily hunted over, many are emptied in rotation or dry out and not all have reed-beds; so, like the Sologne area, this site looks better on a map than on the ground. It also makes it difficult to state definitely which are the best lakes for birds, as this changes from year to year or season to season, depending on water levels.

However, in spite of the foregoing caveat, the Dombes is still a site of international importance for wintering and migratory birds. Thousands of ducks including **Goldeneye** winter there as well as very large numbers of **Coot, Lapwing** and **Cormorant**; migrants include **Black Stork, Red-crested Pochard, Garganey, Cranes, Osprey, Whiskered** and **Black Terns** and numerous species of waders, among them hundreds of **Spotted Redshank**. Breeding birds include a few **Little Bittern,** good numbers of **Night Heron, Grey** and **Purple Heron, Marsh Harrier, Whiskered Tern, Red-crested Pochard, Gadwall, Little, Black-necked** (about 50 pairs) and **Crested Grebes, Hoopoe, Bee-eater, Woodchat and Red-backed Shrikes, Melodious, Great Reed and Savi's Warblers.**

WHEN TO VISIT: It is best to avoid the hunting period, which opens on the first Sunday in September, so between March and the end of May is the best time for waders, ducks and newly arrived summer breeders. Breeding birds and their young will be seen in July and August when migrant waders and raptors also start returning.

ACCESS: VILLARS-LES-DOMBES, on the N83 roughly halfway between Lyon and Bourg-en-Bresse, lies near the centre of the lake area and from here it is feasible to make a circuit by car covering some 100–130 km on minor roads around the better and most accessible lakes in a day or a day and a half. Scan the lakes from the roadside; do not be tempted to trespass as this gives birders a very bad name. Most lakes can be seen from quiet, minor roads with wide grass verges that make parking and walking easy. There is a high-speed rail link between Paris and Lyon and the Dombes area is ideal for cycling; allow at least three days if you want to bird and cycle at a leisurely pace.

Just south of VILLARS, right beside the N83, is a *Parc Ornithologique* (23 hectares, 2000 birds. Open every day form 9.00–19.00 or 17.30 in winter. 38F entry). Even if you do not wish to visit the Bird Park, the Turlet lakes are visible from the free car-park and shelter thousands of duck in winter, no doubt attracted by both the safety and the food. One lake is right beside the car-park; it is necessary to walk a little way back down the road in the direction of Villars to see the one on the other side of the road. More wintering birds can be found on the ponds inside the Bird Park, consorting with pelicans and ibises! The **White Storks** that nest on pylons here and can be seen anywhere in the area are quite wild (even if they are ringed). There is also a **Cattle Egret** roost, attracting in addition a few **Night Heron**, some of which are resident.

There is a helpful Tourist Information Centre by the Bird Park car park where an invaluable map/leaflet in English on the "Dombes Lakes Route" can be obtained. The route is made up of two loops, the northern blue one 65 km in length, the southern purple one 70 km, with a section along the D70 in common. Far and away the easiest way to bird the Dombes is to follow all or part of the suggested routes, which are clearly signed all the way round some very minor roads and lead past lakes that give reasonable viewpoints from the road. Some extra lakes and detours that are generally good for birds are also described below.

Itinerary:
The start of both suggested routes is just outside the Bird Park entrance and takes you back north to Villars but for a birding itinerary taking in the best part of both loops, return to Villars and then turn onto the D2 towards BIRIEUX which lies some 5 km south of Villars. In spring, stop at the crossroads just north of the village and watch egrets and herons flying towards a breeding colony nearby. There are small lakes each side of the road just before the crossroads, good for **Whiskered Tern** and **Purple Heron,** and the occasional **Squacco** in spring. To view the Birieux lakes, continue along the D2 to the village of Birieux. Here you will pick up the purple route markers. At the church at the entrance of the village turn right. Just over I km from the church is a good stop overlooking a lake on the left, covered with yellow waterlilies in summer. On the right a walking track runs between another lake and woods. These are good lakes for **Cormorant**, **Teal** and **Pin-tailed Duck** in winter; **Black-necked Grebe, Garganey, Common** and **Red-crested Pochard and Whiskered Tern** in spring and summer, as well as a colony of **Black-headed Gulls**. Nearby reedbeds may hold **Purple Heron**, **Little Bittern** and **Water Rail**.

The purple trail continues to the crossroads with the N83 in the village of St. MARCEL and goes straight across towards MONTHIEUX. To view this lake, which lies just behind the village, turn down left of the church to a good viewpoint. Continue following the arrows to LAPEYROUSE. Here both routes lead to Villars but first make a detour to two good lakes. Turn right onto the D6B which runs through the Glareins lakes back towards the N83. There are several places to park and scan; the first quite close to Lapeyrouse where among the numerous **Coot, Moorhen, Mute Swans and Black-headed Gulls, Cattle Egret, Marsh Harrier** and **Yellow-legged Gulls** may be seen. Another good stop some 2 km from the N83 has water both sides of the road. **Water Rail, Mediterranean Gull, Black-necked, Little** and **Crested Grebes** and **Red-crested Pochard** have all been found here. This open site is a good raptor viewpoint. **Hobby** are often seen along this road, both perched on poles and hunting. Watch out also for **Hen Harrier** quartering the fields. Glareins lakes are also a good spot for **Black** and **Whiskered Tern** in spring. A few **Great White Egret** are frequently seen here in winter and hundreds of waders use the muddy banks when the lake is dry. Reedbeds hold singing **Great Reed** and **Reed Warbler** in summer as well as **Grasshopper** and **Savi's Warblers**. In August, look for **Spotted Crake** creeping along the base of the reeds.

From these lakes return to VILLARS; again following the "Route de Dombes" arrows turn off the N83 onto the D70 a couple of kilometres north of the town. Follow this road to LE PLANTAY. Make another detour here by taking the D61 to VERSAILLEUX. It passes several small lakes. Both **Ruddy** and **White-headed Duck** have been spotted here and even a wintering **White-tailed Eagle**! Most of the species mentioned above can also be seen. There are numerous **Purple** and **Grey Herons** in summer. The Chapelier/Versailleux lake is about the only non-hunting reserve in the area. In winter **Great White Egrets** and hundreds of ducks appreciate the safety. **Little Bittern** breed here; look for them flying over the reeds, where both **Savi's, Great Reed** and **Reed Warbler** can be seen and heard. **Whiskered Tern** hawk over the water spring and summer. The lake lies just south of the village of VERSAILLEUX. There is a parking area at the end of the village and a wide grass verge to walk along and from which to view the lake.

Return to le Plantay and continue along the signed route towards St. NIZIER-LE-DESERT and through it, still on the D70 towards DOMPIERRE. On the way the route passes the Grand Marais, another large lake partially covered with waterlilies and with a large reed belt. In May, **Black, White-winged Black** and **Whiskered Tern** can be seen over the water, often **Little Gull** is with them. **Purple Heron** and **Little Bittern** breed in the reeds, together with **Savi's, Reed** and **Great Reed Warblers**. It can be especially good for duck, including **Tufted Duck** in August as well as most of the species already mentioned.

After this lake the blue-signed route turns back left towards St. PAUL-DE-VARAX on the N83 and then continues west of the main road along the D17 towards St. ANDRE-LE-BOUCHOUX. Just before the village the route leaves the tarmacked road and twists around some dirt tracks past a lake where there is a **Night Heron** roost (look for them on the posts in the water on the far bank). Check also for **Red-crested Pochard** and **Garganey** in spring, **Osprey** on passage and **Great White Egret** and **Siskin** in winter before rejoining the D67 towards St. GEORGES and turning left onto a very minor road towards MARLIEUX. Between Marlieux and SANDRANS there are several good bird lakes, especially those just before Sandrans village. **Little Bittern** breed and **Spotted Crake** has been seen in late summer. Search the base of any reeds visible around all of these lakes. Crakes creep along the mud as well as walking over thick waterweed cover. If water levels are low, passage waders also favour these lakes. Look on both the islands and muddy banks. Watch out also for **Red-backed Shrike** in this area.

From SANDRANS, the route leads south along the D2 to BOULIGNEUX. As you enter the village it is possible to park on the wide grass verge just before the castle on the left and walk towards the small lake in front of the castle. **Goldeneye, Pochard** and even the occasional **Ferruginous Duck** may be found here in winter and **Black-necked Grebe** in spring and summer.

From Bouligneux the marked route continues to Lapeyrouse and then finishes in Villars.

One more lake complex usually worth exploring lies 8.5 km north of Villars, where the Vavres lakes can be seen on the east (right) of the N83. The D90 runs along their southern edge and off it another minor road, the C105, turns back north through the lakes so they can be viewed from this quiet road. Terns hawk over the surface in spring and at this season they also hold large numbers of **Black-necked Grebe**, as well as **Night** and **Purple Heron** and different species of duck.

If you have time, further exploration from the many minor roads running between lakes may well prove rewarding. Remember to stop wherever there is a gap giving a view over a lake, as there are not too many such openings.

Other wildlife and flora: Many interesting marsh plants can be found in the Dombes area; the irises and waterlilies can be spectacular in spring and summer. It is also good for dragonflies and butterflies. The introduced Coypu is the most likely water mammal to be encountered. Carp, Roach, Tench, Pike and Edible Frogs are common both in the lakes and on the restaurant menus!

<u>Accommodation:</u> There are several hotels in Villars, including a good Logis just beside the N83, and a large campsite nearby. Bouligneux and Saint-Andre-le-Bouchoux also have small hotels. There are numerous restaurants offering local produce, mainly carp and frogs' legs, and excellent local cheeses. This is a region that prides itself on the displays of summer flowers in all the attractive, old villages – "France fleurie".

Site ii.

If you are in the Dombes region in autumn and wish to escape from the hunters shooting all around the lakes, then drive north to **CEYZÉRIAT**, 7 km east of BOURG-EN-BRESSE on the D979, where there is an autumn migration observation site in the hills.

ACCESS: Take the N83 north to Bourg and follow the ring-road round to the east. Do not follow the "All directions" sign but the one for the City Centre, past Brou before turning right onto the D979. (You will know you are on the right road if you pass a large Renault factory on the left). At the end of CEYZÉRIAT village, turn left onto the D52 and almost immediately right onto a minor road signed "*Gare – Mt. July*". Bear right to Mont-July village and continue climbing, following the signs "*Observatoire*" – this is astronomical not ornithological but ends in the same spot, by the satellite mast. It is 3.5 km from the turning in Ceyzériat to the top. Many species of raptors (including **Black** and **Red Kite, Honey** and **Common Buzzard**) as well as passerines going south can be seen close to the ridge or flying over the plain below.

Site iii.

Although there are several good birding sites around Lyon, it is a very large city and the A6 motorway here is one of France's "black spots", both as regards accidents and lengthy hold-ups, so most birders may prefer to give it a miss. However, if you are in the region during the winter or spring, some

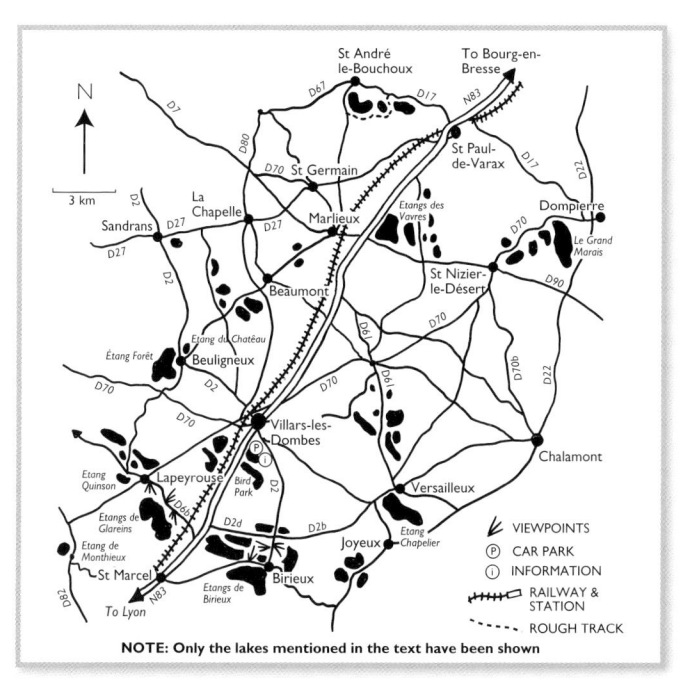

The Centre Area 7 site i. The Dombes. Note: only lakes mentioned in text are shown.

old gravel pits in the **MIRIBEL-JONAGE PARK**, only 12 km from the city centre, are well worth a visit, as they are a no-hunting zone.

To reach them, the easiest way of avoiding built-up areas is to take the A42 motorway (Lyon to Bourg-en-Bresse and Geneva) and leave it at exit 4, clearly signed "Parc de Miribel-Jonage".

The lakes are very large and a scope is needed to scan though all the flocks of birds properly. From November to May thousands of duck species, **Coot**, **Grebes**, **Cormorants** and gulls find refuge here. During cold spells both **Red** and **Black-throated Divers** occur, together with **Red-necked Grebe, Smew, Goosander** and **Red-breasted Merganser**. Rarities have turned up here over the years. From February, **Garganey** start arriving on migration, together with **Black-necked Grebe** and **Red-crested Pochard**. **Osprey** also stop over and a few **Red-footed Falcons** are seen each year at the end of April. Five races of **Yellow Wagtail** have been counted at the end of March each spring, often accompanied by a few **Red-throated Pipits**. **Golden Oriole** and **Black Kite** are two breeding species. August, September and October are the best months to observe the post-nuptial migration of waders and raptors.

Site iv.
The **MONTS DU LYONNAIS**, low hills west and southwest of Lyon are a favourite spot for local walkers. **Stone Curlew** may be seen in the dry, stony fields in summer and **Little Owl** on walls and old buildings, **Red-backed Shrike** perch on hedgerows. There are a few breeding **Hen Harriers** to be seen hunting over the fields and **Black Woodpecker and Short-toed Treecreeper** may be found in the conifer and beech woods. **Hoopoe, Nightingale, Yellowhammer, Skylark, Black Redstart, Tree Sparrow** and **Melodious Warbler** are also to be found.

ACCESS: Take exit 11 off the A 47 from St. ETIENNE south west of Lyon, onto the D42. After 11 km between MORNANT and Montagny turn right onto the D83 and then left up the D83e towards MONTAGNY. Check the fields each side of this minor road for **Stone Curlew**. Return to MORNANT and take the D34 to St. Martin-en-Haut and then the D11 towards St. SYMPHORIEN and CHAZELLE. These roads lead through much suitable habitat with opportunities to park and walk.

If you failed to find Stone Curlew, another likely area is just east of FEURS. From Chazelle take the minor D12a with leads to the N89. After 5 km at BELLEGARDE turn off north onto the D10 with runs through good habitat for 10 km until it reaches the D89. 2.5 km before the junction with the D89, the D18 leads off west towards FEURS. The triangle formed by these three roads east of Feurs contains many small lakes and is another good birding area with many of the DOMBES species here too.

Site v.
Some 60 km south-east, but for convenience grouped under Lyon, as it is easy and quick to reach from the A48 motorway to Grenoble, is the **ETANG DU GRAND-LEMPS RESERVE**, although the "lake" is rapidly turning into marsh with Alder/Birch woodland. This site is included as it is another of the few breeding sites for **Corncrake** in France. **Hen Harrier, Quail** and **Curlew** breed in the surrounding area and **Marsh Harrier** may be seen over the reed-beds where **Grasshopper Warbler** also breed. **Spotted Crake** has been seen here and one or two **Bittern** and **Little Bittern** also breed. Leave the motorway at exit 9 and go back north for 7 km on the D520, which runs parallel to the motorway. In BURCIN village, turn left onto the D73 to view the south and west sides of the Reserve. The D51b runs along the shore. Or continue north up the D520 to CHABONS, then turn left onto a minor road leading to LE LAC, which will take you to the north end of the Reserve.

Site vi.
Also some distance from Lyon, over 60 km due east, is another marshland reserve, the **MARAIS DE LAVOURS.** This peat bog lies below the Grande Colombier massif on the right bank of the River Rhône. It is probably better for invertebrates and amphibians than birds, although 131 bird species have been recorded, of which 76 breed. Since Highland Cattle, Pottock Ponies and Camargue Horses have been introduced to graze the vegetation, bird species

have increased. **Curlew** now breed in the water meadows, as well as **Grasshopper Warbler** and sporadically **Bluethroat**. **Water Rail, Savi's, Sedge, Reed, Great Reed** and **Marsh Warblers** are all found in the reed beds and **Marsh Harrier** is seen occasionally. **Hobby** breed in the damp woodland and patches of bramble hold **Nightingale** and **Melodious Warbler**. Look for **Dipper** and **Kingfisher** along the river.

ACCESS: Take the A42 motorway from Lyon to AMBERIEU, then the N504 and the D904 to BÉON. Take the first right turning after the end of Béon (signed "Marais de Lavours) onto the D37 to CEYZÉRIEU, some 3 km. Turn left in this village (signed "Reserve Naturelle") to AIGNOZ. There is a large car park on the left at the entrance to this village with a map of the reserve. From here you have to walk through the village and cross the River Séran to the edge of the reserve. The only access to the marsh is via a 2.4 km long board-walk. This obviously only allows a very small part of the reserve to be seen, though there are a few places which overlook other parts at the beginning of the D37 just outside BÉON. The southern part of the reserve can only be viewed from the D83 between CEYZÉRIEU and LAVOURS on the D992.

Other wildlife and fauna: 24 species of dragonfly have been recorded here and rare butterflies include the Dusky Large Blue, Scarce Large Blue, Large Copper and False Ringlet. Amphibians are numerous and include Palmate Newt, Natterjack, Parsley Frog, Marsh Frog and Pool Frog in the boggy areas and Fire Salamander, Yellow-bellied Toad, Common Tree Frog and Agile Frog in the flooded woodland. Marsh flora includes Marsh Gentian, Marsh Pea and Spurge, Summer Lady's Tresses, two species of Sundew, Grass of Parnassus and the rare Fen Orchid.

Area 8 **MONTAUBAN**

Site i.

The Aveyron River flows from the Massif Central and joins the Garonne just north-west of Montauban. The **AVEYRON GORGES** are where it has cut through the limestone of the Limogne Plateau. In the stretch between BRUNIQUEL and St. ANTONIN-NOBLE-VAL can be found **Wallcreeper** in winter, breeding **Eagle Owl, Peregrine Falcon, Crag Martin, Alpine Swift, Black Kite, Golden Oriole, Night Heron, Dipper** and **Rock Sparrow**. There may even be small flocks of **Alpine Accentor** in harsh winters as there are sometimes at NAJAC further up river. The cliffs, river, plateau above and the nearby **GRÉSIGNE FOREST** (site ii) south of the gorge (for **Short-toed Eagle, Booted Eagle, Honey Buzzard, Middle Spotted Woodpecker, Crested and Marsh Tit**, **Bonelli's** and **Sub-**

alpine **Warbler, Red-backed Shrike, Tawny Pipit, Hawfinch**) provide a variety of habitats and make this a good birding area with a long list of species. Access is relatively easy from public roads and the forest is criss-crossed with footpaths and forestry tracks. These are ideal for anyone wanting a long walk but the route described below assumes that you want to see as many species as possible in a limited time, so only suggests some short walks and frequent stops.

ACCESS: The D115 runs from MONTAUBAN to BRUNIQUEL and then follows the course of the Aveyron river to PENNE. Leave it at BRUNIQUEL and follow the signs for the chateau and village centre. Park on the outskirts of the village (only residents can take their cars any further). To find the **Wallcreeper**, walk up the steep streets of the picturesque old town towards the chateau (closed November 1 to Easter, open every day July and August, Sundays and Bank Holidays the rest of the year). When you reach the château walk to the right towards the fence which protects you from falling over the cliff. Look back at the château walls and below at the cliff face. Morning is the best time from this viewpoint as the sun will be behind you. A **Wallcreeper** sometimes sits preening on the windowsills! After you have searched for the Wallcreeper walk round the Chateau to the opposite side where you will find the chateau's garden and park (open all year round, no charge). The garden is good for **Cirl Bunting** and **Hawfinch** in winter as well as the usual woodland birds. Beyond the garden is a small wooded area which is a nature reserve. There are tracks through the woods together with viewpoints over the valley. Scan the skies for **Peregrine** and in summer **Alpine Swift**. You may also find Woodpeckers (check that any black and white ones are not **Middle Spotted**) and **Short-toed Treecreeper**. If you did not find **Wallcreeper** on the other side of the chateau try looking back from the woods wherever there is a good view of the chateau. If you have been unlucky with the **Wallcreeper** on the chateau it is possible to view the cliff and chateau from the road below the village.

Return to the D115, drive on toward PENNE and park next to the rubbish container on the right hand side, about 500 metres from where you re-join the main road, and look up at the cliff. There are plenty of **Jackdaws** all year round but also **Alpine Swift** from April to September and **Crag Martins** from February to November. A few pairs of **Rock Sparrows** breed around the villages of Bruniquel and Penne or on sunny rock faces between the two villages. If you want to find them, check all the **House Sparrows** carefully but especially listen out for their distinctive, wheezy call, which always sounds rather mournful, very different from sparrows' cheerful chirping. In winter they leave their breeding areas and form quite large flocks (up to 100), which may be found in the surrounding countryside.

The château at PENNE, a little further along the D115, is another site for wintering **Wallcreeper**. Drive into the village and park below the chateau. Walk through the village and under an arch where there is a sign painted in white indicating old Grain measures. Take the right fork and walk along to where you will find a small open area on the left; there is a small cross on the opposite side. Look up at the chateau walls from here. This site is probably better in late morning or afternoon as the sun will be in your eyes earlier in the morning. It is possible to walk up a footpath to the far end of the chateau and through the ruins where there are other walls to search.

If you are here at dusk from mid December till mid March listen for the deep calls of **Eagle Owl**. Rescued birds have been released both at Penne and near Bruniquel so the stretch of the D115 between them is a good place from which to look and listen, as are the cliffs nearer St. Antonin.

At the foot of PENNE village, cross the Aveyron river and turn right onto the D173 just after the bridge. From here there is a good view (with a telescope) of the cliff below the chateau. This is probably the best place to search for **Wallcreeper** in the morning. In summer, listen for **Golden Oriole** in the tall poplar trees that edge the river. You can continue on the D173 on the left bank of the river; there are some good places to scan the cliffs. At Cazals a bridge crosses the river back to the D115 which runs along the right bank to Saint-Antonin. **Dipper** and **Kingfisher** can sometimes be seen near Saint-Antonin (though Dipper are more common further upstream); **Night Heron** occasionally fly downriver in spring and autumn.

Site ii.

GRÉSIGNE NATIONAL FOREST covers a huge area south-east of the Aveyron Gorge. It can be reached from either Penne or Bruniquel and it is possible to drive in a circular route from one to the other, stopping off to walk through various stretches of the forest along the way. Most of the forest is composed of Sessile Oak and Hornbeam but there are several Beech or Beech-fir woods and a few copses of Sweet Chestnut. Among the smaller woodland birds, look out for **Hawfinch, Middle Spotted Woodpecker, Marsh Tit, Wood** and **Bonelli's Warblers**. In this region **Bonelli's Warbler** breeds in oak woods (unlike the Pyrenees, for example, where it is nearly always found in conifers). Raptors breeding in or near the forest include **Goshawk, Buzzard, Honey Buzzard, Short-toed** and **Booted Eagles**. In large open clearings where trees have been felled, **Hen Harrier** and **Nightjar** may be found and on scrubby slopes **Red-backed Shrike, Dartford** and **Sub-alpine Warbler** breed. **Woodcock** occur in winter.

The forest tracks may be closed at times during the hunting season from the end of October to the end of March; in any case, it is possibly dangerous to use even the footpaths when hunting is taking place, usually at weekends. Both Roe and Red Deer are shot, and Wild Boar hunted with dogs. The deer are quite easy to observe but the Wild Boar are very secretive.

ACCESS: From BRUNIQUEL take the D964 south. After some 5 km (beyond St. Martin) the hamlets of MESPEL and Les Abriols are signed to the right. The sign also indicates a viewpoint. This is 1.3 km up the lane on the right and looks down onto the cliffs above Larroque village. There is space to park on the left verge some 200 m before the viewpoint. The box scrub in this area is good for warblers and shrikes in spring and summer. If you continue up the road through MESPEL (just over 2 km from the junction) the tarmac road finishes and becomes dirt forestry tracks. At a crossroads one such track is signed to Les Abriols; another is the GR 46 footpath which leads to Puycelci in 1 hr 30 m. Walk along these as far as you wish.

Returning to the D964 junction, drive on south towards PUYCELCI. **Scops Owl** may be heard calling around the village on summer nights. Turn left onto the D8 which leads to the village. Do not fork left into the village on the spur road after 2 km but keep on the D8 as it turns sharply right. After another 3 kilometres it turns into a gravel track and shortly after this there is a junction. Continue straight on ignoring the right fork. 2 km from this junction

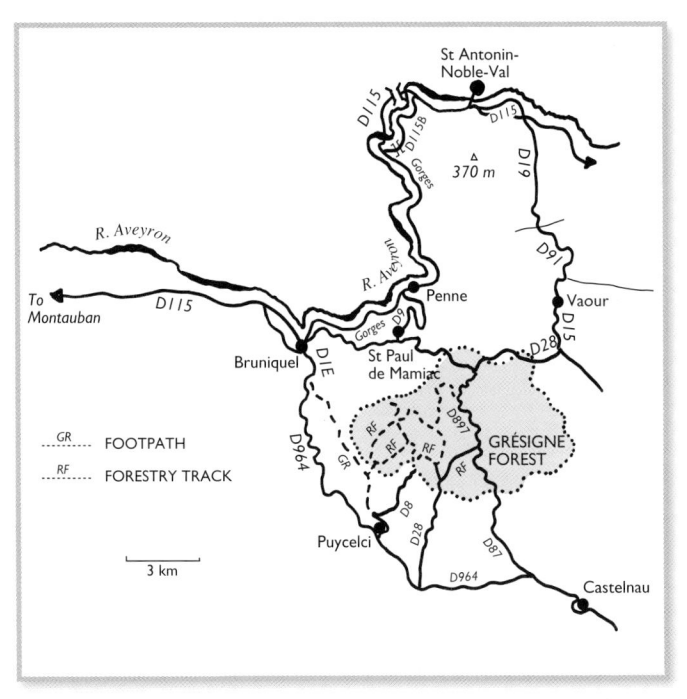

The Centre Area 8 Montauban sites i. and ii. Aveyron Gorges and Grésigne Forest

there is a clearing and a board with a plan at a crossroads by some pine trees (this is the Pins d'Ayrol, marked 17 on the plan). Park here and take the footpath signed to MONTOULIEU. This, at 468 m, is the highest point in the forest. The footpath climbs steeply. Look out for deer. At the top a signed footpath leads back left to Puycelci or right some 100 metres for a view over a large stretch of the forest. Look down over the cleared areas for **Hen Harrier, Hobby** and **Honey Buzzard** flying below. The trees on the plateau are mature beech and fir, good for woodpeckers. **Black Woodpecker** may have started to colonise.

Drive back the way you came and once you have regained the D984 beyond Puycelci continue on for another 10 km until you reach a well-signed crossroads between another St. Martin and 3 km before Castelnau. Turn north on the D87 signed back to PENNE. This road runs straight through the centre of the forest with opportunities to stop and stroll frequently. At the second crossroads (10.5 km on) turn right towards Vaour. Check the woods for the next three or four kilometres for **Middle Spotted Woodpecker**, especially around the hamlet of Haut Serre. They seem to prefer south-facing slopes and mature Oaks. There are also some good viewpoints over the forest along this stretch of road. Return to the crossroads and continue north towards Penne. If you have not found them in the woods, **Hawfinch** can be seen, especially in winter and early spring, around the small hamlet of St. Paul de Mammiac, about 4 km before Penne. **Hawfinch, Marsh Tit** and **Wood Warbler** are common breeding birds in these oak woods but **Hawfinch** become very secretive in the breeding season.

Site iii.

The **GARONNE RIVER** at **SAINT NICOLAS-DE-LA-GRAVE,** southwest of Moissac. The river here forms a reservoir that is also known as the *Lac du Tarn et Garonne*. Much of the lake is used for recreational water sports but it still holds good numbers of birds. There is a hide and a walk along the lakeside towards and beyond the hide can be productive, especially for wintering duck, coots and cormorants and migrant waders in spring. **Kingfisher, Yellow-legged Gull**, **Little Egret** and **Grey Heron** can usually be seen between the harbour and the hide year round, **Night Heron** and **Common Tern** in spring and summer, **Black Tern** and **Little Gull** hawk over the water in April and May.

ACCESS: From Moissac follow the N113 westwards along the north bank of the Garonne. After 5 km turn left over the bridge towards St. Nicholas. Half a kilometre beyond the bridge a turning on the left is signed *"Base de Loisirs"*. Follow the signs for the *Observatoire Ornithologique* to the car park on the lakeside. Walk along the lakeside path on your right towards the hide. It is possible to walk further around the lake but this first stretch plus some time spent in the hide should be sufficient to see most species.

(The stretch of the Garonne west of Grisolles, some 22 km south of Montauban just off the N20, is another ZICO site, noted especially for **Purple Heron, Night Heron** and **Spotted Crake**. However, access to this reedbed and lake is much more difficult).

If you are travelling south along the A62 motorway between Bordeaux and Toulouse, then it could be worthwhile to pull into the *Aire de Forêt de Montech*, which is the last parking area before the Montauban exit. From the car park there is access to an Arboretum. **Black Kite** is one species that is regularly seen here in spring and summer, as well as both **Buzzard** and

Honey Buzzard. Accipiters and other woodland birds can be watched by walking around the woodland.

Other fauna and flora: These sites are some of the best in France for wild flowers, notably orchids, especially between April to June and it follows that there are also plenty of butterfly species. Deer are quite easy to see in Grésigne National Forest, Wild Boar are much more wary.

<u>Accommodation:</u> There are plenty of hotels, including many belonging to the cheaper chains, in Montauban and around the exits from the motorway. There are more expensive ones in Moissac and St. Antonin-Noble-Val, Najac or Caylus (for the Aveyron Gorge). Campsites along the gorge are mainly summer only. There are plenty of "chambres d'hôtes" in and around St Antonin.

Area 9 **TOULOUSE**

Site i.
PARC NATUREL DU CONFLUENT ARIÈGE/GARONNE. The nearest good bird-watching area is surprisingly close to both the city centre and the airport. A series of old gravel pits that lie between the Garonne river and the D4 which runs along its eastern bank due south of the city, have been turned into a small reserve which runs down to the riverside at the junction of the Ariège and the Garonne rivers. It includes not just riverine woodland but also dead flooded trees (favoured by **Night Heron**), ponds, overgrown thickets and open grassy areas. The main attraction is the number of **Night Heron** that breed, but there are also numerous **Nightingales, Zitting Cisticolas, Cetti's, Melodious** and other warblers. **Golden Oriole, Woodchat Shrike, Hobby, Black Kite, Short-toed Eagle, Buzzard, Yellow-legged** and **Black-headed Gulls, Grey Heron** and both **Little** and **Cattle Egrets** are among the species that are regularly seen here. A small colony of **Pallid Swift** breed in Toulouse and they can often be seen flying above the river with the many Common Swift; in spring **Purple Heron** can be seen flying along the river and even **Little Bittern** is a possibility.

WHEN TO VISIT: As the above list of mainly migrant breeders shows, this reserve is best visited in spring and early summer; in winter there is little other than **Grey Heron**, egrets and gulls; there is always the chance of more interesting species on passage.

ACCESS: To reach the reserve leave the ring road (*peripherique*) and take the N20 in the direction of Foix. Cross the Garonne (after some 8 km) and in 2.8 km at the next roundabout turn left onto the D4 towards Lacroix-Falgarde. Zero here. In 1.7 km at the next roundabout turn left following the signs for Toulouse. Carry straight on past the church on your right and after approximately 4 km you will see a pond (part of the reserve) on the left. Go slowly because the entrance, at 4.4 km, is difficult to see from the road, although there is a large signboard. There is a car park with a plan of the Reserve, showing the footpaths and viewpoints. Though a small Reserve, there are several kilometres of tracks.

Walk first towards the river, then along to the left, upstream, towards the viewpoint marking the confluence (junction) of the two rivers, which is a good place to see **Golden Oriole** and **Kingfisher** as well as to watch birds flying along the rivers. You should also find **Night Heron** perched in the dead trees surrounding the old pits. **Nightingales** are common in the damp thickets here and **Melodious Warblers** also like this habitat. Walk back to the main centre path of the Reserve and if you have missed any species, then walk downstream, to the right, to another viewpoint called le Point. There are **Golden Oriole** this side too. **Woodchat Shrike, Stonechat** and **Zitting Cisticola** can be found in more open areas. Keep checking the flocks of Swifts

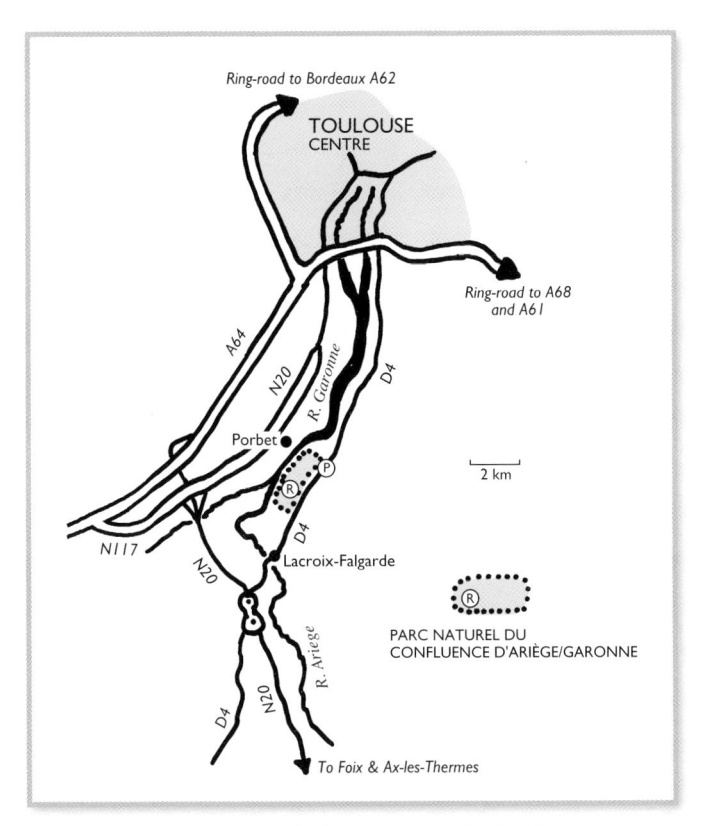

The Centre Area 9 Toulouse site i. Parc Naturel du Confluent d'Ariège/Garrone

over the river for **Pallid Swift**. Raptors can often be seen over the river or the hills to the east.

Site ii.
BOUCONNE FOREST Even closer to the airport, which lies on the west of the city, is Bouconne Forest, only 15 km from the city centre. Although much used by dog walkers, cyclists and riders (avoid weekends) it offers some lovely woodland walks for anyone wishing to get away from the city for a while and also holds good numbers of woodland birds: **Buzzard, Honey Buzzard, Hobby, Sparrowhawk, Green** and **Great-spotted Woodpeckers, Jay, Nuthatch, Short-toed Treecreeper, Firecrest,** thrushes, warblers, finches and tits (Great, Blue, Coal, Marsh and Long-tailed). Of more interest **Nightjar** can be heard on June evenings in recently felled clearings, where **Dartford Warbler** can also be found. **Bonelli's Warbler** is a reasonably common summer breeder; it favours sunny edges of oak and pine strands. In the cereal fields leading to the forest, look out for **Montagu's Harrier** hunting low over the crops, **Corn Bunting** and **Stonechat** sitting on wires. (If you do not find **Montagu's Harrier** here, drive further west along the N624 towards Auch, checking the cereal fields either side of the road).

ACCESS: To reach the forest, take the A624 to AUCH (signed both from the ring-road and from the airport). After 10.9 km from its junction with the ring-road, the D24 leads off on the right and is signed Forêt de Bouconne. There is a large car-park on the right after approximately 6 km. A forestry road (for walkers and cyclists only) runs through the forest and both car parks are sited beside it. However, it is usually more productive to walk around the smaller paths through the woods. There is a small lake (signed) half a kilometre away, and it can be worth walking towards this.

A second car park can be reached from the village of LÉGUEVIN, some 3 km further west towards Auch. Turn right onto the D42 in the centre of the village. It is signed to the Forest. The car park is on the left 3.4 km from the village, where the forestry track crossed the road. This area, which contains some large pines and newly planted conifers, is possibly even better for birds. Check the trees around the car park for Bonelli's Warbler, they are quite numerous here and respond well to a tape.

Accommodation: Toulouse if full of hotels in all price ranges. Many of the cheaper chains have hotels just off the ring-road near the entrances to the motorways.

Site iii.
The Tarn LPO has a Bird Reserve 13 km from CASTRES and approximately 70 km due east of Toulouse, roughly half way between Toulouse and the Cévennes sites described below. The **CAMBOUNET-SUR-LE-SOR BIRD RESERVE** has been formed from several disused gravel-pits; others nearby are still worked and a large lake to the east is a boating and leisure complex. The southern part is a Natural Reserve, the larger, northern lake is a (non)

Hunting Reserve, managed by the *Fédération des Chasseurs*. Together they cover 30 hectares of lakes and woodland, with a footpath running around the boundary and four hides. The Reserve was created in 1990 to protect one of the most important heronries in the region; annually between 500 to 800 pairs of up to seven species of herons breed there. The most numerous are **Night Heron** (in 1997 there were an amazing 675 pairs but the number has since dropped to a couple of hundred, possibly because Cattle Egret numbers have exploded). **Cattle Egret**, which first bred in 1992, increased from 5 pairs to well over 300 in 7 years. There are also fewer (between 40-60) breeding pairs of **Little Egret** and **Grey Heron**, which bred for the first time in 1997. **Purple Heron, Little Bittern** and **Squacco Heron** are irregular breeders, with perhaps only a single pair some years, especially since most of the previously extensive reedbeds have gone. **Coot, Moorhen, Little Grebe** and **Kingfisher** are other water birds to be found all year round. **Bee-eaters** and **Sand Martins** arrive in summer. Raptors observed from the reserve include **Sparrowhawk, Common Buzzard, Kestrel** and **Hen Harrier** year round, plus **Honey Buzzard, Short-toed Eagle, Black Kite, Montagu's Harrier** and **Hobby** in summer. **Barn, Tawny, Long-eared** and **Little Owls** are found on or near the Reserve, with **Scops** an occasional summer visitor. Passage birds include waders, **White Stork, Gargany, Osprey, Marsh Harrier, Whiskered** and **Black Terns** and **Penduline Tit**. Rarities that have turned up include Spoonbill, Glossy Ibis and even Leach's Petrel! In winter several species of duck can be found in the reserve, mainly **Mallard, Shoveler, Teal, Pochard** and **Gadwall** (occasionally Goldeneye or Ferruginous) and several hundred **Cormorant**. Up to a dozen **Night Heron** overwinter and several can be seen even in the severest weather in the trees where the Cormorants roost. Surrounding woods and farmland provide good habitat for many passerines, including **Cetti's** and **Fan-tailed Warblers** as well as large flocks of **Cirl Bunting,** finches and **Skylarks** in winter.

WHEN TO VISIT: From March to August the heronry is the scene of intense activity while in winter the hundreds of Egrets arriving to roost is a remarkable sight, so the Reserve provides good birdwatching all year round. Phone L.P.O. Tarn 05 63 70 40 89 for up-to-date information.

ACCESS: From the N126 some 10 km south-west of CASTRES, turn north onto the D14 (the Reserve is signposted at the roundabout in the direction of CAMBOUNET-SUR-LE-SOR. Just before the town sign for Cambounet turn right over the river bridge and immediately right again; both turnings are clearly signed "Réserve Naturelle". In almost 1 km there is a third sign to the Reserve at a cross signed "La Lieussonnié. Keep left here and continue to a carpark in half a kilometre with a plan of the Reserve, picnic area and small information centre.

Walk around the reserve either clockwise or anti, depending on the position of the sun; there are two hides each on both east and west sides; the whole walk is little more than a couple of kilometres.

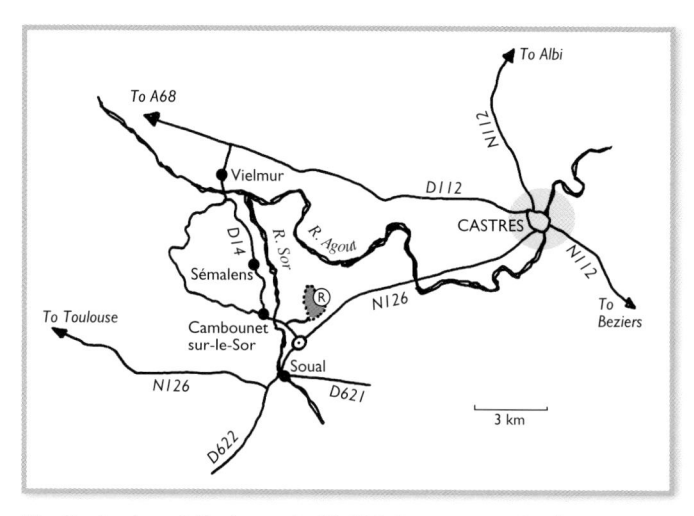

The Centre Area 9 Toulouse site iii. LPO Reserve near Cambounet-sur-le-Sor

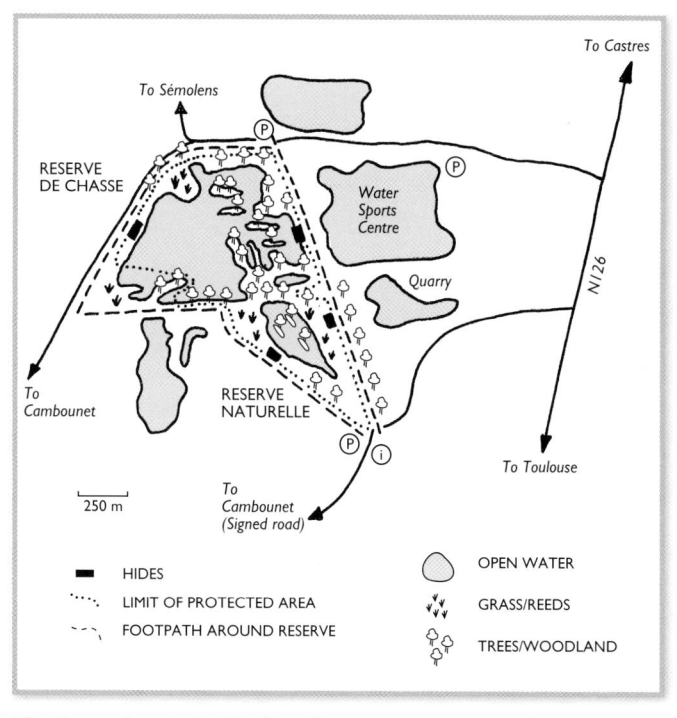

The Centre Area 9 site iii. Plan of LPO Reserve near Cambounet-sur-le-Sor

Area 10 CÉVENNES NATIONAL PARK

The Cévennes are the southernmost tip of the Massif Central; the A75 motorway from Clermont-Ferrand gives quick access. They overlook the Languedoc plain and are under two hours drive, along fast roads, from Montpellier or Nimes. 914 square kilometres, from Mount Lozère (1,169 m) in the north to Mont Aigoual (1,565 m) in the south, form the Cévennes National Park. Surrounding this central area are the "buffer zones" of the Natural Regional Park of the Grands Causses. The *"causses"* are dry, stony, limestone plateaux with, in spring and summer, an incredible wealth of wild flowers and butterflies. Their borders plunge, with dramatic suddenness, into the deep gorges through which flow the rivers Tarn, Arre, Jonte and Dourbie. The gorges are of interest for cliff-nesting birds but it is on the flat tops of the plateaux, covered with Feather-grass *Stipa pennata*, that some of the best birding is to be had, among the rocks, box scrub and scattered pines. **Tawny Pipits** and **Ortolan Buntings** are probably easier to see here than anywhere else in France, four species of shrikes can be found, as well as **Rock** and **Blue Rock Thrush** and Mediterranean warblers. **Griffon Vultures**, after a reintroduction programme, have been breeding in the gorges for some years and it is the only place in France to see **Monk (Black) Vultures,** introduced more recently.

Maps and guide books: The best map, whether walking or driving, that covers the whole park is the IGN (Institut Géographique National) 3615 "Parc National des Cévennes" 1:100,000. Otherwise the IGN green series 1:100,000 covers the area on maps 58, 59 and 65, as does Michelin no .80. IGN blue 1:25,000 walking maps are available locally. The Park Headquarters at Florac and the Belvedere des Vautours (see below) hold a good selection. They both sell the English edition of the guidebook to the park, which provides useful general information and suggests more itineraries than are given below.

WHEN TO VISIT: May-June are excellent months, both for birds, butterflies and flowers. Snow may still be lying on the higher areas at the beginning of May and it can be wet and windy in early spring and autumn. During July and August there are large numbers of tourists and many passerines have stopped singing.

Site i.
BLANDAS is the most southerly *causse* and the first to be reached if driving from the Mediterranean. The small village of BLANDAS, with one hotel, is a good centre from which to explore the region.

From Blandas the D.713 leads south to the CIRQUE DE NAVACELLES, some 2 km. away. Stop at the car park and small restaurant and walk to the top of the cirque. **Nightingale** and **Melodious Warbler** can be found in the trees here, **Blue Rock Thrush** breeds nearby, **Crag Martin, Alpine Swift** and **Red-billed Chough** can be seen around the cliffs and the occasional **Golden** and **Short-toed Eagles** overhead. **Wallcreeper** and **Alpine**

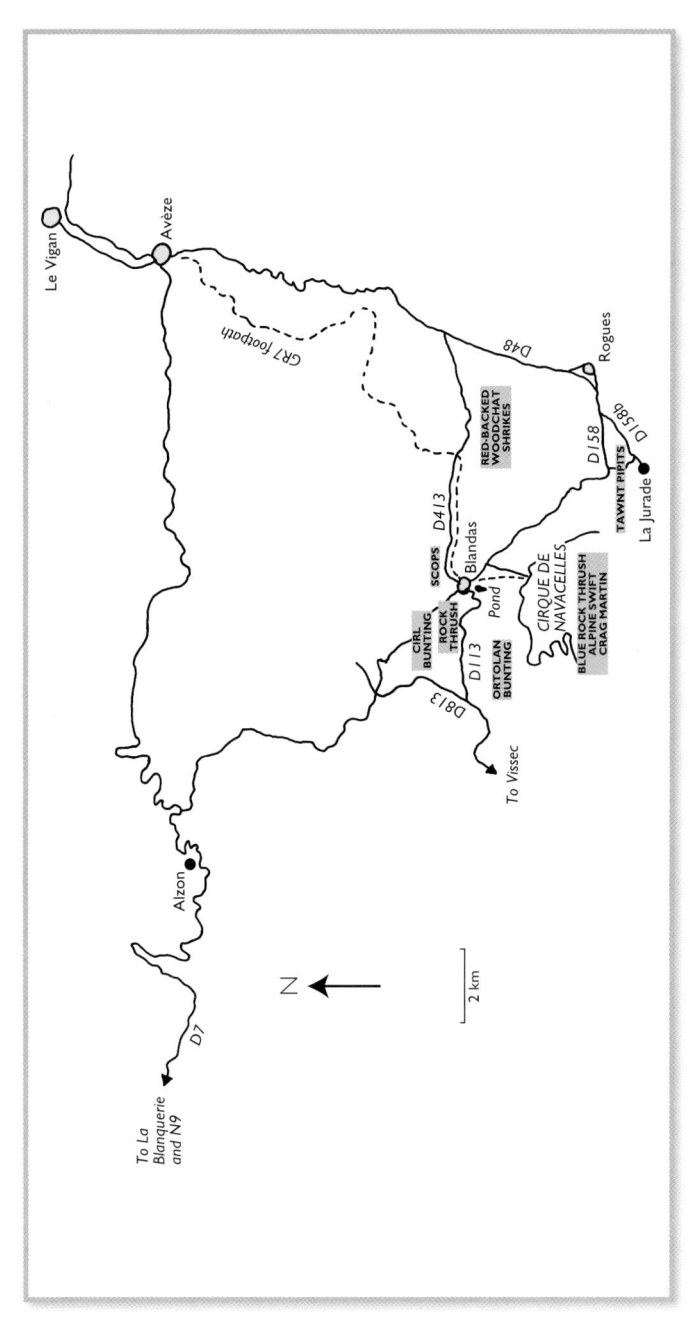

The Centre Area 10 Cévennes site i. Causse de Blandas

Accentor occur regularly in winter and it is worth listening out for **Eagle Owl** at dusk in the early part of the year. The Cirque is also a good spot from which to watch raptor migration in spring. **Scops Owls** call from the trees here or in Blandas village. Just outside the village, going west along the D.113, is a small pond. A short time spent here (with a camera) can be rewarding as large numbers of passerines come to drink: they include **Serin, Yellowhammer, Cirl** and **Ortolan Bunting**. Both **Woodchat** and **Red-backed Shrikes** and **Rock Thrush** can be found in the surrounding area. Just beyond the pond, a footpath signed to the *"Foux Navarelle"* leads over typical causse scenery. Walk as far along it as desired. By car, continue along the D113 for a couple of kilometres and then take the first turning on the right, north along the D813. At the next crossroad, turn back right along the D158 towards Blandas. This triangle will take you over another good stretch of causse. **Hoopoe, Northern Wheatear, Tawny Pipit, Woodlark** are other species that breed. **Subalpine Warbler** can be found in the higher box scrub. **Great Grey Shrike** is rare but those that occur are the southern species *meridionalis*.

Another triangular drive can be taken to the east of Blandas. Go east along the D143, turn south onto the D48 to Rogues village and then west back towards BLANDAS on the D158. The scenery and birds will be similar. It is worth making a short detour just west of Rogues along the "dead-end" D158b, as **Tawny Pipits** are very common here. This lane ends at the Auberge de Jouade, another possible place to stay.

Any strand of pines is worth checking for **Bonelli's Warbler, Crested Tit** and **Firecrest**, as well as other woodland birds. The stretch of the river Arre between Avèze and le Vigan has a footpath running along some stretches and is a likely spot for **Dipper, Kingfisher**, and **Cetti's Warbler**, among other riverside species.

Blandas can be most easily reached by taking the D7 which runs west off the fast N9 dual-carriageway from Montpellier to Millau. The stretch of causse between LA BLAQUERERIE and the turning to LA COUVERTOIRADE, is another good site for steppe birds, including **Stone Curlew** (look around the small piles of stones) and Lizard Orchids.

<u>Accommodation:</u> Apart from the two small hotels mentioned above, there are hotels and campsites in Avèze and le Vigan, some 15 km to the north.

<u>Site ii.</u>
North-west of Blandas, the Gorges of the Tarn and the Jonte meet at the small town of LE ROZIER. This too, like Blandas, lies just outside the boundaries of the Park proper but is an excellent centre for birders. **Griffon** and more recently **Black** or **Monk Vultures** have been re-introduced to this part of the Cévennes since 1981, 40 years after they were extirpated. Today there are some 200 Griffons and 20 Monk Vultures breeding and flying over the gorges north and east of le Rozier. In the past few years, on average, 70 pairs of Griffons have nested and 40 to 50 chicks have been raised. The **Monk**

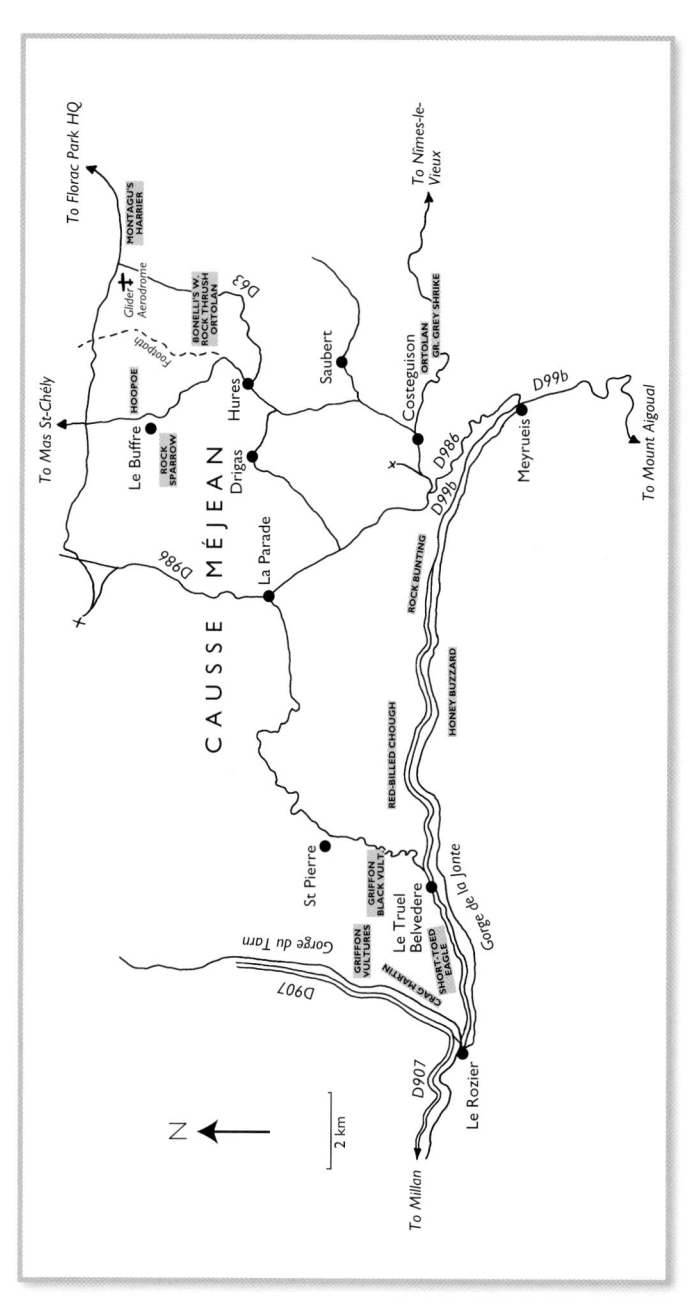

The Centre Area 10 Cévennes sites ii. and iii. Gorges de la Jonte and Causse de Méjean

Vultures have recently only managed 5 nests with one chick; in some years a pair of **Egyptian Vultures** breed. Vultures can be seen almost anywhere over the Park but the gorge near le Rozier is definitely the best location.
If driving north along the GORGES DU TARN, pull in at any of the lay-byes that overlook the gorge. There is a nest-site opposite the second lay-by on the right after the two rock tunnels. Near by is a small café "Chez Louis"; its terrace is an excellent and comfortable viewpoint. **Crag Martin, Alpine Swift, Goshawk** and **Short-toed Eagle** are other species that are likely to be seen here.

The **GORGES DE LA JONTE**, running east, is an even better site. Some 5 kilometres from le Rozier, just before the small hamlet of le Truel, is the recently built "Belvédère des Vautours", a viewing platform and information centre on the vultures. For a charge (26F) visitors can watch a live video of vultures at the nest site and go onto the viewing platform on the roof but equally good sightings can be obtained from the nearby car-park or just outside the building. This is probably the most likely place to see **Monk Vultures** and there are always plenty of Griffons around the cliffs. In addition, **Eagle Owl, Peregrine, Red-billed Chough** and **Blue Rock Thrush** also nest in the cliffs, while **Golden** and **Short-toed Eagles** are frequently overhead. **Honey Buzzard** can be over the woods anywhere in the region. **Rock Bunting** are found in the more open parts of the rocky slopes covered with broom and other low shrubs along the D996 between le Truel and Meyrueis and the D986 going north from Meyrueis. In winter, **Wallcreeper** and **Alpine Accentor** can be found in the gorges. In the summer, between June and September, the Belvedere des Vautours organises various walks morning and evening. One of these, to see vultures and steppe birds, is probably the best way to find **Monk Vulture** or **Stone Curlew**, if you have failed on your own.

A marked footpath, the Sentier Vallée du Tarn, runs north along the river from le Rozier. The species listed above are probably seen better from the roads above but the footpath allows closer views of such species as **Dipper, Grey Wagtail, Kingfisher** and **Common Sandpiper**.

Site iii.

Between the Gorges of the Tarn and the Jonte lies the **MÉJEAN** *causse*. It can be reached from a very minor road twisting up from le Truel or from the D986 running north-west from Meyrueis, which roughly bisects it. The open, stony plateau is perhaps even better than the Blandas Causse for steppe birds such as **Stone Curlew, Montagu's Harrier, Hoopoe, Tawny Pipit, Black-eared Wheatear,** larks, shrikes and buntings. Two rewarding areas to explore lie respectively north and south of the small village of Hures-le Parade.

ACCESS: If starting from the Belvedere at LE TRUEL, take the minor road that twists uphill to LA PARADE. This stretch is mainly wooded. On reaching the D986, it is possible to drive in a large circuit, which will allow you to find most of the steppe birds breeding here. Start by turning left and then after some

5 kilometres turn right. On the open *causse* between the villages of Mas St-Chely, le Buffre and Hures-la-Parade keep stopping and walking. Two kilometres south of LE BUFFRE, where a riding track meets the road, is a very good place for **Ortolan Bunting** and **Rock Thrush**. **Golden Eagles** and **Griffon Vultures** can often be seen hunting over the *causses*, as well as around the higher mountains in the Park. On reaching the D16 turn east towards FLORAC. At the Chanet glider aerodrome, some 5 km further on, turn south onto the D63, following the sign for "Przewalski horses", which can be found near the tiny hamlet of LE VILLARET. This is one of the best areas to search for **Stone Curlew**; listen for them calling at dusk and search the area west of the hamlet. They may be behind the wire in the horses' area, so you will have to scan with a telescope. **Rock Thrush** is often seen near LE VILLARET (or anywhere the terrain is rocky) and **Orphean Warbler** has bred in the few low trees found here. The area around the small glider aerodrome holds **Montagu's Harrier** (and **Hen Harrier** in winter). **Rock Sparrow** and **Short-toed Lark** are two more "steppe-loving" species that can be found on the Causse Méjean in small numbers. Search for the former in the village of NIVOLIERS, just south of the aerodrome or look around the rock outcrops near Aven Armand. Where pine trees have been planted listen for **Bonelli's Warbler** and **Wood Lark**. **Cirl Bunting** is also often near pines or taller bushes. **Dartford Warbler** can be found in the low box bushes. **Wryneck** and **Quail** are more usually heard than seen. The D63 continues to Hures and then through Drigas to the D986.

The D16 continues east from the glider aerodrome to FLORAC. Just where it leaves the plateau and starts to wind down to Florac in a series of hairpin bends is a good site for **Subalpine Warbler**. Park in any lay-by and check the box bushes on the slopes.

South of HURES-LA-PARADE, within the Park boundary, is another good steppe area. Roughly halfway between MEYRUEIS and LA PARADE a very minor road runs east to a series of farms. It is signed "Mas de la Font, Costeguison, Saubert, Hures". Do not take the dead-end road to the first named farm but fork right towards NIMES LE VIEUX, passing through Costeguison. After this hamlet the road forks again; both the right-hand road towards la Citroen and the left one towards Hures and Saubert are worth exploring. **Great Grey Shrike** and **Black-eared Wheatear** are more likely to be seen here than elsewhere. Anywhere on the causses, you are never out of the sound of **Skylark** but **Short-toed Lark** need more searching for. Learn their song or look for them running along the ground.

A walk from the village of HYELZAS, reached by driving up the twisting minor road from LE TRUEL is often productive in the late afternoon. Park near the *fromagerie* (cheese dairy) and walk down the dirt track which leads past some ruined buildings to the very edge of the cliffs above the Gorge de la Jonte. Watch out for vultures, especially **Monk Vulture**, which often fly along the cliffs below, as well as other cliff-dwelling species such as **Peregrine**. Listen at dusk for **Stone Curlew**. Other species likely to be seen

Red-legged Partridge

in box bushes or perched on wires are **Red-backed Shrike**, **Cirl Bunting** and **Sub-alpine Warbler**. **Red-legged Partridge** is quite common in this area.

The higher parts of the park, around Mount Lozère (1699m) and Mont Aigoual (1567m), are surprisingly disappointing for birds although the views and alpine flora are beautiful. **Golden Eagle** is one raptor that is likely to be seen from the tops and **Crested Tit** and **Black Woodpecker** can be found in the wooded slopes.

Site iv.
MOUNT LOZÈRE can easily be reached from FLORAC, or the historic village of PONT-DE-MONTVERT makes a good centre as both the D20 and the D35 lead from the village to higher areas on the mountain. The Chestnut and Beechwoods on the lower slopes of Mt. Lozère are more accessible for woodland birds than most of the wooded gorges and where mixed with pines at higher altitudes contain all the coniferous-loving species mentioned previously, as well as **Crossbill**. The D35 skirts the lower slopes and eventually arrives at the Col de MONTMIRAT, which links the high Mont Lozère plateau with the Sauveterre *causse*. The D20 goes higher and leads to the Col de Finiels (1540 m) and the Chalets du Mont Lozère, a cross-country ski station. **Citril Finch** is one of the many finches (Green, Gold, Linnet, Chaffinch and Serin) that can be found here. **Water Pipit** and **Northern Wheatear** are common birds of the high grassland and the pass is a good spot to raptor watch. **Golden Eagle, Short-toed Eagle, Griffon Vulture, Montagu's** and **Hen Harriers** may all be seen. There are many places to stop, walk and bird along both these road, which run through many different habitats (woodland, pasture, peat-bogs and mountain heathland) along their routes. **Tree Pipit, Yellowhammer, Rock Bunting, Red-backed Shrike, Marsh, Coal** and **Crested Tit** are some of the other species that

should be seen in appropriate habitat on Mount Lozère.

Site v.
MOUNT AIGOUAL (the "rainy mountain") can be visited via a circular tour from MEYRUEIS that also encompasses many different habitats. Leave Meyrueis on the D986, clearly signed to Mt. Aigoual. The first stretch runs through old forest, mainly coniferous. **Black Woodpecker** occurs where the trees are old and large enough. It is most likely to be heard and seen early in the morning or late afternoon. Park in any the various clearings along the D986 leading from MEYRUEIS towards Mt. Aigoual, walk a little way into the woods and listen. There is also a lay-by near the arboretum de la Foux. Fewer species breed in the exotic trees planted here but **Bonelli's Warbler** and **Crested Tit** can both be found. The ABIME DE BRAMABIAU is an abyss where a small river pours from a cleft in the side of a limestone cliff. It can be seen from this road and has **Crag Martins** flying around the cliffs. On the bare summit of Mt. Aigoual around the meteorological station **Yellowhammer, Tree Pipit, Stonechat, Black Redstart, Skylark, Northern Wheatear** can all be found. If you wish to continue the circuit back to MEYRUEIS from the summit, continue on the D18 towards the COL DE PERJURET, stopping at some of the pine woods alongside the road for **Bonelli's Warbler** and **Firecrest**. From the Perjuret pass it is possible to drive up onto the Méjean Causse (follow the signs for NIMES-LE-VIEUX and, by forking right (west) reach the rock formation called NIMES-LE-VIEUX. Turning left at the junction leads to AURES and eventually back to the D986 from where you can turn left back to Meyrueis. This stretch of *causse* is excellent for **Ortolan Bunting, Southern Grey Shrike, Montagu's Harrier** and **Black-eared Wheatear**.

Site vi.
The **DOURBIE GORGE** and River lie to the south of MILLAU between the Causses Noir (to the north) and Larzac. The cliffs are much used by raptors, including vultures from the Jonte and this is another excellent raptor site. The Dourbie Gorge is not so dramatic as the Tarn and Jonte as the road runs alongside the river but this means there is also the chance to see riverside species.

ACCESS: From MILLAU take the D991 which crosses the River Tarn from the centre of the by-pass which runs east of Millau. The Gorge is clearly signed. There are several places to pull off the road to scan the cliffs or walk a short distance in the first 14 kilometres up to ROQUE-ST-MARGUERITE. Besides raptors and vultures, all the cliff-nesting birds mentioned for the Jonte may be seen, including **Raven** and **Chough**. At LA ROQUE-ST-MARGUERITE you can continue along the Dourbie towards NANT and there turn west onto the D999, which climbs up onto the *causse* du Larzac and joins the main N9 at LA CAVALERIE. The *causse* birds mentioned above, including **Black-eared Wheatear** may be found here and it is the most likely area for **Little Bustard**, whose numbers are declining and which has not been seen on the

Causse Méjean for some years. Unfortunately the highest concentration is probably inside the military area "Camp du Larzac" each side of D999. However it is possible to pull onto the verge and scan. Early morning or evening you may spot **Little Bustard** flying. **Stone Curlew** can also be found here; listen for their calls at dusk. South of the military area the Larzac *causse* continues to the D7, already mentioned as the road leading to BLANDAS (site i). Alternative areas of *causse* can be reached by taking the minor road that runs from ROQUE-ST-MARGUERITE to PIERREFICHE and then branches either to ST-MARTIN-DU-LARZAC and BLAQUIERE or to MONTREDON.

Accommodation: This is a tourist region, and there are plenty of good restaurants, hotels in all categories and campsites in and around le Rozier, Florac, Meyrueis as well as all the larger villages near the park. They are only likely to be full during July and August but many will be closed from autumn to Easter. The *Logis* Hôtel du Mont Aigoual in Meyrueis is central and has been recommended by birders as has the Hotel Sources du Tarn at Le Pont de Montvert, nearer Mount Lozère.

Other wildlife and flora: Just off the D63, near the tiny hamlet of le Villaret between Nivoliers and Hures south of the Chanet glider aerodrome, some wild Przewalski horses have been freed, as a first step towards their eventual reintroduction in Mongolia. They also help graze the steppe. The European Beaver has been reintroduced into the River Tarn, but is both secretive and largely nocturnal. Wild Boar, Red and Roe Deer are quite numerous and can be seen in the forests, as are Genets, but these are nocturnal and unlikely to be seen. Red Squirrels abound in the pinewoods. The Montpellier snake *Malpolon monspessulanus* is the main prey of the Short-toed Eagle. Lizards are plentiful and include both Green and Ocellated.

In May and June the causses are covered with wildflowers (a quarter of all the species in France can be found in the Cévennes National Park) and are especially rich in orchids, some dozen species. Pyramidal *Anacamptis pyramidalis* and Military *Orchis militaris* are the most common but Lizard *Himantoglossum hircinum*, Lady *Orchis purpurea*, Monkey *O. simia*, Man *Aceras anthropophorum*, Red Helleborine *Cephelanthera rubra* and different members of the Bee Orchid family are other that can be found. The yellow *Orchis provincialis*, Coralroot *Corallorhiza trifida* and with much searching, Lady's Slipper *Cypripedium calceolus* can be found in clearings in the beechwoods, as well as Martagon Lily and Herb Paris. Several species of Wintergreen, Bird's-nest Orchid *Neottia nidus-avis*, Violet Limodore *Limodorum abortivum* and May-lily *Maianthemum bifolium* are usually found around the coniferous woods.

Not surprisingly, butterflies are numerous on the causses and include the Apollo *Parnassius apollo*, Cleopatra *Gonepteryx cleopatra*, Scarce Swallowtail *Iphiclides podalirius*, Berger's Clouded Yellow, many fritillaries including Spotted, Marbled, Glanville, Pearl-bordered, Cardinal and Queen-of-Spain and

Baton, Provence Chalk-hill, Reverdin's, Escher's, Adonis and Chapman's Blues. The scrubby grassland of the mountain slopes has a slightly different range of butterfly species from the drier causses. Camberwell Beauty, Large Tortoiseshell, Purple-shot and Scarce Coppers, Idas and Silver-studied Blues are relatively common as well as many fritillaries, skippers and ringlets.
The rivers are good for Dragonflies including uncommon species such as *Macromia splendens* and *Boyeria irene*.

The limestone plateaux are riddled with caves or "avens" remarkable for their stalagmites and stalactites, of which the most famous is probably Aven Armand. The Abime de Bramabiau is a cave with an underground river that gushes out of a crevasse. The region also contains many prehistoric dolmens and menhirs.

SOME SPECIAL SPECIES – either birds that are rare in France or those that are frequently sought by British birders

Fulmar *Fulmarus glacialis*. The Fulmar is a recent coloniser; the first birds breeding in the Sept-Îles in 1956. They have continued to expand throughout Brittany, Normandy and along the Channel coast until there are now some 1350 pairs breeding (compared with 570,000 in the British Isles). Sites where they can be seen are les Sept-Îles (Brittany), many Normandy cliffs and Cap Blanc-Nez, Pas-de-Calais, all north of the area covered by this book.

Balearic Shearwater *Puffinus maurentanicus*. Now split from both Yelkouan and Manx Shearwaters. Breeds around the Balearic Islands, so a few can sometimes be seen out at sea in summer along the Roussillon coast. From June onwards they move into the Atlantic and can be see along this coast (Île de Ré, Sables d'Olonne sites), returning to the Mediterranean in late autumn.

Yelkouan or Mediterranean Shearwater *Puffinus yelkouan* nests further east. There are very small colonies breeding on the islands off Marseilles and on the d'Hyères and perhaps a dozen in Corsica. They can be seen off Corsica year-round but are commoner in winter. They are most likely to be seen anywhere around the Mediterranean coast after the breeding period, when they disperse.

Manx Shearwater *Puffinus puffinus* only breed at 4 or 5 sites around Brittany. They can at times be seen offshore from the Atlantic Coast sites.

Cory's Shearwater *Calonectris diomedea* breeds in small numbers off the northern and southern tips of Corsica, the Îles d'Hyères and small islands near Marseilles. They may be seen around Corsica from February to November. The total French population is probably under 1000 pairs. They pass west along the Mediterranean and through the Straits of Gibraltar at the end of October/beginning of November to their wintering quarters in the South Atlantic.

Shag *Phalacrocorax aristotelis*. The Mediterranean sub-species *desmarestii* only breeds on Corsica, where it can be seen throughout the year from Cap Corse in the north all down the west coast to the extreme southern tip.

Little Bittern *Ixobrychus minutus* breeds in small numbers in reedbeds around the Mediterranean coast from Perpignan to the Camargue (the best site) and in Corsica. On the Atlantic coast, where the species has undergone a steep decline since the 1960's, it is most likely to be seen at the Courant d'Huchet (Atlantic Coast Area 11). It is also possible to see them in the Brenne, the Dombes north of Lyons and along the Garonne river (Montauban and Toulouse).

Night Heron *Nycticorax nycticorax* is a relatively common summer breeder in the Dombes (Lyon), Cambounet-sur-le-Sor Bird Reserve near Toulouse, along the Garonne river (Toulouse and Montauban), the Camargue, the Brenne and some Atlantic sites (Grand Lieu, Teich, Orx Marshes).

Cattle Egret *Bubulcus ibis*. This species has been expanding its worldwide range this century but in Europe is still only common in the Iberian peninsular.

In France the main breeding colony is in the Camargue, which, following a succession of mild winters, has grown from some 400 to 4000 nests over the past decade. Much smaller, more recently established but growing colonies can be found at Arcachon (Atlantic coast site 8) and at the Cambounet-sur-le-Sor Reserve, near Toulouse, where birds can often be seen in fields alongside the Garonne river and near the Confluent Reserve.

Squacco Heron *Ardeola ralloides* only breeds regularly in the Camargue, though it has been a very occasional breeder in the Dombes (Lyon) and Gave de Pau. During migration periods can be seen at any wetland along the Mediterranean coast.

Purple Heron *Ardea purpurea* breeds in suitable habitat (large reed beds) all around the Mediterranean from Perpignan to the Camargue as well as some Atlantic sites (Teich, Île d'Oléron and near Rochefort). It is also found in small numbers along the Garonne River (Montauban and Toulouse Areas), where it sometimes has to make do with bushes and willows to nest in.

Black Stork *Ciconia nigra*. Between 20-30 pairs have been observed breeding in France over the past decade but this figure is possibly underestimated. They breed very locally and sparsely in a broad band from the centre of the Atlantic coast (where the population is expanding) running north-east to the German frontier. The forests of Parroy (Meurthe-et-Moselle) and Châtillon-sur-Seine are two nesting areas in the north. Most easily seen during migration periods at Gruissan (Mediterranean Coast Area 3) and southern Atlantic Coast sites, especially Teich Bird Reserve.

White Stork *Ciconia ciconia*. Over 200 pairs breed in France, nearly all along the Channel and Atlantic coasts or the extreme northeast of the country. The Teich Bird Reserve (Atlantic Coast Area 9) is an easily observed nesting site.

Sacred Ibis *Threskiornis aethiopicus*   The feral population in Brittany has grown to well over 350 pairs from the 20 free-flying individuals introduced to the Branféré bird-park in Morbihan, Brittany in 1976, where they nest on an island. They are frequently observed around this area as well as in the Vilaine estuary and the marshes of Trély and Kergenets and even further afield. A few pairs have recently been noted attempting to breed near the Spoonbill colony in Grand-Lieu (Atlantic Coast Area 1).

Glossy Ibis *Plegadis falcinellus*. A very few pairs (between 2 and 4) have bred in the Camargue in recent years, an area where it is usually possible to find several birds in winter – ask at Capillière Information Centre for current location. A few may be seen when on passage at any Mediterranean wetland or in Corsica.

Spoonbill *Platalea leucorodia*. About 50 pairs breed in France and the number seems to be increasing. Some 20 pairs breed in the colony at Grand-Lieu Lake (Atlantic Coast Area 1) and there are a couple of other sites in this area as well as a new, small one in the Orx marshes (Atlantic Coast Area 11). The species now regularly winters in France down the Atlantic Coast, especially in the Parc Ornithologique du Teich (Atlantic Coast Area 9). The entire Dutch breeding population migrates along the Atlantic coast end-February-March and August-September so these are the best periods to see this species.

Greater Flamingo *Phoenicopterus ruber*. The only French breeding site is the Camargue, where about 13,000 pairs breed (though at times the number has risen to 17,000). They can be seen winter and summer feeding not only around the Camargue but at most sites along the Mediterranean coast. The well-wardened breeding site can be observed from a distance in spring.

White-headed Duck *Oxyura leucocephalas*. A re-introduction programme is getting underway in Corsica, so you might spot some on Lake Biguglia in the next few years. A few Ruddy Duck *Oxyura jamaicensis* occur in France, especially around Grand Lieu (Atlantic Coast Area 1) but the reintroduction programme of birds from Spain is conditional on French Ruddy Ducks being exterminated; the Office de Chasse is carrying out the killings.

Goosander *Mergus merganser*. Only breeds in the Haute-Savoie Alps, mainly around Lac Léman. Also look for them on the Rhone near Bellegarde (Alps Area 5 site ii.) and Lac d'Annecy. They winter on many large lakes or sheltered coastal bays, especially during hard winters when the northern and Baltic populations arrive in France.

Honey Buzzard *Pernis apivorus*. Nests throughout France, except the Mediterranean coastal area, in all well-wooded areas. The number of breeding pairs varies from year to year (probably affected by climatic conditions in their wintering quarters or late, wet springs in France). They are far less numerous than Common Buzzard, except perhaps in the well-wooded northeast. Southward migrating birds cross the Pyrenees in huge numbers during the last few days of August and the beginning of September. In spring, pre-nuptial migration is late and much less concentrated. Most breeding birds arrive in mid-May and non-breeders can be seen crossing the Pyrenees as late as mid-June.

Black-shouldered Kite *Elanus caeruleus*. A pair was observed attempting to breed in France for the first time in 1983 and breeding has been confirmed since 1996 at two or three sites in Aquitaine; there are now five breeding pairs. Drive along the roads south of Dax, between this town and Pau and also look around Atlantic Coast Area 11 Les Barthes d'Adour, checking pylons. It chooses areas as much like African savannah as possible; open, cultivated fields with scattered groups of trees, usually near water. A crepuscular species, most active during the three hours before sunset, rather longer in the breeding season, look for it perched on the top of a pine or pylon or hovering nearby. Occasionally an individual is seen crossing the Pyrenean passes and in 1998 a pair bred on the *causses* not far from the Vulture reintroduction site (Cévennes). This area is also very *steppe* or savannah like.

Bearded Vulture or **Lammergeier** *Gypaetus barbatus*. The French do not like the name "Lammergeier", which means, "lamb killer", considering it both misleading and pernicious. Lammergeier has been used in the text, as it is the name by which the bird is generally known to English birders. Numbers have been increasing slowly but steadily over the past decade, largely due to conservation programmes in both France and Spain which combine protection of nesting sites with "vulture restaurants"; the latter in particular helping young birds survive their first few winters. On the French side of the Pyrenees, there are now over 20 breeding pairs and several immature individuals spread the length of the range, with fewer in the east. The Pyrenean National Park, especially the areas around Gavarnie and Vallée d'Ossau, has the highest concentration and is where they are most likely to be seen. Further east, Port d'Aula is another likely site and in the west, Col de Méhatché.

There are 8 pairs in Corsica and the population seems stable, though very low, and the breeding-success rate is poor. They can be seen anywhere in the central, mountainous section with more in the north.

Captive-bred young birds have been reintroduced since 1986 into the Alps and the Alpes-Maritimes (where they have been extinct since the beginning of the century) and one pair has now started to breed in the Haute-Savoie. There are perhaps a dozen other individuals in the Alps and they are most likely to be seen in the Reposoir valley, where they were initially re-introduced, or Sixt reserve, both in the Haute-Savoie and the north-west of Mercantour National Park.

Egyptian Vulture *Neophron percnopterus* is found mainly in the western and central Pyrenees, though there are a few pairs in the Ariège in the east, and the Provence-Alpes. They are cliff nesters and in the Pyrenees often share a Griffon Vulture colony. Some 50 pairs breed in the Pyrenees and about 30 in the Mediterranean region. Vall d'Ossau (Pyrenees Area 5) is a likely spot. The Parc Naturel Regional du Luberon holds about a dozen pairs and two pairs normally breed in the Alpilles. Only one pair bred in the Cévennes vulture colony near le Rozier in 1998 and none in 1999. La Caume in les Alpilles and the rubbish dump at Entressen in the Crau are likely spots to see them along the Mediterranean coast. Egyptian Vultures arrive in March and leave in September.

Griffon Vulture *Gyps fulvus*. Numbers have been increasing spectacularly in the Pyrenees, and this species (though there are far fewer on the French than on the Spanish side) can be seen almost anywhere along the range, being more numerous in the west. They are almost certain at Pyrenees Areas 1, 4,5, 6, 8 and 10 at any time of the year. The species has been reintroduced into the Cévennes, where there are now some 75 pairs and many immatures. They can always be seen from the Belvedere near le Rozier (Cévennes).

Black or Monk Vulture *Aegypius monachus*. The only place this species can be seen in France (apart from a very occasional vagrant to the Pyrenees) is the Cévennes. 25 birds are now flying around the reintroduction site near le Rozier, though only one chick per year has been raised for the past few years.

White-tailed Sea Eagle *Haliaeetus albicilla*. About 20 birds regularly winter in France (most in the northeast). The most famous site is le lac de Der-Chantecoq in Champagne where several birds have been seen each year for well over a decade. More recently a few birds have wintered irregularly along the Atlantic coast (Grand-Lieu lake Area 1), in the southwest in the Barthes d'Adour marshes (Atlantic Coast Area 11) and the Camargue.

Osprey *Pandion haliaetus*. A few pairs of Ospreys have been breeding in central France since 1985, after a gap of nearly 50 years. The breeding range is slightly north of the area covered in this guide, forest areas stretching roughly from Angers to Orleans. The best time to observe this species on the mainland is during their spring and autumn migration, especially the end of March and mid-April when individuals from different European populations can be seen along the river migration routes (the Loire, Allier, Dordogne, Charente) and around the Brenne and the Dombes (Lyon Area) as well as at coastal sites. September is another good month as many birds linger in France for some time before continuing south. Each year between two and three hundred birds use the Allier valley alone. The only other breeding birds are found on Corsica where numbers have increased over the past 25 years and there are now some 25 pairs breeding, all on sea cliffs, in the north-west of the island in the Scandola Reserve.

Spotted Eagle *Aquila clanga*. One or two birds have regularly wintered in the Camargue and the Barthes d'Adour for the past few years.

Golden Eagle *Aquila chrysaetos* is reasonably widespread throughout the Alps (over 150 pairs), the Pyrenees (some 50 pairs) and the Massif Central (12-15 pairs). There are also about 30 pairs in Corsica.

Bonelli's Eagle *Hieraetus fasciatus*. This raptor is virtually restricted to the Mediterranean region. It has suffered a drastic decline in numbers over the past twenty years and there are now only some 24 pairs in France. The best sites are la Caume in the Alpilles and the Petit Luberon (Mediterranean Area 7), or Sainte Victoire mountain east of Aix. This massive limestone mountain (well-known from the paintings of Cézanne) rises to 1000 m and extends for some 20 km. Two, perhaps three pairs of eagles breed there, and birds can be seen flying along the south-facing cliffs near the Information Centre, Maison Sainte-Victoire (exhibitions, café, shop for maps, etc). In winter, birds may hunt over the lowlands towards the sea. *ACCESS*: Leave the A8 motorway at exit 32, turn onto the N7 and head back towards Aix for 1 km (or take the N7 east from Aix for 5 km). Turn north onto the D58 to Beaurecueil. Keep left before the village and then left again to reach the D17 which runs along the base of the mountain. Turn right (east). In the next five kilometres there are two parking places, Plan d'en Chois and Le Bouquet, from where marked paths leads towards the cliffs; there is also a large car park at the Maison. From any of these walk a little way up the paths until you have a clear view of the cliffs. Most of the other species given for the Alpilles can also be seen here.

A pair of Bonelli's Eagles used to breed north-west of Perpignan at Tautavel (Mediterranean Area 4) but the recent expansion of a quarry has probably caused this nest site to be deserted. This species breeds on cliffs in the warmer, limestone ranges, between 100–600m in height, seldom above the Evergreen Oak limit and seems to like water in the vicinity. The best months to see them are from mid-June (when the young are on the wing) to the end of the year, when they start displaying. When they are breeding (mid-February to end of May) they are more difficult to observe. For some reason, they frequently fly in pairs and often at mid-day. One or two immatures often winter around the Camargue and Crau.

Booted Eagle *Hieraetus pennatus* can be found along the Pyrenees, with more at the western end of the range, as well as scattered throughout the centre of the country. An odd individual may over-winter in the Camargue.

Lesser Kestrel *Falco naumanni.* Only likely to be seen on the Crau (Camargue) where the colony continues to increase after declining almost to extinction by the beginning of the 1990's. There are now about 50 pairs that nest in heaps of stones, although attempts have been made to get them to breed in artificial nests placed on the roofs of buildings.

Red-footed Falcon *Falco vespertinus.* No birds have bred in France for some time and at best they were only a very occasional breeder. However it is possible to see this species passing through the Camargue (especially Crau Area 6) every spring at the end of April to the middle of May as well as around Lake Biguglia in Corsica, where they are regular on passage, the majority in May.

Ptarmigan *Lagopus mutus.* Ice-age relicts, the remnant Alpine and Pyrenean populations (different sub-species *L. m. helveticus* and *L. m. pyrenaicus*) keep to the highest mountain tops above 2000 m and a considerable amount of walking, and luck, is always necessary to see this species. Best places are the scree slopes above Néouvielle or Bagnères in the Pyrenees, the Col of Lautaret and Ecrins Park in the Alps and the Haut Giffre in the Haute-Savoie. By the time they are in their winter plumage, end-November and early December, these areas can be dangerous.

Capercaillie *Tetrao urogallus.* There are small relict populations in all the high mountain areas, stranded since the ending of the last ice-age. This species has suffered much disturbance recently through forestry and the spread of off-piste skiing and snowmobiles and is consequently in decline. In the Pyrenees birds can only be found in the central 350 km, between 400 and 2000 m. They seem to prefer the higher mountain pine *(Pinus uncinata)* forests in the woods around Néouvielle (Pyrenees Area 7), Bagnères area (Pyrenees Area 8), Beille plateau (Pyrenees Area 10) and many other Pyrenean forests as well as in the Alps north of Geneva, the Vosges and the Jura. However, they are very difficult to see except by luck or if you should happen to disturb a roosting bird while walking through the forests. In spring, when they lek, sightings are easier but most leks are protected by wardens who will certainly turn you away. The RSPB has recently issued a code of conduct for watching Capercaillies and Black Grouse in Britain, where there too are in decline. It should also be adhered to on the Continent. Avoid disturbing leks from March to May – visit them in autumn instead. Use hides or remain in vehicles wherever possible. Arrive well before daybreak and stay until the lek has finished. Use well-defined paths to avoid disturbing nesting hens and young.

Black Grouse *Tetrao tetrix.* Only found in the Alps, from the Haute-Savoie to the Var between 1000–2100 m. In autumn, when males and females form separate flocks (sometimes numbering up to 30 males), birds may be found up to 2600 m. They can sometimes be seen in the north-east corner of the Queyras Regional Park, above Ristolas. The walk from Les Portes, near la Chapelle in the Ecrins National Park is another site and, with luck, they can be heard and seen among the alder shrubs below the Lautaret pass. See also the Haute-Savoie sites. They favour damp, cool slopes rather than dry, sunny ones and daybreak is the time to hear them calling, when they lek from the end of April through May. There are between 300 and 400 in the Ecrins Park. (But see the RSPB's code of conduct above).

Hazel Hen *Bonasia bonasia.* This secretive game-bird is found in dense forest in the Alps, Jura and Vosges mountains but the populations are very small and scattered. There may even be tiny relict populations in the Massif Central and the Pyrenees. The chances of seeing one, even if you spent days walking through the forests, are slight, except with extreme luck. Tracks or droppings are all most observers see.

Rock Partridge *Alectoris graeca.* Found only in the southern Alps; this species is in regression. It breeds on dry, sunny, rocky slopes above 1500 m but in snowy winters may descent to below 1000 m. Look for it on the slopes facing Ristolas village in the Queyras Park at dawn and in the Ecrins Park above les Portes (The Alps Areas 2 and 3). It displays in May and in autumn family groups often starts moving down towards the villages. In the months between it is very difficult to locate. Beware! In the western and southern parts of the Alps, it pairs with Red-legged Partridge and produces fertile hybrids.

Californian Quail *Callipepla californica.* Corsica is the only place in Europe where this American gamebird has become naturalised. The species has been slowly expanding its range since thousands were released in the early 1960's. The small feral population is to be found on the Aléria plain on the east side of the island, mainly below 200 m. They seem to favour the mixture of low *maquis* and cultivated fields with scrubby cover between Moriani to Ghisonaccia. Their distinctive and far-carrying call can be heard from March to June. Family groups can be seen in the summer.

Spotted Crake *Porzana porzana* breeds locally down the Atlantic coast where suitable habitat occurs. A few **Little Crake** *Porzana parva* and **Baillon's Crake** *Porzana pusilla* may breed in the Camargue but are more likely to be seen along the Mediterranean coast during migration periods.

Purple Gallinule *Porphyrio porphyrio.* This species was reintroduced from the Coto Donaña into the Natural Park of Aiguamolls d'Emporda, Spain in 1989 and 1991. The programme has been extremely successful and numbers are increasing rapidly. In 1996, two pairs (presumably from Aiguamolls) bred in the Etang de Canet-St. Nazaire, near Perpignan; a "first" for France and they continue to be seen there.

Stone-curlew *Burhinus oedicnemus.* This bird of dry steppe-land, dunes and arable land can be found from the north to the south of France in suitable habitat. Some good sites are on the Crau, the *causses* in the Cévennes, the gravel spits on the lower reaches of the Allier River and cultivated fields in the

Loire basin, where about 60% of the French population are found. The quadrangle la Rochelle, Niort, Angloulême, Royan (Atlantic sites) holds good numbers. Listen for its curlew-like call at dawn and dusk.

Collared Pratincole *Glareola pratincola.* Only breeds, in very small numbers, in the Camargue. In 1998 they were down to some six pairs. The best place to see them is between the Domaine de Méjanes and le Paty de la Trinité. On migration, they may be seen at several Mediterranean sites, especially Canet, Perpignan (Mediterranean Area 1).

Little Bustard *Tetrax tetrax.* This species has suffered a drastic decline over the past decade and is currently the object of a LPO campaign to save it and its habitat. There are two main areas where this species can be found. In the centre the greatest number occurs on the flat cereal plains in the west, in Poitou-Charentes, behind the Atlantic coast. In the south it can be found on dry grassland such as the Crau (Camargue) with a few still remaining on the *causses* in the Cévennes. The southern populations are resident but the remainder migrates (mainly to Spain) between September to November, coinciding with the opening of the shooting season. They flock before migrating and this is often the easiest time to see them.

Common Crane *Grus grus.* One of the most impressive birding spectacles is watching skeins of Cranes flying back to roost at dusk at Lac de Der (Northern France) or at Captieux (Atlantic Coast Area 13). During migration (October to early December) there may be many thousands at these sites but several hundred remain there all winter. A few can also be seen at les Barthes d'Adour (Atlantic Coast Area 11) all winter with more during migration periods. They cross the Pyrenees at the end of November and return during February when they can be seen flying over many passes in the centre and west of the range. From east to west these include the Beille plateau (Pyrenees Area 10), the port d'Aula (Pyrenees Area 9), the val d'Aran and Spanish frontier (beside Area 8), the Aure valley (below Area 7) and the three passes in Area 2. They also stop over at lakes in the Pyrenean foothills during both migrations: the lake near Puydarrieux, east of Tarbes; Monbel, 25 km east of Foix and south of Toulouse and Arjuzanx, roughly 75 km (by road) southwest of Captieux (Atlantic Coast Area 13).

Kentish Plover *Charadrius alexandrinus* is a fairly common breeding bird around the Mediterranean where there are sandy beaches and dunes (Mediterranean Areas 1, 2, 4, as well as along the Atlantic coast at Arcachon, the mouth of the Gironde and Bourgneuf and Aiguillon Bay (Atlantic Coast Areas 2 and 4).

Audouin's Gull *Larus audouinii.* This species has been one of Spain's breeding successes. Only 36 pairs bred in the Ebro Delta in 1981; now there are over 7000 pairs. Birds are now regularly seen in France, flying along the Mediterranean coast and in the Camargue, especially before and after the breeding season. Between 20 to 90 pairs (varies from year to year) breed in Corsica, most in the reserve of the Finocchiarola Islands (no access during breeding season), off the north cape but only a few individuals winter in

Corsica. The majority leave during the last week of August and return between mid-March and the beginning of April. Cap Corse is the most likely place to see them flying by but individuals can also be found around the harbours in Ajaccio, St. Florent, Porto and sometimes at Lake Biguglia.

Mediterranean Gull *Larus melanocephalus.* In spite of its name, this is an eastern species with most pairs breeding east of the Black Sea. Since 1965, however, it has started to breed with spectacular success in the Camargue alongside Black-headed Gulls and there are now over 800 breeding pairs. In winter it can be seen almost anywhere along the Mediterranean, Corsican and Atlantic coasts.

Slender-billed Gull *Larus genii* breeds only in the Camargue area, where number have increased from 3 pairs in 1972 to several hundred today. It favours saltpans and the more saline lagoons and can be seen all year round.

Gull-billed Tern *Gelochelidon nilotica* breeds only in the Camargue, around the Salins-de-Giraud and Aigues Mortes, where it can be seen from April to September. Passage migrant elsewhere along the Mediterranean.

Roseate Tern *Sterna dougallii* breeds only around the rocky coasts of Brittany, with most colonies along the north coast. Can usually be seen in Morlaix Bay, Finistère.

Black Tern *Chlidonias niger.* Some 200 pairs breed irregularly in France, mainly in lakes along the Atlantic coast and in the centre: Grand-Lieu (Atlantic Coast Area 1) is a regular site, as is the Reserve of St-Denis-du-Payré (Atlantic Coast. Area 4 site iv), Rochefort marshes, the Brenne and the Camargue. However, they are much easier to see at these sites, and at the Dombes near Lyon, often in large flocks, during spring migration when varying numbers of **White-winged Tern** *Chlidonias leucopterus* may be with them.

Whiskered Tern *Chlidonias hybridus.* Can be found in the same sites as the above species. Between 1000–1500 pairs breed in France and the Dombes and the Brenne are two of the most important sites.

Atlantic Puffin *Fratercula arctica* Only found in three sites along the north Brittany coast: Ouessant and the Morlaix bay, Finistère and the reserve of the Sept-Îles. A few **Common Guillemot** and **Razorbill** may also be found breeding at the same sites, though in winter they are common along the Atlantic coast.

Pin-tailed Sandgrouse *Pterocles alchata* are only found in the Crau (Camargue) where the remaining remnant population numbers some 175 pairs.

Great Spotted Cuckoo *Clamator glandarius.* This summer visitor arrives at the end of February and is often gone by June. Most likely to be seen March-April when its harsh calls give away its presence. Young birds are flying by early May. It parasitises Magpies, so look out when you see a pair getting very excited. It is confined

Great Spotted Cuckoo

Roller

to the Mediterranean area as far east as Marseilles, both the coastal plain and the hills behind. Check the Leucate/Salses, Narbonne, Camargue sites.

Scops Owl *Otus scops*. A summer visitor, this urban little owl is most likely to be seen in town parks and around villages with tall trees. Its "sonar blip" call, given as soon as it is dark, is the best way of locate it. Most numerous around the Mediterranean, it can also be found north of Bordeaux up to Poitiers and scattered throughout the centre of the country.

Tengmalm's Owl *Aegolius funereus*. Found in the Alps and the Jura. A small remnant population was discovered in the eastern Pyrenees as recently as the 1960's; in the 1980's it was found to also breed in the Massif Central and the western Pyrenees. It has also been located in the Massif de l'Aigoual (Montagne du Lingas) in the Cévennes. It seems to be slightly expanding its range and occupying sites from where it was absent up to the '90's. However, an increasing number of observers and their knowledge of the bird's calls has helped locate it. Tengmalm's prefer north-facing slopes above 2000 m. with large, old conifers and normally take over a Black Woodpecker's hole as a nest site; the range expansion of this Woodpecker may have contributed to that of Tengmalm's. They also use nestboxes. Tengmalm's are more common in the Alps, especially the National Parks along the Italian frontier and the Haute-Savoie. They call normally only at night and early in the year when their habitat is inaccessible to walkers, breed irregularly and move around frequently. Consequently they are very difficult to find. Any tree with a hole high up in the right habitat is worth tapping with a stick, to see if a head peers out!

Eagle Owl B*ubo bubo*. This can be a very difficult bird to see, confined basically to the foothills of the Pyrenees, the Massif Central, the Mediterranean hills and the lower Alps and Préalpes. They call mainly between November and February, at or just before dusk, and are relatively quiet when breeding and feeding young, though they may call briefly before flying from the nest site or roost at dusk. They prefer inaccessible and remote cliff faces, sunny but not necessarily very high, for breeding and though a pair stay in the same territory for many years, they move the nest and roosting sites frequently, so giving precise directions is difficult. The best hope of seeing one is to listen at one of the smaller Mediterranean sites, les Alpilles near les Baux, the Petit Luberon or along the Aveyron gorges near Montauban, when they are calling. They are relatively numerous in the Alpilles, so listen by any suitable cliff in this chain. Besides les Baux, try the D24 between Mouries and Eygalières.

Pygmy Owl *Glaucidium passerinum*. Only found in the Alps in coniferous forests up to 1000 m. This tiny owl flies just before it is dusk and calls throughout the year, which makes it easier to spot than a nocturnal owl like Tengmalm's. They are still very hard to find. Try the site south of Besançon in the Bois des Ayes.

Alpine Swift *Apus melba*. This species arrives in the latter part of March and leaves in September-October. It breeds on high cliff faces and can be seen in the central Pyrenees, hills behind the Mediterranean coast, the Alps and Corsica, where it is distributed throughout Cap Corse, the central mountain chain, the south and west coasts.

Pallid Swift *Apus pallidus*. Arrives earlier and leaves later than Common Swift. It can still be seen until October, even the beginning of November. Colonies are found near the Mediterranean around Banyuls (Mediterranean Area 1) and east of Marseilles, and in Toulouse, while a few have recently bred near Biarritz. In Corsica, they are found mainly on rocky coasts in the north and all along the west coast down to Bonifacio in the south. As well as old buildings, rocks and caves, nest sites are sometime old bridges and quays, as this species seems often to be found near water.

Bee-eater *Merops apiaster*. This typically Mediterranean species is most likely to be seen near the Roussillon and Camargue sites and in Corsica although scattered colonies can be found much further north to just south of Paris and on the south Brittany coast. It is present from end-April to September when it breeds colonially in holes in soft banks. Eyne (eastern Pyrenees Area 11) is a good spot for migrating flocks.

Roller *Coracias garrulus*. A scarce bird and possibly in decline. It can be found in dry, open areas around and behind the Mediterranean. It is rare everywhere but the best sites are possibly the Crau (Camargue), Gruissan and Perpignan sites and the southern Causses. Their habit of perching on electric wires makes them easy to spot.

Grey-headed Woodpecker *Picus canus*. Found in a band across the north of the country from inland Brittany to north-east Alsace, but is scarce in the southern part of France covered by this book, except in the Massif Central. Good sites in the north are the woods around the Lac de Der, Fontainebleau and the National Regional Park of Normandy-Maine. Possible sites in this book include the wooded parts of the Sólogne, the Brenne and the woods in the Puy-de Dome range around Clemont-Ferrant. There are a very few pairs in the Forest of Branconne (Angloulême Area). Like the Green, they feed mainly on ants and start displaying and calling as early as January but mainly during February and March. Normally quiet, unobtrusive birds, their "song" is much shorter than the Green's yaffle but their drumming lasts for up to 2 seconds. So if you see an apparently "Green" woodpecker drumming...

Black Woodpecker *Dryocopus martius.* This large woodpecker is relatively common in mixed and coniferous woodland the length of the Pyrenees, the Massif Central and the Alps as well as mature woodland throughout the centre and east of France, such as Lancosme Forest in the Brenne, Moulière Forest north of Poitiers and Branconne Forest, north-east of Angoulême. It has expanded its range westwards considerably since the 1960 and is only absent from the Atlantic and Mediterranean coasts and most of the south-west. The coniferous forest below Mt. Ventoux (Mediterranean Area 8) is probably the nearest site to the Mediterranean.

Pairs are resident but young birds can fly considerable distances to find their own territories during their first autumn and may then be seen outside known territories. A large bird, the Black naturally only nests in mature trees (at least 30-40 cm diameter) and its nesting hole, often 5 metres or more from the ground, is large and distinctively pear-shaped. Listen out for its very loud drumming and take note of dead trees where they have been feeding; look for large areas of stripped-off bark and deep holes. The Black utters a number of very distinctive calls and is often heard before being spotted. In winter and early spring it calls early in the morning and at dusk, just when coming in to roost. From February to May it is at its most territorial and can be heard at almost any time of day. While in the mountains it is to be found in mixed beech/coniferous or coniferous woods, often large Scotch Pines, in the lowlands, while it can be found in large parks or plantations; in mixed deciduous woodland it seems to favour strands of mature Beech.

Middle Spotted Woodpecker *Dendropocus medius. This* species is absent from the Mediterranean plain and hills, the Alpes-Maritimes and Alps south of Geneva, as well as south-west of Bordeaux and most of the Pyrenees, though it can be found in the Forest of Issaux together with the next species. The forest of Grésigne (Montauban Area) holds quite good numbers. Further north, good sites are in the Lancosme Forest in the Brenne, Branconne Forest, north-east of Angoulême and Moulière Forest north-east of Poitiers. Middle Spotted habitually choose old oak woodland (though it is fond in Chestnut woods in the Dordogne) but can also be found in smaller coppices and even groups of tree provided they are mature. In mixed deciduous woods look for it in strands of Oaks. Its "song" is nasal, raucous and very different from the Great-spotted, though its "kick"-call is weak and more like Lesser

Spotted's. It does not drum territorially.

White-backed Woodpecker *Dendrocopus leucotos*. Although it is worth searching any suitable habitat (old beech-fir woods with plenty of decaying trees) in the centre-west of the chain for this, the rarest of the Pyrenean woodpeckers, the site in the Forest of Issaux (Pyrenees Area 4) is the place with the best chance of seeing them. They are very silent birds, rarely calling and reputed to "sing" only in May but have been heard calling in February at Issaux. They also occur further east in the woods south of Bagnères-de-Louchon (Pyrenees Area 8) but are difficult to locate in these steep, dense woods. Take the road leading up to Super-Bagnères ski station. Just after the la Carrière sign is a track on the right *Route Forestière de Techous*. Walk up this track listening and searching clearings with dead and fallen trees.

Three-toed Woodpecker *Picoides tridactylus*. A very rare breeding bird, at the western limit of its range in the Alps and Jura on the Swiss border. It favours cool spruce-deciduous woods, with clearings and plenty of dead trees on the ground. Almost impossible to see because it is retiring, silent for most of the year and the woods where it is found (the Haute-Griffe and Jura around Gex) are usually inaccessible in spring.

Thekla Lark *Galerida theklae*. A bird of stony Mediterranean hillsides and plateaux, only found in the Corbières near Rivesaltes and north of Salses (Mediterranean Area 2) and in the Albères (Mediterranean Area 1).

Crested Lark *Galerida cristata* is widespread around the Mediterranean, up the Atlantic coast as far as the Loire and also around and north of Paris. It is absent from the centre and east, the Alps, Pyrenees and Corsica, being essentially a lowland bird.

Short-toed Lark *Calandrella brachydactyla* is only found around the Mediterranean and very locally along the Atlantic coast at Aiguillon Bay. A very few pairs breed in the coastal regions of Corsica. It is easiest seen on the Crau, on the *causses* of the Cévennes and at Leucate and Gruissan.

Calandra Lark *Melanocorypha calandra*. This large, chunky lark is very local. It is usually seen flying over lowland meadows and arable land when the white trailing edge of its wings is distinctive. It is only found close to the Mediterranean at Cape Leucate (Mediterranean Area 2) – a few pairs, the aerodrome at Lezignan-Corbieres (Mediterranean Area 4) and in the Crau (Mediterranean Area 6).

Red-rumped Swallow *Hirundo daurica*. This species has been gradually extending its very limited range in France but is still difficult to locate as only single pairs breed in widely scattered locations, around Banyuls (Roussillon) in the Albères, the south Corbières, the Cévennes, les Alpilles as well as the north and west coasts of Corsica, below 500 m in altitude. They often nest under a bridge.

Crag Martin *Ptyonoprogne rupestris* is common wherever there are hills and mountains in the south of the country and seems to be expanding its range. It is resident in Corsica and parts of the Mediterranean but in other areas is a partial, altitudinal migrant and most birds move down from the higher breeding grounds in late October-November to return in February, if the weather is mild. It can be seen around gorges, cliff faces and the higher villages, often with House Martins, all along the Pyrenees, the Massif Central, the Mediterranean hills and Alps and pre-Alps in the east.

Alpine Accentor *Prunella collaris.* This resident species is an altitudinal migrant; breeding in rocky scree slopes above 2000–2200 m but descending to ski stations and lower areas in winter. The Cirque de Gavarnie and the nearby Port de Bouchoro and the Haute Savoie site of le Reposoir are two places where they can be seen all year round. They are usually easy to see in the village of Les Baux (Mediterranean Area 7) in winter, as well as round the Spanish frontier passes, especially Pourtalet (Pyrenean Area 5). Several hundred pairs are also to be found in the central mountains of Corsica between 1800–2700 m and wintering on the west coast.

Bluethroat *Luscinia svecica.* The subspecies *cyanecula* with a white spot breeds along the Atlantic coast of France, from Brittany to Arcachon, where the Teich Bird Reserve is probably the best place to see them. During migration they can also be seen right down this coast to the Spanish frontier. There has been sporadic breeding by a few pairs in the Rhône valley – see Lyon and Savoie sites. Check rank vegetation along wet ditches, around salt-pans and under Tamarisk (and other) bushes near the sea walls at all Atlantic Coast sites. Bluethroats are shy, skulking birds so watch for furtive behaviour in reed edges and low vegetation.

Black Wheatear *Oenanthe leucura.* There is only one site for this species in France, on the rocky slopes around the Tour Madeloc near Banyuls-sur-Mer, just north of the Spanish frontier (Mediterranean Area 1). Nearby populations in the Pyrenees have been in general decline in recent years and this is likely to affect the tiny French population which may not survive for long in the twenty-first century if it is not already extinct!

Rock Thrush *Monticola saxatilis.* A summer visitor to the Pyrenees, Alps and Corsica. It arrives in April or the beginning of May and leaves quietly during September. It can be found in both high mountain areas and the lower foothills between April and September. It likes south-facing, rocky slopes with boulders and a few scattered bushes and often sings from a prominent rock or telephone wires in the last two weeks of May and the beginning of June, which is the easiest time to locate it. The Pourtalet pass (Pyrenees Area 5) is one of the most reliable areas, easy to reach without a long climb; others include all the higher Alpine and Pyrenean sites, the central Corsican mountains and Prat de Bouc pass (Parc de Volcans, southern Massif Central).

Blue Rock Thrush *Monticola solitarius.* This resident species is confined to the Mediterranean area and Corsica wherever there are dry and rocky habitats, preferring cliffs and even buildings rather than the rocky slopes chosen by Rock Thrush. It can be seen at la Caume, les Baux, Leucate, Narbonne sites, above Banyuls (Perpignan). It can also be found near the village of Prats-de Mollo (Pyrenees Area 12). In Corsica it breeds on sea cliffs along the west coast, Cap Corse and on buildings in Corté. Search the top of a cliff face or the highest rocks where the male often perches. It has a distinctive long-billed silhouette even when the blue coloration is not obvious (much longer beak than a Blackbird's, for example, whose song is somewhat similar).

Fan-tailed Warbler or Zitting Cisticola *Cisticola juncidis.* Found along the Atlantic coast from Brittany to the Spanish border and all along the Mediterranean area and coastal plains of Corsica flying over arable fields, saltmarsh and reedbeds.

Moustached Warbler *Acrocephalus melanopogon.* A resident species of large reedbeds around the Mediterranean; probably easiest to see in winter when it is the only *Acrocephalus* warbler there. Perpignan and the Camargue are the most likely sites. In Corsica look for it around Lake Biguglia, especially in winter.

Icterine Warbler *Hippolais icterina.* Only breeds in the north-east, outside the area covered by this book. It can sometimes be seen in Corsica and the south when on passage. The widespread *Hippolais* warbler is **Melodious Warbler** *Hippolais polyglotta* which can be found throughout the country except for the highest mountain regions and the coast of Brittany. Look for it in damp woodland or shrubs, especially brambles, near water.

Spectacled Warbler *Sylvia conspicillata.* This rare and local warbler breeds in dry places with low and sparse vegetation, sometimes alongside Dartford Warbler in degraded garrigue, around the Mediterranean and in Corsica, where it is the rarest *Sylvia* warbler. It also favours large stretches of *salicornia* bushes on dry salt flats, as in the Camargue – the easiest place to find it. Its rufous wings and white throat immediately distinguish it (it looks very much like a small Whitethroat).

Subalpine Warbler *Sylvia cantillans.* This migrant breeder reaches the Mediterranean at the end of March and stays until September. It breeds in taller scrub and undergrowth than Dartford and Spectacled Warblers, seeming to have a preference for brambles and drier areas, at low as well as higher altitudes up to about 1200 m. In the right habitat it can be seen at almost all the Mediterranean and Corsican sites described, except high mountain and wetland ones (although tired migrants can be seen in the Camargue in spring). It is, however, very skulking and difficult to see except when the males are singing from the tops of bushes early in the season. The Cévennes, the Crau and the Canigou area of the Pyrenees are other good sites.

Marmora's Warbler *Sylvia sarda.* Found only in Corsica at coastal and inland areas up to 1550 m or even higher in rocky areas where the *maquis* vegetation is sparse or patchy with some taller *Cistus* or other shrubs. It also quickly recolonises recently burnt *maquis.* The best site is the cliff-top *maquis* just south of Bonifacio, where there is a high density; other sites include the Col de Sevi, near Evisa, Galeria and the Regino valley on the west coast.

Western Bonelli's Warbler *Phylloscopus bonelli.* One of the commonest warblers in woodland, found in deciduous and mixed woods as well as pinewoods up to almost 2000 m. It seems to prefer sunny slopes and the edges or clearings of woods but can also be found in plantations. Only absent from the Channel coast, Normandy and Brittany and parts of the extreme north and north-east. It is most easily located by its two-syllable "hoo-eet" call and short single-note trill. In lower areas its range overlaps with that of Chiffchaff but replaces this species at higher altitudes. It arrives in France at the end of March and leaves during August.

Spanish Chiffchaff *Phylloscopus collybita brehmii*. This recently-split species can only be found in the Basque region, from the extreme western end of the Pyrenees to the Atlantic coast. It can only safely be distinguished by its song (Listen to it on the cassette *Oiseaux des Pyrenees* Sitelle). Try Pyrenean Areas 1 and 2 or Atlantic Coast Areas 11 and 12.

Collared Flycatcher *Ficedula albicollis*. At its western limit in France, it only breeds in the north-east, mainly in Lorraine with a few in Champagne and Alsace, well outside the area covered by this guide. Mature oak woodland is its preferred habitat. **Pied Flycatcher** *F. hypoleuca* can be found in suitable woodland in the north-east, the Haute-Savoie Alps, the northern Massif Central, the Cévennes with a few in the western Pyrenees but it is local and scattered.

Bearded Tit *Panurus biarmicus*. Found in reedbeds on Ile de Ré (Atlantic Coast Area 5), Teich reserve (Atlantic Coast Area 9), Chérine Reserve in the Brenne and along the Mediterranean from Perpignan to the Camargue.

Penduline Tit *Remiz pendulinus*. While this species has been contracting its range around the Mediterranean (it has not bred in the Camargue since the 80's), its north-east expansion across Europe means that a few have been breeding in Alsace and Lorraine for ten years. In winter small flocks can be found in reed-beds around the shallow lagoons along the Mediterranean coast, especially in Roussillon. The Perpignan sites (Mediterranean Area 1) are the best bet. It often builds its elaborate tunnel nest in poplars near water.

Corsican Nuthatch *Sitta whiteheadi*. A near-threatened species, endemic to the Corsican Pine forests of this island along the central chain between altitudes of 600 to 1700 m. Outside the breeding season it joins feeding flocks of other woodland birds (Coal Tits, Goldcrest, Treecreeper) and three or four may be seen together. Check any good strands of mature Corsican Pine along the higher roads, especially the Bavella Pass, Asco and Restonica gorges, Vezzani road, Col de Sorba, Col de Veghio and Aitone Forest. A noisy little bird, like all nuthatches, it is most easily located by its calls. Learn to recognise the harsh, drawn-out alarm call it produces when disturbed; it could almost be mistaken for a Jay's! In addition it has a one-note trilling song as well as a trilled contact-call.

Short-toed Treecreeper *Certhia brachydactyla*. Both species of Treecreepers can be found in France. Short-toed Treecreeper is by far the most wide-spread and common, found throughout the country in deciduous and mixed woodland, as well as around parks and gardens, up to an altitude of at least 2000 m in parts of the Pyrenees and Alps, while **Eurasian Treecreeper** *Certhia familiaris* prefers the higher, coniferous forests of the Massif Central,

Alps and Pyrenees and is the only Treecreeper found in Corsica. On the mainland there is an overlap where both occur as the latter species can be found between 900 and 2000 metres. Song is the easiest way to distinguish between them, as their calls can sound similar.

Wallcreeper *Tichodroma muraria.* One of the "most wanted" continental species. It tends to breed at very high altitudes but also favours narrow, shady gorges close to fast flowing water or by waterfalls at lower altitudes. Two such sites are the Gorges de la Corbière, south of Barcelonnette on the D902 (Maritime Alps site ii) and Gavarnie in the Pyrenees National Park. Birds have also been seen in summer on the dam above the Lac du Chevril, a large reservoir near Tignes, northeast of Grenoble in the Savoie Alps. Tignes and the dam can be reached by taking the D87, which leads off the N202.

In winter birds move to lower altitudes and at this season it is often easier to see them when they can be found in the foothills on almost any rocky cliff face or even sea cliffs or tall stone buildings (they seem especially fond of very old castles and Romanesque churches). The Lourdios gorge and the main road between Urdos and the Somport pass in the Pyrenees are some of the areas where they have been seen in winter and spring (Pyrenees Area 4) as well as Pourtalet pass (Pyrenees Area 5). The ruins above the village of les Baux in the Alpilles (Mediterranean Area 7) is a regular wintering site as are both old castles in the villages above the Aveyron Gorge below St. Antonin-Noble-Val, (Montauban Area). Recently also noted on the ramparts of Besançon in the Alps in winter. In Corsica a few are found on the highest mountains (Cinto, d'Oro, Rotondo) from 1750 to 2600 m. In winter they may be seen on seacliffs on the west coast. Listen for their high, thin whistle and watch rock faces and stone facades for a flash of crimson when they flick their wings.

Lesser Grey Shrike *Lanius minor.* A species with a mainly eastern European distribution, it is found at only a few sites in France, all around the Mediterranean. The Crau (Camargue) is where it can be most easily seen and there are one or two pairs around Perpignan. It rarely arrives before the middle of May and leaves by the end of August.

Southern Grey Shrike *Lanius meridionalis.* Now split from *L. excubitor* (which is resident and breeds throughout central and eastern France with an increased winter population of birds from further north), *L. meridionalis* is only found around the Mediterranean area and the low, sunny hills behind the coastal plain as well as the most southerly Cévennes. The Crau (Camargue) is again a good site, so is the Causse de Blandas (Cévennes) and the Maures plain (Mediterranean Area 9) though it is rarer here.

Red-backed Shrike *Lanius collurio* breeds throughout the area covered by this book, except around the Mediterranean. It is the commonest shrike on Corsica, found in low maquis and mountain heath, mainly below 600 m and more common in the north than the south of the island.

Woodchat Shrike *Lanius senator* has a more patchy distribution, being essentially a lowland species and so is found mainly around the Mediterranean, the southern Atlantic coast sites and inland away from mountainous regions. It is less common in Corsica than the previous species and found mainly in the south-east.

Nutcracker *Nucifragaa caryocatactes.* Only found in the Alps. In the southern Alps it is confined to areas where Arolla pine grows, between 1600–2400 m. Sites include the Col d'Izoard and the Queryas Regional Park sites. In the northern Alps and Vosges Mountains, it can be found as low as 650 m in forest clearings and valleys wherever there are abundant supplies of hazelnuts. It is probably easiest to see after the breeding season (end-July, August) when pairs fly noisily around, storing seeds.

Yellow-billed or Alpine Chough *Pyrrhocorax graculus* occurs in the Alps and the Pyrenees (with a couple of thousand in the central Corsican mountains) between 500 m (on the Atlantic side of the Pyrenees) up to 3800 m on Mont Blanc in the Alps. In the Alps they are often found around ski stations in winter. Gavarnie in the Pyrenees is a safe bet as is Val Reposoir in the Haute-Savoie at any time of the year. The **Red-billed or Common Chough** P. *pyrrhocorax* also occurs in the Pyrenees and Alps as well as in the Massif Central but not on Corsica nor in the Haute-Savoie. They can be seen at almost any of the Pyrenean or other Alpine sites. They also breed on sea cliffs in Brittany.

Hooded Crow *Corvus corone sardonius* (the race found eastwards from Italy to the Balkans) breeds only in Corsica, where it is common, especially on the east coast, up to 1200 m. Some "Hoodies" can be seen in eastern France in winter.

Spotless Starling *Sturnus unicolor.* Considered a Spanish bird until quite recently, this species continues to extend its range northwards and a few birds now breed on the north side of the Pyrenees in France. Around Banyuls and Perpignan they can be found side by side with Common Starlings in some places (Mediterranean Area 1). Outside the breeding season they can be difficult to tell apart. The only Starling on Corsica, it can be found in most coastal areas, especially the east coast, and in the Mediterranean vegetation zone. A few Common Starlings may join flocks in winter.

Snow Finch *Montifringilla nivalis.* This large finch only breeds on the highest rocky slopes above 2,200 m. and is very difficult to find at this season. The Col du Galibier above the Col du Lautaret (Alps) is one of the easiest places to see it without a long walk. In the Pyrenees, they are easy to find on the Col de Tourmalet in July (Gavarnie area 6). Park immediately after the summit and check around the pylons on the slopes above the cafe as well as along the toll road to the observatory. It descends lower in winter when small flocks can often be seen around ski resorts in the Alps and Pyrenees, (Cauterets, St. Lary-Soulan, Bagnères-de-Luchon) often in the company of Alpine Accentors. It can be seen at Pourtalet pass (Pyrenees Area 5) as late as March. A very few are found over 2000 m in the Alpine zones of Corsica.

Rock Sparrow *Petronia petronia.* In spite of its name, this species can be found in villages, woods, old ruins, cultivated land as well as on rocky cliffs in

Corsica and throughout the southern half of France, away from the Atlantic coast, the humid Mediterranean along the Côte d'Azur or the higher Alps. It occurs up to 1780 m in the Pyrenees and 2000 m in the southern Alps. Its distribution is local but the Pourtalet site (Pyrenees Area 5) and the village of Brunissard near the Izoard Pass (High Alps Area 2 site iv.) offer a good chance of finding it. The most northerly breeding site, and the nearest to Britain, is the old Abbey of Fontevraud near Saumur on the Loire River. For most of the year a sociable bird, during the breeding season normally only individual pairs will be found, but from August to March quite large flocks can be seen feeding in fallow and stubble fields at lower altitudes, for example south and west of Toulouse. **Italian Sparrow** *Passer domesticus italiae* takes the place of House Sparrow on Corsica and a few are found along France's southern border with Italy. It is always found in areas such as towns and coastal resorts where there is considerable human activity. **Spanish Sparrow** *Passer hispaniolensis* is only found in a small area around Bonifacio in south Corsica.

Citril Finch *Serinus citrinella*. This small mountain finch breeds in low vegetation at the edge of the tree line in subalpine areas above 1500 m. In autumn young birds disperse and may be found above the breeding sites and in winter it flocks with other finches, especially Serins and Siskins, at lower altitudes. They are quite easy to see in the Alps in Mercantour National Park and in many parts of the Pyrenees, especially in the National Park at Gavarnie and Néouvielle. The Corsican sub-species (considered by some to be a full species) *Serinus corsicanus* has a brown (not grey), heavily streaked back. Its habitat is slightly different as it is found in *maquis*, clearings and edges of both deciduous and coniferous forests (especially Corsican Pine) throughout the island from sea level up to 2250 m. In winter quite large flocks may be seen in low *maquis* and grassland in coastal areas.

Common Rosefinch *Carpodacus erythrinus*. This species has recently been found breeding in small numbers at Cap Gris-Nez (Calais), in the northeast and in the Rhône-Alpes (Sixt/Fer-a-Cheval, Haute-Savoie Alps Area 4 site iii.).

Ortolan Bunting *Emberiza hortulana* is a summer visitor to the hillier parts of southern France with the greatest concentration around the Mediterranean and Alps. It can be found in a variety of habitat: dry grassland with scattered bushes, rocky slopes of degraded *garrigue* with juniper, box or rosemary bushes on the *causses* and around the Mediterranean, high alpine meadows in the Alps, even in extensive cereal fields if there are some trees around them, though it prefers areas of more traditional mixed farming with a mosaic of habitats. Not found in Corsica.

Rock Bunting *Emberiza cia* is resident all along the Pyrenees, in the Massif Central and the Alps. It likes dry, sunny, rocky slopes with shrubby vegetation, mainly between 500–2000 m altitudes. In winter, birds from the higher areas normally move down to nearby plains or lower slopes. Males sing between February and April and then are rather silent; listen out for their thin, weak, downslurred "tsii" calls. Not found in Corsica.

BIBLIOGRAPHY AND RECOMMENDED BOOKS

Site Guides
Where to Watch Birds in France. LPO. (Translated by Tony Williams) Christopher Helm.
(I must acknowledge my debt to this book, the first site guide to France. I have used it extensively since the French edition came out in 1989 and it has been invaluable. Inevitably this book covers many of the same sites but I have tried not to plagiarise too much. I have visited all the sites in this book (most of them several times over many years) and have updated when necessary, corrected any errors that slipped into the LPO book and given what I have found to be the best viewpoints or itineraries. The LPO book includes many extra sites both in the south as well as outside the area covered by this guide. However, it is arranged by regions and lacks maps showing the location of the sites within each region, so they are not always easy to find, nor are the instructions to some sites easy to follow.)

Où Observer les Oiseaux en Ariège? Bertrand. ANA 1998 (In French, and only covers this small area of the Midi-Pyrenees but is excellent and detailed.)

Les Oiseaux de la Loire. LPO-Loire is worth purchasing is you are spending any time in the Lyon area. It gives detailed instructions for several itineraries on foot or by car in the Loire department just east of Lyon as well as listing all the birds observed in this department with information on their status.

Birds
The Birds of Britain and Europe. New Edition. Heinzel, Fitter and Parslow. Harper Collins.
Birds of Europe. Jonsson. Helm.
The Birds of Prey of Britain and Europe. Gensbol. Collins.
Collins Bird Guide. Mullarney *et al*.
Guide des Oiseaux d'Europe. Peterson *et al.* Delachaux & Niestlé (The English edition gives French names also).

Flowers
Mediterranean Wild Flowers. Blamey/Grey-Wilson. Harper Collins.
Alpine Flowers of Britain and Europe. New Edition. Blamey/Grey-Wilson. HarperCollins.
Wild Flowers of Britain and Northern Europe. Fitter/Blamey. HarperCollins.
The Illustrated Flora of Britain and Northern Europe. Blamey/Grey-Wilson. Hodder & Stoughton.
Orchids of Britain and Europe. Buttler. Crowood.
Les Flore des Alpes de Haute-Provence. Esi sud/Adri. (Also useful for Cévennes, Alpilles and includes 10 walks).
La Flore Endemique de la Corse. Gamisans & Marzocci. Edisud.

Animals
Mammals of Britain and Europe. Macdonald/Barrett. HarperCollins.
Reptiles and Amphibians of Britain and Europe. Arnold/Burton. Collins.

Insects
Butterflies. Whalley. Mitchell Beazley.
Butterflies and Day-flying Moths New Generation Guide. Chinery. Collins.
Collins Photographic Guide to Butterflies of Britain & Europe. Chinery. Harper Collins.
Guide to the Insects of Britain and Western Europe. Chinery. Collins.
Guide to the Dragonflies of Great Britain. Powell. Arlequin Press. (Equally useful in France).

Bibliography
Guide des Reserves Naturelles de France. Cans & Reille. Delachaux et Niestlé.
Les Zones Importantes pour la Conservation des Oiseaux en France. LPO & Ministère de l'Environnement.
Les Oiseaux de Camargue. Boulin. Lynx.
Les Oiseaux de la Loire. Rimbert. LPO-Loire.
Le Parc Ornithologique le Teich. Conseil Général de la Gironde 1994.
Grands Rapaces et Corvids dels Montagnes d'Europe. Dendaletche Ed. Acta Biologica Montana.
Oiseaux des Pyrénées 2. Dendaletche. ABM.
Col-loqui d'Ornitologia Pirinenca 1995. AND (Andorre).
Rapaces de France. Supplément no. 1. L'Oiseau magazine. 1999.
Où Observer les Oiseaux en Ariege? Bertrand. ANA 1998.
Où Voir les Oiseaux en France. LPO. Nathan. 1989.
Atlas des Oiseaux Nicheurs de France. Yeatman-Berthelot & Jarry. S.O.F. 1995.
Atlas des Oiseaux de France en Hiver. Yeatman-Berthelot & Jarry. S.O.F. 1991.
Atlas des Oiseaux Nicheurs de Midi-Pyrénées. Joachim *et al.* A.R.O.M.P.
Le Livre Rouge des Oiseaux Nicheurs du Poitou-Charentes. Rigaud & Granger. LPO-Vienne.
Oiseaux du Littoral Atlantique. LPO.
Les Oiseaux d'Auvergne. LPO.
The Birds of Corsica. Thibault & Bonaccorsi. BOU checklist series: 17.
The Crau – steppe vivante. Cheylan et al. Jurgen Resch.
Guide Nature de la Brenne. Trotignon, Williams & Desbordes. Parc de la Brenne.

BIRD CHECKLIST

The following check list follows the sequence and nomenclature of the *List of Birds of the Western Palearctic* (British Birds Ltd 1997), which follows those adopted for the new Concise Edition of *Birds of the Western Palearctic*. Extreme rarities and very occasional visitors have not been included but most of the American and eastern vagrants that turn up in Britain have also occurred in France. The order in which the symbols are given indicates the normal status (for example, if the majority of birds are winter visitors but a few may remain to breed, then WV comes first, followed by OB).

Key to Symbols:

RB = Resident Breeder	MB = Migrant Breeder	OB = Occasional Breeder
PM = Passage Migrant	WV = Winter Visitor	AV = Accidental Visitor

BIRDS

English Name	Scientific Name	Status
Red-throated Diver	*Gavia stellata*	WV
Black-throated Diver	*Gavia arctaica*	WV
Great Northern Diver	*Gavia immer*	WV
Little Grebe	*Tachybapus ruficollis*	RB
Great Crested Grebe	*Podiceps cristatus*	RB
Red-necked Grebe	*Podiceps grisegena*	WV
Slavonian Grebe	*Podiceps auritus*	WV
Black-necked Grebe	*Podiceps nigricollis*	RB
Fulmar	*Fulmaris glacialis*	RB, PM
Cory's Shearwater	*Calonectris diomedea*	RB, WV
Balearic Shearwater	*Puffinus mauretanicus*	WV, PM
Yelkouan Shearwater	*Puffinus yelkouan*	RB, PM, WV
Leach's Storm-petrel	*Oceanodroma leucorhoa*	PM
European Storm-petrel	*Hydrobates pelagicus*	RB, WV
Northern Gannet	*Morus bassana*	RB, WV, PM
Great Cormorant	*Phalacrocorax carbo*	RB, WV
Shag	*Phalacrocorax aristotelis*	RB, AV, WV
Great Bittern	*Botaurus stellaris*	RB, MV, WV
Little Bittern	*Ixobrychus minutus*	MB
Night Heron	*Nycticorax nycticorax*	MB
Squacco Heron	*Ardeola ralloides*	MB, PM
Cattle Egret	*Bubulcus ibis*	RB
Little Egret	*Aigrette garzette*	RB
Western Reef Heron	*Egretta gularis*	AV
Great White Egret	*Egretta alba*	WV, PM
Grey Heron	*Ardea cinerea*	RB, WV
Purple Heron	*Ardea purpurea*	MB, PM
Black Stork	*Ciconia nigra*	PM, RB
White Stork	*Ciconia ciconia*	RB, PM
Glossy Ibis	*Plegadis falcinellus*	AV, MB
Sacred Ibis	*Threskiornis aethiopicus*	RB (intro)
Eurasian Spoonbill	*Platalea leucorodia*	PM, MB
Greater Flamingo	*Phoenicopterus ruber*	RB
Mute Swan	*Cygnus olor*	RB

BIRDS

English Name	Scientific Name	Status
Bewick's Swan	*Cygnus columbianus*	WV
Whooper Swan	*Cygne cugnus*	WV
White-fronted Goose	*Anser albifrons*	WV
Bean Goose	*Anser fabalis*	WV, PM
Greylag Goose	*Anser anser*	AV
Barnacle Goose	*Branta leucopsis*	WV
Brent Goose	*Branta bernicla*	WV, PM
Red-breasted Goose	*Branta ruficollis*	AV
Common Shelduck	*Tadorna tadorna*	RB
Eurasian Wigeon	*Anas penelope*	WV, PM, OB
Gadwall	*Anas strepera*	RB, WV, PM
Common Teal	*Anas crecca*	RB, WV, PM
Mallard	*Anas platyrhynchos*	RB, WV, PM
Pintail	*Anas acuta*	WV, PM, OB
Garganey	*Anas quequedula*	PM, MB
Northern Shoveler	*Anas clypeata*	WV, PM, RB
Red-crested Pochard	*Netta rufina*	RB, WV, PM
Common Pochard	*Aythya ferina*	WV, RB, PM
Ferruginous Duck	*Aythya nyroca*	AV, PM
Tufted Duck	*Aythya fuligula*	WV, RB, PM
Greater Scaup	*Aythya marila*	PM, WV
Common Eider	*Somateria mollissima*	WV, PM, OB
Common Scoter	*Melanitta nigra*	PM, WV
Velvet Scoter	*Melanitta fusca*	PM, WV
Goldeneye	*Bucephala clangula*	WV
Smew	*Mergus albellus*	WV
Goosander	*Mergus merganser*	WV, PM, OB
Red-breasted Merganser	*Mergus serrator*	WV,PM
European Honey-buzzard	*Pernis apivorus*	PM, MB
Black-shouldered Kite	*Elanus caeruleus*	AV, RB
Black Kite	*Milvus migrans*	PM, MB
Red Kite	*Milvus milvus*	PM, MB, WV
White-tailed Sea-eagle	*Haliaeetus albicilla*	WV
Osprey	*Pandion haliaetus*	M,MB,RB
Lammergeier	*Gypaetus barbatus*	RB
Egyptian Vulture	*Neophran percnopterus*	MB
Griffon Vulture	*Gyps fulvus*	RB
Black (Monk) Vulture	*Aegypius monachus*	RB re-intro
Short-toed Eagle	*Circaetus gallicus*	MB, PM
Marsh Harrier	*Circus aeruginosus*	RB, WV, PM
Hen Harrier	*Circus cyaneus*	WV, RB, PM
Montagu's Harrier	*Circus pyrargus*	PM, MB
Northern Goshawk	*Accipiter gentilis*	RB, PM, WV
Eurasian Sparrowhawk	*Accipiter nisus*	RB, PM, WV
Common Buzzard	*Buteo buteo*	RB, PM, WV
Spotted Eagle	*Aquila clanga*	WV
Golden Eagle	*Aguila chrysaetos*	RB

BIRDS

English Name	Scientific Name	Status
Booted Eagle	*Hieraaetus pennatus*	MB, PM
Bonelli's Eagle	*Hieraaetus fasciatus*	RB
Lesser Kestrel	*Falco naumanni*	MB
Common Kestrel	*Falco tinnunculus*	RB, WV
Red-footed Falcon	*Falco vespertinus*	AV, PM
Merlin	*Falco columbarius*	WV, PM
Hobby	*Falco subbuteo*	MB, PM
Eleanora's Falcon	*Falco eleonorae*	AV
Peregrine Falcon	*Falco peregrinus*	RB, WV, PM
Ptarmigan	*Lagopus mutus*	RB
Hazelhen	*Bonasa bonasia*	RB
Black Grouse	*Tetrao tetrix*	RB
Capercaillie	*Tetrao urogallus*	RB
Red-legged Partridge	*Alectoris rufa*	RB
Chukar	*Alectoris chukar*	RB intro.
Rock Partridge	*Alectoris graeca*	RB
Grey Partridge	*Perdix perdix*	RB
Common Quail	*Cortunix cortunix*	MB, PM
Californian Quail	*Callipepla californica*	RB intro.Cors.
Common Pheasant	*Phasainus colchicus*	RB
Reeves's Pheasant	*Syrmaticus reevesii*	RB intro.
Water Rail	*Rallus aquaticus*	RB, PM, WV
Spotted Crake	*Porzana porzana*	OB, PM, WV
Little Crake	*Porzana parva*	OB, AV
Baillon's Crake	*Porzana pusilla*	OB, PM
Corn Crake	*Crex crex*	PM, MB(few)
Moorhen	*Gallinula chloropus*	RB
Purple Swamp-hen	*Porphyrio porphyrio*	RB (few)
Common Coot	*Fulica atra*	RB, WV
Common Crane	*Grus grus*	PM,WV,OB
Little Bustard	*Tetrax tetrax*	RB, MB
Oystercatcher	*Haematopus ostralegus*	RB, PM, WV
Black-winged Stilt	*Himantopushimantopus*	MB, PM
Avocet	*Recurvirostra avosetta*	MB, PM, WV
Stone-curlew	*Burhinus oedicnemus*	MB, PM, WV
Collared Pratincole	*Glareola pratincola*	MB (few),PM
Little Ringed Plover	*Charadrius dubius*	MB, PM
Great Ringed Plover	*Charadrius hiaticula*	RB, PM, WV
Kentish Plover	*Charadrius alexandrinus*	RB, PM, WV
Dotterel	*Charadrius morinellus*	MB,(few) PM
European Golden Plover	*Pluvialis apricaria*	WV, PM
Grey Plover	*Pluvialis squatarola*	WV, PM
Northern Lapwing	*Vanellus vanellus*	RB,WV, PM
Red Knot	*Calidris canutus*	PM, WV
Sanderling	*Calidris alba*	PM, WV
Little Stint	*Calidris minuta*	WV, PM
Temminck's Stint	*Calidris temminckii*	PM, AV

BIRDS

				English Name	Scientific Name	Status
				Curlew Sandpiper	*Calidris ferruginea*	PM
				Dunlin	*Calidris alpina*	PM, WV
				Ruff	*Philomachus pugnax*	PM, WV
				Jack Snipe	*Lymnocryptes minimus*	PM, WV
				Common Snipe	*Gallinago gallinago*	RB, PM, WV
				Woodcock	*Scolopax rusticola*	RB, PM, WV
				Black-tailed Godwit	*Limosa limosa*	WV, PM
				Bar-tailed Godwit	*Limosa lapponica*	PM, WV
				Whimbrel	*Numenius phaeopus*	PM
				Eurasian Curlew	*Numenius arquata*	WV, PM, RB
				Spotted Redshank	*Tringa erythropus*	PM, WV
				Common Redshank	*Tringa totanus*	PM, WV, RB
				Marsh Sandpiper	*Tringa stagnatilis*	AV
				Greenshank	*Tringa nebularia*	PM, WV
				Green Sandpiper	*Tringa ochropus*	PM, WV
				Wood Sandpiper	*Tringa glareola*	PM
				Terek Sandpiper	*Xenus cinereus*	AV
				Common Sandpiper	*Actitis hypoleucos*	RB, PM, WV
				Turnstone	*Arenaria interpres*	PM, WV
				Red-necked Phalarope	*Phalaropus lobatus*	PM
				Grey Phalarope	*Phalaropus fulicarius*	PM, WV
				Great Skua	*Catharacta skua*	PM, WV
				Pomarine Skua	*Stercorarius pomarinus*	PM
				Arctic Skua	*Stercorarius parasiticus*	PM, WV
				Mediterranean Gull	*Larus melanocephalus*	WV, PM, RB
				Little Gull	*Larus minutus*	WV, PM
				Black-headed Gull	*Larus ridibundus*	RB, PM, WV
				Slender-billed Gull	*Larus genei*	RB, PM
				Audouin's Gull	*Larus audouinii*	RB, PM
				Common Gull	*Larus canus*	WV, PM, RB
				Lesser Black-backed Gull	*Larus fuscus*	WV, RB, PM
				Herring Gull	*Larus argentatus*	RB, PM, WV
				Yellow-legged Gull	*Larus cachinnans (michalelis)*	RB, PM, WV
				Great Black-backed Gull	*Larus marinus*	WV, RB
				Kittiwake	*Rissa tridactyla*	RB, WV, PM
				Gull-billed Tern	*Sterna nilotica*	PM, MB
				Caspian Tern	*Sterna caspia*	PM
				Sandwich Tern	*Sterna sandvicensis*	RB, PM, WV
				Common Tern	*Sterna hirundo*	PM, MB
				Arctic Tern	*Sterna paradisaea*	PM, MB few
				Little Tern	*Sterna albifrons*	MB, PM
				Whiskered Tern	*Chlidonias hybridus*	PM, MB
				Black Tern	*Chlidonias niger*	PM, MB
				White-winged Black Tern	*Chlidonias leucopterus*	PM
				Common Guillemot	*Uria aalge*	PM, WV, RB
				Razorbill	*Alca torda*	WV, PM, RB
				Atlantic Puffin	*Fratercula arctica*	RB, WV, PM

BIRDS

				English Name	Scientific Name	Status
				Pin-tailed Sandgrouse	Pterocles alchata	RB
				Rock Dove	Columba livia	RB
				Stock Dove	Columba oenas	RB, PM, WV
				Wood Pigeon	Columba palumbus	RB, PM, WV
				Collared Dove	Streptopelia decaoto	RB, PM
				Turtle Dove	Streptopelia turtur	PM, MB
				Great Spotted Cuckoo	Clamator glandarius	MB
				Common Cuckoo	Cuculus canoris	MB, PM
				Barn Owl	Tyto alba	RB, WV, PM
				Eurasian Scops Owl	Otus scops	MB
				Eagle Owl	Bubo bubo	RB
				Pygmy Owl	Glaucidium passerinum	RB
				Little Owl	Athene noctua	RB
				Tawny Owl	Strix aluco	RB
				Long-eared Owl	Asio otus	RB, PM, WV
				Short-eared Owl	Asio flammeus	WV, RB, PM
				Tengmalm's Owl	Aegolius funereus	RB
				European Nightjar	Caprimulgus europaeus	MB
				Alpine Swift	Tachymarptis melba	MB, PM
				Common Swift	Apus apus	MB, PM
				Pallid Swift	Apus pallidus	MB, PM
				Common Kingfisher	Alcedo atthis	RB, WV
				European Bee-eater	Merops apiaster	MB, PM
				European Roller	Coracias garrulus	MB, PM
				Hoopoe	Upupa epops	MB, PM
				Wryneck	Jynx torquilla	MB, PM
				Grey-headed Woodpecker	Picus canus	RB
				Green Woodpecker	Picus viridis	RB
				Black Woodpecker	Dryocopus martius	RB
				Great Spotted Woodpecker	Dendrocopos major	RB
				Middle Spotted Woodpecker	Dendrocopos medius	RB
				White-backed Woodpecker	Dendrocopus leucotos	RB (very local)
				Lesser Spotted Woodpecker	Dendrocopus minor	RB (very local)
				Three-toed Woodpecker	Picoides tridactylus	RB rare
				Calandra Lark	Melanocorypha calandra	RB rare
				Short-toed Lark	Calandrella brachydactyla	MB
				Crested Lark	Galerida cristata	RB
				Thekla Lark	Galerida theklae	RB rare
				Wood Lark	Lullula arborea	RB, PM, WV
				Sky Lark	Alauda arvensis	RB
				Shore Lark	Eremophila alpestris	WV rare
				Sand Martin	Riparia riparia	MB, PM
				Crag Martin	Ptyonoprogne rupestris	RB, WV
				Barn Swallow	Hirundo rustica	MB, PM
				Red-rumped Swallow	Hirundo daurica	AV, OB
				House Martin	Delichon urbica	MB, PM
				Tawny Pipit	Anthus campestris	MB, PM

BIRDS

English Name	Scientific Name	Status
Tree Pipit	*Anthus trivialis*	MB, PM
Meadow Pipit	*Anthus pratensis*	RB, WV, PM
Water Pipit	*Anthus spinoletta*	MB, PM, WV
Rock Pipit	*Anthus petrosus*	PM, WV, RB
Red-throated Pipit	*Anthus cervinus*	PM rare
Yellow Wagtail	*Motacilla flava*	PM, MB
Pied (White) Wagtail	*Motacilla alba*	RB, PM, WV
Grey Wagtail	*Motacilla cinerea*	RB, PM, WV
Waxwing	*Bombycilla garrulus*	WV rare
Dipper	*Cinclus cinclus*	RB
Wren	*Troglodytes troglodytes*	RB
Hedge Accentor	*Prunella modularis*	RB, PM, WV
Alpine Accentor	*Prunella collaris*	RB
Rufous-tailed Scrub-robin	*Cercotrichas galactotes*	PM rare
Robin	*Erithacus rubecula*	RB, PM, WV
Rufous Nightingale	*Luscinia megarhynchos*	MB, PM
Bluethroat	*Luscinia svecica*	MB, PM, WV
Black Redstart	*Phoenicurus ochruros*	RB, PM
Redstart	*Phoenicurus phoenicurus*	MB, PM
Common Stonechat	*Saxicola torquata*	RB, PM, WV
Whinchat	*Saxicola rubetra*	MB, PM
Northern Wheatear	*Oenanthe oenanthe*	MB, PM
Black-eared Wheatear	*Oenanthe hispanica*	MB
Black Wheatear	*Oenanthe leucura*	RB v.rare
Rock Thrush	*Monticola saxatilis*	MB
Blue Rock Thrush	*Monticola solitarius*	RB, PM
Ring Ouzel	*Turdus torquatus*	MB, PM
Blackbird	*Turdus merula*	RB, PM, WV
Fieldfare	*Turdus pilaris*	RB, PM, WV
Song Thrush	*Turdus philomelos*	RB, PM, WV
Redwing	*Turdus iliacus*	PM, WV
Mistle Thrush	*Turdus viscivoris*	RB, PM, WV
Cetti's Warbler	*Cettia cetti*	RB
Zitting Cisticola	*Cisticola juncidis*	RB, PM
Grasshopper Warbler	*Locustella naevia*	MB, PM
Savi's Warbler	*Locustella luscinioides*	MB
Moustached Warbler	*Acrocephalus melanopogon*	RB
Sedge Warbler	*Acrocephalus schoenobaenus*	MB, PM
Marsh Warbler	*Acrocephalus palustris*	MB, PM
Reed Warbler	*Acrocephalus scirpaceus*	MB, PM
Great Reed Warbler	*Acrocephalus arundinaceus*	MB, PM
Icterine Warbler	*Hippolais icterina*	MB, PM
Melodious Warbler	*Hippolais polyglotta*	MB, PM
Marmora's Warbler	*Sylvia sarda*	RB Corsica
Dartford Warbler	*Sylvia undata*	RB, PM, WV
Spectacled Warbler	*Sylvia conspicillata*	MB
Subalpine Warbler	*Sylvia cantilans*	MB

BIRDS

English Name	Scientific Name	Status
Sardinian Warbler	Sylvia melanocephala	RB
Orphean Warbler	Sylvia hortensis	MB
Lesser Whitethroat	Sylvia curruca	MB, PM
Common Whitethroat	Sylvia communis	MB, PM
Garden Warbler	Sylvia borin	MB, PM
Blackcap	Sylvia atricapilla	MB, PM, WV
Western Bonelli's Warbler	Phylloscopus bonelli	MB, PM
Wood Warbler	Phylloscopus sibilatrix	MB, PM
Common Chiffchaff	Phylloscopus collybita	MB, RB, WV
Willow Warbler	Phylloscopus trochilus	MB, PM
Goldcrest	Regulus regulus	RB, PM, WV
Firecrest	Regulus ignicapillus	RB, PM, WV
Spotted Flycatcher	Muscicapa striata	MB, PM
Collared Flycatcher	Ficedula albicollis	MB, PM
Pied Flycatcher	Ficedula hypoleuca	MB, PM
Bearded Tit	Panurus biarmicus	RB, WV
Long-tailed Tit	Aegithalos caudatus	RB
Marsh Tit	Parus palustris	RB
Willow Tit	Parus montanus	RB
Crested Tit	Parus cristatus	RB
Coal Tit	Parus ater	RB, WV
Blue Tit	Parus caeruleus	RB, WV
Great Tit	Parus major	RB, WV
Corsican Nuthatch	Sitta whiteheadi	RB Corsica
European Nuthatch	Sitta europaea	RB
Wallcreeper	Tichodroma muraria	RB, PM, WV
Short-toed Treecreeper	Certhia brachydactyla	RB
Eurasian Treecreeper	Certhia familiaris	RB
Penduline Tit	Remiz pendulinus	RB, PM, WV
Golden Oriole	Oriolus oriolus	MB, PM
Red-backed Shrike	Lanius collurio	MB, PM
Lesser Grey	Lanius minor	MB (local)
Great Grey Shrike	Lanius excubitor	RB, WV, PM
Southern Grey Shrike	Lanius meridionalis	RB, WV, PM
Woodchat Shrike	Lanius senator	MB, PM
Eurasian Jay	Garrulus glandarius	RB, PM, WV
Magpie	Pica pica	RB
Nutcracker	Nucifraga caryocatactes	RB
Red-billed Chough	Pyrrthocorax pyrrthocorax	RB
Yellow-billed Chough	Pyrrthocorax graculus	RB
Eurasian Jackdaw	Corvus monedula	RB, PM, WV
Carrion/Hooded Crow	Corvus corone	RB, WV
Rook	Corvus frugilegus	RB, PM, WV
Common Raven	Corvus corax	RB
Spotless Starling	Sturnus unicolor	RB local
Common Starling	Sturnus vulgaris	RB, WV, PM
House Sparrow	Passer domesticus	RB, PM, WV

BIRDS

English Name	Scientific Name	Status
Italian Sparrow	*Passer italiae*	RB local
Spanish Sparrow	*Passer hispaniolensis*	RB Corsica rare
Tree Sparrow	*Passer montanus*	RB, PM, WV
Rock Sparrow	*Petronia petronia*	RB
Snowfinch	*Montifringilla nivalis*	RB
Common Chaffinch	*Fringilla coelebs*	RB, PM, WV
Brambling	*Fringilla montifringila*	WV, PM
European Serin	*Serinus serinus*	RB, PM, WV
Citril Finch	*Serinus citrinella*	RB
Corsican Citril	*Serinus corsicanus*	RB Corsica
Greenfinch	*Carduelis chloris*	RB, PM, WV
Goldfinch	*Carduelis carduelis*	RB, PM, WV
Siskin	*Carduelis spinus*	WV, RB, PM
Linnet	*Acanthis cannaina*	RB, PM, WV
Common Crossbill	*Loxia curvirostra*	RB, PM, WV
Parrot Crossbill	*Loxia pytyopsittacus*	PM rare
Common Rosefinch	*Carpodacus erythrinus*	OB rare
Common Bullfinch	*Pyrrhula pyrrhula*	RB, WV
Hawfinch	*Coccothraustes coccothraustes*	RB, WV, PM
Lapland Longspur	*Caalcarius lapponicus*	WV
Snow Bunting	*Plectrophenax nivalis*	WV
Yellowhammer	*Emberiza citrinella*	RB, PM, WV
Cirl Bunting	*Emberiza cirlus*	RB, PM
Rock Bunting	*Emberiza cia*	RB
Ortolan Bunting	*Emberiza hortulana*	MB, PM
Reed Bunting	*Emberiza schoeniclus*	RB, WV, PM
Corn Bunting	*Miliaria calandra*	RB, PM, WV

FRENCH BIRD-NAMES

The second check list is in alphabetical order of the French names for most species occurring in France. It is hoped that this will help those whose knowledge of French does not include all the French names as it will be an aid to translating the name quickly when reading information boards at reserves, etc. Some birds have been shown twice to take into account alternative French names.

English Name	French Name
Alpine Accentor	Accenteur alpin
Hedge Accentor	Accenteur mouchet
Rufous-tailed Scrub-robin	Agrobate roux
Booted Eagle	Aigle botté
Spotted Eagle	Aigle criard
Bonelli's Eagle	Aigle de Bonelli
Golden Eagle	Aigle royal
Western Reef Heron	Aigrette des récifs
Little Egret	Aigrette garzette
Calandra Lark	Alouette calandre
Short-toed Lark	Alouette calandrelle
Sky Lark	Alouette des champs
Shore Lark	Alouette haussecol
Wood Lark	Alouette lulu
Northern Goshawk	Autour des polombes
Avocet	Avocette élégante
Osprey	Balbuzard pecheur
Black-tailed Godwit	Barge à queue noire
Bar-tailed Godwit	Barge rousse
Terek Sandpiper	Bargette du Terek
Woodcock	Bécasse des bois
Curlew Sandpiper	Bécasseau cocorli
Temminck's Stint	Bécasseau de Temminck
Red Knot	Bécasseau maubèche
Little Stint	Bécasseau minute
Sanderling	Bécasseau sanderling
Dunlin	Bécasseau variable
Purple Sandpiper	Bécasseau violet
Common Snipe	Bécassine des marais
Jack Snipe	Bécassine sourde
Common Crossbill	Bec-croisé des sapins
Parrot Crossbill	Bec-croisé perroquet
Grey Wagtail	Bergeronnette des ruisseaux
Pied (White) Wagtail	Bergeronnette grise
Yellow Wagtail	Bergeronnette printanière
Red-breasted Goose	Bernache à cou rouge
Brent Goose	Bernache cravant
Barnacle Goose	Bernache nonette
Night Heron	Bihoreau gris
Little Bittern	Blongios nain
European Honey-buzzard	Bondrée apivore
Cetti's Warbler	Bouscarle de Cetti

268

FRENCH BIRD-NAMES

English Name	French Name
Common Bullfinch	*Bouvreuil pivoine*
Snow Bunting	*Bruant des neiges*
Reed Bunting	*Bruant des roseaux*
Rock Bunting	*Bruant fou*
Yellowhammer	*Bruant jaune*
Lapland Longspur	*Bruant lapon*
Ortolan Bunting	*Bruant ortolan*
Corn Bunting	*Bruant proyer*
Cirl Bunting	*Bruant zizi*
Montagu's Harrier	*Busard cendré*
Marsh Harrier	*Busard des roseaux*
Hen Harrier	*Busard Saint-Martin*
Common Buzzard	*Buse variable*
Great Bittern	*Butor étoilé*
Common Quail	*Caille des blès*
Gadwall	*Canard chipeau*
Mallard	*Canard colvert*
Pintail	*Canard pilet*
Eurasian Wigeon	*Canard siffleur*
Northern Shoveler	*Canard souchet*
Nutcracker	*Cassenoix moucheté*
Goldfinch	*Chardonneret élégant*
Greenshank	*Chevalier aboyeur*
Spotted Redshank	*Chevalier arlequin*
Green Sandpiper	*Chevalier culblanc*
Common Sandpiper	*Chevalier guignette*
Marsh Sandpiper	*Chevalier stagnatile*
Wood Sandpiper	*Chevalier sylvain*
Common Redshank	*Chevalier totanus*
Pygmy Owl	*Chevêchette d'Europe/Chouette chevêchette*
Yellow-billed Chough	*Chocard à bec jaune*
Eurasian Jackdaw	*Choucas des tours*
Little Owl	*Chouette cheveche/Chevêche d'Athéna*
Tengmalm's Owl	*Chouette de Tengmalm*
Barn Owl	*Chouette effraie*
Tawny Owl	*Chouette hulotte*
White Stork	*Cigogne blanche*
Black Stork	*Cigogne noire*
Dipper	*Cincle plongeur*
Short-toed Eagle	*Circaète Jean-le-Blanc*
Zitting Cisticola	*Cisticole des joncs*
Thekla Lark	*Cochevis de Thékla*
Crested Lark	*Cochevis huppé*
Californian Quail	*Colin de Californie*
Ruff	*Combattant varié/Chevalier combattant*
Rook	*Corbeau freux*
Shag	*Cormoran huppé*

FRENCH BIRD-NAMES

English Name	French Name
Carrion/Hooded Crow	Corneille noire/manteleé
Great Spotted Cuckoo	Coucou geai
Common Cuckoo	Coucou gris
Eurasian Curlew	Courlis cendré
Whimbrel	Courlis corlieu
Squacco Heron	Crabier chevelu
Red-billed Chough	Crave à bec rouge
Whooper Swan	Cygne chanteur
Bewick's Swan	Cygne de Bewick
Mute Swan	Cygne tuberculé
Black-winged Stilt	Echasse blanche
Barn Owl	Effraie des clochers
Common Eider	Eider à duvet
Black-shouldered Kite	Elanion blanc
European Nightjar	Engoulevent d'Europe
Eurasian Sparrowhawk	Epervier d'Europe
Common Starling	Etourneau sansonnet
Spotless Starling	Etourneau unicolore
Common Pheasant	Faisan de Colchide
Reeves's Pheasant	Faisan vénéré
Common Kestrel	Faucon crécerelle
Lesser Kestrel	Faucon crécerellette
Eleanora's Falcon	Faucon d'Eléonore
Merlin	Faucon émerillon
Hobby	Faucon hobereau
Red-footed Falcon	Faucon kobez
Peregrine Falcon	Faucon pèlerin
Spectacled Warbler	Fauvette à lunettes
Blackcap	Fauvette à tête noire
Lesser Whitethroat	Fauvette babillarde
Garden Warbler	Fauvette des jardins
Common Whitethroat	Fauvette grisette
Sardinian Warbler	Fauvette mélanocéphale
Orphean Warbler	Fauvette orphée
Subalpine Warbler	Fauvette passerinette
Dartford Warbler	Fauvette pitchou
Marmora's Warbler	Fauvette sarde
Greater Flamingo	Flamant rose
Northern Gannet	Fou de Bassan
Common Coot	Foulque macroule
Common Pochard	Fuligule milouin
Greater Scaup	Fuligule milouinan
Tufted Duck	Fuligule morillon
Ferruginous Duck	Fuligule nyroca
Fulmar	Fulmar boréal
Moorhen	Gallinule poule-d'eau
Pin-tailed Sandgrouse	Ganga cata

FRENCH BIRD-NAMES

English Name	French Name
Goldeneye	Garrot à oeil d'or
Eurasian Jay	Geai des chênes
Hazelhen	Gélinotte des bois
Collared Pratincole	Glaréole à collier
Collared Flycatcher	Gobemouche à collier
Spotted Flycatcher	Gobemouche gris
Pied Flycatcher	Gobemouche noir
Herring Gull	Goéland argenté
Lesser Black-backed Gull	Goéland brun
Common Gull	Goéland cendré
Audouin's Gull	Goéland d'Audouin
Yellow-legged Gull	Goéland leucopheé
Great Black-backed Gull	Goéland marin
Slender-billed Gull	Goéland railleur
Bluethroat	Gorgebleue à miroir
Common Raven	Grand Corbeau
Great Cormorant	Grand Cormoran
Great Ringed Plover	Grand Gravelot
Great Skua	Grand Labbe
Capercaillie	Grand Tétras
Eagle Owl	Grand-duc d'Europe/Hibou grand-duc
Great White Egret	Grande Aigrette
Kentish Plover	Gravelot à collier interrompu
Black-necked Grebe	Grèbe à cou noir
Little Grebe	Grèbe castagneux
Slavonian Grebe	Grèbe esclavon
Great Crested Grebe	Grèbe huppé
Red-necked Grebe	Grèbe jougris
Eurasian Treecreeper	Grimpereau des bois
Short-toed Treecreeper	Grimpereau des jardins
Mistle Thrush	Grive draine
Fieldfare	Grive litorne
Redwing	Grive mauvis
Song Thrush	Grive musicienne
Hawfinch	Grosbec casse-noyaux
Common Crane	Grue cendrée
European Bee-eater	Guêpier d'Europe
White-winged Black Tern	Guifette leucoptère
Whiskered Tern	Guifette moustac
Black Tern	Guifette noire
Common Guillemot	Guillemot de Tröil/marmette
Lammergeier	Gypaète barbu
Goosander	Harle bièvre/Grand Harle
Red-breasted Merganser	Harle huppé
Smew	Harle piette
Grey Heron	Héron cendré
Cattle Egret	Héron gardeboeufs

FRENCH BIRD-NAMES

English Name	French Name
Purple Heron	Héron purpré
Short-eared Owl	Hibou des marais
Eagle Owl	Hibou grand-duc/Grand-duc d'Europe
Long-eared Owl	Hibou moyen-duc
Eurasian Scops Owl	Hibou petit-duc/Petit-duc Scops
House Martin	Hirondelle de fenêtre
Sand Martin	Hirondelle de rivage
Crag Martin	Hirondelle de rochers
Red-rumped Swallow	Hirondelle rousseline
Barn Swallow	Hirondelle rustique/de cheminée
Oystercatcher	Huîtrier pie
Hoopoe	Huppe fasciée
Icterine Warbler	Hypolaïs ictérine
Melodious Warbler	Hypolaïs polyglotte
Glossy Ibis	Ibis falcinelle
Sacred Ibis	Ibis sacré
Waxwing	Jaseur boréal
Arctic Skua	Labbe parasite
Pomarine Skua	Labbe pomarin
Ptarmigan	Lagopède alpin
Linnet	Linotte mélodieuse
Savi's Warbler	Locustelle luscinïoïde
Grasshopper Warbler	Locustelle tachetée
Golden Oriole	Loriot d'Europe
Moustached Warbler	Lusciniole à moustaches
Atlantic Puffin	Macareux moine
Velvet Scoter	Macreuse brune
Common Scoter	Macreuse noire
Baillon's Crake	Marouette de Baillon
Spotted Crake	Marouette ponctuée
Little Crake	Marouette poussin
Alpine Swift	Martinet à ventre blanc/alpin
Common Swift	Martinet noir
Pallid Swift	Martinet pâle
Common Kingfisher	Martin-pêcheur d'Europe
Ring Ouzel	Merle à plastron
Blue Rock Thrush	Merle bleu
Blackbird	Merle noir
Rock Thrush	Merle de roche
Long-tailed Tit	Mésange à longue queue
Blue Tit	Mésange bleue
Willow Tit	Mésange boréale
Great Tit	Mésange charbonnière
Crested Tit	Mésange huppée
Coal Tit	Mésange noire
Marsh Tit	Mésange nonnette
Penduline Tit	Mésange rémiz

FRENCH BIRD-NAMES

English Name	French Name
Black Kite	Milan noir
Red Kite	Milan royal
Italian Sparrow	Moineau cisalpin
House Sparrow	Moineau domestique
Tree Sparrow	Moineau friquet
Rock Sparrow	Moineau soulcie
Mediterranean Gull	Mouette mélanocéphale
Little Gull	Mouette pygmée
Black-headed Gull	Mouette rieuse
Kittiwake	Mouette tridactyle
Red-crested Pochard	Nette rousse
Snowfinch	Niverolle alpine
Leach's Storm-petrel	Océanite culblanc
European Storm-petrel	Océanite tempête
Stone-curlew	Oedicnème criard
Greylag Goose	Oie cendrée
Bean Goose	Oie des moissons
White-fronted Goose	Oie rieuse
Little Bustard	Outarde canepetière
Bearded Tit	Panure à moustaches
Rock Partridge	Perdrix bartavelle
Chukar	Perdrix choukar
Grey Partridge	Perdrix grise
Red-legged Partridge	Perdrix rouge
Little Ringed Plover	Petit Gravelot
Eurasian Scops Owl	Petit-duc scops/Hibou petit-duc
Grey Phalarope	Phalarope à bec large
Red-necked Phalarope	Phalarope à bec mince
Sedge Warbler	Phragmite des joncs
White-backed Woodpecker	Pic à dos blanc
Grey-headed Woodpecker	Pic cendré
Great Spotted Woodpecker	Pic épeiche
Lesser Spotted Woodpecker	Pic épeichette
Middle Spotted Woodpecker	Pic mar
Black Woodpecker	Pic noir
Three-toed Woodpecker	Pic tridactyle
Green Woodpecker	Pic vert
Magpie	Pie bavarde
Lesser Grey Shrike	Pie-grièche à poitrine rose
Woodchat Shrike	Pie-grièche à tête rousse
Red-backed Shrike	Pie-grièche écorcheur
Great Grey Shrike	Pie-grièche grise
Southern Grey Shrike	Pie-grièche méridionale
Rock Dove	Pigeon biset
Stock Dove	Pigeon colombin
Wood Pigeon	Pigeon ramier
Razorbill	Pingouin torda

FRENCH BIRD-NAMES

English Name	French Name
Common Chaffinch	*Pinson des arbres*
Brambling	*Pinson du Nord*
Red-throated Pipit	*Pipit à gorge rousse*
Tree Pipit	*Pipit des arbres*
Meadow Pipit	*Pipit farlouse*
Rock Pipit	*Pipit maritime*
Tawny Pipit	*Pipit rousseline*
Water Pipit	*Pipit spioncelle*
Black-throated Diver	*Plongeon artique*
Red-throated Diver	*Plongeon catmarin*
Great Northern Diver	*Plongeon imbrin*
Grey Plover	*Pluvier argenté*
European Golden Plover	*Pluvier doré*
Dotterel	*Pluvier guignard*
Kentish Plover	*Pluvier à collier interrompu*
Ringed Plover	*Pluvier grand-gravelot*
Little Ringed Plover	*Pluvier petit-gravelot*
Purple Gallinule	*Porphyrion bleu/Poule sultane*
Western Bonelli's Warbler	*Pouillot de Bonelli*
Willow Warbler	*Pouillet fitis*
Wood Warbler	*Pouillot siffleur*
Common Iberian Chiffchaff	*Pouillot véloce/iberique*
Cory's Shearwater	*Puffin cendré*
Balearic Shearwater	*Puffin de Baléares*
Yelkouan Shearwater	*Puffin de Mediterranée*
Manx Shearwater	*Puffin des Anglais*
White-tailed Sea-eagle	*Pygargue à queue blanche*
Water Rail	*Râle d'eau*
Corn Crake	*Râle des genêts*
Penduline Tit	*Rémiz penduline*
Goldcrest	*Roitelet huppé*
Firecrest	*Roitelet triple-bandeau*
European Roller	*Rollier d'Europe*
Common Rosefinch	*Roselin cramoisi*
Rufous Nightingale	*Rossignol philomèle*
Robin	*Rougegorge familier*
Redstart	*Rougequeue à front blanc*
Black Redstart	*Rougequeue noir*
Reed Warbler	*Rousserolle effarvatte*
Great Reed Warbler	*Rousserolle turdoïde*
Marsh Warbler	*Rousserolle verderolle*
Garganey	*Sarcelle d'été*
Common Teal	*Sarcelle d'hiver*
European Serin	*Serin cini*
Corsican Nuthatch	*Sitelle corse*
European Nuthatch	*Sitelle torchepot*
Common Redpoll	*Sizerin flammé*

FRENCH BIRD-NAMES

English Name	French Name
Eurasian Spoonbill	*Spatule blanche*
Arctic Tern	*Sterne arctique*
Caspian Tern	*Sterne caspienne*
Sandwich Tern	*Sterne caugek*
Gull-billed Tern	*Sterne hansel*
Little Tern	*Sterne naine*
Common Tern	*Sterne pierregarin*
Common Shelduck	*Tadorne de Belon*
Purple Swamp-hen	*Talève sultane*
Siskin	*Tarin des aulnes*
Whinchat	*Tarier des près*
Common Stonechat	*Tarier pâtre*
Black Grouse	*Tétras lyre*
Wallcreeper	*Tichodrome échelette*
Wryneck	*Torcol fourmilier*
Turnstone	*Tournepierre à collier*
Turtle Dove	*Tourterelle des bois*
Collared Dove	*Tourterelle turque*
Northern Wheatear	*Traquet motteux*
Black-eared Wheatear	*Traquet oreillard*
Black Wheatear	*Traquet rieur*
Wren	*Troglodyte mignon*
Northern Lapwing	*Vanneau huppé*
Griffon Vulture	*Vautore fauve*
Black (Monk) Vulture	*Vautour moine*
Egyptian Vulture	*Vautour percnoptère*
Corsican Citril	*Venturon corse*
Citril Finch	*Venturon montagnard*
Greenfinch	*Verdier d'Europe*

MAMMALS

English Name	Scientific Name
Western Hedgehog	Erinaceus europaeus
Pyrenean Desman	Galemys pyrenaicus
Blind Mole	Talpa caeca
Common Mole	Talpa europaea
Pygmy Shrew	Sorex minutus
Millet's Shrew	S. coronatus
Alpine Shrew	S. alpinus
Water Shrew	Neomys fodiens
Miller's Water Shrew	N. anomalus
Lesser White-toothed Shrew	Crocidura suaveolens
Greater White-toothed Shrew	C. russula
Pygmy White-toothed Shrew	Suncus etruscus
Lesser Horseshoe Bat	Rhinolopus hipposideros
Mediterranean Horseshoe Bat	R. euryale
Greater Horseshoe Bat	R. ferrumequinum
Daubenton's Bat	Myotis daubentonii
Whiskered Bat	M. mystacinus
Long-fingered Bat	M. capaccinii
Natterer's Bat	M. nattereri
Geoffroy's Bat	M. emarginatus
Bechstein's Bat	M. bechsteinii
Greater Mouse-eared Bat	M. myotis
Lesser Mouse-eared Bat	M. blythi
Common Pipistrelle	Pipistrellus pipistrellus
Nathusius's Pipistrelle.	P. nathusii
Kuhl's Pipistrelle	P. kuhlii
Savi's Pipistrelle	Hypsugo savii
Leisler's Bat	Nyctalus leisleri
Noctule	N. noctula
Greater Noctule – rare	N. lasiopteris
Serotine	Eptesicus serotinus
Parti-coloured Bat – rare	Verpertilio murinus
Barbastelle	Barbastella barbastellus
Grey Long-eared Bat	Plecotus austriacus
Brown Long-eared Bat	P. auritus
Schreiber's Bat	Miniopterus schreibersi
Free-tailed Bat	Tadarida teniotis
Brown Hare	Lepus europaeus
Rabbit/Cotton-tail Rabbit (introduced)	Oryctolagus cuniculus/ Sylvilagus floridanus
Red Squirrel	Sciurus vulgaris
Alpine Marmot	Marmota marmota
European Beaver	Castor fiber
Bank Vole	Clethrionomys glareolus
Southern Water Vole	Arvicola sapidus
Northern Water Vole	A. terrestris
Muskrat	Ondatra zibethicus
Alpine Pine Vole	Pitymys multiplex

MAMMALS

				English Name	Scientific Name
				Field Vole	*Microtus agrestis*
				Common Vole	*M. arvalis*
				Pyrenean Pine Vole	*Microtus pyrenaicus*
				Snow Vole	*M. nivalis*
				Garden Dormouse	*Eliomys quercinus*
				Fat (Edible) Dormouse	*Glis glis*
				Common Dormouse	*Muscardinus avellanarius*
				Wood Mouse	*Apodemus sylvaticus*
				Yellow-necked Mouse	*A. flavicollis*
				Harvest Mouse	*Micromys minutus*
				Brown Rat	*Rattus norvegicus*
				Black Rat	*R. rattus*
				House Mouse	*Mus domesticus*
				Coypu	*Myocastor coypus*
				Wild Boar	*Sus scrofa*
				Isard (Pyrenees)/Chamois (Alps)	*Rupicapra pyrenaica/rupicapra*
				Alpine Ibex	*Capra ibex*
				Mouflon/Sardinian Mouflon	*Ovis orientalis/musimon*
				Red Deer	*Cervus elaphus*
				Fallow Deer	*Dama dama*
				Roe Deer	*Capreolus capreolus*
				Wolf	*Canis lupus*
				Red Fox	*Vulpes vulpes*
				Brown Bear	*Ursus arctos*
				Weasel	*Mustela nivalis*
				Stoat	*M. erminea*
				European Mink	*M. lutreola*
				American Mink	*M. vison*
				Western Polecat	*Mustela putorius*
				Pine Marten	*Martes martes*
				Beech Marten	*M. foina*
				Badger	*Meles meles*
				Otter	*Lutra lutra*
				Genet	*Genetta genetta*
				Wild Cat	*Felis silvestris*
				Lynx	*Lynx lynx*
				Striped Dolphin	*Stenella coeruleoalba*
				Common Dolphin	*Delphinus delphis*
				Bottle-nosed Dolphin	*Tursiops truncatus*
				Killer Whale	*Orcinus orca*
				Fin Whale	*Balaenoptera physalus*
				Minke Whale	*Balaenoptera acutorostrata*
				Sperm Whate	*Physeter macrocephalus*
				Risso's Dolphin	*Grampus priseus*
				Long-finned Pilot Whale	*Globicephala melaena*
				Cuvier's Beaked Whale	*Ziphius cavirostris*
				Mediterranean Monk Seal	*Monachus monachus*

AMPHIBIANS and REPTILES

				English Name	Scientific Name
				Hermann's Tortoise	*Testudo hermanni*
				European Pond Terrapin	*Emys orbicularis*
				Moorish Gecko	*Tarentola mauritanica*
				Turkish Gecko	*Hemidactylus turcicus*
				European Leaf-toed Gecko	
				(Corsica)	*Phyllodactylus europaeus*
				Pygmy Algyroides (Corsica)	*Algyroides fitzingeri*
				Large Psammodromus	*Psammadromus algirus*
				Spanish Psammodromus	*P. hispanicus*
				Oscellated Lizard	*Lacerta lepida*
				Green Lizard	*L. viridis*
				Sand Lizard	*L. agilis*
				Viviparous Lizard	*L. vivipara*
				Iberian Rock Lizard	*L. monticola*
				Bedriaga's Rock Lizard	
				(Corsica)	*L. bedriagae*
				Pyrenean Lizard	*L. bonnali (L. aurelioi)*
				Common Wall Lizard	*Podarcis muralis*
				Iberian Wall Lizard	*P. hispanica*
				Tyrrhenian Wall Lizard	
				(Corsica)	*P. tiliguerta*
				Italian Wall Lizard (Corsica)	*P. sicula*
				Slow Worm	*Anguis fragilis*
				Three-toed Skink	*Chalcides chalcides (C. striatus)*
				Montpellier Snake	*Malpolon monspessulanus*
				Western Whip Snake	*Coluber viridiflavus*
				Aesculapian Snake	*Elaphe longissima*
				Ladder Snake	*E. scalaris*
				Grass Snake	*Natrix natrix*
				Viperine Snake	*N. maura*
				Smooth Snake	*Coronella austriaca*
				Southern Smooth Snake	*C. girondica*
				Asp Viper	*Vipera aspis*
				Adder	*V. berus*
				Seoanei's Viper	*V. seoanei*
				Fire Salamander	*Salamandra salamandra*
				Alpine Salamander	*S. atra*
				Pyrenean Brook Salamander	*Euproctus asper*
				Corsican Brook Salamander	*E. montanus*
				Marbled Newt	*Triturus marmoratus*
				Warty Newt	*T. cristatus*
				Alpine Newt	*T. alpestris*
				Smooth Newt	*T. vulgaris*
				Palmate Newt	*Triturus helveticus*
				Yellow-bellied Toad	*Bombina variegata*
				Tyrrhenian Painted Frog	
				(Corsica)	*Discoglossus sardus*

AMPHIBIANS and REPTILES

English Name	Scientific Name
Midwife Toad	Alytes obstetricans
Western Spadefoot	Pelobates cultripes
Common Spadefoot	P. fuscus
Parsley Frog	Pelodytes punctatus
Common Toad	Bufo bufo
Natterjack	B. calamita
Green Toad	B. viridis
Common Tree Frog	Hyla arborea
Stripeless Tree Frog	H. meridionalis
Grass (Common) Frog	Rana temporaria
Agile Frog	R. dalmatina
Pool Frog	R. lessonae
Edible Frog	R. esculenta
Marsh Frog	R. perezi

BUTTERFLIES

English Name	Scientific Name
PAPILLIONIDAE	
Swallowtail	Papilio machaon
Southern Swallowtail	P. alexanor
Corsican Swallowtail	P. hospiton
Scarce Swallowtail	Iphiclides podalirius
Spanish Festoon	Zerynthia rumina
Southern Festoon	Z. polyxena
Apollo	Parnassius apollo
Clouded Apollo	Parnassius mnemosyne
PIERIDAE	
Black-veined White	Aporia crataegi
Large White	Pieris brassicae
Small White	Artogeia rapae
Southern Small White	A. manii
Mountain Small White	A. ergane
Green-veined White	A. napi
Black-veined White	Aporia crataegi
Bath White	Pontia daplidice
Peak White	P. callidice
Freyer's Dappled White	Euchloe simplonia
Dappled White	E. ausonia
Corsican Dappled White	E. insularis
Mountain Dappled White	E. simplonia
Orange Tip	Anthocharis cardamines
Moroccan Orange Tip	A. euphenoides
Mountain Clouded Yellow	Colias phicomone
Moorland Clouded Yellow	C. palaeno
Clouded Yellow	C. crocea
Pale Clouded Yellow	C. hyale

BUTTERFLIES

				English Name	Scientific Name
				Berger's Clouded Yellow	C. australis
				Brimstone	Gonepteryx rhamni
				Cleopatra	G. cleopatra
				Wood White	Leptides sinapis
				Eastern Wood White	L. duponcheli
				RIODINIDAE	
				Duke of Burgundy	Hamearis lucina
				LIBYTHEIDAE	
				Nettle-tree Butterfly	Libythea celtus
				NYMPHALIDAE	
				Two-tailed Pasha	Charaxes jasius
				Purple Emperor	Apatura iris
				Lesser Purple Emperor	A. ilia
				Poplar Admiral	Limenitis populi
				White Admiral	L.camilla
				Southern White Admiral	Limenitis reducta
				Camberwell Beauty	Nyphalis antiopa
				Large Tortoiseshell	N. polychloros
				Small Tortoishell	Aglais urticae
				Comma	Polygonia c-album
				Southern Comma	P. egea
				Map Butterfly	Araschnia levana
				Painted Lady	Cynthia cardui
				Red Admiral	Vanessa atalanta
				Indian Red Admiral	V. indica vulcania
				Peacock Butterfly	Inachis io
				Cardinal	Pandoriana pandora
				Silver-washed Fritillary	Argynnis paphia
				Corsican Fritillary	A. elisa
				Dark Green Fritillary	Mesoacidalia aglaja
				High Brown Fritillary	Fabriciana adippe
				Niobe Fritillary	F. niobe
				Queen of Spain Fritillary	Issoria lathonia
				Twin-spot Fritillary	Brenthis hecate
				Marbled Fritillary	B. daphne
				Lesser Marbled Fritillary	B. ino
				Shepherd's Fritillary	Boloria pales
				Mountain Fritillary	B. napaea
				Cranberry Fritillary	B. aquilonarais
				Bog Fritillary	Proclossiana eunomia
				Pearl-bordered Fritillary	Clossiana euphrosyne
				Small Pearl-bordered Fritillary	C. selene
				Titania's Fritillary	C. titania
				Weaver's Fritillary	C. dia
				Glanville Fritillary	Melitaea cinxia
				Knapweed Fritillary	M. phoebe
				Spotted Fritillary	M. didyma

BUTTERFLIES

				English Name	Scientific Name
				Lesser Spotted Fritillary	M. trivia
				False Heath Fritillary	M. diamina
				Heath Fritillary	Mellicta athalia
				Njickerl's Fritillary	M. aurelia
				Provençal Fritillary	M. deione
				Meadow Fritillary	M. parthenoides
				Marsh Fritillary	Eurodryas aurinia
				SATYRIDAE	
				Marbled White	Menanargia galathea lachesis
				Esper's Marbled White	M. russiae
				Western Marbled White	M. occitanica
				Woodland Grayling	Hipparchia fagi
				Rock Grayling	H. alcyone
				Corsican Grayling	H. neomiris
				Grayling	H. semele cadmus
				Southern Grayling (Corsica)	H. aristaeus
				Tree Grayling	Neohipparchia statillinus
				Striped Grayling	Pseudotergumia fidia
				The Hermit	Chazara briseis
				Black Satyr	Satyrus actaea
				Great Sooty Satry	S. ferula
				Great Banded Grayling	Brintesia circe
				False Grayling	Arethusana arethusa
				Alpine Grayling	Oeneis glacialis
				Dryad	Minois dryas
				Large Ringlet	Erebia euryale
				Sudeten Ringlet	E. sudetica
				Yellow-spotted Ringlet	E. manto
				De Prunner's Ringlet	E. triaria
				Mountain Ringlet	E. epiphron
				Scotch Argus	E. aethiops
				Silky Ringlet	E. gorge
				Gavarnie Ringlet	E. gorgone
				Spring Ringlet	E. epistygne
				Common Brassy Ringlet	E. cassioides
				Spanish Brassy Ringlet	E. hispanica rondoui
				Ottoman Brassy Ringlet	E. ottomana tardeneota
				Woodland Ringlet	E. medusa
				Water Ringlet	E. pronoe
				Lefèbvre's Ringlet	E. lefebvrei
				Larche Ringlet	E. scipio
				Autumn Ringlet	E. neoridas
				Bright-eyed Ringlet	E. oeme
				Piedmont Ringlet	E. meolans
				Dewy Ringlet	E. pandrose
				False Dewy Ringlet	E. sthennyo
				Arran Brown	E. ligea

BUTTERFLIES

			English Name	Scientific Name
			Meadow Brown	*Maniola jurtina*
			Dusky Meadow Brown	*Hyponephele lycaon*
			Gatekeeper	*Pyronia tithonus*
			Southern Gatekeeper	*P. cecilia*
			Spanish Gatekeeper	*P. bathseba*
			Ringlet	*Aphantopus hyperantus*
			Small Heath	*Coenonympha pamphilus*
			Corsican Heath	*C. corinna*
			Dusky Heath	*C. dorus*
			Pearly Heath	*C. arcania*
			Chestnut Heath	*C. glycerion*
			Spanish Heath	*C. iphioides*
			False Ringlet	*C. oedippus*
			Scarce Heath	*C. hero*
			Speckled Wood	*Pararge aegeria*
			Wall Brown	*Lasiommata megera*
			Large Wall Brown	*L. maera*
			Northern Wall Brown	*L. petropolitana*
			Woodland Brown	*Lopinga achine*
			LYCAENIDAE	
			Brown Hairstreak	*Thecla betulae*
			Purple Hairstreak	*Quercusia quercus*
			Spanish Purple Hairstreak	*Laeosopis roboris*
			Sloe Hairstreak	*Nordmannia acaciae*
			Ilex Hairstreak	*N. ilicis*
			False Ilex Hairstreak	*N. esculi*
			Blue-spot Hairstreak	*Strymonidia spini*
			Black Hairstreak	*S. pruni*
			White-letter Hairstreak	*S. w-album*
			Green Hairstreak	*Callophrys rubi*
			Chapman's Green Hairstreak	*C. avis*
			Provence Hairstreak	*Tomares ballus*
			Violet Copper	*Lycaena helle*
			Small Copper	*L. phlaeas*
			Large Copper	*L. dispaar*
			Scarce Copper	*Heodes virgaureae*
			Sooty Copper	*H. tityrus*
			Purple-shot Copper	*H. alciphron*
			Purple-edged Copper	*Palaeochrysophanus hippothoe*
			Long-tailed Blue	*Lampides boeticus*
			Lang's Short-tailed Blue	*Syntarucus pirithous*
			Short-tailed Blue	*Everes argiades*
			Provencal Short-tailed Blue	*E. alcetas*
			Little Blue	*Cupido minimus*
			Osiris Blue	*C. asiris (or sebrus)*
			Holly Blue	*Celastrina argiolus*
			Green-underside Blue	*Glaucopsyche alexis*

BUTTERFLIES

				English Name	Scientific Name
				Black-eyed Blue	G. melanops
				Alcon Blue	Maculinea alcon
				Large Blue	M. arion
				Scarce Large Blue	M. telejus
				Iolas Blue	Iolana iolas
				Baton Blue	Pseudophilotes baton
				Panoptes Blue	P. panoptes
				Chequered Blue	Scolitantides orion
				Silver-studded Blue	Plebejus argus
				Reverdin's Blue	P. argyrognomon
				Idas Blue	Lycaeides idas
				Geranium Argus	Eumedonia eumedon
				Brown Argus	Aricia agestis
				Southern Brown Argus	A. cramera
				Mountain Argus	A. artaxerxes
				Alpine Argus	Albulina orbitulus
				Silvery Argus	Pseudaricia nicias
				Glandon Blue	Agriades glandon
				Gavarnie Blue	A. pyrenaicus
				Mazarine Blue	Cyaniris semiargus
				Furry Blue	Agrodiaetus dolus
				Forster's Furry Blue	A. ainsae
				Damon Blue	A. damon
				Escher's Blue	A. escheri
				Amanda's Blue	A. amanda
				Chapman's Blue	A. thersites
				Ripart's Anomalous Blue	A. ripartii
				Turquoise Blue	Plebicula dorylas
				Meleager's Blue	Meleageria daphnis
				Chalk-hill Blue	Lysandra corydon
				Provence Chalk-hill Blue	L. hispana
				Spanish Chalk-hill Blue	L. albicans
				Adonis Blue	L. bellargus
				Common Blue	Polyommatus icarus
				Eros Blue	P. eros
				HESPERIIDAE	
				Grizzled Skipper	Pyrgus malvae
				Large Grizzled Skipper	P. alveus
				Oberthur's Grizzled skipper	P. armoricanus
				Foulquier's Grizzled Skipper	P. foulquieri
				Olive Skipper	P. serratulae
				Carline Skipper	P. carlinae
				Cinquefoil Skipper	P. cirsii
				Yellow-banded Skipper	P. sidae
				Rosy Grizzled Skipper	P. onopordi
				Safflower Skipper	P. carthami
				Alpine Grizzled Skipper	P. andromedae

BUTTERFLIES

				English Name	Scientific Name
				Dusky Grizzled Skipper	*P. cacaliae*
				Red Underwing Skipper	*Spialia sertorius*
				Sage Skipper	*Syrichtus proto*
				Mallow Skipper	*Carcharodus alceae*
				Marbled Skipper	*C. lavatherae*
				Southern Marbled Skipper	*C. boeticus*
				Tufted Marbled Skipper	*C. flocciferis*
				Dingy Skipper	*Erynnis tages*
				Large Chequered Skipper	*Heteropterus morpheus*
				Chequered Skipper	*Carterocephalus palaemon*
				Large Chequered	*Heteropterus morpheus*
				Lulworth Skipper	*Thymelicus acteon*
				Essex Skipper	*T. lineola*
				Small Skipper	*T. flavus*
				Silver-spotted Skipper	*Hesperia comma*
				Large Skipper	*Ochlodes venatus*
				Pigmy Skipper	*Gegenes pumilio*
				Mediterranean Skipper	*Gegenes nostrodamus*

NOTES

OTHER TITLES AVAILABLE FROM ARLEQUIN PRESS

A Birdwatching Guide to MALLORCA by GRAHAM HEARL

Written by the RSPB representative on the Island this guide is unsurpassed in its detailed coverage of the area with maps and clear directions. Includes colour photographs and full checklist of the 309 documented species recorded on the Island over the last 20 years. Now 92pp.

£9.95 +p&p

A Birdwatching Guide to MENORCA, IBIZA & FORMENTERA
by GRAHAM HEARL

This guide covers the smaller Balearic Islands, all important staging posts for migrants crossing the mediterranean. Menorca is especially good for seeing Egyptian Vulture, Red Kite and Booted Eagle. Ibiza which hosts all the typical Balearic resident specialities and Formentera is important for its breeding colonies of Mediterranean Shearwater. 56pp, site maps, colour habitat photographs.

£8.95 +p&p

A Birdwatching Guide to SOUTHERN SPAIN
by MALCOLM PALMER

Covering the provinces of Almeria, Grand, Jáen, Málaga, Cadiz, Murcia and part of Cordoba and Sevilla. Sites which offer the most interesting birdwatching opportunities are included. Specific list and habitat guide, checklist, maps, colour habitat photographs. 92pp.

£9.95 +p&p

A Birdwatching Guide to MOROCCO
by PETER COMBRIDGE & ALAN SNOOK

Morroco remains an exciting and interesting country to visit. This guide is aimed at those with limited time and want to see a cross section of habitats and find a good selection of species. 64pp, maps, checklist, colour habitat photographs.

£9.95 +p&p

A Birdwatching Guide to CYPRUS
by ARTHUR STAGG & GRAHAM HEARL

Ideally situated in the Mediterranean the Cyprus bird list is long, it currently stands at 363 species. Notable among the endemics and resident species are Cyprus Warbler, Cyprus Pied Wheatear and Griffon Vulture. Summer visitors include Eleonoras Falcon and Red rumped Swallow. In winter Flamingo and a wide variety of wildfowl. In all respects Cyprus is a truly a year round birdwatching venue. 88pp.

£9.95 +p&p

A Birdwatching Guide to THE PYRENEES
by JACQUIE CROZIER

Written by a resident of the area, this excellent guide covers the entire area from the Atlantic to the Mediterranean. Not only detailing the best sites to visit for birdwatching but includes information about other flora and fauna. 92pp.

£9.95 +p&p

A Birdwatching Guide to CRETE
by STEPHANIE COGHLAN

Crete offers a great deal to the birdwatcher, botanist and general naturalist. It is very mountainous and many of the mountains are cut by impressive gorges which from the birdwatchers point of view offer breeding areas for Griffon Vultures, Lammergeier and Blue Rock Thrush as well as good observation points. This guide features the most productive birding sites on the Island, includes maps, checklists for birds, mammals, amphibians, reptiles, butterflies and orchids.

£9.95 +p&p

A Birdwatching Guide to EXTREMADURA
by JOHN MUDDEMAN

The essential guide to the area including illustrations by John Busby, colour habitat photographs and checklists. 120 pp.

£10.95 +p&p

All of the above titles measure 148.5mm x 210mm.

Available from all good book shops *or* direct from
Subbuteo Natural History Books, The Rea,
Upton Magna, Shrewsbury, SY4 4UR.
Tel 0870 010 9700 Fax 0870 010 9699
www.wildlifebooks.com